Language and Mediated Masculinities

Reinventing Identitites: The Gendered Self in Discourse
Edited by Mary Bucholtz, A.C. Liang, and Laurel A. Sutton

Pronoun Envy: Literacy Uses of Linguistic Gender
Anna Livia

Japanese Language, Gender and Ideology: Cultural Models and Real People
Edited by Shigeko Okamoto and Janet S. Shibamoto Smith

Language and Women's Place: Text and Commentaries
Revised and Expanded Edition
By Robin Tolmach Lakoff
Edited by Mary Bucholtz

From the Kitchen to the Parlor: Language and Becoming in African American Women's Hair Care
Lanita Jacobs-Huey

Gender, Sexuality, and Meaning: Linguistic Practice and Politics
Sally McConnell-Ginet

Queer Excursions: Retheorizing Binaries in Language, Gender, and Sexuality
Edited by Lal Zimman, Jenny Davis, and Joshua Raclaw

Language, Sexuality, and Power: Studies in Intersectional Sociolinguistics
Edited by Erez Levon and Ronald Beline Mendes

From Drag Queens to Leathermen: Language, Gender, and Gay Male Subcultures
Rusty Barrett

queerqueen: Linguistic Excess in Japanese Media
Claire Maree

Language and Mediated Masculinities: Cultures, Contexts, Constraints
Robert Lawson

LANGUAGE AND MEDIATED MASCULINITIES

Cultures, Contexts, Constraints

Robert Lawson

OXFORD
UNIVERSITY PRESS

OXFORD
UNIVERSITY PRESS

Oxford University Press is a department of the University of Oxford. It furthers
the University's objective of excellence in research, scholarship, and education
by publishing worldwide. Oxford is a registered trade mark of Oxford University
Press in the UK and certain other countries.

Published in the United States of America by Oxford University Press
198 Madison Avenue, New York, NY 10016, United States of America.

© Oxford University Press 2023

Library of Congress Cataloging-in-Publication Data
Names: Lawson, Robert, 1982– author.
Title: Language and mediated masculinities : Cultures, Contexts, Constraints / Robert Lawson.
Description: New York, NY : Oxford University Press, [2023] |
Series: Studies in language gender sex series |
Includes bibliographical references and index.
Identifiers: LCCN 2022040739 (print) | LCCN 2022040740 (ebook) |
ISBN 9780190081041 (hardback) | ISBN 9780190081058 (paperback) |
ISBN 9780190081072 (epub) | ISBN 9780190081089 (oso)
Subjects: LCSH: Men—Language. | Language and languages—Sex differences.
Classification: LCC P120.M45 L39 2023 (print) | LCC P120.M45 (ebook) |
DDC 306.440811—dc23/eng/20221013
LC record available at https://lccn.loc.gov/2022040739
LC ebook record available at https://lccn.loc.gov/2022040740

DOI: 10.1093/oso/9780190081041.001.0001

9 8 7 6 5 4 3 2 1

Paperback printed by Marquis, Canada
Hardback Printed by Bridgeport National Bindery, Inc., United States of America

For Rebecca, Bethany, and Georgia

CONTENTS

Series Foreword   ix
List of Figures   xi
List of Tables   xiii
Preface   xvii
Acknowledgments   xxiii

1. Contexts, Cultures, and Constraints: Language and Mediated
   Masculinities in the Twenty-First Century   1
2. Setting the Scene: Some Key Ideas in Language and Masculinities Studies   19
3. Approaches to Analyzing Language and Masculinities: Data, Theories,
   and Methods   39
4. Representations of 'Hard Man' Masculinity and Ideologies of Toughness
   in the British Press   59
5. Being a 'Real Man' on /r/The_Donald: Masculinity, Ethnic Identity,
   and the Alternative Right   85
6. "Alphas Get Treated Like Bygone Emperors and Betas Live
   Lives of Quiet Desperation": Toxic Masculinity and Discourses of
   Gender in the Manosphere   120
7. Positive Masculinity and Brooklyn Nine-Nine: Reconfiguring Dominant
   Gender Tropes in Television Comedy   167
8. The Language of Fatherhood 2.0: Discourses of Caring Masculinities
   on an Online Fathers' Forum   199
9. Conclusion: Where Next for Language and Masculinities Studies?   219

References   237
Index   285

SERIES FOREWORD

Oxford's series Studies in Language, Gender, and Sexuality provides a broad-based interdisciplinary forum for the best new scholarship on language, gender, and sexuality. The mandate of the series is to encourage innovative work in the field, a goal that may be achieved through the revisitation of familiar topics from fresh vantage points, through the introduction of new avenues of research, or through new theoretical or methodological frameworks. The series is interdisciplinary in its scope: volumes may be authored by scholars in such disciplines as anthropology, communication, education, feminist and gender studies, linguistics, literary studies, psychology, queer studies, race and ethnic studies, sociology, and other fields.

FIGURES

1.1   Piers Morgan's tweet, posted January 14, 2019   13

2.1   Jessica Walton's tweet, posted February 7, 2019. Reproduced by permission from: Jessica Walton   22

3.1   A collocation network for "summer" and "spring" displayed in GraphColl   47

4.1   Top lexical frequency rankings in the *HarM* corpus   72

4.2   GraphColl results for "hard man" in *The Guardian* subcorpus   78

4.3   GraphColl results for "hard man" in *The Scotsman* subcorpus   81

5.1   Andy Swan's tweet, posted January 23, 2017   100

6.1   The 'Manogrid'   130

6.2   Positive male gendered terms across the manosphere corpus   140

6.3   Neutral male gendered terms (generic) across the manosphere corpus   146

6.4   Neutral male gendered terms (relational) across the manosphere corpus   148

6.5   Negative male gendered terms across the manosphere corpus   150

6.6   Neutral female gendered terms (generic) across the manosphere corpus   156

6.7   Neutral female gendered terms (relational) across the manosphere corpus   159

6.8   Negative female gendered terms across the manosphere corpus   160

6.9   Negative female gendered terms across the manosphere corpus used in fewer than three subreddits   163

6.10   Comparison of male and female referents across the manosphere corpus   165

7.1   'Real'. Reproduced by permission from: Christopher O'Grady, *Lunarbaboon*, http://www.lunarbaboon.com/comics/real.html   171

7.2   Number of words by speaker across six seasons of *Brooklyn Nine-Nine*   180

7.3   Number of turns by speaker across six seasons of *Brooklyn Nine-Nine*   180

7.4 Radar chart of main keyword categories for Peralta, Holt, Boyle, and Jeffords   183

7.5 Wide shot of Diaz and Peralta's reaction to Boyle's 'threesome' statement   189

7.6 Close up shot of Diaz and Peralta's reaction to Boyle's 'threesome' statement   189

7.7 Wide shot of Peralta and Boyle performing "My Hunch"   191

7.8 Jeffords in Season 1, Episode 3 ("The Slump")   194

TABLES

3.1	Selected concordance lines for "summer" displayed in #LancsBox	48
4.1	Breakdown of the *HarM* corpus (ranked by total number of words)	63
4.2	NMF topic model analysis in *The Guardian* subcorpus	64
4.3	NMF topic model analysis in *The Scotsman* subcorpus	66
4.4	Topic comparison across the *HarM* corpus	69
4.5	Breakdown of "hard man" variants in the *HarM* corpus	70
4.6	Top keywords in *The Guardian* subcorpus	74
4.7	Top keywords in *The Scotsman* subcorpus	75
4.8	Selected concordance lines for "hard man" in *The Guardian* subcorpus (five-word L/R span)	79
4.9	Main collocates of "hard man" in *The Guardian* subcorpus (within a five-word L/R span)	79
4.10	Selected concordance lines for "hard man" in *The Guardian* subcorpus (within a five-word L/R span of "reputation")	80
4.11	Main collocates of "hard man" in *The Scotsman* subcorpus (within a five-word L/R span)	81
5.1	Breakdown of /r/The_Donald subcorpus (ranked by total number of words)	97
5.2	Top twenty collocates for "men" in the *men* subcorpus (ranked by frequency)	101
5.3	Selected concordance lines for "men are" in the *men* subcorpus (variable L/R span)	102
5.4	Selected concordance lines for "liberal men are" in the *men* subcorpus (variable L/R span)	102
5.5	Top fifteen 3-grams in the *men* subcorpus (ranked by frequency)	103
5.6	Selected concordance lines for "I don't" in the *men* subcorpus (variable L/R span)	104
5.7	Concordance lines for "a bunch of" in the *men* subcorpus (variable L/R span)	105

5.8   Top twenty collocates for "men" in the *White men* subcorpus (ranked by frequency)   106

5.9   Concordance lines for "hate white men" in the *White men* subcorpus (variable L/R span)   107

5.10 Concordance lines for "white men" in the *White men* subcorpus (variable L/R span)   108

5.11 Concordance lines for "invented" in the *White men* subcorpus (variable L/R span)   109

5.12 Top collocates of "Muslim" in the *Muslim men* subcorpus (ranked by frequency)   112

5.13 Selected concordance lines "Muslims are" in the *Muslim men* subcorpus (variable L/R span)   113

5.14 Top collocates of "black" in the *Black men* subcorpus (ranked by frequency)   118

6.1   Breakdown of the manosphere corpus (ranked by total number of words)   138

6.2   Selected concordance lines for "bro" in the manosphere corpus (variable L/R span)   141

6.3   Selected concordance lines for "dude" in the manosphere corpus (variable L/R span)   141

6.4   Selected concordance lines for "brother" in the /r/MGTOW subcorpus (variable L/R span)   141

6.5   Selected concordance lines for "an alpha" in the /r/TheRedPill subcorpus (variable L/R span)   144

6.6   Selected concordance lines for "alpha(s)" in the /r/TheRedPill subcorpus (variable L/R span)   144

6.7   Selected concordance lines for "guys" in the manosphere corpus (variable L/R span)   145

6.8   Selected concordance lines for "you guys" in the manosphere corpus (variable L/R span)   145

6.9   Top twenty collocates for "men" in the manosphere corpus   147

6.10 Selected concordance lines for "boyfriend" and "husband" in the /r/MGTOW subcorpus (variable L/R span)   149

6.11 Selected concordance lines for "boyfriend" in the /r/TheRedPill subcorpus (variable L/R span)   149

6.12 Selected concordance lines for "father" in the /r/Incels subcorpus (variable L/R span)   150

6.13 Selected concordance lines for "Chad" in the /r/Incels subcorpus (variable L/R span)   151

6.14 Selected concordance lines for "beta" in the manosphere corpus (variable L/R span) 152

6.15 Selected concordance lines for "simp," "cuck," "white knight," and "faggot" in the manosphere corpus (variable L/R span) 153

6.16 Selected concordance lines for "cuck" in the manosphere corpus (variable L/R span) 153

6.17 Selected concordance lines for "faggot(s)" in the manosphere corpus (variable L/R span) 153

6.18 Selected concordance lines for "white knight" in the manosphere corpus (variable L/R span) 154

6.19 Selected concordance lines for "unicorn" in the manosphere corpus (variable L/R span) 155

6.20 Selected concordance lines for "princess" in the manosphere corpus (variable L/R span) 155

6.21 Selected concordance lines for "NAWALT" in the manosphere corpus (variable L/R span) 156

6.22 Top twenty collocates for "women" in the manosphere corpus (ranked by log-likelihood score) 157

6.23 Selected concordance lines for "bitch" in the manosphere corpus (variable L/R span) 161

6.24 Selected concordance lines for "cunt" in the manosphere corpus (variable L/R span) 162

6.25 Selected concordance lines for "feminazi" and "hamster" in the /r/MensRights and /r/TheRedPill subcorpora (variable L/R span) 163

6.26 Selected concordance lines for "femoid," "roastie," and "Stacy" in the /r/Incels subcorpus (variable L/R span) 164

7.1 Overview of *Brooklyn Nine-Nine* corpus by season 178

7.2 Top twenty keywords for Peralta, Holt, Boyle, and Jeffords 182

7.3 Selected concordance lines for "Jakey" in the *B99* corpus (variable L/R span) 186

7.4 Selected concordance lines for "buddy" in the *B99* corpus (variable L/R span) 187

7.5 Selected concordance lines for the use of "love" and "hate" by Jeffords in the *B99* corpus (variable L/R span) 195

8.1 Overview of *DadInfo* corpus (ranked by number of topics) 209

8.2 Top twenty keywords across the *DadInfo* corpus 210

8.3 Selected concordance lines for "not fair on" in the *DadInfo* corpus (variable L/R span) 211

8.4   Selected concordance lines for "congratulations" in the Relationships
      subforum (variable L/R span)   212

8.5   Top ten collocates of "father" across the *DadInfo* corpus   212

PREFACE

Before the main part of the book, there are a few things I'd like to get out of the way first, primarily to help explain some of the background to the book and the actual process of writing it. These issues aren't central to the main aims of the book, but (I think) they're important in terms of the context in which it was written. If you prefer, you can skip over this preface and I'll be none the wiser. But as I go on to note, both here and in the chapters that follow, this book is a product of who I am and the life I've lived, and the process of writing it is not divorced from that reality. To that end, this preface will give readers a better understanding of how this book came about and how it is situated within the broader structural context of academia.

First, writing this book has been, without a shadow of a doubt, the single most difficult personal and intellectual endeavor I've ever undertaken. Not only did I write the vast majority of the book during a prolonged period away from my family and friends as a Junior Visiting Professor at the University of Jyväskylä (a point I discuss in more detail later on), but there is also a profound pressure in coming up with new ideas, seeing things in different ways, and ultimately writing something that other people are hopefully going to find a valuable, interesting, and useful contribution to knowledge. And since I don't consider myself especially talented, innovative, or clever, it's been doubly awful, because I've had to contend with constantly comparing myself to the brilliant writing that I have had to read for this book (and having an acute case of Impostor Syndrome doesn't help with this!). Theodore Roosevelt once opined that comparison is the thief of joy, yet comparison looms large in academia, where ideas are currency and setting yourself out as different is an occupational necessity.

So, to anyone reading this who thinks that writing a book is easy, please take it from me that it's anything but. On the other hand, I don't think I'm anything special, so if I can do it, then you definitely can do too. One thing that kept me going through the long days, nights, and weekends of writing was something that my parents told me when I was growing up: as long as you try your best, then no one can ask any more of you. This book is absolutely the best that I could have done; I hope it's enough.

Second, over the course of writing this book, the UK higher education sector was embroiled in strike action in November 2019, February 2020, December 2021, and again in November 2022, partly in response to planned changes to pensions and partly in response to increasing precarity, workplace stress, and the yawning gap between education as a commodity and education as a social good. The strikes were not one-issue campaigns, but rather responses to the culmination of years of underinvestment, overwork, and a series of increasingly unrealistic demands on staff. After years of mismanagement by governmental agencies and ministers who variously introduced a variety of 'innovations' like the National Student Survey, the Teaching Excellence Framework, and other metrics, academics across the UK decided that they could no longer tolerate the slow erosion of the values and expertise that has made the UK higher education sector one of the best in the world.

While there's an argument to be made that the 'innovations' introduced by government agencies encourage a high-quality teaching environment, the other side of the argument is that they detract from the core university focus of teaching, research, and writing, leading to short-term thinking couched primarily in terms of league tables and rankings (see Jones 2019 for a discussion of the marketization of British higher education). Moreover, academics are increasingly squeezed on all sides, barely able to keep up with the demands of teaching, planning, preparation, committees, meetings, marking, tutorials, office hours, emails, outreach, and public engagement, never mind reviewing, writing, editing, collaborating, and dealing with other research-related activities (see UCU report 2020 for a sobering review of academics' opinions on university research culture). These constant pressures have an effect on staff morale, mental health, and well-being, sometimes culminating in devastating consequences. The suicide of Dr. Malcolm Anderson, a lecturer at Cardiff University, in February 2018 is one such tragedy, and there are countless others struggling under unsustainable workloads, unrealistic targets, constant emails, and the difficulties of doing more with less, leading to significant increases in depression, anxiety, and general poor mental health across the sector (see Morrish 2018; Adron 2019; Smith and Ulus 2020; Erickson, Hanna, and Walker 2021; UCU report 2022 for discussions about workload pressures and well-being in academia). The COVID-19 pandemic further exacerbated long-standing pressures, alongside the emotional and psychological toll of lockdowns, quarantines, virus testing, and isolation from friends, family, and colleagues.

Don't get me wrong, I'm incredibly privileged to have the job that I do. I love working with my students and helping them reach their goals. My colleagues, both at BCU and further afield, are wonderful educators and incredible researchers and I am proud to work alongside them. I find research tough, but I get a fair amount of personal and professional satisfaction from seeing an idea through to final publication. I have reasonable job security, I'm able take on projects that I believe in, and I think that what I do as a teacher, lecturer, and researcher is socially valuable and adds something to the world (however small that contribution might be!). Unfortunately, I know of far too many exceptionally talented colleagues who do amazing and important teaching and research on precarious fractional contracts, who have to jump from job to job with no long-term security, and who are not able to plan for their futures (see Gupta 2019; Jones 2020; McKie 2020; Megoran and Mason 2020 for discussions of the impact of casualization and academic precarity). I also know of too many colleagues who, even with secure contracts, find it difficult to keep up with the range of competing demands placed upon them. Academia certainly isn't the only sector suffering from these issues, reproduced as they are in health care, policing, transport, primary and secondary education, social work, and many other professions. While it's difficult to ward off the temptation to argue about who's got it worse, it's important that people stand together and push for real change across all sectors, rather than engage in a race to the bottom.

All of this takes me to my third point, which concerns the Junior Visiting Professor post I took at the University of Jyväskylä (JYU). As I mentioned earlier, writing this book was far from easy, most particularly because I lived apart from my wife Rebecca and our daughter Bethany for the six months of my research leave in Finland. There were a few reasons for making this decision. First, it didn't seem like a great idea to uproot the entire family and move to a country where we didn't know anyone, didn't speak the language, didn't know our way around, and didn't know if we'd make it through the long dark months of a Finnish winter. Second, we knew that without accepting the post, writing this book would have to happen in the small chunks of time I had in between meetings, teaching, commuting, and my regular work responsibilities, alongside spending evenings and weekends trying to make progress, something which didn't really appeal to either of us.

Deciding whether or not to the opportunity on offer from JYU was one of the most difficult decisions Rebecca and I have ever had to make together, especially since the longest we'd been apart from one another in nearly ten years was just over a week. In terms of positives, the post would mean that I would have nearly six months to dedicate to the book, alongside the opportunity to share my research and build new connections with an academic community I hadn't previously had the chance to work with. In terms of negatives, it meant that Rebecca would have to take on six months of looking after our daughter by herself, a full-time job substantially tougher than what I had to deal with in Finland, while we would be apart as a family for the duration of my stay. The personal cost for all of us should be obvious at this point.

I say all of this because it's easy to be critical of someone who has upped sticks to gallivant off to another country for research purposes. For example, in one of the few academic articles on acknowledgments, Callaci (2019, 2) observes that they "offer a glimpse into the political economy of academic life, revealing truths that we intend to share, as well as many that we do not." Callaci goes on to wryly note that acknowledgments written by male scholars sometimes seem to blur the boundary between a genuine thank you letter and a heartfelt confessional, suggesting the following as a more accurate rendering of traditional acknowledgments:

> Dear reader, I exploited my wife's re-productive labor, neglected my children and aging parents, shifted departmental service onto my colleagues, extracted knowledge from people in a distant country, contributed to the warming of the planet by flying all over the world, and withdrew from my community, all in order to bring you this book.

I read Callici's article about halfway through writing the book and it has stayed with me ever since, especially because, at least in my case, there was more than the sting of truth in her argument. Support of my wife? Check. Leaving her to take on all the child-caring duties? Check. Spending time away from my daughter? Check. Leaving colleagues to take on my work responsibilities? Check. Traveling via airplane to a far-flung international locale? Check. Didn't see friends or family for months? Check. I fit, in quite a worrying way it has to be said, what Callici calls (mostly tongue-in-cheek, I think) the 'ideal scholar', one who is flexible, mobile, has a passport from a powerful nation, can rely on a partner for childcare, and is not providing for extended family or elderly, sick, or vulnerable parents.

It is true that I have benefited enormously from the privilege of international mobility, the invitation of a research post at a prestigious international institution, and the support of my wife who took on the individual responsibility of raising our daughter, while working at a university which allowed me to take time away from my normal duties and having colleagues who could cover my responsibilities. While all of this is perhaps commonplace in academia, especially for male scholars, it nevertheless raises a number of issues concerning equality of opportunity, privilege, and reciprocity.

I could, of course, overlook all of this and instead present the writing of this book as the neat packaged up story that we all know and love. And this is Callici's argument—most people do exactly that, a process which simply erases the structural contexts (and struggles) within which academic work emerges. By confronting some of these issues, we can at least start to ask the question, as Callici (2019, 2) does, "Was this book really worth it?" And doing so requires us to deal with some of the less salutary aspects of academic life and to consider some of the broader structural contexts of academia, which Callici's main thesis arguably overlooks.

This, ultimately, takes me to my fourth and final point. I think it's something of an open secret to say that academia is a ridiculously competitive club. There is a constant need to be 'research active' and to climb the greasy ladder of something called 'success'. Ultimately, research outputs in the form of journal articles, books, edited volumes, chapters, and so on are worth something in the eyes of the academy and in the eyes of institutions who employ you. In the precarious and shifting sands of higher education, publications influence promotions, confer status, and often determine job security. Failure to publish can raise questions about your performance, your competency, and your ability to conduct research, so the pressure is on to write. But how do you fit something as demanding as a book alongside all of the other responsibilities that one might have? Unfortunately, with great difficulty.

While the earliest rumblings of this book go all the way back to 2013, I eventually started working on it in earnest during my research leave in late 2018, where I was able to complete rough drafts of every chapter by the time my sabbatical ended. From January 2019 to August 2019, I didn't have any time for the book at all due to major structural changes at BCU, preparing for teaching new modules, plus a host of other day-to-day activities that I needed to do just to keep my head above water (from January 2014 until January 2020, I oversaw the entire English degree program as part of my job at BCU, so it was a very intense and student-focused role). In 2018, I also took the decision to limit the amount I worked at evenings and weekends in order to spend time with my family, rather than working the fifty- or sixty-hour weeks that I had been previously. So, it wasn't until I arrived at JYU in August 2019 that I was able to make any significant headway on the book, where I had time to read, learn new methods, analyze data, and write almost every day, including weekends, for nearly six months straight (and it was time that I needed!).

To go back to the post at JYU, the question Rebecca and I kept returning to was a simple one—could we afford to turn it down? Without taking the post, the likely publication date of this book would have been closer to 2026. As it is, it's out in 2023, a full three years earlier and hopefully much closer to the contemporary contexts I discuss in the different chapters.

I am, nevertheless, conscious of the extra work that Rebecca took on to make the visit to Finland (and by extension, the book) possible in the first place—FaceTime, Skype, and pictures helped with the loneliness we both felt, but it's never quite the same as being in the there-and-now. The guilt of being an absent husband and father, knowing that I was missing out on precious time with my daughter and my wife, is not an experience I'd ever like to go through again. But as Rebecca reminded me during one evening of soul-searching, opportunities like visiting professor posts (junior or otherwise) very rarely come along and it would have been silly to have turned it down.

I'd certainly be the first to acknowledge that my privilege made it possible for me to finish this book, but I think it's reasonable to say that this is only part of the story. To that end, I hope what I've covered in this preface has provided more of an insight into the personal and professional contexts within which this book has been written. This kind of openness is much needed in academia, even if it is scary to stick your head above the parapet.

REFERENCES

Andron, Sabina. 2019. "I Adore my Work, Yet I Consider Quitting Every Day: This Is Teaching." *Sabina Andron* (blog), November 18, 2019. https://sabinaand ron.com/2019/11/18/i-adore-my-work-yet-i-consider-quitting-every-day-this-is-teaching/.

Callaci, Emily. 2019. "On Acknowledgements." *The American Historical Review* 125 (1): 126–131.

Erickson, Mark, Paul Hanna, and Carl Walker. 2021. "The UK Higher Education Senior Management Survey: A Statactivist Response to Managerialist Governance." *Studies in Higher Education* 46 (11): 2134–2151.

Gupta, Kat. 2019. "On Strike and on Striking." *Mixosaurus*, November 26, 2019. http://mixosaurus.co.uk/2019/11/on-strike-and-on-striking/.

Jones, Lee. 2019. "The Seven Deadly Sins of Marketisation in British Higher Education." *Medium*, November 28, 2019, https://medium.com/@drleejones/the-seven-deadly-sins-of-marketisation-in-british-higher-education-c91102a04a8f.

Jones, Steven. 2020. "UK Academics Must Stand Up to Stop Universities Becoming Sweatshops." *The Guardian*, January 28, 2020, https://www.theguardian.com/education/2020/jan/28/academics-must-stop-uk-universities-sweatshops.

McKie, Anna. 2020. "Casualised Staff 'Dehumanised' in UK Universities." *Times Higher Education (THE)*. January 20, 2020. https://www.timeshighereducation.com/news/casualised-staff-dehumanised-uk-universities.

Megoran, Nick, and Olivia Mason. 2020. *Second Class Academic Citizens: The Dehumanising Effects of Casualisation in Higher Education*. London: University and College Union.

Morrish, Liz. 2019. "Pressure Vessels: The Epidemic of Poor Mental Health Among Higher Education Staff." *HEPI number Occasional Paper* 20: https://www.hepi.ac.uk/2019/05/23/pressure-vessels-the-epidemic-of-poor-mental-health-among-higher-education-staff/.

Smith, Charlie, and Eda Ulus. 2020. "Who Cares for Academics? We Need to Talk About Emotional Well-Being Including What We Avoid and Intellectualize Through Macro-Discourses." *Organization* 27 (6): 840–857.

University and College Union. 2020. *What Researchers Think About the Culture They Work In*. London: Shift Learning/Welcome Trust.

University and College Union. 2022. *Workload Survey 2021: Data Report*. London: University and College Union.

ACKNOWLEDGMENTS

As everyone knows, acknowledgments are one of the nicest bits of a book, where the author gets to thank everyone who has contributed, either directly or indirectly, to getting the final version of the manuscript to publication. Consequently, they're an insight into the life of the author, charting the sacrifices they've made, the challenges they've overcome, and the help they've received along the way. Acknowledgments are immemorial in academia and for good reason—even though writing is usually framed as a solitary activity, a book isn't just the result of one person's exertions, but a collective effort forged from a scholar's personal and professional community. The image of the lonely academic hunched over a laptop typing into the wee hours of the morning is certainly a common one, but in my case, that's only part of the story. Writing this book has put me in the company and friendship of so many people that it's difficult to know how to thank all of them. All I can do, though, is try.

First and foremost, I would like to express my gratitude to Monika Bednarek, Kat Gupta, Bernie Hogan, Scot Kiesling, Jack LaViolette, Alon Lischinsky, Jai McKenzie, and Ashley Morgan, all of whom read drafts of various chapters or helped out with queries while I was writing. Their feedback made a massive difference to the end product, helping me to organize my thoughts, clarify my arguments, and refine my writing. Particular thanks go to my 'writing pact' partner Melissa Yoong, who provided mutual advice and encouragement as we both tackled our respective book projects, and the anonymous reviewer of the manuscript, whose insightful comments considerably improved the final version. I would also like to extend my sincerest thanks to Ursula Lutzky, Norma Mendoza-Denton, and Ruth Page, all of whom provided me with some much-needed mentoring at particularly difficult times during the project.

My colleagues at BCU were incredibly supportive while I tackled this book. In particular, I'd like to thank Joseph Anderton, for taking over my course director responsibilities; Esther Asprey, for leading on my undergraduate modules; Matt Gee, for his assistance with the numerous technical problems and programming quandaries I encountered; Mark McGlashan, for helping me through BCU's ethical review process; and Andrew Kehoe, for reviewing the entire manuscript and offering guidance and comments on each chapter with care, good humor, and an eye for detail. Without the help of these colleagues, this book would have taken much longer to finish.

To the numerous students I have taught over the years in my undergraduate classes at BCU, thank you for letting me present some of the ideas I cover in this book and for providing me with valuable feedback on what worked and what didn't. Parts of the book were also presented as conferences papers and invited talks to colleagues at the University of West of England, Sheffield Hallam, the American Anthropology Association conference, the International Pragmatics Association, and more. The questions, insights, and comments offered during these presentations helped guide my thoughts and strengthened a number of the points made in the chapters.

In terms of the nuts and bolts of publishing the book, I'd like to thank Meredith Keffer for her editorial help and expertise; Lal Zimman for his comments on various proposals and drafts; Alexcee Bechthold, Ryan Egan, Macey Fairfield, Suma George, and Kavitha Yuvaraj for proof-reading, copy-editing, and preparing the manuscript for publication; Nicola Lennon for arranging the index; and OUP's design team for the front cover artwork.

Sadya Z helped with fine tuning three of the graphs in the book; Pauliina Nihtilä helped with data preparation for Chapter 7; and Muhammad Hamza Qureshi helped with the data collection for Chapter 8, all of which made a massive difference to the pace of progress. Thanks also to Ian Soars, the CEO of dad.info, for giving me permission to work on the site, and to the contributors of dad.info for sharing their thoughts about fatherhood.

Finally, I'd like to thank Jessica Walton for their permission to reproduce the tweet discussed in Chapter 2 and Christopher Brady for his permission to reproduce his *LunarBaboon* comic discussed in Chapter 7. Copyright for all media content analyzed in this book remains with the original authors/creators and such data has been used exclusively for the sole purpose of criticism and scholarship.

In 2019–2020, I was fortunate enough to be invited to take up a Visiting Junior Professor post as a member of the Research Collegium for Language and Changing Society (ReCLaS) at the University of Jyväskylä in Finland. To that end, I am enormously indebted to JYU and ReCLaS for their financial, pastoral, and research support during my stay, and to Sarah Wood and Alison Honour at BCU for supporting an extended leave of absence to allow me to take up the opportunity JYU represented. Not only I was able to not only dedicate a large portion of my time to completing this book, but I was also able to share my research with a new community of scholars who had a common interest in the social relevance of linguistics. To Rodrigio Camargo Aragão, Nettie Boivin, Josep Soler Carbonell, Sigurd D'hondt, Ulla Heiskanen, Päivi Iikkanen, Chris Jarvis, Leila Kääntä, Gavin Lamb, Mika Lähteenmäki, Laura McCambridge, Joe McVeigh, Anne Pitkänen-Huhta, Tarja Nikula-Jäntti, Nora Schleicher, Kate Sotejeff-Wilson, Laura-Maija Suur-Askola, Eszter Szenes, and Tomi Visakko, thank you for your collegiality and friendship.

My time in Jyväskylä was also made all the more enjoyable though the company of the Riggs family (Dominque, Ahti, Mielikki, and Väinö), boardgame nights with Veera Laine, Lauri Laine, Aino Karppanen, and Jaakko Tähtinen, visits to Teerenpeli Bar under the watchful stewardship of manager Alex 'Allu' Tabell, and outings with members of the Anglo-Finnish Guild of Jyväskylä, including Chloe Wells and Graham Burns. Special mention goes to Dave Sayers, Kerry Garman, and their two children

Anna and Ben, who very kindly acted as a surrogate family and helped stave off the various bouts of homesickness I endured. I'm particularly grateful for their generosity and hospitality, which ran the gamut from advising me on the practicalities of Finnish life though to helping out with problems both major and minor during my time in Jyväskylä. To you all—kiitos teille kaikille!

While writing this book I was fortunate enough to visit Università degli Studi di Bari Aldo Moro in Italy, supported by the Erasmus+ staff mobility program. Thanks go to Annarita Taronna, Gino Lorenzelli, Antonio Eduardo Favale, and all the staff and students I met during my stay for a wonderful week of scholarship and collaboration, with numerous opportunities for me to practice my Italian. Un forte abbraccio e grazie!

Outside of my academic life, a number of friends have been there along the way to help take my mind off the relentless schedule of writing, revising, and editing, both for this project and countless others. To Pelham Carter, Leigh Deas, Andy Deas, Dan Eke, Sarah Eke, Gary Hazeldine, Jill Molloy, Dale Ricketts, Erin Shore, Ross Shore, Gordon Stewart, Laurie Stokes, and Gethin Williams, thank you for your texts, phone calls, messages, conversations, weekend dinners, visits to the pub, and much more. I would also like to thank Pete Wellington, Hanh Hodgson, Katie Sharp-Fisher, Richard Fryer, and Penny Fryer, who all helped support Bethany and Rebecca in matters big and small while I was away in Finland. There are so many others who have been an important part of my life over the years, and it would take a lot more pages than I've got to thank them all. Wherever you are, from Glasgow to Birmingham, Arizona to Pittsburgh, and everywhere else in between, thank you for your friendship.

To my extended family, the Hering Clan (Peter, Linda, Marcus, Claire, Paige, and Reid), your encouragement and support has been a massive help over the years, keeping my mood up when the going got tough. Here's to good company and many more days and nights of Aperol Spritz and stays at the caravilla. To my brother Kris Lawson and my sister-in-law Sarah Lawson, thank you for your quality banter about 'widden pallets', which always put a smile on my face. To my Mum and Dad, you have been a constant source of love, guidance, and inspiration throughout my life. You taught me to use my brain and always encouraged me on to higher things. Who I am today is because of you both—thank you.

The last people I'd like to thank are the most important people in my life—my wife Rebecca and our children Bethany and Georgia. To Rebecca, you are an incredible mum, an amazing wife, my soul mate, my best friend, and so much more besides. To Bethany and Georgia, thank you both for bringing so much light and joy into my life. To all three of you—I love you more than words can say and I hope that I've made you proud. This book is dedicated to you.

CHAPTER 1

Contexts, Cultures, and Constraints

Language and Mediated Masculinities in the

Twenty-First Century

TRUMP, 'PUSSYGATE', AND CONTEMPORARY MASCULINITIES

In late 2016, *The Washington Post* released a video of presidential candidate Donald Trump and *Access Hollywood* host Billy Bush discussing women, dating, and relationships. Captured during a bus ride while both Trump and Bush's microphones were switched on, this conversation saw Trump brag about his fame, his wealth, and his attempts at having sex with a married woman, offering a candid insight into his views regarding his celebrity status, the construction of sexual privilege, and his objectification of women. As the bus stops, one moment in the conversation stands out, where Trump and Bush start talking about the host who is meeting them, Arianne Zucker, an actress and model best known for her role in the American soap opera *Days of our Lives*.

1	Trump	Yeah that's her with the gold.
		I better use some Tic Tacs just in case I start kissing her.
		You know I'm automatically attracted to beautiful . . .
		I just start kissing them.
5		It's like a magnet.
		Just kiss.
		I don't even wait.
		And when you're a star they let you do it.
		You can do anything.
10	Bush	Whatever you want.
	Trump	Grab them by the pussy.
		You can do anything.

Language and Mediated Masculinities. Robert Lawson, Oxford University Press. © Oxford University Press 2023.
DOI: 10.1093/oso/9780190081041.003.0001

	Bush	Yeah, those legs.
		All I can see is the legs.
15	Trump	It looks good.
	Bush	Come on shorty.
	Trump	Oh nice legs huh.
	Bush	Get out of the way honey.
		Oh that's good legs.

After identifying Zucker, Trump says that he should take some breath fresheners just in case he starts kissing her, before talking about how being a celebrity means that he can do anything he wants to women, even *grab them by the pussy* (line 11). In the process of reducing Zucker to her physical appearance (lines 7–11), coupled with comments about grabbing and kissing, Trump and Bush appear to condone sexual assault, abuse, and groping, ignoring issues of mutual consent and appropriate professional conduct (see also Cameron 2020 for a more detailed discussion of this incident).

The video, originally recorded in 2005 but released in the run-up to the second presidential debate between Hillary Clinton and Donald Trump, drew criticism from across the social and political spectrum. House Speaker Paul Ryan stated that "women should be championed or revered, not objectified" while John Oliver, host of the late-night political satire show *Last Week Tonight*, called Trump "one giant, salivating, dick-size-referencing, pussy-grabbing warthog in a red power tie." On the other side of the pond, controversial public commentator Katie Hopkins argued that "Trump is (a very flawed) human—big deal. I'd rather be grabbed by the pussy than governed by one."

In subsequent interviews, Trump defended his statement, arguing that it was "locker room banter" typical of the kind carried out by men in private settings, where they brag about their sexual activities and their sexual partners. But even this generated widespread disagreement, especially among athletes, coaches, and other sporting professionals. For example, NFL player Chris Conley tweeted, "just for reference. I work in a locker room (every day) . . . that is not locker room talk," while NBA player Kendall Marshall announced, "PSA: sexual advances without consent is NOT locker room talk."

The video not only reignited debates about sexual privilege, consent, and how men in positions of power exploit their status, it also raised broader questions about men and masculinities in the twenty-first century, captured most prominently in ex-boxer Floyd Mayweather's defense of Trump, who argued that "[Trump] speak like a real man spoke. Real men speak like, 'Man, she had a fat ass. You see her ass? I had to squeeze her ass'" (see Wells 2017). Did the video really represent how men talk to one another in private? Were Trump and Bush men simply guilty of being men? And how did their conversation map on to cultural expectations surrounding (White) masculinity in contemporary Western societies?[1] These questions once again came to the fore less than a year later during the #metoo movement, a social

---

1. With the exception of lowercase forms if they have been used in quotes or in excerpts of data, the terms 'White' and 'Black' are capitalized throughout the book (see also McIntosh

media campaign which sought to highlight the sexual abuse and harassment faced by women from all walks of life, including politics, academia, and the media and entertainment industries.

MEN AND MASCULINITIES IN THE PUBLIC EYE

We have seen an increase in Western media coverage about 'bad men' in recent years, with social commentators, politicians, and journalists critiquing, challenging, or contesting 'toxic masculinity', the age of 'aggressive masculinity', and the 'problem of men' (Peters and Besley 2019). A cursory look at the discourses of (and about) men (particularly White heterosexual men, the focus of this book) would suggest that they play a major role in almost every contemporary social problem, from climate change to the global financial crash, from wars and civil conflicts to inner-city crime, and from interpersonal domestic violence to mass shootings. And there is arguably some truth in this.

For example, all of the mass shootings in the US between 2000 and 2018 were carried out by men (Kimmel 2017, 72; Kiesel 2018; Vito, Admire, and Hughes 2018, 1), many very often preceded by a history of domestic abuse and misogyny (Bosman, Taylor, and Arango 2019). Internationally, most violent crime is carried out by men, including (attempted) murder, rape, sexual assault, robbery, and terrorist offences (Office for National Statistics 2021a, 2021b); most institutional and workplace sexism is carried out by men (Stamarski and Son Hing 2015); most instances of domestic violence and assault are perpetrated by men (Dragiewicz and Lindgren 2009; although see Dutton 2012 for a contrary perspective); those responsible for the global economic turndown and the subsequent financial scandals which followed, including the bankruptcy of Lehman Brothers investment bank in 2008, the renationalization of the Royal Bank of Scotland in 2009, the LIBOR case in 2012, the JPMorgan Chase trading loss in 2014, the HBOS fraud case in 2016, and the HSBC tax evasion and money laundering scheme in 2017, were almost exclusively men (Griffin 2013; Noonan et al. 2017); and male CEOs have been jailed for a variety of offenses over the years, such as tax evasion, securities fraud, theft, insider trading, investment misselling, and environmental crimes (see also Maclean 2016).

Alongside these problems, boys and men tend to be disproportionally represented across a variety of other social ills. For example, British boys perform worse academically than girls (Hillman and Robinson 2016); in almost every country, men are more at risk of committing self-harm and suicide (Murray et al. 2016, 1493); men are more likely to suffer from drug, gambling, or alcohol addiction (Cotto et al. 2010; Hughes, Wilsnack, and Kantor 2016; Merkouris et al. 2016); men have higher incarceration rates compared to women (Loesche 2017; Sturge 2018); men are more likely to be the victim of violent crime, particularly in areas of high deprivation (Rossetti,

and Mendoza-Denton 2020, xix and University of Chicago Press Editorial Staff 2020 for related discussions of capitalization in relation to ethnonyms).

Dinisman, and Moroz 2016); men take more risks in sex, driving, sports, outdoor pursuits, and a range of other activities (Byrnes, Miller, and Schafer 1999; Rhodes and Pivik 2011; Charness and Gneezy 2012); men are less likely to seek out help for depression, anxiety, and stress (Doward 2016); men from socially disadvantaged backgrounds have poorer health outcomes in terms of disability, chronic illness, and injury rates compared to women in the same contexts (Evans et al. 2011); and men have a shorter life expectancy than women (Austad 2006; Inoue et al. 2008).

Of course, whether these statistics are due to biological or sociological factors is an open question—do men have a shorter life expectancy than women because they have a biological predisposition to higher cholesterol levels, for example, or is it because they pursue riskier behaviors which are likely to lead to an earlier death? Do men pursue these risky behaviors because competition and bravado are so ingrained as part of the 'masculine ideal'? Do boys perform academically poorer than girls because being clever is seen as 'less manly' or are there neurological differences which explain this patterning? I return to some of these points in Chapter 2, but for the moment it is enough to say that this division between biological and sociological explanations of gendered behavior has dominated the research literature for decades.

CHANGING MASCULINITIES?

Going beyond the statistics above, it would be reasonable to say that the traditional touchstones of male identity, such as aggression and risk-taking, are becoming increasingly problematized, challenged, or disputed (although these cultural touchstones also vary depending on age, social class, and background). This is not new though. Men's lives have long been changing, from the loss of traditional laboring jobs from the mid-1970s onward (Beckwith 2001; Johnston and McIvor 2004a, 2004b; Iacuone 2005) and the subsequent rise of technical and nonmanufacturing specialisms (Lohan and Faulkner 2004; Mellström 2004), through to the shift in sexual relations (Seidler 1989; Garlick 2003; Flood 2008; Hyde et al. 2009) and changing familial and domestic patterns which de-emphasize the role of the traditional male 'breadwinner' (Aitken 2000; Thébaud 2010; Walsh 2011). Even as far back as 1987, Shepherd Bliss, a key figure in the mythopoetic men's movement, claimed that "the consensus about what it means to be a man in America today is eroding, a development that some applaud and others bemoan" (Bliss 1987).

In the mid-1980s through to the late-1990s, these "Men's Movements" organizations and consciousness-raising groups, influenced by writers like Robert Bly and Michael Mead, called for a return to a form of 'primal' masculinity more connected to nature and spiritualism (Kimmel and Kaufman 1993; see also Fox 2004 for an overview of the men's movement between 1970 and 2000). Drawing on storytelling, rituals, poetry, sports, and crafts, such groups gave men the opportunity to gather together for friendship and connection and to reflect on the supposed changes that were affecting their lives (although see Boise 2019 for a discussion of antifeminist stances in the men's movement). That said, the men's movement as a whole was firmly entrenched in the "crisis of masculinity" discourse, where the shifting sands of contemporary gender relations seemingly left men without a place in the world (see Kimmel 1987; Mac an Ghaill 1996; Hearn 1999; McDowell 2000; Robinson 2000; Morgan 2006 for further discussion).

Even though the men's movement more or less stalled in the late 1990s, it is, of course, worthwhile questioning the contention that men were (or are) in 'crisis' (Connell 2002, 91; Flood 2010, 329; Walsh 2010, 7; Milani 2011, 183), particularly given the abundant social capital that is usually afforded to them. While a common refrain, it is difficult to sustain any argument that places men, especially White men, in a 'victim' position, even if many do not feel they benefit from any degree of social privilege (I return to these issues in later chapters). As author John Scalzi (2012) points out in one of his blog posts, "in the role-playing game known as The Real World, 'Straight White Male' is the lowest difficulty setting there is and it is difficult to argue the contrary."

Nevertheless, this "crisis of masculinity" discourse (which tends to center on White Western masculinities) is a beguiling one and one that still crops up in contemporary discussions about men and their position in society (de Coning 2016). Drawing on this discourse, a variety of groups have pushed back against what they consider to be the ongoing demonization and marginalization of men, men who feel they are shunted to the side-lines (Kimmel 2017, 23). These groups include (radical) men's rights organizations; the newly coined, predominantly male-led, political 'alt-right' movement; online 'seduction' communities; individuals who identify as involuntary celibates or 'incels' (i.e. men who, despite wanting to, have never had sex or have not been in a sexual relationship with another person); and advocates of 'men going their own way' (conventionally known as the MGTOW movement), that is, men who reject marriage, common-law partnerships, and nuclear male/female relationships.

Finding a home in the 'manosphere', a loose collection of male-authored websites and blogs concerned with "men's issues," these groups promote the reclamation of a 'primal' form of masculinity and a return to traditional gender norms and relations. By extension, many sites uphold an ideology of male supremacism which sees women as biologically and intellectually inferior to men, "incompetent yet conniving and manipulative . . . [reducing] women to their reproductive function and simultaneously shaming women for having sex while believing that sex is something women owe men or that should even be coerced out of them" (Southern Poverty Law Center 2021). For example, manosphere blogger Daryush Valizadeh (more commonly known as Roosh Valizadeh or Roosh V; see Southern Poverty Law Center, 2018) argued that women should have their behavior and decisions overseen by close male relations.

As long as we continue to treat women as equals to men, a biological absurdity that will one day be the butt of many jokes for comedians of the future, women will continue to make horrible decisions that hurt themselves, their families, and their reproductive potential. Unless we take action soon to reconsider the freedoms that women now have, the very survival of Western civilization is at stake. (Valizadeh 2015)

The post received over 450 responses, with the vast majority supportive of Valizadeh's points. A brief review of posts and user submissions on websites like *The Red Pill*, *A Voice for Men*, *The Return of Kings*, *Men Going Their Own Way*, and other manosphere outlets provides numerous examples of men blaming women for the social ills that men face, coupled with anger about men's perceived loss of status and position (Rensin 2015). Unsurprisingly, views like this have led the Southern Poverty Law Center to classify certain male supremacist websites as extremist organizations (Smith 2018; Southern Poverty Law Center 2021).

SO WHY THIS BOOK NOW?

So why write a book about language and masculinities? What do we get by looking at this intersection of language and gender? What can a linguistic analysis uncover about contemporary social practices associated with men and masculinities? And what can this book offer in terms of furthering our knowledge about the mediated representations and lived realities of men in the twenty-first century?

As noted previously, there has been an intense media spotlight on men and masculinities in recent years, including extensive discussion of their behavior, attitudes, beliefs, and ways of interacting with others. People are interested in (and sometimes exasperated, frustrated, or angered by) what men do. Over the past ten years, a lot of ink has been spilled about toxic masculinities, fragile masculinities, aggressive masculinities, and other forms of masculine identities, while male violence against other men, as well as homophobic and transphobic violence perpetrated by men, have been raised as significant public health issues (Blondeel et al. 2018; Harper et al. 2022). Men are often cast as villains of the piece, while at the same time, there is a general view that dominant ways of being a man are changing and that the traditional strongholds of male identity are becoming unviable. Organizations such as the *Men's Health Network* and the *Good Men Project* are conscious of the social and psychological damage that these traditional expressions of masculinity can wreak, advocating for healthier configurations of masculinity. The quarrel about what it means to be a man plays out most dramatically in online media contexts, where people (mainly men) argue about how, for example, men are becoming more effeminate or are losing their sense of masculine pride.

This growing debate surrounding men and masculinities has been captured in a number of outputs directed at the general public. For example, artist Grayson Perry's documentary *All Man* (Crombie and Cary 2016), and his companion book *The Descent of Man* (Perry 2016), offers an autobiographical account of Perry's life and his struggles to deal with normative conceptions of masculinity as he navigates his way through his own gender identity as a "man in a dress." In a similar vein, comedian Robert Webb's (2017) autobiography *How Not to Be a Boy* examines the pressures men and boys are under to uphold certain standards of masculinity, wryly noting that the rules for being a man are straightforward—"don't cry; love sport; play rough; drink beer; don't talk about feelings." This idea of artifice and 'maskcraft' is also the subject of athlete Lewis Howe's *The Mask of Masculinity* (2017), which deals with the intersection of masculinity and emotional vulnerability, with Howe contending that "there are many things that our definition of masculinity inhibits, but the damage it does to our relationships and sense of self, and therefore to our chances of success in life, should be enough to make you reconsider the stereotypical definition of 'masculinity'" (Howe 2017, 13; see also Bola 2019 for a discussion of masculinity and the mask metaphor).

Beyond these general public outputs, there is also a burgeoning academic scholarship on the topic, including a number of edited volumes and books dedicated to exploring the intersection between masculinities, cultures, and contexts. These include (to name just a few) *Studying Men and Masculinities* (Buchbinder 2012), *Men, Masculinities and Violence* (Ellis 2015), *Masculinities under Neoliberalism* (Cornwall, Karioris, and Lindisfarne 2017), *Marginalised Masculinities: Contexts, Continuities and Change* (Haywood and Johansson 2017), *Angry White Men* (Kimmel 2017), *Gender Hate Online: Understanding the New Anti-Feminism* (Ging and Siapera 2019), and *Gender, Sexuality, and the Cultural Politics of Men's Identities* (Mundy and Denny 2020), alongside a host of journals about masculinities studies (e.g. *Masculinities: A Journal of Identity and Culture*, *Masculinities and Social Change*, and *Psychology of Men and Masculinity*).

So, there is certainly no shortage of both academic and nonacademic work on men and masculinities. But while this body of research forms an important foundation to some of the issues discussed later in this book, what is often missing from these accounts is any detailed treatment of the role language plays in how men construct their identities and how language functions as the primary channels through which they live their lives. And although there are a great many individual articles, edited volumes, and chapters concerned with language and masculinities (e.g. Edley and Wetherell 1997, 1999; Johnson and Meinhof 1997; Wetherell and Edley 1999; Bucholtz 1999; Evaldsson 2002; Benwell 2003; Bamberg 2004; Kiesling 1998, 2004, 2005, 2006, 2018; Andersson 2008; Lawson 2013, 2015, 2020; Milani 2015; Baker and Levon 2016; Levon, Milani, and Kitis 2017), there are almost no single-authored books about the topic (some notable exceptions include Coates 2003 and Coffey-Glover 2019, on male narratives and representations of masculinity in women's magazines respectively). *Language and Mediated Masculinities*, then, is one of the few book-length attempts at examining contemporary masculinities in the twenty-first century to answer the question of how language is implicated in the performance, maintenance, and construction of masculinities, focusing particularly on online and offline media contexts. More specifically, I believe that the critical study of language is central to a discussion about masculinity for several reasons.

WHY LANGUAGE?

First, language is a key part of how people *do* identity, where linguistic resources are used to construct raced, sexed, gendered, and classed identities (and intersections thereof—aspects of identity cannot easily be unlinked from one another, Preece 2016). When people talk, they are not just communicating a particular idea or concept, they are telling their interlocutor(s) about who they are and where they are from. Sometimes this can be their use of a certain word, phrase, or grammatical structure, other times it can be the way that they say something. Whatever it might be, the way a speaker uses language gives other people (broad) information about their identity.

This focus on language as a constituent component of identity has been a well-established part of sociolinguistic theory for over three decades, building on the pioneering work of Butler (1990) and Eckert and McConnell-Ginet (1992). I go into more detail about this in Chapter 2, but for the moment, it is enough to say that this approach views language as a social practice, as something people do as they go about their day-to-day lives. Thinking more specifically about men and masculinities, an in-depth analysis of language can help us better understand the linguistic means through which masculine gender identities are constructed and the different strategies men adopt to *do* masculinities. In the context of twenty-first century gender relations and the ways that masculinities are presented in online and off-line spaces, it is vital that we know more about the role that language plays in these contemporary gendered identity projects.

Second, we can use a linguistic analysis to examine how language is implicated in a broader system of social power and gender politics, how contemporary gender relations are constituted, and how the privileged position of men is maintained. This perspective also falls under the auspices of Critical Discourse Analysis (van Dijk 1993), where linguistics is used to uncover hidden or implicit systems of inequality. For example, although many aspects of everyday talk are typically unremarkable, they nevertheless yield incredible power, subtly influencing our decision-making, our world views, and our opinions (Kiesling 2007, 655). How people talk about one another and the words they use to refer to others can tell us a lot about the assumptions and expectations that are packed up alongside these terms. For example, the terms *alpha* and *beta*, commonly used within seduction communities as a way of ranking supposedly "dominant" and "submissive" men, are not only a way of identifying (or claiming) that an individual holds particular character traits, but they are also used as internal measures of hierarchy and difference (an example of what Christensen and Jensen 2014 called *internal hegemony*). Similarly, the term *thot* ('that ho [whore] over there') has become a derogatory term within the manosphere to shame and belittle women for their sexual behavior, with those using it tapping into a broader set of discourses to do with (often contrary) standards of promiscuity and sexual attractiveness. Consequently, the study of language and masculinities can help uncover how different groups are marginalized and subjugated through linguistic means, including women, gay men, and ethnic minorities. This, in turn, can help us better understand the power dynamics which underpin gender relations.

Finally, a linguistic analysis can shed light on normative notions of masculinity and how certain standards of masculinity are monitored, policed, and enforced. Men tell one another not to be *fags* or *queer* or *pussies*, *alphas* and *hard men* are celebrated, while men who are *bitches* or *betas* or *cucks* are not real men at all. The more we know about what these standards are and how they are communicated through language, the more we are able to challenge the promotion of essentialist ideas about masculinity (see also Lawson 2022). The fact there are calls in some quarters for a return to traditional gender relations, such as women staying at home as caregivers, means that it is ever more important to chart where this is happening and connect it to broader processes of social change.

Drawing on data collected from newspapers, social media sites, television programs, and online forums, this book presents a discussion of language and masculinities across a range of social and mediated contexts. In offering a critical evaluation of the intersection between language, masculinities, and identities in contemporary society, three key questions underpin the chapters:

- How are contemporary masculinities discursively constructed, in both public and semipublic spheres?
- What can a linguistic analysis tell us about the representation and evaluation of masculinities in different media contexts?
- How does language (re)create gender ideologies and what might this language tell us about the state of contemporary gender relations?

I consider these questions over the course of the book and, in typical academic fashion, the final chapter offers a comprehensive discussion of the implications of these questions, in addition to outlining future research directions.

In taking a critical perspective on men and masculinities and the role that language plays in contemporary constructions of masculinities, the book adopts a data-driven approach throughout, drawing on critical discourse analysis, corpus linguistics, sociolinguistics, and other relevant analytical methods (fair warning should also be given to readers that a number of the textual examples used in this book articulate explicitly sexist, racist, and misogynistic positions). As Cameron (1997) shows, however, it is possible to arrive at two very different interpretations on the same piece of data, so it is likely that there will be disagreement about what the analysis shows, or even with my interpretation of what the data is telling us. Where possible, then, I have also used analytical triangulation, or the process of "measuring or investigating a phenomenon from different perspectives" (Todd 2016, 153). It should also go without saying that each chapter has been peer reviewed by a number of colleagues in order to get a range of perspectives on what I have written. It is very easy to get wrapped up in one's own worldview and positionality when writing a book, so having outside eyes has been helpful in moderating my analytical process.

WHO IS THIS BOOK FOR?

As might be imagined, the primary target audience of this book is other linguists, sociolinguists, and linguistic anthropologists, particularly those interested in language and masculinities, language, gender, and sexuality, language and identity, language and the media, linguistic variation, stylistics, corpus linguistics, and more. The book shows how we can productively combine a variety of methodological approaches to develop a holistic picture of masculinities in the twenty-first century across different social and mediated contexts.

The work presented in this book should also be of interest to researchers in the fields of anthropology, sociology, media, history, criminology, public policy, communication studies, and education. In particular, how we can better illuminate the lived reality of men through the analysis of language should find application across a range of disciplines to do with (mediated) performances of gender, intersectionality, and gender politics. I also hope to demonstrate how a richer understanding of masculinities can be developed through the application of insights drawn from across disciplines.

I have also written this book with undergraduate and postgraduate students in mind, especially those taking classes in language, gender, and sexuality, sociolinguistics, and linguistic anthropology. The research presented in this book spans a range of contemporary contexts, including online forums, comedy shows, newspapers, and different social media sites, much of which I am anticipating readers recognizing. What I want to show is that gender relations, and the politics which undergird everything, are out there in the here and now, ready to be picked apart and examined. I hope what follows might inspire students to reflect on the myriad ways that language is used to perform, enact, and construct different types of masculinity and to consider how the findings in this book might help inform students' own projects and studies.

Beyond academia, there is a growing interest in masculinities more generally, so I hope the book will also appeal to those looking to learn about language and masculinities and its relevance to their own experiences, including educational organizations, charities, policy groups, social workers, teachers, and parents, as well as those who have a broader interest in gender, masculinities, identity and/or sociolinguistic research. I imagine that it is uncontroversial to say that we have all met boys or men in our past who did things we could not understand or said things that were sexist, hurtful, derogatory, or abusive. Conversely, I am sure we have all encountered men and boys who have stood out because they have not followed traditional or dominant ideas about what it is to be masculine. While I cannot claim to have any answers for why men do what they do, I hope that what is here will give readers an insight into the current state of the field. Ultimately, I will always be in the dark about who bought this book and why. Whatever people's interest or motivation in picking up it might be, I hope that there is something of value within its pages.

A FEW WORDS FROM THE AUTHOR

Before going any further, though, I know that this book is likely to be polarizing (and that might even be an understatement), so it is worthwhile noting a few preliminary caveats. I hope that these points are taken in the spirit in which they are intended, which is to clarify some of the choices I have made and the underpinning motivations for the book.

The first thing to say is that the predominant focus in the book is primarily on English speaking, White, heterosexual, cis-gendered[2] men, rather than non-English speaking and queer, homosexual, or non-White masculinities. And it would be reasonable to ask why, especially given recent work on gay masculinities, queer masculinities, female masculinities, and more (cf. Baker and Balirano 2018). Milani (2011) discusses this point at length, arguing that the "critical perspective on heterosexual men is necessary because, from the point of view of queer theory, we should not only pay attention 'to the cases in which bodies/relations/desires "deviate" from the norm, but also those cases in which they do not'" (Milani 2011, 183, citing Cameron and Kulick 2003, 149). The majority of the data I discuss in this book promotes a particular perspective on what it is to be a (White) man and what masculinity entails in twenty-first century society. Not only are these perspectives packaged up as 'normal' and 'everyday', but those who deviate from them are often classed as 'not real men', lacking fundamental masculine qualities. Interrogating the lines between 'successful' masculinity and 'failed' masculinity is an important undertaking which allows us to "[shake] the profound foundations on which the gender and sexual orders are built" (Milani 2011, 184; see also Johnson 1997, 25).

The second thing is that while I use 'men' as a collective term in this chapter and elsewhere, partly for efficiency and partly for ease of reading, I do not mean to imply that what I discuss applies to all men, or even that all men do x, y, or z. Even this position needs some unpacking, though, because it dovetails with some of the counter-politics of the #metoo movement in late 2017 and early 2018 and the associated #notallmen backlash which accompanied it (see also Boyle 2019 and Jones et al. 2022).

Since the #metoo movement played out in the public arenas of Twitter, Facebook, and other social media sites, many men started asking what they could do as allies to reduce the rates of sexual abuse and harassment women were experiencing. Although this was a much welcome change from the 'blame the victim' discourse that is popular in discussions of sexual violence toward women, a less savory strand of discourse emerged at the same time—that of 'not all men' (and the associated hashtag #notallmen). This statement was initially intended to highlight the fact that not all men were rapists, murderers, or likely to commit sexual assault or harassment but, understandably, the general sentiment quickly came under fire as an attempt to divert the conversation away from the problems and issues faced by women. For example, Ford (2018) argues that 'not all men' has become a "notorious battle cry some men bellow whenever women start speaking about the impact misogyny has on our lives," while Proudfoot (2021) points out that the hashtag "[derails] the conversation and [twists] the wave of women speaking up about street violence into 'man hating'" (see also Godwin 2018; Spratt 2021).

The murders of Sarah Everard and Sabina Nessa in 2021 further highlighted the continued problem of male violence toward women and, once again, the specter of

2. That is, men whose biological male sex assignment aligns with their own personal sense of gender identity as a man.

#notallmen trended across social media. While criticisms of the hashtag followed much the same lines as those expressed during the 2017 #metoo movement, there nevertheless appeared to be some shift toward men critically reflecting on their roles in sustaining cultures of male violence and privilege (Alexandra 2021; Burrell, Westmarland, and Buxton 2021; Ferguson 2021; Morgan 2021). To what extent this results in sustained and concrete change remains to be seen, but it represents at least tentative progress toward reframing violence against women as a men's issue rather than as a women's issue (see also Katz 2012, 2019).

As might be expected, I do not wish to align myself with the #notallmen position, but at the same time, I am conscious of following what Johnstone (2000, 5) calls the "grammar of particularity," or the need to distinguish "particular observations from generalized speculations" (Gordon 2005, 958). Consequently, I try to make it clear when my discussion relates to specific communities of men or even specific users and when it is used in a more generic fashion, as far as is reasonably possible.

The third point to note is that I do not think men are inherently bad or that being a man is somehow the worst thing in the world. This book is not meant as an attack on men, and while criticizing certain forms of masculinity is often conflated with criticizing men, there is a marked distinction between 'men' and 'masculinities' (I discuss this distinction further in Chapter 2). But this distinction is not always observed and very often 'men' and 'masculinity' are collapsed together. I would like to discuss just one brief example of this.

In early 2019, shaving company Gillette released an advert challenging certain practices related to what has since come to be termed 'toxic masculinity', including bullying, casual sexism, and suppressing emotional vulnerability. The tag line of 'the best a man can get', known by millions of men and teenage boys across the world, was reformulated to 'the best that men can be', with the advert attempting to send a positive message that being a man does not mean having to beat others up or catcall women on the street. The reaction, however, was far from positive, with many men boycotting the company and criticizing the advert on social media (see Taylor 2019 for a discussion of Gillette's marketing strategy and why it was so poorly received by the target audience). For example, at the time of writing, the advert has over 37.5 million views on YouTube and nearly 500,000 comments, with 840k thumbs up and 1.6 million thumbs down (there have also been accusations that Gillette were censoring comments and deleting downvotes to image-manage and manipulate perceptions of the campaign; incidentally, the video is now closed to comments). Perhaps the most high-profile opponent to Gillette's message was journalist and television presenter Piers Morgan, who wrote the following on Twitter (Figure 1.1).

Morgan's choice of words, including 'virtue-signaling', 'global assault', and 'PC guff', has all the hallmarks of trivializing the message behind the advert. And, like Morgan, many men on social media viewed the advert as an attack on men, arguing that it was replete with harmful stereotypes and superficial characterizations of men as bullies and harassers. Commenting on Gillette's $8 billion write-down due to falling sales apparently caused by the advert, one YouTube poster argues that "this is the price you pay for demonising White male customers," while another states that

Piers Morgan ✔
@piersmorgan

I've used @Gillette razors my entire adult life but this absurd virtue-signalling PC guff may drive me away to a company less eager to fuel the current pathetic global assault on masculinity.
Let boys be damn boys.
Let men be damn men.

Figure 1.1. Piers Morgan's tweet, posted January 14, 2019

"gender equality activists making all the males feel bad about being who they are" (see also Trott 2020 for further discussion of responses to the advert).

I would argue, however, that these comments miss the point of the advert. The advert was not trying to stop "boys being damn boys" or "men being damn men." It was instead trying to draw attention to some of the negative practices of what being a boy or a man normatively entails and to promote "positive, attainable, inclusive and healthy versions of what it means to be a man" (Gillette press release 2019). I do not think it is controversial to assert that bullying is bad, casual sexism is bad, or emotional detachment is bad. Nor do I think it is controversial to say that these are behaviors most commonly associated with boys and men, rather than with girls and women; the history of cinema, television, video games, literature, and advertising has innumerable examples of men doing exactly the kinds of practices flagged up in the Gillette advert, as does real life.

In my reading, the advert was not implying that all men, or even most men, did these kinds of things, far from it. Very often, though, these kinds of practices are bound up with expectations of what it is to be 'manly'—be physically intimidating, objectify women, disavow your emotions—and it was this that Gillette was trying to dismantle. The point the advert was trying to make was that one can still be a boy or a man and avoid, challenge, or discourage these kinds of practices. As Ted Bunch, cofounder of the charity *A Call to Men*, pointed out, the advert "wasn't an indictment on men, it's actually an invitation to men to be different, to be better . . . Men have been challenged to reflect, to challenge our privilege, our entitlements, to look at how we impact other people" (CBS *This Morning* 2019; although see Edmond Jr. 2019 for an alternative take).

In the same way, this book is not meant to suggest that all men are awful, terrible people or that being a man is an awful, terrible thing, and it should not be taken as a manifesto against men and masculinities. Full disclosure: I am a man and I enjoy being one (although I am conscious that this enjoyment is concomitant with certain privileges I have based on my sex, my sexuality, my social class, my ethnicity, my language, and more). But my identity as a man does not mean that I cannot cast a critical eye on particular forms of contemporary masculinities or how some of the practices traditionally associated with masculinity are problematic or should be challenged.

As such, I would argue that not everything associated with men and masculinities should be viewed negatively. Consequently, some of the chapters deal with what could be regarded as the more positive aspects of masculinities studies, including male friendship, caregiving, fatherhood, and homosociality (although the latter has its problems, as discussed in Bird 1996; Kiesling 2005; Cameron 2018; Loofbourow 2018). I also spend some time talking about how masculinity is being reconfigured and reformulated and the role that charity organizations are taking on to promote different, and arguably healthier, conceptualizations of masculinity.

Of course, it is worthwhile mentioning that considering the positive side of masculinity might be considered problematic, especially given how men are often bound up with systems of power, hierarchy, and inequality and the extent to which White heterosexual men in particular benefit from what Connell (2005) calls the 'patriarchal dividend'. As Englar-Carlson and Kiselica (2013, 401) note,

> For many individuals, the idea of empowering men or identifying strengths may seem foreign or downright antithetical to someone who is working to reduce male power, privilege, and sexism. A central concern could be that advocating for a positive psychology of men, or positive masculinity, may gloss over the dark side of masculinity and may be associated with supporting patriarchal structures.

My aim in including chapters oriented around 'positive masculinities' is not an attempt to rehabilitate men, to advance a 'both sides of the story' angle, or to provide some naïve sense of balance. Instead, I suggest that we cannot fully understand the more troublesome components of masculinity without interrogating those practices that are more broadly concerned with positive or progressive outlooks. If what it is to be a man in the twenty-first century is based on a state of tension, then we need to examine the different components that construct this tension. But perhaps more important, these parts of male life and experience are hugely under-investigated in language and masculinities studies. If we are serious about expanding the scope of the field, then these are the kinds of areas that need attention.

WHO AM I TO WRITE THIS BOOK?

In most academic books, the author's background is normally left out, usually for good reason. Some people do not feel comfortable putting that much of themselves into the public eye or are wary of giving up too much information about themselves in case of 'doxing' (that is, personal or private information being released into the public domain), while others think that it is irrelevant to the main focus of the book. In sociolinguistics and linguistic anthropology, however, there has been a shift toward more explicitly stating one's positionality (Mendoza-Denton 2008, 44; Russell 2021, 12). This is not borne from a desire to engage in useless navel gazing, but rather to demonstrate that academic work is never neutral and is shaped by the author's life history and lived experiences. As Spilioti and Tagg (2017) note in their discussion of online ethics, researchers should be more explicit about their positionality, agenda, perspective, and ideologies. As such, it would be foolhardy of me to claim that this book is an objective account; no academic work is, even though the hard sciences might disagree (see Hetherington 1983; Fausto-Sterling 2000; Mendoza-Denton 2008, 4 for discussions of these positions). I'll be honest, though, putting myself out there like this has caused me some sleepless nights and I am not sure how I feel with all of this being written down. At the very least, I hope it gives readers some sense of who I am and where this book comes from, even if it is not an especially interesting account of my history!

So, who am I? Like most introductions, I should probably start with my name. I am Rob, although I grew up as 'Robert' and did not really start using 'Rob' until I was in my late twenties in an attempt to reinvent myself after a break-up. My parents still call me 'Robert' and it is what I use as my publishing and professional name, but most of my colleagues, students, and friends know me as 'Rob'. Whether it is Rob or Robert, I was born in Scotland in 1982, which makes me the ripe old age of 40 at the time this book came out, firmly in the middle-age bracket of life.

I had a largely uneventful childhood growing up in a small Scottish village, before moving to a larger town of around 13,000 when I was eight. Both my mum and my dad are from traditional working-class backgrounds and wanted me to have a better life than them when I grew up. I had a positive male role model in the form of my dad, who worked as a stonemason for the local council and then latterly as a roads and lighting inspector, while my mum worked a variety of jobs in the local community and instilled in me the importance of hard work, persistence, and discipline. I enjoyed reading all through primary school and high school and I really did not like sports (although this changed when I realized that it was possible to enjoy sports as a spectator rather than as an active participant), fighting (whether play or real), or getting dirty running around outside, all typical pursuits for most young boys in the central belt of Scotland. Consequently, I was a bit of an outsider and was bullied when I was younger, especially in high school, both for rejecting stereotypical 'boy' activities and for daring to engage with the learning process the school represented. In Paul Willis's terms, who wrote the classic 1977 sociological text *Learning to Labor*, I would have been an *ear 'ole*—the studious, obedient pupil who followed the rules and did his homework. Thankfully, I found a group of friends with whom I shared some interests, particularly video games and movies, which helped take the sting out of the worst of the bullying.

In 1994, I joined the Air Training Corp, an affiliation which started me down the path of wanting to join the RAF. Unfortunately, I was diagnosed with exercise-induced asthma in 1999, which put the brakes on those plans. My teachers and parents encouraged me to come up with an alternative and I decided to do a degree in English Literature at the University of Glasgow (I was the first in my family to go to university), with the aim of becoming a teacher. During university, though, literature and I had a falling out and I found surprising solace in linguistics, which ended up being my main focus, alongside a wee dabble in Scottish Literature. Throughout my studies, I had a range of jobs, including a trainee electrician, a cashier at Somerfield (a now-defunct supermarket some UK-based readers will recognize), a customer service representative at the Glasgow Science Center, and a summer camp counselor in America, so I would like to think I had fairly broad exposure to a variety of people, cultures, and ideas.

I finished my undergraduate degree in 2004, but not before being jumped (or assaulted, for those readers unfamiliar with the vernacular of casual street violence) by a group of young men as I was on my way to the gym one Friday evening. Thankfully, that story has a happy ending in that I was not seriously injured and the encounter ultimately inspired my postgraduate research on language, masculinity, and violence (Lawson 2009, 2011, 2013). As might be expected, though, it was pretty scary at the time and I genuinely thought I was going to be stabbed or worse. As it was, I 'only' got a belt buckle whipped across my face, a few punches, and a good story to tell. I finished my MPhil in 2005 and my PhD in 2009, before being offered a post as a lecturer at Birmingham City University, where I have been ever since.

Now as if all that was not personal enough, here's a bit more. Over the course of my life, I have lived in Scotland, England, America, and Finland, sometimes with people, sometimes by myself; I have tried (unsuccessfully) to learn German, Spanish, and French, but I have had better success with Italian; I am generally politically apathetic but would class myself as left-leaning; I enjoy movies, gaming, beer, whisk(e)y, cycling, rugby, running (when my knees let me), barbequing, and reading; I have identified as a Scottish, White, cis-hetero male all my life, or at least since I was able to articulate that kind of thing; I would probably categorize myself as middle-class now, but I cannot say I like the label; I have had three serious relationships, met my wife at a music festival in 2009, and we married in 2015.

So why am I telling you all of this, as though this is a bad daytime talk show rather than a serious academic book? It is not just to pad things out or add to the word count, honestly. Instead, it is to show you that this book is the product of all of the experiences I have had over the course of the past forty years. It has not always been an easy life, nor has it been sheltered, but it is certainly not been as difficult as it could have been. And all of these experiences have undoubtedly influenced my gender identity in adulthood. I do not like violence or confrontation; I do not enjoy taking risks; I do not like being a leader or an *alpha*; and I do not like dominating people or 'winning'. At the same time, I am aware that I embody certain aspects of identity which put me at a social advantage—I am university-educated, I am White, I am male, I am straight, I am middle-class, I am English speaking (see also Elsherif et al. 2022 on their 'Academic Wheel of Privilege'). In some circles, I would probably be described as a 'brainwashed soyboy beta cuck' (what these terms mean will be covered in later chapters).

I also wanted to write this history to show that I am a real person, just like your brother, friend, father, son, nephew, spouse, or colleague. And I say this because, and this might be the paranoia talking, it is likely there will be readers out there who will disagree with what I have to say, who will argue that I have been bought off by a shadowy organization to write this book, or who will see it as part of some left-wing feminist conspiracy to undermine (Western) masculinity. Part of me is worried, naturally, by any potential backlash because I have dared to question some of the less salubrious aspects of masculinity, especially as this pertains to digital spaces (see also

Bothwell 2020). And unfortunately, I do not think this concern is misplaced, having spoken with other colleagues who have received hate mail and online harassment following publication of work critical of particular constellations of masculine practice (see Sculos 2017a for a discussion of this and Oksanen et al. 2022 for an overview of online harassment in academic contexts more generally). Disagreement is to be expected in academia, but I would argue that trolling, harassment, doxing, and personal abuse have no place in the canon of civil discourse. Yet I have been online for far too long to know that these practices are common, and hugely damaging, tools in the armory of online argumentation and can have irrevocable consequences for those who find themselves in the firing line. Call me ridiculous, but I could do without all of that in my life. That does not make me a snowflake; it just makes me human.

For what it is worth, I have not been brainwashed by some radical liberal philosophy that has blinded me to the way that the 'real world' works. I am just a lad who grew up in a small town in Scotland who wanted to write a book I thought was important. Whatever your political or personal philosophies are, I hope you will engage with the book in the spirit it is intended.

OUTLINE OF THIS BOOK

Before finishing this chapter, I want to set out a synopsis of each chapter to introduce the data, methodological approaches, and underpinning frameworks used in the book. My aim here is to outline the structure of the book and the general focus of each chapter, so readers know what is coming and how it all fits together.

In Chapter 2, I discuss a number of key terms used throughout the book, including *sex, gender, men, and masculinity*, alongside setting out some of the history of masculinities studies and the trajectory of language and masculinities research over the past twenty years. This chapter aims to contextualize the book against existing research trends and show how the analysis chapters contribute to our understanding of the intersection of language, gender, and sexuality.

Chapter 3 sets out the methodological and theoretical 'nuts and bolts' which underpin the analyses presented in Chapters 4–8. Chapter 3 also presents an overview of the ethical and legal dimensions of the study and issues related to managing researcher safety.

Chapter 4 is the first of the analytical chapters and offers a discussion of one of the exemplars of 'tough' masculinity in Britain, that of the 'hard man'. Tracing how discourses of tough masculinity are deployed in two British broadsheet newspapers, the chapter investigates how the figure of the 'hard man' is used across the different domains of entertainment, sports, politics, and true crime.

Chapter 5 considers a more contemporary context in the form of /r/The_Donald, an online community on the social media site Reddit, to examine the intersection of right-wing masculinities and nationalism. Drawing on four subcorpora, the chapter charts the range of normative masculinities which exist on the subreddit and discusses how these are connected to notions of protectionism and national identity.

Chapter 6 turns to the broader scope of the 'manosphere' and considers data collected from four Reddit manosphere communities. More specifically, the chapter discusses the concept of 'toxic masculinity' and examines how men and women are represented in these communities and what these representations tell us about the nature of online gendered hierarchies.

Chapter 7 discusses the concept of 'positive masculinity' and looks at how masculinity in the twenty-first century is being reconfigured away from the more extreme practices related to 'toxic masculinity'. This chapter also presents an analysis of the comedy show *Brooklyn Nine-Nine* to explore how television can challenge hegemonic notions of masculinity, particularly in the realms of homosociability, friendship, and nonromantic same-sex affiliation.

Chapter 8 examines fatherhood and masculinity through the analysis of dad.info, an online forum dedicated to all aspects of fatherhood and parenting. Examining discourses of new fatherhood, this chapter contributes to the growing body of literature which falls under the umbrella of 'Fatherhood 2.0' research.

Finally, Chapter 9 discusses some broader implications of the book, outlines what we might learn from the insights the book has offered and relates the book to the general scope of men and masculinities research. It also imagines some of the potential future research trajectories in the field.

CONCLUSION

In addition to outlining the contribution this book makes to current debates about men and masculinities, this chapter has attempted to situate the book within a broader context of contemporary gender politics. As I hope I have been able to articulate, this book is timely given the reestablishment of traditional (masculine) gender values among the newly coined 'alt-right' and manosphere movements (Kelly 2017), recent media coverage of sexual abuse and harassment carried out by high-profile men in the political and entertainment spheres (Blumell and Huemmer 2017), and the argument that Western society has reverted to an age of 'aggressive masculinity' (Peters and Besley 2019).

Against a backdrop of rising neoliberalism, ethnic nationalism, online radicalization, and fractious gender relations, not only is a critical discussion about masculinities much needed, but the increased attention on the politics of identity, sexuality, class, power, and more, all refracted through the lens of gender, means that there is a moral imperative to examine contemporary masculinities and how language in implicated in the construction, maintenance, and mediation of such masculinities. It is only by doing so that we can start to unpack the kinds of discourses which surround men and masculinities and to better understand the (usually hidden) processes of hierarchy, differentiation, and discrimination. I hope this book represents one small step in that direction.

CHAPTER 2

Setting the Scene

Some Key Ideas in Language and Masculinities Studies

INTRODUCTION

In this chapter, I introduce the theoretical foundations on which the rest of the book is built. To that end, the chapter has four main purposes. First, it offers a discussion of some key terms used throughout the book, including *sex*, *gender*, *men*, *male*, and *masculinity*. While the meaning of these terms might seem obvious, they have in fact been the subject of some contestation in the literature. Second, it describes some of the approaches in the study of men and masculinities, including hegemonic masculinity (Connell 1987, 2005), positive masculinities (O'Neil 2010; Englar-Carlson and Kiselica 2013), toxic masculinities (Kupers 2005), and caring masculinities (Elliott 2016). Third, it sketches out a brief history of language and masculinities studies (LMS hereafter), showing how this work becomes part of the broader field of language, gender, and sexuality and how attention to the communicative practices of men emerges in response to their relatively uncritical position within linguistics. Finally, the chapter sets out a discussion of men, masculinities, and gender politics, particularly in relation to power and violence.

THE PROBLEM OF DEFINITIONS

While the terms *sex*, *gender*, *men*, *male*, *masculine*, and *masculinity* all seem relatively unproblematic, at least on the surface, as Clatterbaugh (2004, 201) notes, "it may well be the best-kept secret of the literature on masculinities that we have an extremely ill-defined idea of what we are talking about." What is the difference between 'sex' and 'gender'? What is a 'male'? What is a 'man'? How should 'masculinity' be defined? Can only men be masculine? Why talk of 'masculinities' in the plural? Since

Language and Mediated Masculinities. Robert Lawson, Oxford University Press. © Oxford University Press 2023.
DOI: 10.1093/oso/9780190081041.003.0002

we are wading into a terminological minefield, then, the first thing we need to tackle is what it is we are actually talking about (cf. Schrock and Schwalbe 2009, 279).

SEX AND GENDER: SOME PRELIMINARY IDEAS

In almost any introductory language and gender textbook, you will find definitions of the terms 'sex' and 'gender' and a discussion of how they are related to one another. For example, Litosseliti (2006, 10–11) notes that "sex refers to biological maleness and femaleness, or the physiological, functional and anatomical differences that distinguish men and women, whereas gender refers to the traits assigned to a sex— what maleness and femaleness stand for—within different cultures and societies." Similarly, Talbot (2019, 7) points out that "according to the sex-gender distinction, sex is biologically founded, whereas gender is learned behaviour." From these two quotes, we can start to identify some of the dominant discourses of how 'sex' and 'gender' have been used in the literature.

The first is that 'sex' is something rooted in biology, usually a constellation of chromosomal features, hormonal traits, and reproductive anatomy. A great deal of sociobiological research has examined a range of sex-based differences (see, for example, Geary 2010 for a discussion of the evolution of human sex differences), but generally speaking, a categorization as 'male', particularly from a medical perspective, means to be in the possession of a penis and testes, alongside XY sex chromosomes and specific hormonal traits, such as higher levels of testosterone. Being 'female', however, is based on the absence of the Y chromosome, the presence of a womb, ovaries, and vagina, and lower levels of testosterone (and it is important to note that in this schema we have evidence of the 'male-as-norm' discourse;[1] see also Fausto-Sterling 1987; Wilkinson 1997; Ely 2015). During puberty, these differences become further pronounced through secondary sexual characteristics; for example, males generally have larger bodies compared to females and can expect to grow thicker and darker facial and body hair, alongside increased muscle mass and a heavier bone structure. This differentiation approach seems 'common sense' and something people learn from a very early age (Speer 2005, 68). Such accounts of sex as a biological category are enticing, built as they are on a (seemingly infallible) foundation of science (cf. Hasinoff 2009).

Gender, on the other hand, is something which builds on biological sex but is expressed through social action. In basic terms, it is the fluid and dynamic assemblage of behaviors, practices, traits, and attributes that people use and adopt in their everyday lives that allows them to be 'read' as masculine or feminine (although even this schema is problematic, since it assumes gender is a binary dichotomy when in reality it is much more of a plurality or a continuum; see Eckert and Podesva 2011).

---

1. This is the idea that the male category is the default and that other categories (e.g. women) are deviations from the norm.

In many ways, gender is something that we do, rather than something that we have, simultaneously both a conscious and habitual practice (Bucholtz and Hall 2005).

This perspective treats gender as a social endeavor—something that has to be enacted or performed—rather than as something that is inherent and stable. This framing draws heavily on Goffman's (1977) idea of affirmation and Butler's (1990) notion of performativity, whereby individuals construct (or perform) their social identities through practice, including speech. In their ground-breaking article which introduced the concepts of performativity and practice into language and gender research, Eckert and McConnell-Ginet (1992) highlight the numerous ways in which speakers draw on linguistic materials to construct their identities as particular types of men and women. This project consequently inspired a whole tranche of new research, broadly conceived as 'third wave sociolinguistics' (Eckert 2012, 2018; Hall-Lew, Moore, and Podesva 2021).

And while biological sex does not causally determine gender identity, scholarship is now interrogating how the body and gender performance are interrelated. This interrelation is particularly apparent among individuals who identify as nonbinary, queer, or genderqueer, where their biological sex categorization assigned at birth does not align with their gender identity and expression. Recent work has examined how such individuals strategically play with and reconfigure gender practices, from adopting the symbols more commonly associated with the opposite of their assignment, to adjusting their bodies to better align with their gender identity (see also Kiesling 2019, 27). Zimman (2017b) is a good example of how speakers who present a variety of masculine gender identities utilize both linguistic and nonlinguistic practices to emphasize or downplay their alignment with traditional masculine norms (for further discussion of how speakers destabilize and dislocate language, see Barrett 2017 on drag queens and Balirano and Baker 2018 on queering masculinities).

Bringing all of this together, Kiesling (2019, 23) offers a useful summary of what gender encompasses, arguing that:

> Gender is a lot more than a person's individual biology . . . Gender is comprehensive—a system that involves an individual, their habits (including speaking), their feelings, and how they experience the world. But it is also involved in more collective human aspects such as economies, nations, and institutions like families. Gender is not located in one place, then, but is an aspect of human existence that suffuses itself through most aspects of our lives.

And almost everything we do is gendered or related to gender identity in some way, even things we normally take as innocuous. As a society, we are invested in maintaining gender differences—hobbies, jobs, sports, toys, institutions, music, food, drink, make-up, jewelry, clothing, colors, movies, television shows, and more all have gendered dimensions. We even have gender reveal parties for unborn babies and it is usually the first thing that people ask about a newborn. Because gender permeates almost every aspect of our lives, it is sometimes hard to recognize that a practice, or even an object, has anything to do with gender in the first place. The

Jessica Walton - They/Them ⚡
@JessHealyWalton

I just heard a grown man change his order from a hot chocolate to a coffee because his other grown man friends teased him for his "embarrassing" order. Wtf, toxic masculinity? Have you gendered hot chocolate?

1:38 AM · Feb 7, 2019 · Twitter for iPhone

23K Retweets **2,000** Quote Tweets **106.9K** Likes

Figure 2.1. Jessica Walton's tweet, posted February 7, 2019. Reproduced by permission from: Jessica Walton

following tweet (Figure 2.1) is a good example of how even something mundane as hot drinks can have gendered associations.

So why might ordering a hot chocolate be 'embarrassing'? Although we do not get any information about the background to the event reported in the tweet, it is possible to make some sensible inferences. First, sweet drinks like hot chocolate are commonly associated with children, juvenility, and immaturity, so it would make sense the drink would be avoided by people who want to present themselves as mature, experienced, and worldly-wise. But perhaps more relevant here is that as a broad food category, chocolate is strongly associated with women and femininity. Many chocolate adverts are, for example, explicitly designed for, and marketed toward, female audiences and there is a whole set of cultural discourses about femininity and chocolate consumption (Robertson 2010). By extension, then, hot chocolate is embarrassing primarily because it is something women and girls drink.[2] Coffee, on the other hand, should be the (nonalcoholic) drink of choice for men who want to present themselves as normatively masculine (see Davies 2018 for a discussion of the gendered distribution of coffee in television shows and movies; Korobov 2018 for the management of 'manly' and 'girly' drinks in heterosexual dating interactions; and Staples 2020 for an overview of 'gendered' snacks more generally).

This snippet speaks to the broader point that in order to construct a desirable masculine identity, men must assiduously avoid 'feminine' gendered practices (Kimmel 1993, 28; Cheng 1999, 298). As Berdahl et al. (2018, 428) point out, "masculinity is proven through manly displays and feats as well as by eschewing and devaluing traits, characteristics, or interests that are culturally coded as feminine" (see also

2. Following a discussion with the author of the tweet, this interpretation was further supported when they noted that the man's friends "called his order embarrassing and girly." I am thankful to the author for discussing the tweet with me and agreeing for the original tweet to be reproduced here.

O'Neil 2008). Indeed, masculinity and femininity are often defined in relation (or perhaps more accurately, in opposition) to one other. For example, Mills (2008, 130) notes that masculinity "has often been posited as the direct opposite of femininity," while Sunderland (2004) reminds us that the gender differences discourse is an important lens through which people view reality (see also Kimmel 1994; Real and Verner 2011).

While even something like drinks is part of the policing of social norms surrounding gender, these systems of gendered associations are arbitrary and thus open to potential change over time, as social trends and preferences ebb and flow. But while they exist, they have ramifications for how society organizes itself and determines what is 'proper' or 'natural' and there is significant social pressure brought to bear on individuals to follow the cultural scripts at the heart of what is considered 'normal' and 'desirable' gendered behavior. As Kiesling (2019, 27) notes, "if you transgress the right combination of performative practices (especially those that are not ideologically aligned with your genital configuration) you are likely to have huge real-life bodily consequences." The hot chocolate case is a relatively innocuous example of a culturally normative script, but we get into much more difficult territory in cases where technical skills are coded as masculine or caregiving skills as feminine, since these kinds of associations can often reinforce existing social hierarchies and inequalities (see also Kiesling 2019, 70).

This kind of deterministic viewpoint has a long tradition in scholarship which argued for the existence of a causal link between sex and gender, where an individual's biological sex was viewed to have significant implications for their life opportunities (see Maney 2016 for a brief overview of some of this scholarship). Developed in the work of sociologist Talcott Parsons (Parsons 1940), perhaps one of the most influential models in this regard was the concept of the sex role, or the "personal qualities, behavioral characteristics, interests, attitudes, abilities and skills which one is expected to have because one occupies a certain status or position" (Hartley 1959, 457). As might be expected, a number of scholars have rallied against these claims.

In one early rebuttal, Klein (1950, 3) undercuts the notion of a unitary 'feminine type', arguing instead that "society carries, as part of its ideological baggage, a stereotype of Woman, a sort of rough model purporting to contain the *essential* characteristics, while all the *existential* features are but variations on a theme" (emphasis in original).

Nevertheless, sex role theory proved to be a particularly seductive addition to psychology and sociology, where men and women were believed to best occupy particular social roles in society based on their biological sex. This perspective also found a home in the fields of sociobiology and evolutionary psychology, alongside the claim that contemporary sex roles and gender characteristics are the result of evolutionary pressures and processes. For example, Buss and Schmidt (1993) argued that males developed an evolutionary adaptation in which they desire short-term relationships more than women do, due to the lower investment cost in child-rearing, while Greengross (2014) claims that humor is a sexually selected trait for men which increases their potential to attract a female mate (the "differences between men and women" genre is a well-established one—see, for example, Gray 1992; Pease and

Pease 2001; Baron-Cohen 2003; Brizendine 2008, 2011; Locke 2011). This returns us to a point raised in Chapter 1 regarding the tension between nature and nurture. Do, for example, boys perform poorer academically than girls because being clever is seen as 'less manly', or are there neurological differences which can explain this patterning?

Although claims like these have not been without their detractors, many of these discourses are in play even now, particularly as they relate to gender. Seduction artists (also known as 'pick-up artists', that is men who pursue women purely for the purposes of sexual relations) draw heavily on discourses from evolutionary psychology, from the idea that women are more likely to be attracted to a 'natural leader' to the belief that there is an inherent predisposition for women to want to be positioned as subordinate to men. It is also easy to see how these perspectives feed into the narrative that women should 'know their place' in the gender hierarchy.

Within the "men going their own way" (MGTOW) movement (and the manosphere more generally), women's behaviors (and alleged failures of character) are often similarly claimed to be rooted in evolutionary psychological causes. This runs the gamut from women being 'naturally' disposed to cheating and manipulation, through to views about their different moral standards, their selfishness, and their ultimate inferiority to men. This viewpoint is condensed in the acronym AWALT ('all women are like that', or the "absolutist assertion that states females are hard-wired to respond to certain situations in a certain way; and that, more specifically, if given the opportunity, they will tend to behave as manipulative, abusive, sociopathic, destructive, drama-oriented liars. To the extent that women differ from one another, it is in how and to what extent (rather than whether) they manifest these traits when they are allowed to do so" (Rational Wiki 2019).

The attraction of evolutionary psychology is that, like other branches of positivist inquiry, the field is viewed as promoting a scientific approach to the study of human behavior, one based on replicable and measurable methodologies (see Confer et al. 2010 for a discussion of the scientific basis of evolutionary psychology; Fine 2010 for a subsequent critique of "neuroscientific discourse"; and Russell 2021, 219–223 for an overview of scientific discourse strategies in relation to masculinity).

Many individuals in manosphere communities are consequently suspicious or critical of social constructionism, identity politics, and other 'leftie' concepts, since they lack the apparent validity of more scientific approaches (see, for example, Tomassi 2019). Furthermore, evolutionary psychology can be an attractive way of reasoning about the world. For men who might have been cheated on, who have not had a long-term partner, or who have gone through divorce and the concomitant loss of financial resources and regular access to their children, evolutionary psychology arguably offers some comfort that the world is as it is because of nature not nurture. For others, evolutionary psychology is a way of seeing the world for what it really is, rather than being contaminated by a liberal agenda that hides the truth of reality.

This idea is taken up most literally in the manosphere subreddit /r/TheRedPill, which draws on a key piece of symbolism from the movie *The Matrix*. For readers unfamiliar with the premise of the movie, the world in which the protagonist (Neo) exists is a shared simulated reality known as the 'Matrix', whereas the real world is a postapocalyptic warzone controlled by sentient AI machines who have enslaved humanity. During an exchange between Neo and his mentor Morpheus, Neo is offered a choice between a blue pill or a red pill and ultimately a choice between staying in his current world or taking a leap of faith to see the 'real world'. If Neo takes the blue pill, Morpheus tells him that "the story ends, you wake up in your bed and believe whatever you want to believe." But if Neo takes the red pill, "you stay in Wonderland, and I show you how deep the rabbit hole goes." This imagery has since been co-opted by *The Red Pill* subreddit to distinguish those who know the truth of the world, those who have been 'red-pilled,' and 'blue-pilled', those who are still laboring under a mass social delusion (see Read 2019; Hoffman, Ware, and Shapiro 2020, 568; I also return to some of these ideas in Chapter 6).

A key goal of feminist scholarship has been, of course, to challenge these positions, including the idea that biology comes first in the list of explanations for how we are how we are or that sex is the absolute determinant of human behavior, alongside broader critiques of biological sex categorization and problematizing the neat terminological split between sex as biological and gender as social. Examining the research on brain structure and its effect on human behavior, for example, Fine (2010) introduces the concept of 'neurosexism' and argues how a great deal of this research simply maintains the social status quo in what women and men are supposedly 'good' at. In her discussion of the impact of fetal testosterone on male's apparently lower communicative capacity, she observes that "this kind of portrayal is just new 'advertising copy' for the old stereotype of females as submissive, emotional, oversensitive gossips. And a different, nicer way of saying that female brains are designed for feminine skills rather than those necessary for excellence in masculine pursuits" (Fine 2010, 100). Looking more specifically at language use, Cameron (2007) presents a comprehensive critique of what she calls the 'Stone Age Myth', arguing that invoking evolutionary explanations for human behavior is tautological, since evolutionary psychology relies on using contemporary contexts to explain humans behavior in the distant past, but we have no direct observation of past behavior. As she puts it, "[evolutionary psychologists] are obliged to construct narratives about our ancestors based on a mixture of what we think we do know about their lives, what we observe among modern humans, and what are understood to be general principles of evolution. At the same time, they assume that the behaviour of modern humans must be explained as a more-or-less direct continuation of what went on among prehistoric ones" (Cameron 2007, 105).

Discussing the biological basis of sex determination, Lorber (1993, 569) makes the point that "neither sex nor gender are pure categories. Combinations of incongruous genes, genitalia, and hormonal input are ignored in sex categorization and Eckert and McConnell-Ginet (2013, 2–4) argue that even the biological classification of an individual as 'male' or 'female' is very much driven by cultural, rather than scientific, beliefs and that there is no "single objective biological criterion for male or female sex." In a similar vein, Fausto-Sterling (2012) discusses the difficulties of placing individuals born with combinations of chromosomes, genitals, and other biological characteristics into either the male or the female sex category. Carlson (2016, 20) even goes so far to argue that "female and male are not natural but social categories" (see also Wijngaard 1997, 3; Garlick 2003, 164; Cameron 2005, 486; Reeser 2010, 12–13; Sara C 2019). Finally, Eckert and McConnell-Ginet (1992, 463) unpick the separation of sex as biological and gender as social, noting that "what looks like laudable terminological clarity in the service of workable analytical distinctions turns out to mask intellectual confusion. Bodies and biological processes are inextricably part of cultural histories, affected by human inventions ranging from the purely symbolic to the technologic." Despite this work, however, the notion that biology maps on to sex in a straightforward and unitary way is thoroughly embedded in contemporary society and one that has proved exceptionally difficult to dislodge (see also Ainsworth 2018).

It is, of course, important to note that I am *not* saying that biological differences do not exist. There is no doubt that bodies are real, and scholars in sociolinguistics and linguistic anthropology are now starting to investigate the intersection of embodiment, gender, and linguistic performance, challenging perceived wisdoms about this relationship (e.g. Zimman 2014; Bucholtz and Hall 2016; Mendoza-Denton et al. 2017). And while Maney (2016) reminds us to accurately report the influence on behavior of claimed sex differences, we also have a responsibility to ask not just what sex (or gender) differences there are, but what difference sex (or gender) makes (from Cameron 1992).

MALES, MEN, AND MASCULINITIES

So, what does all of this have to do with masculinities? Primarily, it allows me to set out the general theoretical background that is needed to contextualize the next section of this chapter. More specifically, without a clear articulation of what sex and gender mean and the extent to which they are related, it is difficult to tease apart terms like 'male', 'men', and 'masculinity'. With that proviso, we can now move on to consider how these terms have been used in the men's studies literature.

As noted previously, the biological category of male is typically predicated on the basis of possessing a penis and testes alongside having a higher level of testosterone (although as Eckert and McConnell-Ginet 2013, 3 note, the requirements for male genital designation are more stringent than the requirements for female genital designation; see also Zimman 2014, 23). The bodily basis of 'maleness' typically continues through the life-span and a great number of men express concerns about the extent to which they measure up to particular standards of male biology, from penis length to muscularity, height, and body weight (Lawler and Nixon 2011; Johnston, McLellan, and McKinlay 2014). Moreover, there are often a range of normative pressures for men to achieve particular bodily configurations and standards. This can be seen through popular media representations of men in movies (Bruzzi 2013), television shows (Feasey 2008, 2009; Dallesasse and Kluck 2013), video games (Dill and Thill 2007), magazines (Ricciardelli, Clow, and White 2010), the rise of male beauty products (Barber 2008; McNeill and Douglas 2011) and the emergence of a health and wellbeing industry which is more explicitly targeted toward male consumers, covering everything from supplements and dietary advice to gym memberships and lifestyle magazines. This is all part of what Alexander (2003) calls "branded masculinity," a gender construct "rooted in consumer capitalism wherein corporate profit can be enhanced by generating insecurity about one's body and one's consumer choices and then offering a solution through a particular corporate brand" (Alexander 2003, 535). While it would be tempting to suggest, as Garlick (2003) does, that 'man' is at the intersection where biological sex (male) meets gender identity (masculinity), this misses the point that bodies are not just biological realities, but instead are comingled with social evaluations of what is 'right', 'normal', and 'ideal'.

So far, I have used the term 'men' rather uncritically, so it is worthwhile unpacking this, especially since the discussion so far shows how the apparent dividing line between 'male' (sex) and 'men' (gender) can start to break down. First, it is usually the case that the term 'male' is culturally and discursively connected with the associated gender construct of 'men' (cf. Clatterbaugh 2004, 202)—that is, individuals who claim "rights and privileges attendant to membership in the dominant gender group" (Schrock and Schwalbe 2009, 279). In that case, being a 'man' is part of positioning oneself as a member of the dominant gender order and enjoying what Connell (2005, 79) calls the "patriarchal dividend or "the advantage men in general gain from the overall subordination of women." While Kiesling (2007, 660) notes that most men do not feel as though they benefit from the sociocultural privileges of being a man (see also Kiesling 2019, 4–5), Connell argues that even men who do not oppress women or engage in discriminatory behavior still enjoy the concomitant social privileges of being a man.

In general terms, then, being a man is an ongoing process of identity construction—it is something one does, usually via the deployment of a range of strategies and practices broadly conceived as 'masculine'. Of course, having a male body as a symbolic asset can strengthen claims to being a 'man' (see Connell 2005, 50–58 for a discussion of the interplay of the body, science, and society), but the latter does not necessarily follow on from the former. Having a male body does not categorically mean that one identifies as a man or is invested in constructing an identity as a man. Conversely, the lack of a male body does not mean that one *cannot* identify as a man. By dislocating the term 'male' from 'man', not only can intersex, nonbinary, and trans individuals be 'men', 'males' can agentively opt not to be 'men' (cf. Kiesling 2007, 656). Being a 'man', therefore, goes beyond the possession of particular reproductive organs and instead centers on the kinds of practices and behaviors that individuals might need to adopt in order to be normatively 'read' as a man (Schwalbe 2005).

If we take the view that being a man is an ongoing identity project constituted through discursive interaction and, to some extent, bodily practice, then we can start to make sense of the idea that 'manhood' is something that needs to be proven on a regular basis, where being a man is fragile, tenuous, and ephemeral. In his discussion of men and manhood across a range of historical and cultural contexts, for example, Gilmore (1990, 17) notes that:

Among most of the people that anthropologists are familiar with, true manhood is a precious and elusive status beyond mere maleness, a hortatory image that men and boys aspire to and that their culture demands of them as a measure of belonging. Its vindication is doubtful, resting on rigid codes of decisive action in many spheres of life: as husband, father, lover, provider, warrior. A restricted status, there are always men who fail the test. These are the negative examples, the effete men, the men-who-are-no-men, held up scornfully to inspire conformity to the glorious ideal.

Although there are legitimate criticisms to make of Gilmore's work regarding the utility of cross-cultural comparisons (see, for example, Connell 2005, 33), I would argue that there is a grain of truth in his overall point—many men often feel the need to 'prove' themselves against an arbitrary constellation of behaviors, something typically encouraged through a host of cultural pressures, including family and caregiver views, media representations, peer group friendships, and more. In a number of communities, this process of becoming a man is a rite of passage, marked out through ceremony and celebration.[3] In some respects, the men's movement of the 1980s represented an attempt to develop Western 'rites of passage', based particularly on an engagement with the natural world (Bonnett 1996), but these failed to catch on across broader society. The fact that contemporary Western Anglosphere societies do not have formalized rites of passage to mark the transition from boy to man is often part of the "crisis of masculinity" discourse, where men have 'lost their way' because they have no structured process by which 'manhood' is bestowed upon them (see, for example, the discussion presented in McKay and McKay 2010; Winton 2018; Mashabane and Henderson 2020). Such discourses are again replicated in the manosphere, where the supposed failure of masculinity is due to the lack of these ritualized processes.

Finally, just as 'male' can be dislocated from 'men', the same principle of dislocation can be applied to 'men' and 'masculinity', since "all things that men do are not masculine, and all things masculine are not necessarily done by men" (Kiesling 2007, 654). This takes us neatly to a discussion of the thorny term 'masculinity'.

WHAT ABOUT MASCULINITIES?

Although some scholars have argued that defining masculinity and masculinities is a "fruitless task" (MacInnes 1998, 2), this has not stopped many from trying. Indeed, a number of approaches to defining masculinity have been set out over the years. Connell (2005, 68–70) summarizes four common frameworks—*essentialist*, *positivist*, *normative*, and *semiotic*—and examines how masculinity has been operationalized in different fields. In the mythopoetic men's movement, for

---

3. These rites of passage include Vanuatu land diving, Hamar cow jumping, and the Satere-Mawe bullet ant glove (I will leave readers to research these initiations for themselves), while circumcision is viewed as part of the transition to being a man in a number of religions (see Brown 2017 for a discussion of rites of passage in different cultures).

example, essentialist definitions of masculinity are typical, where particular characteristics are taken as core to men's identities (e.g. risk-taking or aggression). In the social sciences and psychology, a more positivist definition is applied in an attempt to find out what men are really like (leading to things like 'more male/more female' scales). In areas like media studies, normative definitions tend to predominate; that is, masculinity is defined as what men ought to be (such presentations abound in movies and television shows in which traditional male leads are physically strong, tough, and courageous). Finally, semiotic definitions are common within psychoanalysis and post-structural cultural analyses of gender, in which masculinity is defined as "not femininity."

Connell (2005, 68–70) points out, however, that each of these approaches comes with its own set of problems. Essentialist definitions are arbitrary, positivist definitions are based on assumptions, normative definitions are unrepresentative, and semiotic definitions are limited. Connell argues that scholars should instead approach masculinity through an examination of the processes and relationships through which men live their lives. So, rather than seeing masculinity as an object of study, it is more productive to see it as "simultaneously a place in gender relations, the practices through which men and women engage that place in gender, and the effects of these practices in bodily experience, personality and culture" (Connell 2005, 71). Relatedly, Kiesling (2007, 659) defines masculinity as "social performances which are semiotically linked (indexed) to men, and not to women, through cultural discourses and cultural models." One of the benefits of this definition is that individual characteristics, traits, and behaviors are not specified; rather, the definition remains flexible across time periods and cultures.

Consequently, the field has embraced the idea of masculinities as multiple, fractured, and dislocated—a thinking initially inspired by Mort (1988, 195), who observes that "we are not dealing with masculinity, but with a series of *masculinities*" (emphasis in original; see also Clatterbaugh 2004, 200, who discusses the political dimension of this reframing). In a similar vein, Milani (2015, 10) notes that "masculinity is never in the singular, but is instead a set of performances that one carries out by employing linguistic and other meaning-making resources within normative constraints about how a man should sound, appear and behave."

HEGEMONIC MASCULINITY

Perhaps the most influential framework in masculinity studies over the past thirty years has been that of *hegemonic masculinity*, introduced in R. W. Connell's work in the mid-1980s. The idea of hegemonic masculinity grew from a dissatisfaction with the literature on the "male sex role" and the lack of theorizing about the intersection of men, power relations, and labor politics (Connell 1987, 1992). More specifically, Connell argued that constellations of characteristics, traits, and behaviors of men tend to be culturally exalted, valorized, and dominant. While the specific targets of this exaltation might change over time (Connell 1992, 736), what remains constant is the fact that there exists in most societies a "most honored way of being a man [which requires] all other men to position themselves in relation to it" (Connell and Messerschmidt 2005, 832). In Western contexts, this idea of masculinity has been variously configured. For example, Goffman (1963, 128) suggests that hegemonically masculine men are "young, urban, white, northern heterosexual, Protestant father, of college education, fully employed, of good complexion, and a recent record in sports" (see also Kimmel 1994). In a similar vein, Cheng (1999, 298) notes that "hegemonic masculinity is the defining gender performance of Euro-American males; in addition to being white and male, important demographic characteristics (or, include being able-bodied, heterosexual, Christian perhaps Jewish), first world (as opposed to colonized men), and ranging in age from 20 to 40 (although the upper end is rising as baby boomers get older)."

Hegemonic masculinity is context-dependent, thus the features and characteristics which mark out a male athlete (strength, competitiveness, athletic ability and so on) are different to those which mark out, for example, a male army officer (authority, decision-making power, ability to command others). Both are hegemonic, although they draw on different practices to mark out this hegemonic orientation (Connell 2005; Talbot and Quayle 2010). And it is typically the case that the characteristics associated with hegemonic masculinity—physical strength, courage, authority, aggression, (compulsory) heterosexuality, risk-taking, competitiveness, virility, emotional restraint, toughness, and so on—are lauded as elements of a desirable masculine identity. Hegemonic masculinity is positioned as what a man *ought* to be, maintained through a variety of social pressures and implicit consent rather than outright coercion, and is a central element of maintaining the patriarchal structures of contemporary Western society.

Hegemonic masculinity is also bound up with the policing, and subsequent marginalization and subordination, of other masculine identities, including gay men and men from ethnic minorities (Hillman and Henfry 2006; Jensen 2010). Thus, hegemonic masculinity is implicated in a system of hierarchies of difference, where certain constellations of behavior and personal characteristics are given more social value and are thus valorized as more desirable. And these processes of marginalization are refractive, so even marginalized masculinities can come to compete with one another. For example, in her analyses of race and ethnicity in Brazil, Roth-Gordon (2012, 2017) discusses how young Brazilian men manage the opposing identities of the *mano* ('black brother') and the *playboy* ('white wealthy male youth') through a range of semiotic practices that include language, jewelry, clothing, hairstyle, and music. While these two masculine identities are differently valued within young black male communities (generally speaking, mano positively and playboy negatively), young men exploit the mano/playboy cline for specific interactional goals, such as using the playboy identity to align themselves with authority and privilege.

As useful as hegemonic masculinity has been in developing our understanding of how men position themselves in relation to one another and the underpinnings of masculine gender politics (Connell 2005, 37–38; Balirano and Baker 2018, 5), the concept has nevertheless been criticized for its lack of specificity and for the fact that it is difficult to identify particular practices as hegemonic (Hall 2002; Christensen and Jensen 2014). In an extensive appraisal of the concept, Demetriou (2001) even goes so far as to argue that "hegemonic masculinity is united by its ugliness and negativity and by its opposition to femininity and subordinate masculinities." An arguably stronger critique, however, is that while hegemonic masculinity is a dominant gender identity and a significant cultural reference point, most men do not meet the standards of hegemonic masculinity. Most men are not movie stars or world-leading athletes or CEOs or captains of industry. Most men are not in a position to command large numbers of people or to lead with authority. And to some extent, most men are not supposed to be able to meet these standards. Instead, striving to attain these standards is part and parcel of pursuing the cultural project of 'manhood' (Cornwall 2016, 5). In many cases, these demands can be managed effectively, where men are able to balance the various expectations laid upon them (or imposed by themselves). In others, these pressures can lead to a range of negative psychological outcomes where men feel as though they have 'failed' to live up to social normative scripts. Alternatively, the pursuit of extreme versions of hegemonically masculine practices (e.g. aggression to the point of interpersonal violence or the subordination of women to the point of misogyny) arguably characterizes what has recently been termed 'toxic masculinity'. While we should ask how useful a theory of masculinity is when it does not account for most men's lived realities, later chapters will show how the underlying notion of an 'ideal' masculinity remains an important orienting point for many men.

THE HISTORY OF LANGUAGE AND MASCULINITIES RESEARCH

While the study of men and masculinities was developing along the lines set out previously, it took some time before this critical gaze established itself within sociolinguistics. In early quantitative work, for example, speaker sex was treated mainly as a static social variable in models of linguistic variation, where the primary focus was on how this correlated with the use of standard and nonstandard variants (e.g. Labov 1963; Trudgill 1972; Macaulay 1977). It was not until the mid-1970s that other domains of linguistics started to pay attention to the politics of language and gender, building on general concerns in feminist scholarship about the role of language in the maintenance of patriarchy, structural inequality, and representation. A landmark moment in this regard was the publication of Lakoff (1973) and her discussion of how women's marginality and lack of social power was reflected in the way they were expected to speak. In this "deficit" approach, however, the predominant assumption was that men's language was the de facto standard against which all other speakers should be evaluated (see Johnson 1997, 12).

Lakoff's work ultimately started a broader consideration of the intersection of language and gender, as her linguistic claims were put to the empirical test. In what has since come to be known as the "dominance" framework, research sought to examine the ways in which language was part of a comprehensive (and insidious) system of control, power, and hierarchy (see Zimman 2017a for an overview of some of this research). This work analyzed a range of linguistic phenomena, including conversational dominance (Zimmerman and West 1975; Brooks 1982; West 1984; Smith-Lovin and Brody 1989), topic management (Fishman 1977, 1978), male bias in English (Spender 1980), control of the conversational floor (Edelsky 1981), and questions (Harris 1995).

This work was useful in charting some of the ways men use language to conversationally dominate women, but as Johnson (1997, 11) points out, "within the dominance paradigm . . . a kind of 'all-purpose male oppressor' is constructed in the guise of a mysterious individual who talks too much, interrupts and generally dominates conversations with women." Men were conceptualized in fairly one-dimension terms and there were limited attempts to properly problematize the multiplicity of masculine identities (although see Eckert and McConnell-Ginet 1992, 482 for an early call to examine men's language more critically). Moreover, by implicitly promoting the male-as-norm discourse, the deficit and dominance approaches offered only partial answers to how men were implicated in structures of power and inequality. For example, Kiesling (2007, 662–665) argues that there is a danger in proposing a one-to-one relationship between a linguistic feature and its interactional function since the same feature (e.g. silence) can be put to very different uses, depending on the interlocutors, the relative degree of power between them, the social and conversational context, and so on. As Kiesling (2007, 663) goes on to note, "we expect men to use speech that creates dominance in some way, but we cannot specify exactly what features men are going to use to do this, because the same linguistic feature can index different things depending on context." Thus, men's powerful position in society is not because of how they speak, but rather because they are afforded social and institutional authority. Finally, in assuming that interactions involving men were primarily about domination, the nuance of men's discourse was overlooked, including the ways they enact friendship, alignment, and connection with one another.

The publication of Johnson and Meinhof's foundational volume *Language and Masculinity* (1997) was the first serious attempt to address these limitations (although see Sattel 1983 and Kaminer and Dixon 1995 for some preliminary observations on the nature of men's language). Adopting an explicitly feminist perspective, contributions to the volume offered critical analyses of men across a variety of contexts, from the nature of male gossip (Cameron 1997) to the intersection of language and male power (Kiesling 1997). By more explicitly critiquing men and their associated linguistic and social practices, the volume shed light on the ways in which masculine identities are constructed through language. As Johnson (1997, 13) notes, "[I]f it is male power we wish to contest, then it is all aspects of the male order that we must comprehend." Ultimately, the volume became the catalyst for a new wave of language and masculinities scholarship, developing key ideas which have helped us advance our understanding of the strategic deployment of linguistic practice by men and the different ways masculine identities are enacted.

THE DISCURSIVE CONSTRUCTION
OF MASCULINE IDENTITIES

As noted earlier in the chapter, one of the key theoretical concepts in contemporary sociolinguistic thought is the idea that language is a practice through which speakers *do* identity. Broadly framed as the 'performative turn', the introduction of this concept was a radical break from established thinking in early sociolinguistic research. For example, Trudgill's (1972) analysis of (ing) reduction in Norwich found that male speakers used higher rates of the nonstandard alveolar nasal variant [n], whereas female speakers used higher rates of the standard velar nasal variant [ŋ], irrespective of social class. This use of [n] or [ŋ] was subsequently taken to reflect particular social categories and speakers, with speakers using certain patterns of variation *because* they were male or female. As later work argued (e.g. Eckert 1989), however, this overlooked issues of power and identity and never properly explained *why* speakers would adopt one variant over another.

This idea of identity as constituted through practice, initially introduced in Eckert and McConnell-Ginet (1992), built on Goffman's work on affirmation, which pointed out that "every physical surround, every room, every box for social gatherings, necessarily provides materials that can be used in the display of gender and the affirmation of gender identity. But, of course, the social interaction occurring in these places can be read as supplying these materials also . . . More important, the management of talk will itself make available a swarm of events usable as signs" (Goffman 1977, 324). This argued that gender was not just a pre-existing resource, but rather something that was displayed through the deployment of interactional and other semiotic resources. A major step forward in formalizing the idea of identity as constituted through social action was the work of Judith Butler (1988, 1990), who introduced performativity theory as a theoretical framework. As Butler (1988, 519) put it, "gender is in no way a stable identity or locus of agency from which various acts proceed: rather, it is an identity tenuously constituted in time—an identity instituted through a *stylized repetition of acts*" (emphasis in original).

Drawing these different strands together, Eckert and McConnell-Ginet (1992) proposed that speakers use linguistic resources and interactional phenomena as a way of constructing their identities as particular kinds of gendered individuals. More specifically, their work encouraged "a view of the interaction of gender and language that roots each in the everyday social practices of particular local communities and sees them as jointly constructed in those practices" (Eckert and McConnell-Ginet 1992, 462). Viewing Trudgill's results from this angle, male speakers do not use [n] *because* they are men, but instead, use [n] to perform a (particular) masculine identity which draws on the association of nonstandard variants with stereotypical working-class characteristics such as toughness, physical strength, courage, and so on.

Treating language as a social practice through which identity is constructed also relies on the concept of indexical social meaning—that is, "the connection between a linguistic feature and meaning that is not denotational" (Kiesling 2007, 660). Linguistic practices of all sorts can function as indexicals. A good example is vocal pitch. Most men have low vocal pitch because their vocal tracts are, on average, longer than women's vocal tracts. But vocal pitch is also something under some degree of conscious control, so a man who might wish to enact a more masculine identity may choose to lower his pitch. This might index not only a more masculine identity but also stereotypically masculine characteristics, like authority, dominance, aggression, and strength (Eckert and McConnell-Ginet 2013, 5). As Kiesling (2007, 661) notes, "masculinity is expressed in language through features of language indexical of cultural discourses of masculinity, or through features directly indexical of certain kinds of men."

This practice-based approach has since come to dominate contemporary sociolinguistic thought, particularly in relation to masculinities. This work has advanced our understanding of the diversity of masculine experience and how the lived realities of men play out across a range of contexts. For example, Kiesling's (1997, 2001, 2004, 2005) ethnographically-informed analyses of the linguistic behavior of fraternity men at an American college outlined how they manage orientations toward ideal masculine identities (as breadwinners, as physically strong) and how different types of power (e.g. economic power, knowledge power, structural power) are implicated in their discourse. Bucholtz (1999) examined how toughness is discursively constructed as a valued aspect of masculinity. Analyzing a narrative by a White American high school student (Brand One) about a confrontation with an African American male antagonist who attempts to steal his backpack, Bucholtz show how the speaker strategically crosses over into African American Vernacular English (AAVE), exploits cultural stereotypes of African American men as strong, physically powerful, and aggressive, and integrates these socially positive character traits into his own gendered identity as a man. Similar work by Edley and Wetherell (1999), Bamberg (2004), Korobov (2005), and Sidnell (2011) investigates how speakers align with (or more typically, resist) hegemonic macho masculinity. More recent research (for example, the collected chapters in Milani 2015 and Baker and Balirano 2018) push the discussion beyond heterosexual men, offering an examination of masculinities at the intersection of linguistics and queer theory. Drawing on this lineage of intellectual thought, this book adopts an explicit social constructionist stance—in sum, men use language to construct themselves as particular types of men. This construction might (dis)align with notions of hegemonic masculinity or other forms of masculinity and a linguistic analysis can tease out exactly the discursive means through which such identity projects are realized.

As useful as the constructivist framework might be, though, identity is not simply an additive process of being. We do not start from the position of 'male' and then add working-class, young, rural, and so on. Thus, running through the analytical chapters is the idea that masculinities are multidimensional, "always intertwined with race and other supposedly separate categories of identity and experienced and interpreted differently in different contexts" (Cooper 2012, 97).

A framework mainly used in the legal field (e.g. Hutchinson 2000; Cooper and McGinley 2012; Mutua 2013; McGinley 2016), multidimensionality shares a number of features with intersectionality, including its antiessentialist perspective and seeing forms of subordination as inter-related phenomena. But where it differs is in its examination of heteronormativity, heterosexism, and homophobia as axes of subordination, particularly in relation to partially privileged identities. For Cooper (2011, 4), "multidimensionality theory allows for the consideration of how people are not just multiply subordinated, but often both subordinated and privileged at the same time." In a comprehensive discussion of intersectionality vs. multidimensionality, Hutchinson (1997, 641) notes that,

> intersectionality . . . *subtly* implies a convergence, particularly in the lives of people of color, of otherwise separate and independent categories, . . . thus [suggesting] a separability of the host of identities and forces that define social groups and social power. I therefore prefer multidimensionality because it more effectively captures the inherent complexity and irreversibly multilayered nature of *everyone's* identities and of oppression (emphasis in original).

While there is an argument to be made that multidimensionality is to masculinities what intersectionality is to feminism (Mutua 2013), a range of work has set out the theoretical utility that multidimensionality affords. For example, Cooper's (2012) analysis of the television show *The Wire* shows how alternative masculinities can sometimes be hegemonic in particular contexts, while Kim (2014) argues that multidimensionality is useful in unpacking the racial dimensions of normative masculinities.

GENDER POLITICS, POWER, AND VIOLENCE

The processes of identity construction are not independent of the social context in which they happen—identity is rooted in the milieu of contemporary life. As such, what men do is inevitably connected to everyday gender politics. As I noted in Chapter 1, gender politics have very much been in the media spotlight in recent years, from the #metoo movement through to the casual sexism of Donald Trump and much more besides. Not only has this coverage been important in highlighting the continued gender inequalities which exist in contemporary society, it has also raised a number of questions about masculinities and what men do. How are women represented and talked about by men? How do men talk about other groups of men? How are internal and external gender hierarchies maintained though language?

At the heart of contemporary gender politics is the role of power and domination. Contesting male power and patriarchy has been, of course, a central plank of feminist scholarship since its inception. The entire premise of the dominance approach in language and gender research, for example, was predicated on challenging how language encoded gendered systems of privilege, power, and hierarchy. By examining both the explicit and implicit means through which power is maintained, early feminist linguistic scholarship aimed to raise awareness of how language was implicated in gender inequalities and sexist discrimination, a goal which continues to be pursued in contemporary feminist work.

This scholarship has argued that one of the main ways in which the power of men is sustained is through (potential or actual) violence, including domestic abuse, sexual assault, rape, murder, harassment, and physical attacks (Kimmel 2001). As Connell (2005, 83) notes, "it is, overwhelmingly, the dominant gender who hold and use the means of violence." And not only does use of violence maintain power by men over women, but also between different groups of men. Thus, violence is a means through which internal hierarchies of masculinity are created, where the willingness to use violence is considered to be a hallmark of manliness. For example, in my discussion of masculinity in Glasgow (Lawson 2013), I show how discourses of violence are positively evaluated, even by young men who typically do not engage in violent social practices such as fighting.

Violence, however, need not be explicit or physical for it to have an effect on the world. Forms of symbolic violence (Bordieu 1979) are often key ways through which power is sustained. For example, homosociality is often predicated on the marginalization, relegation, and sexual objectification of women and thus can be seen as a central component of modern patriarchy (Bird 1996). Recent high-profile media cases have brought this into sharp relief, including Donald Trump's infamous "grab them by the pussy" episode with Billy Bush (as discussed in Chapter 1). This interaction can perhaps most productively be read as a substantiation of symbolic violence and male bonding through the verbal denigration of the two women who were the focus of the exchange, reducing them to their bodies and their sexual desirability. The use of laughter, boasts, sexually explicit insult terms, and mutually appreciative evaluative comments by Trump and Bush are part of the linguistic means through which misogynist and verbally violent "locker room banter" is perpetuated, contributing to the participants' co-construction of an intended sexually confident masculinity. These strategies of what Loofbourow (2018) calls "toxic homosociality" are strategies through which "males [woo] other males over the comedy of being cruel to women" (see also Coates 2013, 547–548; Tolentino 2018).

Such symbolic violence can also be part of policing and enforcing particular standards of masculinity. In many online manosphere communities, for example, there is almost no scope for resisting the dominant community conceptualization of masculinity, usually one based on extreme hegemonic features. Those who try to resist these discourses are regarded as failed men, lacking in the essential qualities needed to be successfully masculine. This tyranny of homogeneity, or the pressure for men to conform to a set of arbitrary standards and protocols about masculinity, carries a great deal of social power. There is often no space for difference or divergence and dissent against the 'norm' is quickly shut down by the community (I deal with this in more detail in Chapter 6). Understanding the linguistic means through which this policing is carried out and how male power is exercised through discourse should be, I believe, one of the key aims of language and masculinities research.

OTHER THEORIES OF MASCULINITY

In this closing section, I outline some of the other relevant theoretical frameworks to do with masculinity, including toxic masculinities (Sculos 2017b), positive masculinities (Kiselica and Englar-Carlson 2010), and caring masculinities (Hanlon

2012; Elliott 2016; Hunter, Riggs, and Augoustinos 2017), and sketch out how they relate to the later analytical chapters. Consequently, the following discussion does not represent an overview of different masculinities theories where one approach chronologically follows on from the other but is instead intended to form the backdrop to the six analytical chapters (that is, Chapters 4–8). It is also worth saying that in some cases, a number of different frameworks apply to one chapter, so bringing them together here provides some degree of discursive coherency.

First, Chapter 4 discusses how the notion of 'tough masculinity' in operationalized in a series of British newspaper articles, particularly through the term 'hard man'. Indeed, violence and aggressive behavior is often cited as a hallmark of powerful (and hegemonic) masculinity in a range of contexts, from inner-city street gangs to football hooligans (Spaaij 2008; Baird 2012; Patton, Eschmann, and Butler 2013), and from sport to war (Messner 1990; Hutchings 2008). By charting the dispersion of 'hard man', we can see how the associated practices and characteristics of the 'hard man' are deployed across a range of news coverage and consider what this tells us about idealized masculine types in the British press.

Chapter 5 moves on to consider the intersection of masculinity and right-wing nationalism, examining how ethnicity and cultural notions of whiteness are bound up with masculine identities. Building on work from Enloe (1998), Nagel (1998), and Banerjee (2005, 2012), this chapter explores how masculinity is connected to 'White is right' discourses and how White masculinity in particular is reified as the most exalted form of masculinity. As might be obvious, the racialized dimension of gender identity is central here, an issue growing in importance with the rise of the 'alt-right' and other right-wing nationalist movements in Western contexts.

In Chapter 6, I bring in the idea of 'toxic' masculinities, typically defined as a constellation of behaviors associated with men which is destructive, violent, and socially harmful (Kupers 2005, 714). Sculos (2017b, 3) offers a definition of toxic masculinity, noting that the term "is used to refer to a loosely interrelated collection of norms, beliefs, and behaviors associated with masculinity, which are harmful to women, men, children, and society more broadly." This can include homophobia, excessive violence, chauvinism, misogyny, sexual entitlement, hyper-competitiveness, a belief in male superiority, and so on. While there has been some work on toxic masculinities from a linguistic perspective (e.g. Hess and Flores 2016; Myketiak 2016), the linguistic practices associated with toxic masculinity are somewhat underinvestigated, especially in context of the manosphere.

Chapter 7 utilizes the concept of positive masculinities, or what Englar-Carlson and Kiselica (2013, 401) define as "the adaptive character strengths, emotions, and virtues of men that promote well-being and resiliency in self and others." In this approach, practices related to dominant and traditional forms of masculinity are replaced with a healthier and less destructive concept of masculinity. This chapter considers how media outputs help promote positive masculinity and explores how the kinds of linguistic practice used in a comedy television show subvert dominant tropes of hegemonic masculinity.

Finally, the framework of caring masculinities forms the basis of Chapter 8 and the analysis of fatherhood in online forums. Central to caring masculinities is the "rejection of domination and [the] integration of values of care, such as positive emotion, interdependence, and relationality, into masculine identities" (Elliot 2016, 241). While there has been a great deal of work on fatherhood (e.g. Johansson 2011; Miller 2011), we know little about how fatherhood is interactively constituted in online spaces such as discussion forums (although see Johansson and Hammarén 2014; Andreasson and Johansson 2016 for a discussion of fatherhood on blogs). By examining one of the central aspects of men's emotional lives, we can see how connection, vulnerability, and care are part of men's identity projects. As Hanlon (2012, 66) observes, "we cannot appreciate masculinities without understanding relations of power and dominance, but we cannot understand power and dominance without also appreciating men's emotional lives. Moreover, we cannot deconstruct male power without reconstructing the emotional lives of men."

CONCLUSION

This chapter has attempted to set out some of the relevant background literature to the critical study of men and masculinities, drawing on both sociological and linguistic perspectives. In doing so, one of the main arguments developed is that while hegemonic masculinity remains an important theoretical concept, new frameworks have much to offer in terms of how we understand the embedded reality of men's lives. By using these frameworks to contextualize the research sites tackled in Chapters 4–9, we can develop a richer account of exactly how masculinity is constructed and the linguistic means used to do so.

Furthermore, this chapter has briefly discussed contemporary gender politics, noting that there is a need to interrogate gender politics and to challenge existing hierarchies, binaries, and expectations. If we are, as some have claimed, in a new age of aggressive masculinity, then this undertaking becomes ever more important against a growing context of online and offline violence against women and minorities, online radicalization, and the promotion of masculine identities based on discrimination, misogyny, and violence toward others.

Ultimately, by combining a more critically informed perspective on men and masculinities with close attention to linguistic practice, we can contribute to a socially transformative research agenda that seeks to unpack the normative assumptions underpinning masculinities in contemporary life. And it is to the linguistic tools we can use to achieve this that I turn to in Chapter 3.

CHAPTER 3
Approaches to Analyzing Language and Masculinities

Data, Theories, and Methods

INTRODUCTION

This chapter introduces the scaffolding on which the book is built and the underpinning methodological nuts and bolts used in the analyses. In doing so, my aim is to contextualize the research questions presented in Chapter 1 and to relate the book to existing studies in the field of language and masculinities. More specifically, the chapter does the following things. First, it outlines the data which form the basis of the analytical accounts in Chapters 4–8, from newspaper articles and television shows to social networking sites and online forums, setting out why these are useful locales for the study of language and masculinities. Second, it introduces the different methodologies which are used to explore these data sets, including critical discourse analysis and corpus linguistics, showing how existing research in these areas has contributed to our understanding of language and masculinities. Third, it discusses a number of issues related to ethics, the impact of the EU General Data Protection Regulation (GDPR) on linguistic research, working with 'unlikeable subjects', and the question of researcher safety and managing risk.

DATA

In order to examine the construction of masculinities across a range of contexts, the data discussed in Chapters 4–8 have been collected from a variety of sources, including television shows, newspaper archives, online forums, and social networking sites. The choice of data is motivated by three things. First, by examining multiple contexts where masculinities intersect with language use, we can get a better

Language and Mediated Masculinities. Robert Lawson, Oxford University Press. © Oxford University Press 2023.
DOI: 10.1093/oso/9780190081041.003.0003

understanding of how similarities and differences in gender norms, relations, and hierarchies are realized across different contexts. Second, in considering such a diverse range of data, we can get a better handle on the extent to which strategies of marginalization, othering, and other forms of discrimination are altered, refracted, and reformulated for new contexts, settings, and formats. Finally, if we want to better understand the socially damaging processes of marginalization, sexism, violence, and harassment, then it is incumbent on us to examine contexts where such divisive, abusive, and contentious social practices manifest. While each of the contexts are discussed in more detail in the respective chapters, it is worthwhile outlining them here to help set the scene.

First, Chapter 4 looks at how discourses of tough masculinity are presented in two corpora of British newspaper articles collected from *The Scotsman* and *The Guardian*. In particular, I discuss the semiotic and ideological associations bound up with the term 'hard man', an archetypical construction of masculinity in urban contexts (Young 2007; Fraser 2015) and trace how this concept is used across UK print media outlets.

Chapter 5 moves to an online context and examines data collected from the social media networking site Reddit, and specifically a subreddit called /r/The_Donald, originally developed for supporters of Donald Trump and his 2016 presidential bid.

Chapter 6 continues this focus on Reddit and deals with data collected from four manosphere communities on the site: /r/Incels, /r/MGTOW, /r/MensRights, and /r/TheRedPill.

Chapter 7 presents an analysis of masculinities in the television show *Brooklyn Nine-Nine*, a police procedural comedy which follows the lives of police officers in New York's fictional 99th precinct. Concentrating on seasons one through six, the analysis examines how the male characters in the show resist, and sometimes align themselves with, hegemonic discourses of masculinity and how their talk might shed light on the integration of a positive masculinity perspective in the show.

Finally, Chapter 8 deals with dad.info, a UK-based website and forum founded in 2008 which offers a range of help, advice, and guidance for fathers. Drawing on corpus linguistic and discourse analytic methods, the chapter presents one of the first linguistically informed analyses of fatherhood in digital spaces.

CRITICAL DISCOURSE ANALYSIS

Having set out the different forms of data considered in this book, the discussion turns to think about how we can actually go about analyzing this data. This section deals with two approaches which are particularly useful in examining the intersection of language and masculinities—critical discourse analysis (CDA hereafter) and corpus linguistics. These methods are augmented by additional approaches as set out in the relevant chapters.

First and foremost, the study of language and masculinities is inherently a critical project (Johnson 1997). As stated in Chapter 1, there is substantial concern about how particular masculinities are celebrated and valorized in contemporary Western society, especially in online spaces, where hegemonic standards of masculinity are bound up with being White, heterosexual, sexually active, and having a strong sense of nationalistic identity, among other features. Those who do not meet these arbitrary standards of masculinity are typically deemed as 'failures'. A critical perspective can help uncover how these strategies of normalization are packaged up across different discursive domains and offer some challenge to these discourses.

This critical attention on language and masculinity follows a long line of work concerned with addressing social problems through the application of language research, a lineage which can be traced back to the publication of *Language and Power* (Fairclough 1989). This book is widely regarded as the beginning of CDA and the first step toward helping "correct a widespread underestimation of the significance of language in the production, maintenance, and change of social relations of power" (Fairclough 1989, 1).

The field of CDA is best thought of as an interdisciplinary collection of methods (Fairclough 2001a; Wodak 2004; Fairclough 2012), with the overarching goal to examine "the role of discourse in the (re)production and challenge of dominance" (van Dijk 1993, 250) and the "non-obvious ways in which language is involved in social relations of power and dominance" (Fairclough 2001b, 229). As such, CDA draws on a variety of approaches to interrogate the role language plays in the maintenance of social inequality and discrimination, to bring to light the hidden processes though which these inequalities become unremarkable elements of everyday life, and then (ideally) to effect social change (van Dijk 1993, 252–254). As Pennycook (1990, 25–26) highlights, "If we are concerned about the manifold and manifest inequities of the societies and the world we live in, then I believe we must start to take up moral and political projects to change those circumstances. This requires that we cease to operate with modes of intellectual inquiry that are asocial, apolitical or ahistorical."

To achieve these aims, Fairclough (1989) outlined a framework which considers the implicit linguistic means through which power is encoded, maintained, and communicated. Most influentially, he advocated for an approach which examines not just the microlevel of the text (that is, the linguistic content of a newspaper article, poster, news broadcast, etc.), but also who produces, markets, promotes, and consumes a particular text (the mesolevel) and how a text relates to broader sociocultural events within which the text exists (the macrolevel). This moved the field of textual analysis away from treating texts as disembodied artifacts toward critically examining how texts are constitutive of social reality. Later work expanded on these approaches, including van Dijk's cognitive turn (van Dijk 2016) and Wodak's discourse-historical approach (see also Reisigl and Wodak 2016).

Recent work in language and masculinities research has demonstrated the utility of CDA, outlining how particular constructions of masculinity become positioned as ideal, desirable, or socially appropriate. For example, Baker and Levon (2015) use CDA and corpus linguistic approaches to investigate the discursive representation of masculinities in the British press, while Conradie (2011) draws on social actor theory and the notion of 'underlying assumptions' to discuss male sexualities in the magazine *FHM*. In a similar vein, Stibbe (2004) adopts a CDA perspective in her analysis of health and the social construction of masculinity in *Men's Health* magazine, showing how the discursive positioning of cooking methods (e.g. barbeques instead of kitchen-prepared meals) and particular foods (e.g. beer and red meat) are co-opted as markers of desirable masculine characteristics (see also Crawshaw 2007). Thus, CDA uncovers the role language plays in constructing masculinities across a range of texts and how the discursive representation of men and masculinities is woven into broader cultural discourses of what it is to be a man in contemporary social life.

CORPUS LINGUISTICS

CDA draws on an interdisciplinary range of methods to investigate social problems based on situated language use. To that end, it is difficult to talk of a unitary approach which underpins CDA research. Instead, CDA scholars adopt different methods to address their specific research context. For example, Machin and Mayr (2012) show how CDA can be conducted through multimodal approaches, while the intersection of CDA and digital humanities research has led to the development of the relatively new field of 'critical technocultural discourse analysis' (Brock 2018).

One methodological approach which has seen a significant increase in CDA work is that of corpus linguistics (see Nartey and Mwinlaaru 2019 for a review of CDA work which draws on corpus linguistic methods, sometimes termed *corpus-assisted critical discourse analysis*). One of the reasons for this rise is that corpus methods offer a more quantitative perspective over large bodies of data, allowing us to tease out the regular, repeatable, and systematic patterns which exist in the data (Partington, Duguid, and Taylor 2013). In this section, I present a brief background on corpus linguistics, before setting out some of the key linguistic features which form the basis of the later analysis chapters.

At its core, corpus linguistics is the "study of language based on examples of 'real life' language use" (McEnery and Wilson 2001, 1) and "empirical, analysing the actual patterns of use in natural texts" (Biber, Conrad, and Reppen 1998, 38). But perhaps what makes corpus linguistics distinct from other branches of linguistics is that it is based on the "computer-aided analysis of very extensive collections of transcribed utterances or written texts" (McEnery and Hardie 2012, i), allowing a quantitative, replicable, and reliable analysis of the linguistic patterning of a particular piece of data. As O'Keeffe and McCarthy (2010, 3) point out, corpus linguistics is "most readily associated in the minds of linguists with searching through screen after screen of concordance lines and wordlists generated by computer software, in an attempt to make sense of phenomena in big texts or big collections of smaller texts."

From this discussion, then, we can identify several distinguishing features of corpus linguistics. First, corpus linguistics examines a large collection of data known as corpus (or 'corpora' if it is being used in the plural), either written or spoken, usually digitized in a machine-readable format and often reaching into the multimillion or billion word range. Second, these corpora can either comprise texts by different authors (e.g. newspaper articles or courtroom proceedings) or texts by a single author (e.g. the CLiC Dickens Corpus, Mahlberg et al. 2016). Third, corpus linguistics uses specialized computer software to 'mine' the data to develop insights about patterns of usage (Collins 2019, 1). Some of these software tools are open-source and free to use, such as AntConc (Anthony 2020) or #LancsBox (Brezina, Timperley, and McEnery 2018), while others are proprietary programs, such as Sketch Engine (Kilgarriff et al. 2014) and WordSmith Tools (Scott 2020). Whichever software is used, they all have in common the ability to produce standard analytical outputs in the form of word lists, keywords, n-grams, concordances, and collocations, which form the backdrop of most analytical accounts (I return to these terms later). In this book, the main pieces of software used are AntConc and #LancsBox.

While there has been much discussion concerning whether it is best to view corpus linguistics as a set of methods or as a coherent theory, this debate is beyond the scope of this book (for relevant work, see Chapter 1 of McEnery and Wilson 2001; and McEnery and Hardie 2012, 147–149). What is clear, however, is that the approaches promoted in corpus linguistics have found a home in a range of sociolinguistic projects. Baker (2010) and Murphy (2010) are probably two of the earliest accounts of this intersection, outlining the productive ways in which corpus linguistic methods can answer a range of questions to do with sociolinguistic variation, interpersonal communication, and social discourse. Following Baker (2010) and Murphy (2010), a number of other publications have demonstrated the value of uniting corpus linguistics and sociolinguistics, including Andersen (2012), Friginal and Hardy (2014), Brezina, Love, and Aijmer (2018), and Friginal (2018), to name but a few (although there are several early nods toward this partnership in McEnery and Wilson 2001; Hunston 2002; Beeching 2006, 200; Xiao and Tao 2007; Mair 2009).

More recently, corpus methods have been deployed in the analysis of language and masculinities. For example, Baker (2015) discusses the changing representations of American masculinities in the *Corpus of Historical American English*. Expanding this theme, Baker and Levon (2015, 2016) set out an intersectional approach to masculinities in UK newspapers which uncovers how the hierarchies between different types of men are sustained through reference to race and class (see also Levon, Milani, and Kitis 2017 for a discussion of the South African context using similar methodology). While Black and Asian men tended to be described as violent and criminal, working-class White men were characterized as being unfairly excluded from society, a position which becomes even more acute for working-class White men through their association with violence. In their comparison of masculinities and femininities in the UK press, Baker and Baker (2019) show how the British press celebrate, promote, and privilege masculinity over femininity, not only in terms of making more references to it as a concept, but also through its association with prestige, status, and power. Analyzing representations of men and masculinities in women's lifestyle magazines, Coffey-Glover (2015) found that the main ideologies of masculinity in these publications included men being heterosexual, dominant in relationships, and driven by their sexual desires (see also Coffey-Glover 2019). Bogetić (2013), meanwhile, analyzes patterns of word co-occurrence to examine how dominant and marginal ideologies of masculinity are expressed in the personal ads of Serbian gay teenagers. This study argues that even among homosexual men, discourses of hegemonic masculinity still have massive cultural sway, while the cultural stigma associated with homosexuality is shifted only to nonmasculine gay men.

All of this work demonstrates how corpus linguistics can shed light on the different ways in which a specific substantiation of masculinity is represented, uncovering the "ideological framework for masculinity the texts serve to instantiate" (Baker and Levon 2016, 113). This is part of a general analytical approach known as *discourse prosody* or *semantic prosody* (from Louw 1993; although see Hunston's 2007 suggestion of *semantic preference* or *attitudinal preference*). As Collins (2019, 60) notes, "Semantic prosody is said to capture some of the implicit attitude or evaluation of the speaker/writer and it is argued that when a word collocates with another word that expresses positive or negative evaluation, this positivity/negativity is transferred to the node word." For example, Baker and Levon (2016) show how the words *inarticulate*, *Glasgow*, *average*, and *White* typically co-occur with *working-class man*, demonstrating the (occasionally negative) semantic associations in articles where working-class men are the focus. Having outlined some of the relevant background of corpus linguistics, the discussion now turns to discuss some of the main fundamentals of corpus methods, including word frequency, keywords, collocations, and topic analysis.

WORD LISTS

Word list analysis is the cornerstone of corpus linguistics and one of the first steps in understanding the distribution and usage of words in a corpus (Säily and Suomela 2017). Word lists can be generated in a number of ways, by order of first occurrence (the sequence and distribution of words in a corpus), alphabetically (A–Z order), or frequency (most common words through to less common words). Usually, high frequency grammatical words (e.g. articles, determiners, prepositions) are omitted using stop-word lists, but analysts can retain certain words if they believe them to be linguistically important (for a discussion of corpus linguistics and word frequency, see Baron, Rayson, and Archer 2009).

Word lists are usually normalized in terms of incidence rate per X thousands of words (incidence rates of 10,000, 100,000, or even 1,000,000 words are common). This means that we can compare the use of a word (or words) across corpora that might be of very different sizes, providing a more accurate sense of how (un)usual a word is. A related procedure is determining how a term is distributed across the individual texts that make up a corpus. Of particular danger is that an individual text in a corpus might have a significantly high incidence rate of one term. Consequently, this term will be returned as a high frequency item in the *whole* corpus, even if it is never used in the other texts that make up the corpus. This has been referred to as the 'whelks problem' (from Kilgarriff 1997; see also Evans et al. 2016). To address this issue, #LancsBox has the 'whelk tool' option, which provides information about absolute and relative frequencies of search terms in a corpus and its constituent texts.

As useful as word lists are, however, relying on them poses a number of problems. As mentioned, word list frequencies must be normalized before any meaningful comparisons can be made. Second, high frequency words might not be useful in terms of understanding the content of a corpus. Third, the top-ranked words might not be the most analytically important words. But perhaps most crucially, word lists do not give us any information about the context in which term occur (Collins 2019, 9). In many senses, word lists are divorced from the context in which they occur. In order to better understand how words are connected to other words in a meaningful way, we need to turn to two other methods: keywords and collocation.

KEYWORDS

While frequency lists allow us to identify the most frequent words in a corpus, they do not allow us to see which words are special to one corpus or how one corpus might differ to another corpus. As Kilgarriff (2009, 1) observes, "We very often want to know which words are distinctive of one corpus, or text type, versus another." In order to achieve this, we need to rely on a different measure, that of keywords. A keyword is a word which "occurs with unusual frequency in a given text" (Scott 1997, 236), or within a given corpus. The term "unusual" is important here, since a keyword is determined though comparing the target corpus against a reference corpus. This reference corpus can be "a representation of 'general' language use [which] establishes a baseline norm for how frequently we might expect a language feature to appear" (Collins 2019, 66), or it can be a specialist corpus focusing on a particular genre or topic (for example, comparing articles from Newspaper A against articles from Newspaper B). The determination of a word as key is consequently based on comparing the relative frequency of terms in the target corpus against how often those terms appear in the reference corpus. This ultimately leads to two outcomes— positive keywords (that is, words which appear more frequently in the target corpus, when compared against the reference corpus) and negative keywords (that is, words which appear less frequently in the target corpus, when compared against the reference corpus).[1]

By calculating the keywords of a corpus, we can use this as a basis for "drawing inferences regarding the culture these texts spring from" (Scott 1997, 235). More specifically, keyword analysis is one of the means of identifying important concepts, themes, and ideas in a text, which "may help to highlight the existence of types of (embedded) discourse or ideology" (Baker 2004, 347). Thus, keyword analysis is part of uncovering how discourses are embedded in a group of texts and how these might set up particular contextual framings of individuals and groups. More succinctly, "keyword analysis is a useful tool for identifying subtle differences in the lexical profiles of two corpora, and thus the ideological and/or attitudinal differences these profiles reflect" (Levon, Milani, and Kitis 2017, 519). In the analysis chapters, keywords are identified by the use of SMALL CAPS.

---

1. The statistical basis for keyword analysis is not especially relevant to this discussion, but readers interested in this are advised to consult Gabrielatos (2018).

COLLOCATION

Like frequency lists and keywords, collocation is central to corpus linguistic analyses, broadly referring to the co-occurrence of words in a repeatable and regular pattern. As Firth (1956, 11) famously observed, "You shall know a word by the company it keeps," and there is a tendency in English for particular words to appear alongside one another. For example, Sinclair (1998, 18) demonstrates that *budge* tends to co-occur with negative auxiliary verbs like *won't, can't,* and *didn't* as well as other nonpositive words like *refuse,* while Kehoe and Gee (2007) show that although the word *credit* has strongly collocated with *card* since the mid-1980s, the global recession in 2008–2009 sparked new and socially productive collocations with *crunch, crisis,* and *squeeze.*

Collocates are an important means in accessing both general and specific social meanings of a text. As Bogetić (2013, 338) points out, "repeated collocations implicitly reflect social meanings which can even be in direct opposition to what is claimed overtly. Furthermore, words that collocate with particular linguistic items have an influence over the meaning of those items" (see also Romaine 2001; Hunston 2002, 2010; Levon, Milani, and Kitis 2017). Thus, the study of collocation can give us an insight into the specific lexical means through texts construct ideological positionings.

Over the years, a number of criteria have been established to facilitate the identification of collocates—(i) distance, (ii) frequency, (iii) exclusivity, (iv) directionality, (v) dispersion, (vi) type-token distribution, and (vii) connectivity. For our purposes, it is enough to briefly set out what each of these criteria mean, but for an extended discussion of these dimensions, see Gries (2013), Brezina, McEnery, and Wattam (2015), and Collins (2019, 58–59).

First, distance refers to how far away a collocate is in relation to the 'node' word (that is, the term being examined in the corpus), usually within a one- to five-word span. In almost every piece of corpus software, it is possible to look at words to the left and to the right of this 'node' word to investigate which words come before and which words come after. This approach is typically paired with an analysis of how frequently a collocate occurs in a corpus. A minimum frequency can be set to filter out collocates, so that a baseline number of results is returned.

But words frequently occurring together does not always mean that they are analytically useful or textually important, so we need other measures for collocational strength. For that, we can use measures such as exclusivity, which refers to the extent to which the relationship between the words in a collocation is restricted. For example, Brezina, McEnery, and Wattam (2015, 140) discuss exclusivity in relation to the phrase *in love.* While *in love* is a frequent phrase in English, *in* occurs with lots of other words as well, so the relationship between *in* and *love* is not exclusive. There are, however, other words which have a stronger relationship with *love,* such as the noun *affair.* As Brezina, McEnery, and Wattam (2015, 140) point out, "*love* is much more strongly and exclusively connected with the noun *affair*; when the word *affair* appears in text, there is a large probability that the preceding word is *love.*" In this case, we would say that the relationship between *love* and *affair* is more exclusive than the relationship between *in* and *love.*

This distinction also raises questions about the direction of attraction between a node word and its collocates, or in other words, whether "[a] node word has a stronger attraction to a collocate or vice versa" (Collins 2019, 59). We can illustrate this by looking at the phrase *of course*. This phrase is made up of two words—*of* and *course*—but *of* also co-occurs with other parts of speech, including noun phrases ("a summit *of* European leaders," "the MP was kicked out *of* the party"), verb phrases ("the arithmetic *of* getting the deal through," "in terms *of* consulting the right people"), and so on. *Course*, on the other hand, is more likely to co-occur with *of*, so we can say that *course* has a stronger attraction to *of* than the other way around. As Gries (2013, 144) puts it, "*of* occurs with very many different types and a large number of tokens, but *course*'s distribution is much more restricted and, thus, *course* is a better cue to *of* than vice versa."

We also need to consider the issue of dispersion, or how distributed a node word and its collocates are throughout a corpus—are they found in one text or across numerous texts in a corpus (this is similar to the 'whelks problem' discussed previously)? Type-token distribution refers to the issue of what other words could potentially occupy a slot next to, or near, a collocate. For example, *love* can be preceded by more words other than *affair*—*in love, to love, my love, first love, true love, unrequited love*—so type-token distribution captures the level of competition around the node word (Brezina, McEnery, and Wattam 2015, 141; note that there are nearly 13,000 collocate types for *love* in the British National Corpus).

Finally, Brezina, McEnery and Wattam (2015, 141) introduce the notion of connectivity, noting that "Collocates of words do not occur in isolation, but are part of a complex network of semantic relationships which ultimately reveals their meaning and the semantic structure of a text or corpus." Taking the example of *affair*, they point out that while this word does not collocate with *unrequited, undying,* or *madly*, it is connected to these terms through the word *love*, since this word collocates with *affair* and the three other terms (see also Renouf 1996).

This system of semantic network connections is an important way readers derive textual and interactional meaning. Brezina, McEnery, and Wattam (2015) develop this concept through their work on the GraphColl (graphical collocations) tool, which is a way of visualizing collocational networks. Figure 3.1 is a basic graph of the node word *summer* and its collocates, drawn from the Lancaster-Oslo-Bergen (L-O-B) corpus. GraphColl displays three dimensions—strength, frequency, and position. Strength is indicated by the length of the line between the node word (or phrase) and the collocates, where stronger collocates are closer to the node and weaker collocates are further away. The darker the shading, the more frequent the collocation, while the

Figure 3.1. A collocation network for "summer" and "spring" displayed in GraphColl

position of a collocate indicates whether it is found predominantly left or right relative to the node word (words which can appear either left or right are located in the middle position). In Figure 3.1, for example, *in summer* is more frequent than *last summer* in the L-O-B corpus, while *during summer* and *summer evening* are more typical word orders compared to, for example, *one summer during a monsoon* or *evening summer jobs*.

GraphColl can be used alongside concordance lines (also known as Key Words in Context), a more established method of examining collocational results. A concordance line is where the node word is listed in the center column, with context words to the left and right which can be ordered alphabetically, in order to determine patterns of usage (Table 3.1).

Table 3.1. SELECTED L-O-B CONCORDANCE LINES FOR 'SUMMER' DISPLAYED IN #LANCSBOX (FIVE-WORD SPAN)

. . . leafed tree in the dark	summer	evening, sometimes showing the wet . . .
. . . and enlivened hearth interiors during	summer	months when the burnished steel . . .
. . . year, but especially during the	summer	months, these clubs hold costume . . .
. . . stage. Before that again, last	summer	the established government of Turkey . . .
. . . primitive nature, where cooking in	summer	was done in a home-made . . .

TOPIC ANALYSIS

Although not strictly a corpus linguistic method, topic modeling has started to make inroads into corpus linguistic and discourse analytic accounts of language use (Jaworska and Nanda 2018; Murakami et al. 2017; Carter et al. 2019, 2021). In topic modeling, a body of texts is automatically categorized into discrete topics by identifying "lists of words which have a high probability of co-occurrence within a 'span' that is set by the researcher" (Murakami et al. 2017, 244). The end result is lists of words which are then mapped onto researcher-identified 'topics'. For example, in their analysis of a corpus of academic papers published in the journal *Global Environmental Change*, Murakami et al. (2017, 244–245) suggest that the following words are organized around the topics of (a) forestry conservation and deforestation; (b) physical risk and hazards; and (c) resource distribution (although it is important to note that not all words in the model output will necessarily be linked to a specific topic).

(a) *forest, carbon, deforest, tropic, land, area, cover, conservation, forestry, timber*
(b) *risk, health, disaster, effect, hazard, disease, people, affect, reduce, potential*
(c) *should, right, principle, this, distribution, not, equitable, which, justice, or*

While other topic modeling frameworks use a probabilistic and non-deterministic method (e.g. Latent Dirichlet Allocation, Blei, Ng, and Jordan 2003), this book adopts a topic modeling approach known as Nonnegative Matrix Factorization (or NMF; see Lee and Seung 2000). In practice, NMF is less random than other methods, leading to higher-quality topic generation (Chen et al. 2019, 11).

As Xu, Zong, and Yang (2013) describe, the underlying principle of NMF is that the input data (i.e. the corpus) is rendered as a matrix (i.e. an array of rows and columns), where the words of the corpus are the rows and the documents are the columns (for arguments sake, let's say that our input matrix is 10,000 rows and 500 columns, so 500 documents indexed by 10,000 words). The NMF algorithm is then asked to find, for instance, ten features, generating two things in the process—a features matrix (W = 10,000 rows and 10 columns, or the topic clusters discovered from the documents) and a coefficients matrix (H = 10 rows and 500 columns, or the membership weights for the topics in each document). By multiplying the features matrix and the coefficients matrix (WH), we get a matrix (V) of 10,000 words and 500 columns which, if the factorization process works correctly, should be roughly approximate to the input data. In mathematical terms, this can be formalized as $V = WH$. Following these steps, we can posit that each column in the product matrix (WH) is a linear combination of the ten column vectors in the features matrix W, with coefficients supplied by the matrix H. It is this final step which is the basis of NMF, "because we can consider each original document in our example as being built from a small set of hidden features. NMF generates these features" (Xu, Zong, and Yang 2013, 42). In other words, NMF works by decomposing a large data set into smaller chunks which we ultimately interpret as topics (see Bakharia et al. 2016; Chawla 2018; Herrero 2019 for discussions of the mathematical underpinning of NMF).

Newspaper articles typically have a very definite 'aboutness' based on specific individuals, events, or occasions (e.g. a sporting event, a movie release, a criminal investigation), which makes them amenable to topic modeling. The topic outputs generated, however, should not be seen as the end point of analysis, but rather as a starting point which should be augmented with close attention to individual sentences in the constituent texts. In particular, Brookes and McEnery (2019, 16) caution that "topic word-lists alone are of limited use for interpreting the topics produced by the computer," echoing a similar point made by Jacobi, van Atttevelt, and Welbers (2015, 14) that topic modeling analyses should be manually inspected. On the other hand, Murakami et al. (2017, 272) argue that topic modelling can be "particularly useful in the initial exploration of corpora that are of large enough scale to preclude a manual approach such as reading each text." Topic modeling analysis, consequently, is combined with other approaches which focus more on word, phrase, and sentence level in order to give more contextual grounding to the texts under consideration.

THE LEGAL DIMENSION: COPYRIGHT, FAIR USE, AND DATA REGULATION

Having set out the kinds of data examined in this book and methods deployed in the analysis, the discussion now turns to some of the overarching legal and ethical issues.

This is important given that two of the chapters deal with publicly available media data (Chapter 4 on *The Guardian* and *The Scotsman* and Chapter 7 on *Brooklyn Nine-Nine*), while other chapters examine data drawn from online sources. Setting out how the book aligns with relevant legal and ethical frameworks is necessary to show how compliance with these frameworks has been achieved. In this section, I discuss the legal dimension of collecting and analyzing publicly available media data, before introducing the EU's General Data Protection Regulation (GDPR hereafter) and its implications for academic research.

First and foremost, the legal issues are (relatively) straightforward for television shows, newspapers, and the like, although there are a number of issues related to copyright, monetization, and fair use (see also McEnery and Hardie 2012, 57–60; Zanettin 2012, 52–55; Crawford and Csomay 2015, 76–78). More specifically, since such data are in the public domain, no ethical approval or legal consent is needed from individual shows, television networks, or newspaper companies to analyze or reproduce excerpts in an academic analysis, provided any excerpts meet fair use (or 'fair dealing' in the UK), where the "amount of the material quoted is no more than is necessary for the purpose of the review" (UK Copyright Service 2020). This doctrine of fair use also applies to still images, where the reproduction of images and stills is permitted in order to criticize, review, or analyze the work in question. For example, the still images of *Brooklyn Nine-Nine*, which augment the analysis presented in Chapter 8, fulfill the fair use doctrine, since such images are only used for the purpose of academic research.

Things become less clear when *building* corpora based on media data. For the corpus of *Guardian* and *Scotsman* articles (Chapter 4), this comprises only a small subset of data collected via the publicly available online newspaper article repository *LexisNexis*, while the *Brooklyn Nine-Nine* corpus was built using a combination of fan-produced scripts, new transcripts, and transcripts collected from a script repository website, following similar procedures set out in Bednarek (2018, 2020). In each case, these corpora have been constructed for nonprofit purposes and have not been distributed or shared in an online repository or otherwise.

Beyond issues of copyright and fair use, of particular (legal) importance is the introduction of the GDPR, a relatively new piece of EU legislation and, arguably, the most significant change to the legal landscape of research in the past twenty years. This directive was introduced in May 2018 to tackle a range of problems to do with user privacy and control of user data across different platforms. For example, a user might sign up for an online service and unknowingly have their personal data sold to another company for the purposes of conducting targeted market research. With the growth of a range of integrated online services (e.g. banking, insurance, household bills), the emergence of 'cloud-based' file storage systems (e.g. iCloud, Dropbox, Google Drive), and the inconsistency of privacy directives across European member states, coupled with a number of major privacy breaches, data leaks, and the threat of governmental surveillance, GDPR was intended to give more rights and protections to individuals in terms of how their personal data was collected, stored, accessed, and processed (European Commission 2019, 1). Thus, GDPR does not apply just to online services, but rather any situation where an individual might offer up personal data (e.g. their name, their email or postal address, pictures). It enshrines in law eight rights for individuals—the right to be informed, the right of access, the right to rectification, the right to erasure, the right to restrict processing, the right to data portability, the right to object, and rights in relation to automated decision-making and profiling.

In basic terms, this means that individuals (also known as 'data subjects' in GDPR terms) have the right to be informed about the collection and use of their personal data, that sites must provide information about why their personal data is being collected, for how long and who it will be shared with, and that individuals must explicitly consent to having their personal data collected (this last point is a particularly important one). Individuals also have the right to request a copy of their personal information from a company, to rectify mistakes in their personal data, to request that their personal data be deleted, and to stop their data being used for direct marketing. Furthermore, companies and organizations now need to have a lawful basis for collecting and processing personal data and are obliged to safeguard users though strong anonymization to ensure that data cannot be linked to identifiable individuals (see chapter 3, article 12–23 of the GDPR for a more comprehensive discussion of the rights of the data subject).

The implications of GDPR for linguistics research are potentially far-reaching, but because GDPR is a relatively new addition to the research process, discussion about its effects on data collection, processing, and analysis is almost entirely absent in the literature (although see Collins 2019: 35–36 for an exception). Is 'informed consent' always required in every situation under GDPR? Can researchers analyze anonymous comments posted online without permission? What do GDPR restrictions mean for analytical approaches like discourse analysis? If the focus is ostensibly on texts and not on the authors, can 'informed consent' be forfeited? If the community is not named, does that satisfy ethical requirements? How do we balance the critical examination of 'problematic' discourses with the rights of the community? Ultimately, how can researchers carry out socially valuable work without falling foul of GDPR requirements?

In an attempt to resolve some of these tensions, the directive sets out special conditions for institutions conducting academic research, stating that such research is a "task in the public interest" (UK Research and Innovation 2020, 5) and so organizations such as universities have a lawful basis for processing personal data. Furthermore, this personal data may be processed, without consent, when such "processing is necessary for the purposes of the legitimate interests pursued by the controller or by a third party" (Information Commissioner's Office 2020; see also Maldoff 2016). The requirement for consent also interacts with the extent to which users have expectations of privacy—thus, posting on Reddit is more public than posting on a closed forum group, where membership is approved by a moderator or administrator. Consent does not necessarily have to be secured in the former, but it would be more likely in the latter, provided that the researcher has a lawful basis for investigating these communities.

Nevertheless, universities and researchers have a responsibility to implement appropriate safeguards and to put in place measures to ensure that they process only the personal data necessary for research purposes. Not only does this mean that anonymization must be used, but it also means deleting (or not collecting) identifiable metadata about a user (e.g. IP address, email address, specific geolocations, and so on). This process of anonymization is key to GDPR regulations, since once personal data is fully anonymized,

> it is no longer personal data. In this context, anonymised means that it is not possible to identify an individual from the data itself or from that data in combination with other data, taking account of all the means that are reasonably likely to be used to identify them. . . . The issue is not about eliminating the risk of re-identification altogether, but whether it can be mitigated so it is no longer significant. (Information Commissioner's Office 2014, 58)

In bringing a more explicit legal dimension to ethical decision-making, GDPR has changed the research landscape considerably and linguists are still figuring out how best to uphold legal and ethical requirements while being able to continue the socially valuable work an informed analysis of language in its social context offers. That said, the issue of legitimate interest gives some flexibility for researchers, provided other interventions are implemented, as I go on to discuss.

ONLINE COMMUNITIES AND THE ETHICS OF DIGITAL RESEARCH

Since its inception, sociolinguistics has been concerned with the ethics of data collection, including issues to do with anonymity, confidentiality, informed consent, representation, and social responsibility. This stance is primarily borne from the fact that researchers work closely with community members and that continued access to these communities is predicated on the ethos of 'do no harm' (see the exchange between Cameron et al. 1993 and Rickford 1993 for an early discussion of ethics in sociolinguistic research). While this ethos has tended to be the driving force which underpins ethical decisions in sociolinguistics research, online and digital forms of data has muddied the waters, particularly in terms of informed consent and confidentiality.

More specifically, a common position among researchers collecting data from online forums and social networking sites has been that users forgo any rights to privacy or confidentiality because such data is in the public domain. Consequently, this data becomes available for collection, analysis, and dissemination via articles, conference presentations, books, and chapters (see Stommel and Rijk 2021 for a general discussion of social media and ethical practice in linguistics). In their analysis of Reddit data, for example, Derksen et al. (2017, 2) report that "according to the University of Auckland Human Participants Ethics Committee policy, this work did not require ethical approval, as it involved analysis of publicly available data. Consent was not obtained from individuals or Reddit, as the posts are available in the public domain and were made voluntarily from individuals who could not be identified."

Park and Conway (2018) also adopt a similar position, stating that "research using publicly accessible social media data (such as Reddit) is typically granted exemption from review by IRBs in the US context."

Yet the blurring of the private/public boundary in online spaces, where individuals share personal information in public-facing outlets, coupled with increased attention concerning individuals' expectations of privacy in digital media, has meant revisiting some of the assumptions about online data collection (see Collins 2019, 34–38 for a discussion of the ethics of online research from a corpus linguistic perspective). Accordingly, the field has shifted toward treating ethics as a case-by-case, contextualized, and ongoing process of decision-making based on guidelines, instead of a box-ticking practice based on codes and rules (Markham and Buchanan 2012, 5; Mackenzie 2017, 294; Page 2017, 316). At the heart of this shift lies the argument that the binary 'public/private' schema is an oversimplification (briefly, the oversimplification being that all public data is public and fair game and that all private data is not) and that researchers should instead consider what people's reasonable expectations of privacy might be (Markham 2012). As Markham and Buchanan (2012, 8) ask, "if access to an online context is publicly available, do members/participants/ authors perceive the context to be public?" Building on Nissenbaum's (2004) framework of 'contextual integrity', Mackenzie (2017, 297) argues that researchers have a responsibility to establish the 'informational norms' which undergird the community under analysis, that is the "identifiable patterns of expectation, achieved in social context, about the normal and appropriate use of data."

For the purposes of this book, there are two spaces where such 'informational norms' need to be determined. The first is Reddit (discussed in more detail in Chapters 5 and 6), an online social media and networking space which is organized along the lines of specialized subreddits dedicated to a range of topics and interests. At the time of writing, active membership of Reddit is estimated to be around 330 million monthly users, all of whom are under no compulsion to use their real names as their Reddit handle (although this is usually not the case for celebrities, politicians, journalists, authors, and other public-facing individuals who use Reddit as a PR platform; see also van der Nagel's 2017 and 2020 discussions of pseudonymity, identity, and identification on Reddit). The sheer size of Reddit raises a number of practical problems in securing informed consent from every user, as well as the fact that a number of accounts either lie dormant, have been banned by the site's admin, or have been deleted by the user. Moreover, a cursory look at any given Reddit community would suggest that the interactions do not appear to be intimate and private, with users aware that there is a broader audience engaging with the content they post. Even Reddit's own privacy policy, to which users are directed when they first sign up to the site, states that when users, "submit content (such as a post or comment or public chat) to the Services, any visitors to and users of our Services will be able to see that content, the username associated with the content, and the date and time you originally submitted the content" (Reddit Inc. 2020). Furthermore, it is possible for a subreddit to implement a private setting to make it inaccessible to members of the general public (for example, /r/Top1000Users is an invite-only subreddit), while those users wishing to have fully private conversations are encouraged to use the site's direct messaging system. Each of these facts suggests there exists a clear demarcation between 'public' and 'private' Reddit spaces.

The second online community for which we need to figure out the 'Informational norms' is the dad.info forum, which forms the basis of Chapter 8. As briefly mentioned earlier in the chapter, this is a fathers' support forum and, as such, is fundamentally different to Reddit. Like Reddit, members of dad.info are not required to identify themselves by their real name, but the site is much smaller in size than Reddit, with only 40,000 registered users. With its focus on fatherhood, the site is perhaps best considered a semipublic space, especially given the reasons why a father might initially post to the site (for example, seeking guidance on child custody issues), even though the site's privacy policy states that "the forum area is where you as an individual can post information/thoughts/comments that are then in the public domain and visible to all." Reviewing the site, it is clear that these are much more intimate interactions, where users disclose feelings of vulnerability, issues with their physical and mental health, and worries about fatherhood, relationships, and parenting. As such, the ethical approach adopted for Reddit data cannot be the same as the ethical approach adopted for dad.info, given that they are two very different communities in function and form. In the next section, I outline in more detail the ethical interventions adopted in this book.

ETHICAL PRINCIPLES ADOPTED IN THIS BOOK

In almost any project which deals with real people, the guiding principle of do no harm prevails, where the researcher has a responsibility to mitigate or minimize the potential for harm to be caused to community members (harm, here, can be defined as embarrassment, reputational damage, prosecution, or being faced with abuse or threatening behavior, Collins 2019, 37). While some scholarship on online communities takes the view that there is minimal potential for harm in dealing with anonymous digital data, there is still a need to consider how best to protect such communities, balancing this against broader practical issues.

In this book, a number of strategies have been implemented to address a range of ethical concerns. First, ethical approval was secured from my institutional review board, which examined the ethical practices set out below and aligned the project against relevant GDPR standards. This also meant that all data had to be stored on a password-protected laptop to which only I had access and none of the data were stored on cloud-based servers.

Second, I have tried to balance the principle of do no harm against legitimate public interest. With the exception of public-facing people (e.g. celebrities and journalists), I have not identified specific individuals, nor have I collected data that would allow the identification of individual people. Moreover, all data has been anonymized (or reanonymized if needed for discussion purposes) and any identifying information has been removed, reducing the possibility of linking any one username to an identifiable individual.

The third point relates to informed consent. While it was simply not practical to collect informed consent from Reddit posters due to the size of the site and the number of members, for the smaller community of dad.info, consent was obtained to include extended quotes from users. This followed the standard consent process which set out the research project, the nature of participants' involvement, their right to withdraw from the study at any point, and how their data was stored and protected.

Fourth, while I have principally relied on aggregating linguistic data and reporting only general trends and findings using approaches such as keyword analyses, frequency lists, collocations, n-grams, and similar methods of analysis (Derksen et al. 2017; Smith, Bulbul, and Jones 2017; Collins 2019, 36), discussions are augmented with excerpts and concordance lines when focusing on the qualitative dimension of the data.[2] To this point, none of the excerpts or concordance lines are attributed to an individual user or identified as belonging to a particular username. Additionally, the nature of the analysis is such that specific users are not individually scrutinized, nor are individuals identifiable on the basis of direct quotes. It is also worthwhile adding that /r/The_Donald was banned in June 2020, meaning that posted content no longer appears on a Google or Reddit search (in any event, Google searches are very poor at finding content posted to Reddit, while Reddit's search function is notoriously unreliable).

Finally, none of the corpora in this book have been made publicly available and will not be distributed via an online repository or otherwise. This does, of course, raise some issues concerning data reuse and replication, but on balance, wider distribution of the data would likely cause more problems than it solves.

'UNLIKEABLE SUBJECTS' AND RESEARCHER RISK

Beyond the ethics of accessing and using online data, there has also been an increased focus on issues related to working with communities which not only skirt the edges of reasonable civil behavior, but go into the realms of criminality, hate speech, misogyny, sexism, sexual deviancy, extremism, racism, ethno-nationalism, and male supremacism. Not only do we have a responsibility as researchers to confront the more insalubrious elements of society, such research also has a "critical role to play in exploring and questioning social, cultural and economic structures and processes (for example relating to patterns of power and social inequality, and institutional dynamics and regimes that disadvantage some social groups over others, intentionally or not)" (Economic and Social Research Council 2015, 28).

While (socio)linguistics has historically not engaged with these kinds of communities, especially compared to disciplines like anthropology, ethnography, criminology, policing, and sociology (although see Hardaker 2013; Hardaker and

---

2. With the exception of the composite accounts, excerpts and concordance lines are reproduced verbatim.

McGlashan 2016; Grant and MacLeod 2016, 2020 for some recent exceptions, as well as Rüdiger and Dayter's 2017 discussion of working with 'unlikeable subjects'), conducting research on these communities raises a number of issues concerning researcher risk and dealing with potential backlash, from the dangers of being doxed (that is, the publication of personal information such as home address or phone number), through to harassment, threats, and online abuse (see Ketchum 2020). These issues become even more pronounced in digital contexts, since social media has arguably become the principal vector through which networked harassment and abuse occurs, even as funders and institutions increasingly encourage researchers and academics to use these spaces for the purposes of dissemination and outreach strategies, in order to increase public engagement of research with nonacademic audiences (see also Page 2017, 319). These dangers were raised in a Special Session at the 2019 American Sociological Association meeting about social justice and social media, which noted that "in an era of both pronounced inequality and rapid technological change, social media is an integral means of reaching a wide population outside of academia and sharing ideas that might otherwise be confined to this particular space. Yet academics who use this platform also risk backlash in the form of doxing, hate emails, or threats" (Wingfield 2019).

In a form of 'backlash politics', a number of journalists, social commentators, and scholars working in feminism, gender studies, ethnic studies, and so on have faced a variety of personal online and offline attacks, sometimes in relatively high-profile cases (see also Spring 2021; Alibhai-Brown 2021; Gerald 2021). For example, media critic Anita Sarkeesian and video game developers Zoë Quinn and Brianna Wu were subjected to an intense period of harassment, doxing, and death threats in what has since come to be known as the Gamergate Controversy (Wu 2019; see also Massanari 2017 on toxic technocultures; Warzell 2019 for a discussion of the cultural impact of Gamergate; and boyd 2019 for a reflection of sexual abuse and misogyny in the tech industry), while academic Kate Starbird was sent a range of threatening and abusive messages following the publication of her work on election integrity and dis/misinformation in online spaces (see Starbird 2022). Similarly, Bryant Sculos faced a range of harassing behavior after the publication of his article on toxic masculinity in Disney's *Beauty and the Beast* (Sculos 2017b). In a response about the reception of his article and subsequent media coverage, he notes that "because the many articles linked to my personal information, I received a number of hateful, mocking emails that had surprisingly few spelling errors, and several voicemails that ranged from politely oppositional to verbose and incoherent" (Sculos 2017a, 5). In more recent work, Ketchum (2020) provides an overview of how marginalized scholars have been malignantly targeted on the basis of their academic work and the range of sexist and racist abuse such scholars face, including doxing, invasions of privacy, trolling, and cyberbullying (see also Mantilla 2013; Megarry 2014; Mulcahy, McGregor, and Kosman 2017; Veletsianos et al. 2018; Worth 2020 for further accounts of researcher harassment).

Beyond these threats, though, there are also the psychological and emotional risks researchers face through regular encounters with sexist, homophobic, racist, misogynistic, and supremacist content. In cases where researchers have to engage with this data in order to produce a detailed analytical account, this threat becomes even more pronounced, as the problem of what I call the "density of awful data" can cause significant harm in terms of mental well-being and psychological security. This is particularly relevant for work which adopts corpus linguistic or critical discourse analytic approaches, where such fine-grained attention to linguistic detail is par for the course.

Reviewing these issues, it would seem important to consider how to mitigate researcher risk. Unfortunately, this is where ethics guidelines in sociolinguistics arguably fall short. For example, although the British Association of Applied Linguistics (BAAL)'s list of recommendations has a brief section on dealing with distressing data, it does not outline any practical safeguards, while the ESRC research guidelines (2015) offer only a passing reminder to consider "risks to the research team without any specific suggestions of a) what these risks might be or b) how to manage these risk."

Some areas of healthcare and the social sciences are much further along the path of managing researcher risk. For example, Fahie (2014) is a useful exposition of ethical reflexivity and dealing with physical, psychological, and reputational risks (see also Lee-Treweek and Linkogle 2000; Dickson-Swift et al. 2007; Mitchell and Irvine 2008; Kaye 2018; Massanari 2018), while a range of online resources have been made available by the VOX-Pol Research Network, which carries out research on violent online political extremism (see VOX-Pol Network of Excellence 2020). These resources cover guidelines on online security through to researcher well-being and digital privacy and are a valuable starting point for anyone conducting research on forms of online extremism. More specifically, peer support and regular meetings with colleagues or supervisors to discuss difficult or distressing data, are key parts of looking after your mental health (see also Lawson forthcoming).

But perhaps the most helpful set of guidelines is offered by Marwick, Blackwell, and Lo (2016), who provide a comprehensive discussion of the dangers of online harassment, as well as concrete suggestions about how to manage and mitigate these risks. These strategies include limiting online personal identifying information; removing phone numbers and addresses from public CVs, websites, and online profiles; creating an email alias on your institutional or professional domain that points to your primary email address; using a Google voice number instead of your personal phone number; setting up two-factor authentication on email; and having a trusted friend monitor social media accounts. The guidelines also highlight the importance of institutional leadership, department chairs, and administrative support in developing a proactive communication plan for dealing with online harassment, arguing that researcher safety is also an institutional responsibility (see also Ketchum 2020 for guidance for university PR departments). Consequently, managing risk is perhaps best seen as a holistic framework, rather than something which is only the responsibility of an individual researcher.

Of course, explaining the strategies I have adopted to manage potential risk would seem to defeat the purpose of adopting these strategies in the first place, so I hope my lack of transparency is understandable. Nevertheless, one would hope that none of the risks of harassment, doxing, or online abuse would ever come to pass.

Once a piece of research is out there in the public eye, however, it is very difficult to know what kind of reception it will receive and what people's reactions might be, measured or otherwise. Therefore, it is incumbent on researchers to manage and mitigate personal risk with the same level of rigor as would be applied toward research participants.

CONCLUSION

My aim in this chapter has been to introduce the data analyzed in the book, outline the methodological tools that will be used in the upcoming analyses, and discuss how the book sits within the broader legal and ethical context. In doing so, this chapter forms the methodological foundation for the following chapters, where the elements discussed here are put into practice. In the next five chapters, we see how these frameworks are deployed to provide a multimethod analysis of language and masculinities across a range of different media contexts.

CHAPTER 4

Representations of 'Hard Man' Masculinity and Ideologies of Toughness in the British Press

INTRODUCTION

As noted in Chapter 2, one of the hallmarks of hegemonic masculinity is the deployment of violence, whether physical, verbal, or symbolic. This chapter draws on corpus linguistic methods to examine one of these exemplars of violent masculinity, that of the 'hard man'. Although perhaps most commonly associated with Scottish working-class male identities (Lawson 2013), the trope is also used in other parts of the UK, drawing on a cultural constellation of excessive aggression, violence, and toughness.

Using data collected from *The Scotsman* (aimed at a Scottish audience) and *The Guardian* (aimed at a non-Scottish audience), the chapter presents a diachronic analysis of a corpus of news articles to outline how the term has been used in print media in the UK as a type of enregistered characterological figure (cf. Johnstone 2017). By investigating how 'tough' masculinities are constructed at a national level, the chapter considers the role of the press in (de)legitimizing public performances of masculinity, how particular evaluative stances are encoded in newspaper discourse, and the complex web of social meanings associated with the term 'hard man'. While the focus in this chapter is on British newspapers, the chapter has broader relevance to contexts further afield, particularly in terms of how specific forms of masculinity are constructed in the mass media.

The chapter begins by outlining a brief history of the 'hard man'. Following this, I discuss some of the extant work on masculinities in newspapers, showing how the mediatized construction of men and manhood in the press is realized discursively, both in the UK and elsewhere. The chapter then introduces the newspaper corpus on which the analysis is based, before working through four primary features—topic modeling, word frequency, keywords, and collocations. The chapter ends with some

Language and Mediated Masculinities. Robert Lawson, Oxford University Press. © Oxford University Press 2023.
DOI: 10.1093/oso/9780190081041.003.0004

observations concerning the shifting social indexes of 'hard man' masculinity, paying particular attention to the Scottish context.

THE GLASGOW 'HARD MAN' AND DISCOURSES OF VIOLENCE IN URBAN SPACES

In his travelogue of the United Kingdom in the early 1700s, Daniel Defoe (1753, 122) famously described Glasgow as "one of the cleanest, most beautiful, and best-built Cities in Great Britain," a description befitting its Gaelic etymology of 'dear green place'. By the turn of the twentieth century, however, the city had come to be more associated with urban squalor, overcrowding, crime, and violence (Davies 2013). This image of 'criminal Glasgow' finds its first major media treatment in the novel *No Mean City: A Story of the Glasgow Slums* (McArthur and Kingsley-Long 1935), which charts the rise and fall of Johnnie Stark, the infamous 'razor king' of the Gorbals, a working-class neighborhood in the south of the city. Although variously praised and disparaged as a literary moment, *No Mean City* kickstarted the genre of Scottish gangster literature, with 'hard man' masculinity at its core. As Crawford (2009, 591) points out, "though many West of Scotland writers have sought to counter or modulate its influence, the 'hard man' novel *No Mean City* with its influential urban Scottish gangsterism did leave literary legacies to later Glasgow authors and to generations of Scottish urban crime writers from William McIlvanney to Ian Rankin, not to mention the Irvine Welsh of Edinburgh's *Trainspotting*" (see also Fraser 2015, 59–60 for a discussion of Glasgow's reputation as a city of crime and violence).

The 'hard man' trope has since been taken up in a variety of media over the years, from plays like *The Hard Man* (McGarth and Boyle 1977) and *The Slab Boys* trilogy (Byrne 1978, 1979, 1982), to the famous street detective *Taggart* and movies such as *Small Faces* (MacKinnon 1995), *Trainspotting* (Boyle 1996), *Neds* (Mullan 2010), and *The Wee Man* (Burdis 2013). The hard man has also dominated the true crime genre, with a range of books about the lives of infamous Glaswegian criminals like Walter Norval, Jimmy Boyle, Paul Ferris, Thomas McGraw, and Jamie Daniel (see Boyle 1977; Ferris and McKay 2001, 2005; Ferris, Wheatman, and Wraith 2018; Jeffrey 2006, 2008, 2011; Leslie 2011; McKay 2006, 2007). More light-hearted representations can be found in the characters of Rab C. Nesbitt, an unemployed and alcoholic Glaswegian 'street philosopher', The Big Man' from *Chewin' the Fat*, the scary uncles from *Burnistoun*, the southside gangsters of *At It*, and even Groundskeeper Willie from *The Simpsons*. This trope has become part of a number of creative video mashups, where innocent characters are revoiced into Glaswegian English, including the famous Dolmio puppets and various Pokémon characters. There are even websites dedicated to the numerous incarnations of the 'violent Glaswegian', with the website TV Tropes (n.d.) going so far as noting that "Glaswegian is a very good dialect for uttering threats."

The 'hard man' has come to be an important cultural touchstone for many men in Scotland and one of the most persistent themes in the social history of Glasgow

(Johnston and McIvor 2004a; Young 2007). Associated with working-class street culture, the status of being a 'hard man' relies on the intersection of several different practices, including physical strength, fearlessness, violence, aggression, toughness, criminality, and social competitiveness. The loss of industry in Glasgow is regularly cited as one of the principal reasons why 'hard man' masculinity, and gangs more generally, are a central part of Glasgow's social fabric, since "deindustrialization has meant that the ability for working-class male adolescents to express their masculinity via the workplace is no longer possible" (McLean and Holligan 2018, 3).

The cultural identity of the 'hard man' affords some benefits, from discouraging potential attacks to promoting local community identity and status (McLean and Holligan 2018, 12), even though it comes with a variety of social costs, including incarceration, serious injury, and social marginalization. In his discussion of what he terms the "Glasgow gang complex," Fraser (2015, 184) observes that "the masculine bravado in 'gang talk' serves to confirm, consolidate, and legitimize the violent aspects of gang identity," noting that violence is one of the most persistent features of street-based cultures in the city (see also Rafanell, McLean, and Poole 2017 on the emotional dimension of gang affiliation). While the 'hard man' is something of a celebrated identity among working-class male communities in Glasgow, a number of scholars have argued that it should be seen as a more complex substantiation of class-based masculinities (sometimes described as a 'protest masculinity'; Holligan and McLean 2018), rather than as a straightforward expression of violent masculine practice (see, for example, Milton 1997 and Fraser 2015, 186 who problematize the intersection of class and violence).

MASCULINITIES IN PRINT

To date, research on Scottish masculinities has mainly been within the fields of history, criminology, and sociology, including work on gang cultures (Fraser 2013; Bartie and Fraser 2017a, 2017b), youth crime (Fraser et al. 2010; Bartie and Jackson 2011; Fraser 2015), and health care (Johnston and McIvor 2004a, 2004b, 2007). In terms of linguistic studies, Lawson (2013) examines 'tough' masculinity in narratives collected from male Glaswegian adolescents, noting that "none of the speakers . . . offer a more general rejection of 'tough' masculinity . . . suggesting that such an identity is accepted as the hegemonic one for young men in the city" (Lawson 2013, 390). In their project on gang masculinities in Glasgow, McLean and Holligan (2018) develop a qualitatively informed analysis of masculinity and violence which gives more nuance to the lived realities of gang members and how they understand their individual masculine projects as bound up with organized crime and casual street violence. Beyond this, however, there have been limited attempts to chart the use of the term 'hard man', particularly how it is deployed as a broader cultural resource. This is surprising given the social significance of the term and how it encodes particular configurations of aggressive, rebellious, and violent masculine practice.

This is not to say, of course, that masculinities in the public sphere have not been of interest to linguists. Analyses of media representations of masculinities are now commonplace within CDA, corpus linguistics, and sociolinguistics, mainly because mass media formats (such as newspapers, magazines, television, and movies) are powerful means though which discourses of masculinity (and gender more broadly) are normalized. For example, Baker and Levon's (2016) study of masculinities in nine different British newspapers between 2003 and 2011 analyzed the intersectional nature of masculinity in the UK. Of particular relevance is their finding that working-class men were typically positioned as unsuitable or undesirable, noting that "the more implicit positioning of working-class men as 'beleaguered' has the effect of producing a discourse of working-class men in the subsample as 'forgotten' members of society who, as a result, have come to occupy a morally deviant space within the ideological landscape of masculinity" (Baker and Levon 2016, 129).

Part of the social power of mass media is derived through the fact it employs an ongoing process of repetition and reiteration. Thus, audiences are subject to repeated instances of 'this is the way the world is', usually via a multitude of outlets. As Baker and Baker (2019, 363) point out, mass media has "long-term effects on audiences that compound over time due to the repetition of images and concepts . . . repeated use of language helps to construct and solidify particular understandings of masculinity as 'received wisdom.'" Similarly, Macarro (2002, 13) suggests that "As individuals, we are all influenced, our opinions shaped, reinforced and altered by our exposure to the media." Thus, news becomes socially constitutive "through shaping understandings, influencing audience attitudes and beliefs (particularly through their reinforcement), and transforming the consciousness of those who read and consume it" (Richardson 2007, 29).

While it is possible to make some general inferences, based on cultural knowledge and other media representations, about how 'hard man' is used in the British press, developing an empirically grounded analysis means that we are able to chart with more precision the cultural discourses surrounding the term and the extent to which meanings associated with violence, criminality, and aggression have coalesced (or have been resisted) in these media formats. The fact that the 'hard man' identity is more salient in Scotland potentially suggests different patterns of usage. The Scotsman is an interesting case in this regard, because such newspapers were one of the principal ways violence was reported in Scotland. As Jeffrey (2006, 2–3) reports, "the [news]papers themselves relied heavily on crime to sell. At the top end of the scale there were undignified scrums outside the High Court as rival hacks fought to buy up the stories of participants in major trials . . . At the other end of the crime-scale, [stairhead fights] and minor feuds were reported in great detail. These were the days of hot-metal journalism with the popular papers heavily staffed with crime reporters, a breed who spent their proprietors' cash with abandon building up the allegedly vital contacts book."

DATA AND CORPUS CONSTRUCTION

The data for this chapter were downloaded through the online newspaper archive LexisNexis, with a date range of 1984 to 2018 for The Guardian and 1993 to 2018 for The Scotsman, using the compound noun hard man as a search term (and possible variants hardman and hard-man). While it would have been preferable to have had a longer time span to examine early attestations of 'hard man', this was not possible for a number of reasons. First, although both newspapers have online archives going back to the earliest issues, none of this has been optimized with optical character recognition technology (OCR). This means that it was not possible to convert these digital images to machine-readable format where the text of an article could then be extracted for the purposes of linguistic analysis. Second, *The Scotsman* has no digitized archive between 1950 and 1993, so any linguistic analysis would need to be conducted on microfilm or bound volumes of hard copies (at the time of writing, deputy editor Donald Walker confirmed that *The Scotsman* intended to digitize the rest of their archive, but this was a longer-term plan, Walker, p.c.). With the number of articles in each issue, it would have been impossible to search through an archive spanning forty years to find every instance of 'hard man' in print.

The data were extracted to text files, duplicate entries deleted, and articles cleaned, which involved removing the by-line, publication date, links, social media comments, and so on (McEnery, Xiao, and Wong 2006, 73). Articles where 'hard' functioned as a premodifying adjective were also manually removed from the corpus (e.g. 'Even his enemies admit he is a *hard* man to stop'). After these steps, the final 'Hard Man Corpus' (*HarM* corpus hereafter) totaled over two million words (Table 4.1).

Table 4.1. BREAKDOWN OF THE *HarM* CORPUS (RANKED BY NUMBER OF WORDS)

	Number of articles	Number of words
The Guardian	1304	1,329,286
The Scotsman	715	727,297
Totals	2019	2,056,583

ANALYSIS OF *THE GUARDIAN* AND *THE SCOTSMAN*

In the analysis which follows, my interest is in unpacking the semiotic foundations upon which the ideological construct of the 'hard man' is built. In doing so, it is necessary to examine how *hard man* is deployed across the range of news stories in the *HarM* corpus and to interrogate how the term co-occurs with other linguistic material. This allow us to examine how a specific substantiation of masculinity is represented and uncover the "ideological framework for masculinity the texts serve to instantiate" (Baker and Levon 2016, 113).

To conduct the analysis, the programs #LancsBox (Brezina, Timperley, and McEnery 2018) and AntConc (Anthony 2020) were used, looking at four main features—topic analysis, frequency lists, keywords, and collocation. By working from the macro level (i.e. topics) to the micro level (i.e. words in context), we can trace the structuring discourses of 'hard man' masculinity in the corpus and how specific lexical items are associated with these discourses.

TOPIC MODELING

For the first stage of the analysis, we want to determine which kinds of topic 'hard man' is associated with. As noted in Chapter 3, NMF topic modeling was implemented, using the Scikit-learn and Python programming packages (Pedregosa et al. 2011; van Rossum 2020). In terms of number of topics set, Murakami et al. (2017, 250) note that "There is no agreed way to automatically decide the number of topics. In other words, the decision on how many topics a corpus will be deemed to contain is a subjective one and the answer may be defended on the grounds of usefulness but not on the grounds of accuracy."

Reviewing *The Guardian* UK website reveals six top-level topics (news, opinion, sport, culture, lifestyle, and 'more'), with a further 58 subtopics, while *The Scotsman* has eight top-level topics (news, sport, business, arts and culture, lifestyle, food and drink, heritage, and Future Scotland), and 39 subtopics. References to 'hard man', however, are not likely to be found in the fashion section, so it is possible to omit certain subtopic categories as potential sites. Accordingly, the number of topics was set to 20, based on the top 20 subtopics of 'news' and 'sport', while the number of words to be returned was set to 15 (again, it is worthwhile noting that not all of the words returned in the output will align with the overarching topic). Using these parameters, the following results were obtained (Table 4.2):

Table 4.2. NMF TOPIC MODEL ANALYSIS IN *THE GUARDIAN* SUBCORPUS

Topic	Interpretation	Representative words
1	Miscellaneous items	SAYS PEOPLE JUST LIFE PRISON MAN YEARS GOT GET NOW THINK KNOW TIME MEN WOMEN
2	English sports (mainly football/soccer)	PLAYERS CUP ENGLAND FOOTBALL TEAM GAME LEAGUE CLUB SEASON PLAYER UNITED CHELSEA ARSENAL RUGBY LIVERPOOL
3	French politics	PAGES POLL RONNIE NICK FRANCE PAGE VICTORY OH EASY NATIONAL PLAY WORLD HARD MAN SARKOZY
4	Ray Winstone movies	FILM MOVIE MOVIES FILMS DIRECTOR ACTOR BRONSON WINSTONE STARS HOLLYWOOD COMEDY RAY HARDMAN CINEMA DRAMA
5	Vinnie Jones movies	JONES VINNIE HOLLYWOOD BARRELS LOCK STOCK SMOKING ROLE LANDS SOCCER LANDED STARRING ACTOR POUNDS THRILLER
6	*EastEnders*	VIEWERS AUDIENCE MILLION SOAP EPISODE SHARE AVERAGE SHOOTING EASTENDERS CHANNEL TUNED VIC PULLED MEL AUDIENCES
7	Gordon Brown's April Fools article	APRIL NO-NONSENSE FOOL POSH FOOLS BROWN PUNK GORDON TRICK LETTER PLEASE DESPERATE STORIES HARD-MAN APPROACH
8	Russian politics	PUTIN CHECHNYA RUSSIAN RUSSIA PRESIDENT KREMLIN VLADIMIR MOSCOW NATO ABUSES FATHER ASSASSINATED SECURITY REBELS RIGHTS

Table 4.2. CONTINUED

Topic	Interpretation	Representative words
9	Managers of English football teams	WORLD-CLASS KEANE INTERNET ROY HITS MANAGER BENITEZ RAFAEL SUNDERLAND ARSENE MOURINHO WENGER JUDGED QUALIFY JOSE
10	Hunting	HUNT PROTESTERS ESSEX FOX INJURED POLICE DELAYED PROVOKE BULLY BATTLES CRUEL HIRED OFFICERS ARRESTED TACTICS
11	Boxing	BOXING CHAMPION FIGHT TITLE HATTON LEWIS HARRISON COLLINS KHAN WORLD FIGHTER RING TYSON EUBANK FIGHTS
12	Andy McNab	FOOD MCNAB GUIDE PICK STUFFED MORRISON GUESTS PERMANENTLY QUEST MONDAY AMBASSADOR FIND TRANSITION AFFECT ATTITUDES
13	Newspaper industry	GALLAGHER TELEGRAPH EDITOR DAILY PAPER MAIL MEDIA MURDOCH DIGITAL TONY LATEST EXECUTIVES JOURNALISTS EXECUTIVE DERRY
14	Pubs and alcohol	PUB NIGHT CAPER LANDLORD CHEERY FRANTIC RECESSION RELENTLESS MALES COSY DRUNKEN RICKY FORCING STRAW REFLECTS
15	Non-UK football	MIN BLOCK BALL RONALDO GOAL CORNER PORTUGAL ARSENAL WIDE CROSS DOWN RIGHT CZECH REAL SUNDERLAND
16	Serial killers and murders	GAY SERIAL KILLER VICTIMS SIGNIFICANT AGED APPEARANCE PICTURE BROWN CLAIMED POLICE HAIR RESPONSE RECEIVED SHOWS
17	(British) politics	LABOUR GOVERNMENT MINISTER PARTY BLAIR SARKOZY SAID ELECTION PRIME BROWN POLITICAL NEW SECRETARY TORY JOHNSON
18	Irish politics	IRA SINN IRELAND FEIN BELFAST NORTHERN ADAMS MCGUINNESS ULSTER UNIONIST IRISH REPUBLICAN PEACE TRIMBLE REPUBLICANS
19	Ross Kemp	KEMP ROSS WADE SUN EDITOR EASTENDERS MS GANGS MCFADDEN KILLING NEWS MEDIA GUARDIAN KIDS TV MITCHELL
20	Donal MacIntyre	MINS MACINTYRE DONAL DOMINIC CERT FILM GANGSTER MUSIC REVIEWS SOPRANOS FAINTLY DOCUMENTARY BOAST FILM-MAKER EXPOSE

Examining these topics, we can make a number of observations. First, there is generally coverage of a wide range of topics in *The Guardian*, including sports, politics, and entertainment. Not only does this reflect the newspaper's more global position and wider readership, but it also highlights where *The Guardian* writers see fit to deploy the idea of the 'hard man'. Interestingly, however, this does not accord with the general image of the true crime 'hard man' as discussed previously. For example, of the 20 topics, 10 are related to entertainment (sports, movies, soap operas, documentaries, and books), five are related to politics, and the remaining five are split up across serial killers, hunting, the newspaper industry, journalistic language, and a non-specific category. Topics related to criminality, violence, or delinquency are generally not a major focus in *The Guardian*, with the exception of topic 16 (serial killers). Instead, the 'hard man' is often utilized in relation to a more generic sense of 'toughness'.

> Another day, another hardman pose: here's Vladimir Putin with the Russian bob-sleigh team. (*The Guardian*, February 20, 2012)

> Ex-footie hard man Vinnie Jones is incapable of saying anything without it sounding as if he is about to twist your testicles off. (*The Guardian*, December 17, 2005)

> Then the legendary hard man [Andy McNab] revealed something truly shocking. He is a massive *Thomas the Tank Engine* fan. (*The Guardian*, May 30, 2006)

The term 'hard man' is also used in articles about Grant and Phil Mitchell (from the television show *EastEnders*), Hollywood hard men Vinnie Jones and Ray Winstone (who appeared as gangster characters in the movies *Lock, Stock and Two Smoking Barrels* and *Sexy Beast* respectively), Donal MacIntyre's[1] documentaries *A Very British Gangster* and *MacIntyre's Underworld: Gangster* (about British gang activity), and Ross Kemp's[2] documentary *On Gangs*. In the context of entertainment media about gangsters (both real and scripted), it makes sense that 'hard man' would feature predominantly in these kinds of articles.

For *The Scotsman* subcorpus, on the other hand, the following set of topics were returned (Table 4.3):

Table 4.3. NMF TOPIC MODEL ANALYSIS IN *THE SCOTSMAN* SUBCORPUS

Topic	Interpretation	Representative words
1	Miscellaneous	SAYS JUST FILM PEOPLE TIME NOW GOT GET REALLY FIRST THINK EVEN LIFE BACK KNOW
2	*EastEnders* soap opera	ARREST MITCHELL PHIL EASTENDERS STEVE PARTNER WEDNESDAY DAUGHTER PICKED CLAIMS ACTOR PLAYS POLICE STAR TV
3	Scottish football	RANGERS PLAYERS SOUNESS CLUB CELTIC MANAGER CUP TEAM LEAGUE FOOTBALL GAME HEARTS PLAYER SEASON FERGUSON
4	Politics	LABOUR MINISTER PARTY BLAIR BROWN GOVERNMENT SECRETARY DEWAR SCOTTISH PRIME POLITICAL REID TORY ELECTION LEADER

1. Donal MacIntyre is an investigative journalist who covers a variety of crime-related topics.
2. Ross Kemp also plays the character of Grant Mitchell in *EastEnders*.

Table 4.3. CONTINUED

Topic	Interpretation	Representative words
5	*Trainspotting* movie	WELSH BEGBIE TRAINSPOTTING IRVINE FRANCIS NOVEL BOOK CHARACTER CARLYLE ISSUE STORY BIG PAPERS EXCLUSIVE DESCRIBE
6	Alcohol and health	DRINKING ALCOHOL EXECUTIVE GBP WOMEN CAMPAIGN ADVERTISING CULTURE LAD MILLION POUNDS AGED ESTIMATED RESEARCH COSTS
7	Michael Stone	STONE COURT SAID DOUGLAS EVIDENCE GUILTY JURY TOLD SHOT DEAD POLICE QC STRANGER ADMITTED HEARD
8	Vinnie Jones movies	JONES VINNIE HOLLYWOOD ROLE FORMER GLOVES OSCAR STARRED FOOTBALL AL PULLS REPORTEDLY ADMITTING SIGHTS JOINING
9	Return of Grant Mitchell to *EastEnders*	KEMP EASTENDERS MITCHELL ROSS GRANT DAME BRIEF SOAP FINAL RETURN ON-SCREEN ACTOR MOTHER EPISODES STORYLINE
10	Glasgow/Scottish violence	GLASGOW CITY CRIME CENT VIOLENCE PEOPLE POLICE SCOTLAND STRATHCLYDE KNIFE SAID VIOLENT STREETS GREATER HEALTH
11	Prison and incarceration	PRISON ROOF UNIT PETERHEAD INQUIRY PRISONER PRISONERS PROTEST GOVERNOR JAIL HOURS INMATES STAFF SENTENCE SCOTTISH
12	English football	KEANE COLE UNITED MANCHESTER BUTT GOAL FERGUSON PREMIERSHIP FOOTBALL BOOK ROY REFEREE MINUTES TRAFFORD CELTIC
13	Knife crime	MEN WALLACE MALES BLAMED KNIVES YOUNG STARK HARD COMMIT KNOCK LAY STUDY JUSTICE ENGLAND MINISTER
14	Billy Connelly movies	BOYLE BILLY CONNOLLY FILM COLLECTOR DEBT SUE JIMMY REFUSED SIGN GORBALS RIGHT MACDONALD SAYING HODGE
15	Phil Mitchell's shooting in *EastEnders*	EPISODE SOAP PHIL SHOOTING EASTENDERS MITCHELL AUDIENCE ALBERT MILLION BBC SQUARE VIEWERS CENT MEASURED STEPS
16	Music and festivals	MUSIC HALL NOVEMBER EDINBURGH GLASGOW CLASSICAL FESTIVAL BAND CONCERT STEVE QUEEN KIRK VENUES PIANO PREMIERE
17	Rugby	RUGBY CUP GAME COACH SCOTLAND ENGLAND WORLD LIONS ITALY BLACKS IRELAND TOUR ZEALAND SIDE SQUAD
18	*Trainspotting 2* movie*	FILMING COM TRAINSPOTTING FILM ACTOR EWAN MCGREGOR LOTHIAN CARLYLE SPOTTED SET BEGBIE DANNY STORE PLAYS
19	Miscellaneous crimes	SHOT BOXING STRANGER DEAD SHOOTING TRIGGER INDIAN WANTED RANDOM QC ALLEGEDLY ENTERED JURY GUN STUDENT
20	Ronnie Cray coverage	RONNIE GAY RELEASED DETECTIVES SEXUALITY RUN-UP ASSOCIATE GANGSTER CRIME BIOGRAPHY TWIN CLARK REVELATION TRIAL CHARLES

*The town of Blackburn in (West) Lothian was the filming location for *Trainspotting 2*, so this output has been treated as separate to topic #5.

First off, there are some notable similarities with *The Guardian* results. For example, articles about *EastEnders* and 'hard man' movies (covering *Trainspotting, Trainspotting 2, The Debt Collector*, and movies featuring Vinnie Jones) are regularly discussed, while sports (mainly Scottish and English club football) and Labour party politics feature prominently. There are also topics which relate to major political events, such as the imprisonment of Michael Stone,[3] a Northern Irish loyalist who was jailed in 1988 for three counts of murder at an IRA funeral and, after he was released in 2000, the attempted murder of two prominent Irish politicians in 2006. What is revealing, however, is the extent to which true crime stories about the 'hard man' are situated more fully within the Scottish and Glaswegian context. This is further apparent in the range of articles which focus on the general conditions underpinning Scotland's 'hard man' social culture, including articles about knife crime, alcohol-related violence, criminality, prisons, and incarceration.

> Alcohol and the cult of the "hard man" were identified yesterday as key factors behind Scotland's high murder rates, after a report revealed that the number of homicides committed by men here was more than twice the number in England and Wales. (*The Scotsman*, March 4, 2000)

> Justice Secretary Kenny MacAskill has argued that minimum pricing for alcohol would most affect harmful and hazardous drinkers. He said: "We need to change the culture of looking up to the heavy-drinking hard man." (*The Scotsman*, June 3, 2009)

> The 25-year old, who is serving a seven-year sentence, spent four hours on the roof of a special "hard man" unit in the Peterhead Prison complex. (*The Scotsman*, August 9, 1997)

Thus, 'hard man' masculinity is not positioned as an entertainment product, but rather as something more connected to the real world. In particular, the idea of the 'hard man' is typically found in articles related to knife crime, alcohol, and casual violence, all regularly cited public health problems in Scotland (Skott and McVie 2019). The articles in *The Scotsman* reflect a broader cultural preoccupation with these concerns, particularly as they relate to young men in Scotland, rather than as some distant form of titillating and vicarious entertainment. The 'hard man' in *The Scotsman* is, arguably, something more 'real' than the 'hard man' in *The Guardian*.

Bringing the two analyses together, we can compare topics across the two newspapers (Table 4.4).

---

3. Michael Stone is also the name of a suspected serial killer who was convicted in 1997 of the murders of Dr. Lin Russell and her daughter Megan Russell.

Table 4.4. TOPIC COMPARISON ACROSS THE *HarM* CORPUS

The Scotsman	The Guardian
Narrower sports coverage—Scottish club football, English club football, rugby	Broader sports coverage—English club football, football managers, non-UK football, boxing
Narrower politics coverage—Labour	Broader politics coverage—Labour, Ireland, Russia, France
Narrower entertainment coverage—*EastEnders, Trainspotting, Trainspotting 2*, Vinnie Jones movies, Billy Connelly movies	Broader entertainment coverage—*EastEnders*, Vinnie Jones movies, Ray Winstone movies, Ross Kemp and Donal McIntyre documentaries, Andy McNab books
Broader coverage of criminal violence—prisons, knife crime, alcohol-related violence, gun violence, miscellaneous violence	Narrower coverage of criminal violence—Serial killers

Although Table 4.4 is based on some subjective decisions about aggregating topics, I have tried to keep like-with-like in order to generate umbrella categories. Generally speaking, we can say that the topic coverage in *The Guardian* is broader in scope, including a wider pool of sports articles, political discussions, and entertainment coverage. In almost every respect, *The Scotsman* has much narrower coverage in these topics. Perhaps the most marked difference between the two corpora is in the realm of criminality and violence, with a broader range of articles about these topics in *The Scotsman*. This suggests that the 'hard man' is more explicitly related to real-world issues in *The Scotsman*, while the 'hard man' is more commonly conceptualized as a fictional entertainment figure in *The Guardian*.

As discussed earlier in this chapter, though, it is not enough to rely on topic modeling as the start and end point of an analysis. As such, we will now look more closely at the lexical level to examine the overall distribution and patterning of language use in the corpus.

FREQUENCY

First, although every article in the corpus contains some variant of the phrase "hard man," it is useful to chart the overall distribution in terms of density across both newspapers (Table 4.5). In other words, does one newspaper have a higher use of 'hard man' variants than the other? Using the Whelk Tool in #LancsBox, we find that there are 2234 instances of all 'hard man' variants across both corpora, broken down as follows (interestingly, the parallel construction of 'hard woman' simply does not exist as an ideological reference point, with only two instances of this phrase in the entire *HarM* corpus):

As might be expected, there is a higher overall use of all 'hard man' variants in *The Guardian*, reflecting the fact that there is more data for this newspaper, with the form *hard man* predominant and *hard-man* the least common. This pattern of *hard*

Table 4.5. BREAKDOWN OF 'HARD MAN' VARIANTS IN THE HarM CORPUS

	hard man	hardman	hard-man	Total
The Guardian	869 (6.54 per 10k)	398 (2.99 per 10k)	154 (1.16 per 10k)	1421
The Scotsman	512 (7.04 per 10k)	208 (2.86 per 10k)	93 (1.28 per 10k)	813
Total	**1381**	**606**	**247**	**2234**

man>hardman>hard-man is echoed in *The Scotsman*, suggesting that *hard man* is the most typical form for both Scottish and English newspapers.

Looking at the individual variants and the rate per 10,000 words, there is a slightly higher use for *hard man* and *hard-man* in *The Scotsman* compared to *The Guardian*. This does not, however, represent any major difference in usage, as the following examples illustrate (each with *Scottish* functioning as a premodifying adjective; the same holds true for other words in prenominal position):

> Edinburgh's Lothian Road- once a notorious trouble-spot- has been reclaimed for the decent citizen. The **Scottish hard man**, it seems, has had his stamping ground pulled from under his bovver-booted feet. (*The Scotsman*, June 4, 1998)

> The image of the dour **Scottish hardman** beating his miscreant wife has long been a part of Scottish folklore. (*The Scotsman*, December 11, 1998)

> We will soon be recalling that sad day when the **Scottish hard-man** image took a knock as James IV's forces were annihilated. (*The Scotsman*, August 21, 2013)

What is noteworthy, however, is that *hard man* is the most likely variant to be rendered as *"hard man"* (with either single or double quote marks) in both corpora, with 52 instances in *The Guardian*, 14 instances of *"hardman,"* and four instances of *"hard-man."* This pattern is repeated in *The Scotsman*, with 55 instances of *"hard man,"* compared to only seven for *"hard-man"* and five for *"hardman."*

> Gerry Kelly, one of the key players in Sinn Fein and part of its negotiating team at Stormont, was jailed in the Seventies for his part in a bombing campaign in London, yet this **"hard man"** of the delegation, alleged still to be actively involved with the IRA at a high level, is talking to ministers. (*The Scotsman*, January 9, 1998)

> I remember reading, some years later, the memoirs of the 1980s Portsmouth **'hard man'** Mick Kennedy, as serialised in the *Sun*. (*The Guardian*, August 9, 1996)

> Renowned for his work ethic and **'hard man'** reputation, Gallagher joined the *Telegraph* in 2006, becoming editor in 2009. (*The Guardian*, July 25, 2011)

Although other variants are commonplace, we can ask why *"hard man"* might be marked out as separate from the rest of the text through the use of quote marks. The 'hard man' is, in many ways, a folklore symbol, an urban legend of sorts (Fraser

2015), valorized as a culturally important form of masculinity. It is, in Agha's terms, a "characterological figure," identified through a recognizable and socially meaningful constellation of linguistic and non-linguistic practices (Agha 2007, 177; see also Agha 2003). Characterological types abound in society, from the Pittsburgh *Yinzer* (Johnstone 2013, 2017), through to the Beijing *Smooth Operator* (Zhang 2008), the Californian *Valley Girl* (D'Onofrio 2015), and the gay *Sassy Queen* (Ilbury 2020). While the concept of the 'hard man' is bound up with particular configurations of linguistic and non-linguistic practice (particularly in Scotland, Lawson 2016), newspapers cannot report 'voice' in the same way a televised news segment can. In the absence of these embodied resources, newspapers have to rely on other means of marking out 'hard man' as newsworthy. Features like topic (as discussed above) and co-occurring words (as I go on to discuss later in the analysis) can help in this semiotic positioning, but since 'hard man' is such a well-entrenched social stereotype, simply evoking the name is often enough to call up its associated social practices for an acculturated readership.

Having set out the distribution of 'hard man' and its variants, we can now consider other frequent lexical items which occur in the corpus. This analysis was carried out using AntConc, since this program can omit high frequency words, an option unavailable in #LancsBox. Rather than discuss every word, this section teases out some of the more important lexical items and how these might be used in news coverage (where necessary, I also discuss some of the main collocates of the words included in Figure 4.1).[4]

It is perhaps no surprise that the most frequent lexical item is *man*, since every article contains at least one instance of the phrase 'hard man', as well as more generic instances of *man* (e.g. *young man*, *family man*, *leading man*). The next items on the list (*time* and *said*) are comparable across both corpora, indicating two things. The first is that journalistic writing relies on verbs which introduce direct speech, the most common of which is *said*. This word simultaneously allows a journalist to avoid subjectivity in their reporting and facilitates them "staying out of the story" (Bradshaw 2017). Across both corpora, *said* almost exclusively introduces or closes direct speech:

Judge Antony Balston **said**: "I have no doubt at all that you are an extremely dangerous man. You have an appalling record for dishonesty and violence." (*The Scotsman*, October 24, 1998)

"These charges are all invented," the 28-year-old **said**. "I have never hurt anybody, let alone murdered someone." (*The Guardian*, November 18, 2011)

While *said* is relatively neutral, examining the collocates reveals some interesting patterns. For example, *he said* is more common than *she said* (465 vs. 90 occurrences in *The Guardian* and 312 vs. 59 occurrences in *The Scotsman* respectively), reflecting a predominantly male focus in both corpora. Although this is potentially an artifact of the corpus construction, it nevertheless dovetails with the findings of Baker and

4. All graphs in the book were produced using Python and the Matplotlib graphics package version 3.1.1 (Hunter 2007).

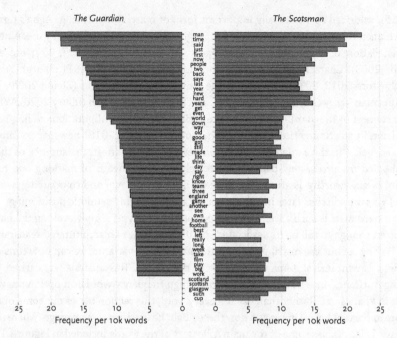

Figure 4.1. Top lexical frequency rankings in the *HarM* corpus

Baker (2019), who argue that British newspapers privilege and advantage men more than women.

Second, news stories are typically located in a chronological place or bounded by a particular temporal context. In many cases, this is achieved by the word *time,* but there are other high frequency words which relate to specific timeframes (e.g. *day, week,* and *years*). Furthermore, not only is *time* used to mark out major life events or socially important moments (*first time, last time, next time, one time, hit the big time*), but it is also connected with duration (*long time, no time, lot of time*). Given the number of references to *prison* (142 in *The Guardian* and 253 in *The Scotsman*) and the fact that it emerged as a salient topic for *The Scotsman,* it is surprising that the euphemistic phrase 'to do time' (that is, to be imprisoned) only appears four times in *The Guardian* and once in *The Scotsman.*

> The man who was prepared **to do time** as an anti-poll tax protestor and who this week led an angry mob of demonstrators to Glasgow City Chambers. (*The Scotsman,* March 13, 1997)

> The truth is that few prisoners really want trouble with staff. Most just want to "do their bird" and get back out again. Sadly, **doing time** is rarely that simple. (*The Guardian,* July 17, 2003)

There is also an intersection between *time* and *football,* as found in the phrases *half time, full time,* and *extra time,* all referring to specific stages of a football match. The social significance of football is marked in both corpora, with words such as *cup, game*, *play*, *team* appearing in the top 50 words (football was also returned as important in the topic modeling).

A final observation is the extent to which *The Scotsman* is more concerned with specific geographical spaces. For example, *The Guardian* only has *England* as the top geographical place name (although this could also be related to international football), while *The Scotsman* has both *Scotland* and *Glasgow*, suggesting a more locally grounded concentration. Perhaps more important, however, is how place names in *The Scotsman* are used to premodify *hard man*, emphasizing its connection to the city.

This is why the story of Hugh Collins is so apposite at this moment in the political argument about crime and punishment. For Collins was born into crime. His father was a **Glasgow hard man**. Collins became a Glasgow hard man. Now he is not. (*The Scotsman*, February 2, 1997)

Documents previously kept from the public described the **Glasgow hard man's** time in jail at Aberdeen and Inverness in the 1960s and police files from his home city. (*The Scotsman*, January 15, 2010)

Charlie managed to maintain his **Glasgow hard man** image, assuring his injured underling: "That was done by a razor. I know what these things can do." (*The Scotsman*, April 24, 1994)

KEYWORDS

We now move on to examine keywords in the corpus. This analysis was conducted using AntConc to generate a list of 25 words, based on the log-likelihood statistic, the p-value threshold set at $p \leq 0.0001$ (with Bonferroni correction), and Hardie's Log Ratio for the calculation of effect size (see Gabrielatos 2018 for a discussion of these parameters in relation to keyword analysis). Rather than use a general reference corpus (like the BNC, for example) to determine keywords, *The Guardian* and *The Scotsman* were compared against one another. Consequently, the number of keywords is slightly different in each analysis (words in parentheses were not key but are instead included to give more contextual information about a specific person or event).

Comparing the keywords analysis for *The Guardian* (Table 4.6) with the earlier topic analysis reveals some complementary findings. In particular, the predominant focus is primarily sports and sportsmen, a finding which also emerged in the topic modeling. In the keyword analysis, however, more specific sportsmen are identified, suggesting two things.

The first is that in occupying a 'hard man' position, these sportsmen are positioned as proficient at intimidating the opposition and using their physicality to contribute positively to their team and the outcome of the game.

Saracens salute Borthwick, a hard man in the Johnno mould: Second row puts unhappy times behind him to play a leading role for country and new club. (*The Guardian*, September 4, 2008)

Table 4.6. TOP KEYWORDS IN *THE GUARDIAN* SUBCORPUS

Sports-related terms	AFRICA, ARSENAL, BALL, CRICKET, ENGLAND, FIVER, INDIA, MIN, MINS, PAKISTAN, SUNDERLAND, TOTTENHAM, WICKET
Sportsmen	(JONNY) BAIRSTOW, (NICK) COMPTON, (ALASTAIR) COOK, (QUINTON) DE KOCK, (MOHAMMAD) HAFEEZ, (DIETER) KLEIN, (LIONEL) MESSI, (SAMIT) PATEL, (DANE) PIEDT, (JOE) ROOT, (MATTHEW) WADE
Politics	(DONALD) TRUMP, CHINA, ENGLAND, LABOUR, (VLADIMIR) PUTIN, (NICOLAS) SARKOZY, ZACARIAS (MOUSSAOUI)
Miscellaneous	JOHNSON, PM, POUNDS

A strangled appeal first up as Abbott swings one a wee bit back into Cook and it clatters between pad and thigh pad via a thick inside edge. That probably hurt, but Cook is a hard man. (*The Guardian*, January 23, 2016)

The second is that these sportsmen are often in the position of facing other 'hard men' on the pitch or in the ring, where again physicality, aggression, and toughness are evaluated as positive character attributes.

"Actually, we had about six different plans," said Hatton afterwards. "It was a case of getting in there and adapting to what Tackie could do. He is a hard man with a dangerous right hand, so I knew I would be playing into his hands if I went in there and started hurling left hooks at him and left myself open." (*The Guardian*, December 15, 2003)

Asked to name the hooker he respects most, it turns out to be Wood, his head-to-head adversary tomorrow. "He's great. He's probably the only hooker I admire, because he wants to do the same things as me, chuck the ball about, slot drop goals and things. We chat during games." Swapping hairdressing jokes, presumably? "He's a hard man but he's a top boy as well. He's someone after my own heart." (*The Guardian*, February 4, 2000)

All of this ultimately resemiotizes aggressive behavior as a positive character trait, dovetailing with other work which has argued for sport as a key site for the performance of normative masculinities (Levon, Milani, and Kitis 2017, 520).

The other significant arena of 'hard man' masculinity is politics, with a number of male politicians identified as key, including Nicolas SARKOZY, Vladimir PUTIN, and Donald TRUMP. Like sports, politics is often seen as a realm where aggression, toughness, and machismo are feted as desirable qualities required to push through domestic agendas and to protect national interests (Franke-Ruta 2013; Chollet 2016).

Unions and the left yesterday accused Sarkozy of deliberately forcing workers onto the streets for a showdown over pensions reform in order to portray himself as a hard-man reformer who is prepared to stand his ground. (*The Guardian*, November 13, 2007)

Some with knowledge of the negotiations suggested it was Trump's son Eric who had pushed the company's unwavering stance. Others pointed to his carefully guarded image as a straight talking hardman that he was unlikely to relinquish for the duration of the presidential race. (*The Guardian*, May 11, 2016)

The new president, Vladimir Putin, is part economic liberal, part traditional Russian hard man. (*The Guardian*, July 10, 2000)

In comparison to *The Guardian,* a much broader range of keywords are returned for *The Scotsman* (Table 4.7). More specifically, the analysis identifies Scottish football teams (ABERDEEN, CELTIC, RANGERS, HIBS), football stadia (HAMPDEN, IBROX, PITTODRIE), and 'legendary' figures in Scottish sports (Jim TELFER, Alex FERGUSON, Jock STEIN). Several politicians are also returned, including Donald DEWAR (former First Minister for Scotland) and Michael FORSYTH (former Secretary of State for Scotland), although these figures were more involved in Scottish affairs than international ones.

For Mr Dewar, consulting with No 10 comes easier than consorting with his own backbenchers. He is not a natural grassroots politician. Behind a gauche exterior lies a hard man, ready to exercise power ruthlessly. (*The Scotsman*, May 28, 1999)

APE can exclusively reveal that Home Secretary Michael Forsyth cannae hold his drink. After just 14 Malibu and tequila slammers the Scottish Terror loses his hard man pose, as well as the intellectual rigour for which he is so justly famed, and becomes maudlin. (*The Scotsman*, February 4, 1997)

Table 4.7. TOP KEYWORDS IN *THE SCOTSMAN* SUBCORPUS

Sport	ABERDEEN, CELTIC, DUNDEE, DUNFERMLINE, HEARTS, HIBS, HIGHLAND (GAMES), RANGERS, SRU, (ST) JOHNSTONE
Stadia	HAMPDEN, IBROX, PARK, PITTODRIE, TYNECASTLE
Sportsmen	(MARTIN) BUCHAN, (JOHN) CUMMING, JIM (HERMISTON), (ALEX) FERGUSON, (ALEX) RAE, (GRAHAM) SOUNESS, (JIM) STEIN, (JIM) TELFER
Politics	SNP, (DONALD) DEWAR, (YEVGENY) PRIMAKOV, (MICHAEL) FORSYTH
Entertainment	BEGBIE, (ROBERT) CARLYE, HAMISH (MACBETH), (PETER) MCDOUGALL, TAGGART, TRAINSPOTTING, (IRVINE) WELSH
Law enforcement crime	BARLINNIE, (RONNIE) COULTER, (JAMES) FIENNES, (WILLIAM) MOONEY, (WILLIAM) RAE, (MICHAEL) STONE, (SPECIAL) UNIT
Places/nationality	COUNTRYSIDE, EDINBURGH, GLASGOW, SCOTLAND, SCOT, SCOTTISH, STRATHCLYDE
Miscellaneous	GBP, (ANDREW) GROSSART, TEN, WEE

The media 'hard man' is also flagged up in *The Scotsman* subcorpus, including BEGBIE (the psychopathic hard man of Irvine Welsh's novel *Trainspotting*), playwright Peter MCDOUGALL (famous for his plays *Just Another Saturday* and *Just a Boy's Game*, which explore intergenerational violence and sectarianism in Glasgow), and Scottish television detective Jim TAGGART.[5]

> In the way of its predecessor, *Trainspotting* also turns out to be a tale of comradeship and betrayal with Renton's future depending on how much distance he can place between himself and figures like Robert Carlyle's chillingly convincing hardman Begbie and Johnny Lee Miller's James Bond-obsessed Sick Boy. (*The Scotsman*, February 4, 1996)

> "The hard men are still out there," says Peter McDougall, whose powerful Seventies dramas of life and death on Scotland's mean streets, *Just Another Saturday* and *Just a Boy's Game*, earned him the nickname the 'Bard of Hard'. (*The Scotsman*, June 4, 1998)

> Although Detective Taggart is routinely contemptuous of life in general, like many west of Scotland males, this is often emotional armour protecting a soft centre. Like the average hardman, he is more complex than first appears. (*The Scotsman*, May 31, 1994)

There are also more references to incarceration (BARLINNIE prison and the Barlinnie and Peterhead SPECIAL Units), criminals (Hugh COLLINS, Ronnie COULTER), and victims of crime (James FIENNES, William MOONEY), showing how the idea of the 'hard man' is interwoven with discourses relating to violence, gang activity, and criminality.

Finally, we see more specific name referents in *The Scotsman*. For example, the two major cities of Glasgow and Edinburgh function as geographical place name identifiers (e.g. *streets of Glasgow*, *in Glasgow*, *suburb of Edinburgh*), and as specific political and cultural organizations (*Glasgow City Council*, *Glasgow Health Board*, *Edinburgh District Council*, *Edinburgh Festival*). Only *Glasgow*, however, is used as a 'hard man' premodifier (31 times in *The Scotsman*), while Edinburgh is never used as a premodifier.

> The **Glasgow hardman** is simultaneously deplored and celebrated, at once the brutalised product of the system and a magnificent challenge to it. (*The Scotsman*, April 4, 1993)

> But the **Glasgow hardman** [Thomas Shanks] still yearned for action. His requests to go to the frontline were refused on the personal instructions of General Sir Peter de la Billiere, commander of British forces in the Gulf. (*The Scotsman*, April 20, 2000)

5. The titular character of the BBC Scotland television series *Hamish Macbeth*, played by Robert Carlyle, is identified as key. This is because articles about *Hamish Macbeth* also typically refer to Carlyle's role as the 'hard man' Begbie in the movie *Trainspotting*.

Still, Charlie managed to maintain his **Glasgow hard man** image, assuring his injured underling: "That was done by a razor. I know what these things can do." (*The Scotsman*, April 24, 1994)

Other place names refer to organizations such as *Strathclyde Police*, formerly Scotland's largest police force, while *Scot* and *Scotland* are understandable given the newspaper's geographical focus.

COLLOCATION

The final part of the analysis examines collocates of *hard man* (given their low frequency, *hardman* and *hard-man* were not considered). While there are a variety of ways to calculate the strength of association between *hard man* and other words, collocates were obtained using a statistical measure known as Mutual Information (MI). This was chosen because it calculates the extent to which words co-occur compared to the number of times they appear separately. One criticism of MI is that low frequency words can have high MI scores, returning misleading results. In order to address this limitation, #LancsBox allows the user to set a minimum threshold to ensure that only collocates above this number are returned. For this analysis, the threshold was set to five, covering a span of five words either side of the node phrase. The GraphColl results for both corpora are presented first, followed by a more fine-grained breakdown based on concordance lines.

Figure 4.2 presents the GraphColl results for *hard man* in *The Guardian* subcorpus, with a span of five words. From this, we can see that premodifiers related to place and nationality (*Irish, Scottish, Glasgow*), profession (*Hollywood, Wimbledon* [football club]), and stance (*notorious, legendary, self-styled*) appear to the left of the node phrase. Conversely, most of the collocates to the right of the node phrase are to do with fictional characters, most notably Phil and Grant Mitchell from *EastEnders* and the actor Vinnie Jones, who tends to play tough, 'hard man' gangster roles in Hollywood movies and can be read as normative, unobtainable, and idealistic exemplars of 'tough' masculinity (see also the selected concordance lines in Table 4.10).

The strongest associations (i.e. the collocates closest to the node phrase) relate to the evaluation of 'hard man' masculinity, either as something to be gained (*reputation*), as something claimed for oneself (*self-styled*), or the idea of social importance (*legendary*). *Soft*, interestingly, appears to be used as a contrastive element and as a strategy for humanizing the subject of an article.

So does this hard man of business have a soft centre? "Well, it takes a bit of digging through but it's there—it's most definitely there. Always has been and always will be." (*The Guardian*, April 3, 2004)

There is also a range of characteristics we would normally associate with 'hard man' masculinity, including *tough* and *ruthless*, while the general associations with football

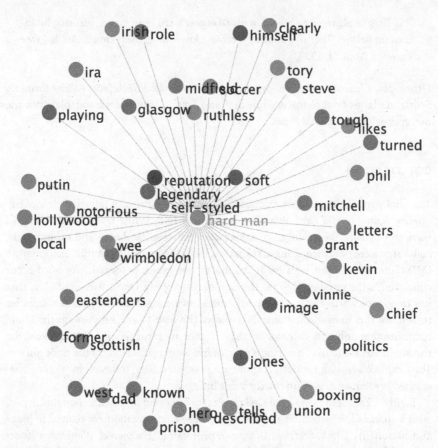

Figure 4.2. GraphColl results for "hard man" in *The Guardian* subcorpus

and politics identified in the topic modeling and the keyword analyses also emerge in the collocational analysis (Table 4.8).

Based on the GraphColl results, we can aggregate the strongest collocates under the categories of 'evaluation', 'sports', 'politics', 'entertainment', 'male identifiers', 'place', and 'miscellaneous', that is, words which do not fit into any one category (Table 4.9). Numbers in parentheses indicate how many times this word collocates with the node phrase and how many times the word itself appears in the corpus overall—so *reputation* appears 50 times within a five-word span of *hard man* and 237 times in the corpus as a whole (rankings are ordered by collocation frequency).

For *The Guardian* subcorpus, one of the strongest collocates is *reputation*, followed by *Vinnie Jones* and *Phil* and *Grant Mitchell* from *EastEnders* (Table 4.10). Reference to place names is less regular, although when *Glasgow* or *Scottish* appears, there is an approximately a 1 in 10 chance that *hard man* will appear close by.

Even within these selected lines, we can see references to issues associated with violence (e.g. *assault, bullied, crushed, fighter, knife, prison, tackle, temper*). Furthermore, 'reputation' is something which is *gained, earned,* or *built*, constantly pursued and

Table 4.8. SELECTED CONCORDANCE LINES FOR 'HARD MAN' IN *THE GUARDIAN* SUBCORPUS (FIVE-WORD L/R SPAN)

. . . Campbell, a well known **Glasgow**	"hard man"	and Steele, have always pleaded. . .
. . . it was predictable. The **Irish**	hard man	who likes a drink himself. . .
. . . in the way. A **legendary**	hard man	, Yates is expected to use. . .
. . . the life of the **notorious**	hard man	and perpetual British prisoner, this. . .
. . . Butler's toughest gig. The **Hollywood**	hard man	thinks he knows what backbreaking. . .
. . . Arguably, the Wales and **Wimbledon**	hard man	started playing the role of. . . .
is best known for his role as	hard man	**Grant** Mitchell in *EastEnders*. ITV. . .
. . . out who shot the EastEnders	hard man	**Phil** Mitchell in a special. . .
. . . but for now the football	"hard man"	**Vinnie** Jones is starting off. . .
. . . IRA assassin and feared	hard man	**Kevin** McGuigan was shot dead. . .

Table 4.9. MAIN COLLOCATES OF 'HARD MAN' IN *THE GUARDIAN* SUBCORPUS (WITHIN A FIVE-WORD L/R SPAN)

Evaluation	reputation (50/237), image (23/248), former (23/754), soft (22/99), legendary (13/60), tough (12/266), known (10/308), self-styled (6/21), hero (5/176), notorious (5/73), ruthless (5/47), wee (5/41),
Sports	midfield (9/130), wimbledon (9/74), boxing (5/216), soccer (5/70)
Politics	politics (8/256), ira (7/247), putin (6/169), union (5/224), tory (5/126)
Entertainment	jones (22/389), playing (16/501), vinnie (13/180), role (10/358), Mitchell (9/92), eastenders (8/162), grant (8/98), hollywood (7/199), phil (6/149),
Male identifiers	himself (27/902), steve (8/182), kevin (6/107), chief (5/213), dad (5/204)
Place	local (13/357), glasgow (11/153), scottish (7/182), prison (9/420), irish (5/218)
Miscellaneous	turned (11/386), west (11/523), clearly (5/212), described (5/188), letters (5/92), likes (5/144), tells (5/177)

having to be proven, aligning more broadly with discourses of masculinity as a precarious social status.

Figure 4.3 presents the GraphColl results for *hard man* in *The Scotsman* subcorpus. Because this subcorpus is smaller than *The Guardian* subcorpus, it is not surprising that fewer collocates are returned. Nevertheless, some interesting patterns emerge. Like *The Guardian*, the strongest left collocate is *reputation*, while there is a constellation of entertainment figures in the forms of *Vinnie Jones*, Phil/Grant *Mitchell*, and *Begbie* from the movie *Trainspotting*, also notable in the words *role* and *playing*. There are, however, more references to *culture* and the figure of the *Glasgow hard man* is more common in terms of raw frequencies (11 in *The Guardian* and 30 in *The Scotsman*). Sports is surprisingly absent in the collocation network, with only five instances of *Leeds* and none for Scottish football teams, suggesting that while

Table 4.10. SELECTED CONCORDANCE LINES FOR 'HARD MAN' IN *THE GUARDIAN* SUBCORPUS (WITHIN A FIVE-WORD L/R SPAN OF 'REPUTATION')

. . . gaining a **reputation** of a	hard man	who would stop at nothing . . .
. . . he had a **reputation** as a	hard man,	with an SAS background, who . . .
. . . his long-held **reputation** as a	hard man	with a nasty temper. The . . .
. . . made his **reputation** as a	hard man	who crushed fundamentalists, is vehemently . . .
. . . has a **reputation** as a	hard man	who could tackle corruption and . . .
. . . with a **reputation** as a	hard man,	was that he had systematically . . .
. . . gained a **reputation** as a	hard man.	The Englishman, people at the . . .
. . . had a **reputation** as a	hard man	that was well-founded but . . .
. . . himself a **reputation** as a	hard man.	Savile, the most Jewish Catholic . . .
. . . built a **reputation** as a	hard man:	prison terms for assault and . . .
. . . Fletcher's **reputation** as a	hard man	precedes him and, while convinced . . .
. . . Tandy, whose **reputation** as a	hard man	preceded him. Originally from Rotherham . . .
. . . with a **reputation** as a	hard man	on union relations after his . . .
. . . his **reputation** as a boardroom	hard man.	Right now, there is no point . . .
. . . a **reputation** for being a	hard man	who takes no prisoners. He . . .
. . . big **reputation** as being the	hard man,	street fighter, the gangster. My . . .
. . . here seems to be to a	hard man	's **reputation**. Does the episode . . .
. . . skinhead image bolstered his political	hard man	**reputation**. But critics accused him . . .
. . . for his work ethic and	"hard man"	**reputation**, Gallagher joined the Telegraph . . .
. . . he is revelling in his	"hard man"	**reputation**. He has a knife . . .
. . . The Welsh international with the	"hard man"	**reputation** both on and off . . .

'hard man' masculinity might be relevant at a broader topic level, it is not necessarily substantiated at the level of specific team collocates.

Given the lower number of collocates in *The Scotsman*, the aggregate categorization presented in Table 4.11 is less nuanced than Table 4.9, but it is still possible to identify common themes, particularly around evaluative language, entertainment, and place.

THE 'HARD MAN' IN SCOTTISH MEDIA: RECONFIGURATION AND REINVENTION

Bringing all of the different elements together, we can offer a few observations. First, the collocational analysis suggests that there is a wider range of collocates in *The Guardian* and a narrower range in *The Scotsman*. This finding aligns with the topic modeling analysis, which found that *The Guardian* articles tended to use the 'hard

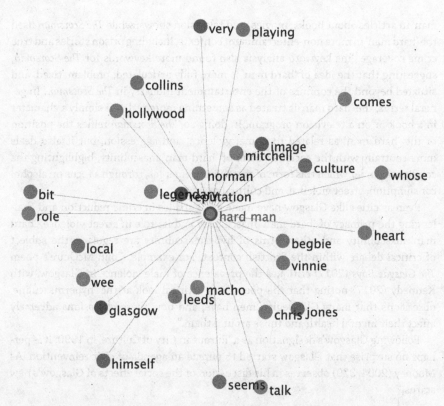

Figure 4.3. GraphColl results for "hard man" in *The Scotsman* subcorpus

---

Table 4.11. MAIN COLLOCATES OF 'HARD MAN' IN *THE SCOTSMAN*
SUBCORPUS (WITHIN A FIVE-WORD L/R SPAN)

Evaluation	reputation (24/137), image (16/182), heart (6/181), wee (5/126), macho (5/48), legendary (5/42)
Sports	leeds (7/83)
Entertainment	jones (11/225), playing (7/306), vinnie (6/70), begbie (6/61), role (5/218), hollywood (5/118), mitchell (5/43)
Male identifiers	himself (11/457), collins (7/512), chris (6/97), norman (5/31)
Society	culture (9/136)
Related to place	glasgow (30/757), local (8/185)
Miscellaneous	very (16/716), seems (8/271), bit (7/303), whose (6/238), talk (5/201), comes (5/196)

man' in articles about books, movies, and television shows, while *The Scotsman* used the 'hard man' in more non-entertainment contexts, including prison stories and true crime coverage. The keyword analysis also found more keywords for *The Scotsman*, suggesting that the idea of 'hard man' is more fully articulated, problematized, and situated beyond the confines of the entertainment industry in *The Scotsman*. In general terms, the 'hard man' is treated as something more real, not simply a character in a book or on a television program. In doing so, *The Scotsman* reifies the position of the 'hard man' as related to crime, violence, and aggression, but it also deals more centrally with the social problem of 'hard man' masculinity, highlighting the conditions under which this form of masculinity emerges, through a focus on alcohol consumption, street violence, and cultural pressures.

Even as cities like Glasgow have made great strides in crime reduction and challenging the primacy of 'hard man' masculinity and its role in street violence, 'hard man' masculinity and other forms of hypermasculinity are regularly the subject of critical debate within the Scottish context. For example, Colin McGuire's poem *The Glasgae Boys* (2017) critiques the prevalence of male violence in Glasgow, with Kennedy (2017) noting that the poem "is a satirical look at the 'hypermasculine' obsessions that many Glaswegian men have, and how these obsessions adversely affect their mental health and those around them."

Following Glasgow's designation as a 'European City of Culture' in 1990, it is perhaps no surprise that Glasgow started to pursue an agenda of civic reinvention. As Mooney (2004, 329) observes in his discussion of the social effects of Glasgow's new status,

> Throwing off its long-term image as a place of grim urban decay, poverty, violence and industrial unrest, Glasgow was re-imagined as a 'vibrant', 'post-industrial', 'fashionable' city. In the various celebratory discourses that emerged, the 'new' Glasgow was constructed and sharply contrasted with the 'old Glasgow'.

Media culture was a key element of this strategy and a range of outputs started to poke fun at the Glaswegian 'hard man', including comedy shows like *Rab C. Nesbitt* (1990–2008) and *Chewin' the Fat* (1999–2005), which offered a contrary narrative of masculinity compared to the true crime genres represented by *No Mean City* and its ilk. Hall (2002, 15) is particularly instructive here, noting that "the rather slippery behavior of the press, broadcasting and general cultural industries suggests quite strongly that, within the parameters of market logic, they are adaptable, durable and independent power-brokers with a keen eye for changes in the zeitgeist."

The subversion of dominant tropes of 'hard man' masculinity continues to this day, with programmes like *Burnistoun, Still Game,* and online comedy sketch show *At It* showing the flaws of 'hard man' masculinity and transforming it into a figure of fun and ridicule, rather than as a desirable masculine identity (albeit these 'hard man' characters remain staunchly White, working-class, violent, and heterosexual, raising some questions as to the extent they are truly transformative). Shows like *Gary: Tank Commander* go even further, where the main character presents "confident and uninhibitedly camp sensibility, in opposition to the 'conventional' Scottish masculinity considered [in other comedy shows]" (Irwin and Smith 2018, 55).

There is, then, a tension in Scottish media, where 'hard man' masculinity is simultaneously promoted and problematized. This tension is perhaps best captured in a *Scotsman* article about *Front* magazine's story about the UK's most violent cities, with Glasgow ranked number 1.

> Yet *Front*'s cover story, which would have been pulled together for a laugh, serves only to maintain the macho image of a city that is bleeding to death. . . . Yet, in Scotland, we, too, are guilty of maintaining the city's reputation. You just have to look at the best-seller lists in bookstores to see our fascination with Glasgow's true crime and tales from the violent underworld. There is an argument that such books serve to perpetuate the culture of violence, but this leaves all of us who enjoy *GoodFellas* and *The Soprano* [and] frown on Glasgow's Hard Men to a charge of double standards. (*The Scotsman*, April 26, 2007)

Ultimately, media forms like newspapers and television shows play a key role in communicating normative forms of masculinity, but they are also sites where these forms of masculinity can be challenged, critiqued, or resisted. The analysis presented in this chapter has also demonstrated that even reified identities like the 'hard man' are positioned in complex ways in the British press, particularly in relation to larger social concerns like entertainment, politics and sport. Applying linguistic methods to shed light on these processes means that we are able to come to a more nuanced understanding of an important ideological facet of masculinity in the UK and how this is distributed across time and space.

CONCLUSION

This chapter has mapped out how the ideological construct of the 'hard man' is deployed across a corpus of English and Scottish newspaper articles, drawing on corpus linguistic methods to examine topics, word frequencies, keywords, and collocations. While each approach provided a slightly different perspective on the data, a number of interesting findings were uncovered. Of course, analyzing one term is much more specific than the analyses presented in, for example, Baker (2015), Baker and Levon (2016), Levon, Milani, and Kitis (2017), and Baker and Baker (2019), and it could be argued that this focus neglects a broader consideration of Scottish and English masculinities in newspaper media. On the other hand, we now have a more detailed understanding of how a culturally important category of masculinity is deployed in the British press and how this construct relates more broadly across the entertainment industry, politics, and sports.

Because this analysis only deals with the very specific context of Scotland and England, across a limited sample of two newspapers, it consequently raises further questions as to how masculinities are realized discursively in other forms of media, especially at the intersection of place, nationality, and ethnicity. In particular, how might other forms of 'ideal' masculinity be constituted, how might these ideals form part of contemporary political discourse, and how can these discourses become weaponized for the purposes of recruitment to radical and extremist groups? These questions form the basis of the next chapter, which examines online masculinities in the context of the 'Alternative Right'.

CHAPTER 5

Being a 'Real Man' on /r/The_Donald

Masculinity, Ethnic Identity, and the Alternative Right

INTRODUCTION

This chapter examines the intersections of masculinity, ethnicity, and nationalism on /r/The_Donald, a community on the social networking site Reddit. In particular, the chapter traces how different types of men are represented in this community and what this might tell us about broader discourses of masculinity in the 'alt-right', a political movement which pits itself against left-wing liberalism, feminism, and multiculturalism. A well-established refrain within this community is that only 'real men' can protect their country from immigration and cultural dilution. For example, Daniel Friberg, one of the alt-right's leading figures, wrote the following in a 2017 blog post:

> Europe is enveloped in twilight—an utterly grave situation that demands real men
> for its solution, men who are willing to accept their traditional roles as defenders of
> family, folk, and civilisation. It is your responsibility to become such a man. What
> follows is concrete advice on how to take the first steps to transform yourself into
> the kind of man Europe needs and deserves. (Friberg 2017)

This excerpt raises a few points worth discussing. First, the statement that Europe is "enveloped in twilight" draws on the metaphorical frame of LIGHT/DARK to evoke a positive/negative binary, a common reference point in depictions of GOOD/BAD and PROGRESS/REGRESSION. As El Refaie (2014, 150–151) notes, "we all experience a connection between the absence or presence of light and our subjective sense of well-being, resulting in a universal tendency to understand and describe negative experiences and emotions in terms of darkness." Second, Europe's position is framed as a "grave situation," further amplifying the preceding claim as a point of significant social concern. Finally, the excerpt sets up a problem-solution pattern, where

Language and Mediated Masculinities. Robert Lawson, Oxford University Press. © Oxford University Press 2023.
DOI: 10.1093/oso/9780190081041.003.0005

only White men can transform themselves into exemplars of masculinity to defend European culture and values.[1] For Friberg, 'real' masculinity (framed as a particular configuration of White masculinity) cannot be divorced from the nationalist project, where 'real' masculinity is needed to defend against, as the rest of the article implies, the apparently growing threat of multiculturalism, migration, and ethnopluralism (see also Sunderland 2022).

Friberg's tactics are part of a long-standing tradition of equating ideal masculinity with whiteness and the framing of masculinity as something 'lost' and needing to be 'reclaimed' (Ferber and Kimmel 2000; Jackson 2002). As Ferber (1998, 137) notes, "male readers' masculinity is frequently assaulted in order to invite them to become 'real men' by joining the white supremacist movement." Being a 'real man' in nationalist and White supremacist contexts entails idealized traditionally hegemonically masculine traits such as physical strength, explicit heterosexuality, intellectual rationality, and emotional control. This conflation of White national identity with normative notions of masculinity has been highlighted as one possible reason for the increased numbers of young men involved with right-wing politics (Devega 2015).

One corollary of this is that desirable right-wing masculinity becomes juxtaposed against the 'weak' masculinity of those on the liberal left, as well as gay men and men from ethnic minority backgrounds, many of whom are subsequently viewed as failed or deviant in terms of their physicality, sexuality, intellectual capacity, appearance, morality, and more. Such stances are encoded in the language used by alt-right political commentators, as well as posters on Twitter, Facebook, Reddit and other social media spaces, as a way of demarcating (un)acceptable forms of masculinity, particularly in relation to national and ethnic identities (see also Romano 2018).

That said, we know little about the linguistic means through which men and masculinities are evaluated in 'alt-right' spaces. To that end, this chapter contributes to the growing body of work on how ethnic and national identities become bound up with masculinity politics (Riabov and Riabov 2014; Andersen and Wendt 2015; Enloe 2015), as well as adding to our understanding of how 'banal nationalism' (Billig 1995) is expressed in gendered terms. In the context of growing extremist right-wing political ideology (Wodak 2015; Norocel et al. 2018) and the spread of White nationalist discourse (Brindle 2016; Eriksson 2017; Johns 2017; Johnson 2018), such a project is ever more socially relevant.

THE 'ALT-RIGHT'

Although the term 'alternative right' (typically abbreviated as 'alt-right' in contemporary usage) was first coined in 2008 by paleoconservative political theorist

---

1. Although White masculinity is implicit in the article, through references to the 'West', 'European', and the German concept of 'Männerbund' (or male bonding; see Kim 2019 for a discussion of this in relation to the alt-right and White surpremacism), its evocation becomes more explicit in the comments. For example, one commenter suggests that "White men need to learn how to fight and if need be, to kill," with Friberg posting a (chilling) one word response of 'agreed'.

Paul Gottfried (see Hartzell 2018, 17–19), the publication of *The Alternative Right* webzine in 2010 by White supremacist Richard Spencer[2] can be thought of as the beginnings of the 'alt-right' as a political movement. The alt-right has been defined by the Southern Poverty Law Center (2017) as a "set of far-right ideologies, groups and individuals whose core belief is that 'White identity' is under attack by multicultural forces using 'political correctness' and 'social justice' to undermine White people and 'their' civilization," while Lyons (2017) suggests that it is "a loosely organized far-right movement that shares a contempt for both liberal multiculturalism and mainstream conservatism; a belief that some people are inherently superior to others; a strong internet presence and embrace of specific elements of online culture; and a self-presentation as being new, hip, and irreverent" (see also Lyons 2018).

Repackaging White nationalism and White supremacism under a more socially palatable label (Ehrenfreund 2016; Barnes 2017; Hartzell 2018), the alt-right has positioned itself as a mischievous *agent provocateur*, broadening its scope to include a variety of ideologies, including antisemitism, misogyny, and male supremacism (see also McIntosh 2020, 2). As such, it is not a uniform, unitarian, or monolithic movement; it has no leader, no coherent organizational structure, and no clear articulation of its aims, goals, or objectives (Marantz 2017). It is amorphous, undirected, and sometimes contradictory, uniting a variety of individuals under its banner, including conservatives, neo-Nazis, White supremacists, antiglobalists, men's right activists, and antiprogressive gamers.

The line demarcating the alt-right and other right-wing and conservative commentators is arguably blurred. For example, while commentators such as Ben Shapiro, Jordan Peterson, Stefan Molyneux, and Steven Crowder do not identify as alt-right,[3] they share a critical perspective on a number of common sociopolitical concerns, including identity politics and 'social justice warrior' culture. Others still, like Gavin McInnes (the former leader of the Proud Boys, a men-only far-right neofascist organization see Burnett 2022 for a discussion of McInnes and his politics), were originally positioned as part of the alt-right, but have since distanced themselves from the movement, claiming "They care about the White race. We care about Western values" (McInnes, cited in Marantz 2017).

Perhaps the alt-right's most telling characteristic is that it is offensive and provocative, happy to "crack jokes about the Holocaust, loudly—albeit almost entirely satirically—[express] its horror at 'race-mixing', and [denounce] the 'degeneracy' of homosexuals . . . while inviting Jewish gays and mixed-race *Breitbart* reporters to their secret dinner parties" (Bokhari and Yiannopoulos 2016). Through "high

2. Spencer is also the president of the National Policy Institute and director of Washington Summit Publishers, both White nationalist organizations. See Coaston (2019) and Gais (2019) for discussions of Spencer's political views.

3. Ribeiro et al. (2019) present a taxonomy of what they call *contrarian communities*, including the alt-right (e.g. Faith Goldy, Mark Collett, The Golden One), the alt-light ("the alt-right without the sieg heils and the white ethnostate," Lynskey 2018, which include media personalities like Steven Crowder, Stefan Molyneux, and Paul Joseph Watson), and the Intellectual Dark Web (e.g. Ben Shapiro, Jordan Peterson, Owen Benjamin). See also Hawley (2017, 139–158).

energy" memes, jokes, and mashups, alt-right members create and distribute offensive social commentary while standing behind a defense of plausible deniability and a "for the lulz" façade ("a sharper form of offensive humour directed by online activists," May and Feldman 2019, 26). Primarily existing in a variety of niche outlets (e.g. 4chan, *Daily Stormer*, *Occidental Observer*, *Radix Journal*) until around 2014, three major events catapulted the alt-right into public consciousness (for a comprehensive history of the alt-right, see Hawley 2017; Nagle 2017; Neiwert 2017; Lyons 2018).

The first was the 2014 Gamergate controversy, where several women in the videogame industry were targeted in a campaign of harassment by the (predominantly male) gaming community (see also Poland 2016; Massanari 2017; Hampton 2019). The harassment was initially directed at developer Zöe Quinn following the release of her game *Depression Quest*, stoked in part by articles written by Milo Yiannopoulos in the alt-right outlet *Breitbart News* (see Yiannopoulos 2014). Not only did the game generate antagonism within the community for its supposed political intrusions by being about mental health, but a former boyfriend published a blog post accusing Quinn of sleeping with a reviewer in exchange for favorable reviews. Although this accusation was later found to be false, the damage had been done, leading to claims of nepotism, conflicts of interest, and a subversion of gaming's merit-based review system (see Burgess and Matamoros-Fernández 2016 for a discussion of competing frames during Gamergate).

Further harassment was directed at other developers and critics who defended Quinn, including developer Phil Fish, who had his personal information hacked and posted online, and critic Anita Sarkeesian, who had previously faced harassment following her YouTube series about sexism in videogames. In late 2014, developer Brianna Wu became caught up in the controversy, while actress and gamer Felicia Day had her home address and phone number posted online following her criticism of Gamergate (see Day 2014 and Hamilton 2014 for a discussion of fears about doxing and the pressure to be silent, and Quinn 2017 for an insight into the personal cost of Gamergate, the impact of 'crowdsourced abuse', and her efforts to address online harassment at an industry level). In many ways, Gamergate was the opening salvo of the new online culture wars which have since come to dominate (un)civil discourse, where open misogyny and sexism are not only tolerated, but celebrated and communally encouraged (see also Siapera 2019). A number of commentators have since noted how Gamergate became a focal point for alt-right supporters, particularly due to their shared overlap of entitlement and defense of a culture under threat. As Romano (2018) observes, "Gamergate foreshadowed the alt-right's rise—and created an unsettling template for the movement to expand."

The second event which helped propel the alt-right was negative fan-reaction following the release of the 2016 *Ghostbusters* reboot, featuring an all-female cast. The epicenter of this fan-reaction was a review by Milo Yiannopoulos (2016), which argued that the movie pandered to feminism and media diversity, suggesting that the movie advanced an ideology where "the enemy is *all men*, while the government ends up playing dad." The evocation of man-bashing, coupled with the assertion that the

movie was yet another example of creeping political correctness, found rapid acceptance among the fan community. Yiannopoulos then took to Twitter and facilitated
further trolling of Leslie Jones, one of the main cast members. With over 300,000
followers, Yiannopoulos caused a mass brigading of Jones's Twitter account, leading
her to abandon the site. Yiannopoulos was consequently banned from Twitter, amid
accusations that the platform was restricting free speech. The saga established itself
as the next stage of the online culture wars, although this time inflected by racism
and ethnic discrimination (Romano 2016).

The third, and arguably the most prominent, factor was the election of Donald
Trump as the forty-fifth President of the United States, whose campaign built
on "right-wing narratives of anti-immigration, hyper-nationalism and anti-
globalisation" (Williams 2018, 7), alongside a strategy of American exceptionalism
and protectionism. As Williams (2018, 8) goes on to argue, "although independent
of Trump, the alt-right's White nationalist/neo-Nazi agenda is explicitly and implicitly supported by the now president." While Trump publicly disavowed the alt-right
in an effort to distance himself from the movement (Barrow 2016), his presidential
bid is inextricably linked to the emergence of the alt-right, and particularly /r/The_
Donald, the alt-right's most prominent online space. The subreddit ended up playing
a major part in establishing the alt-right as a force in everyday political conversations
in the US, before, during, and after Trump's election success (although see Marwick
and Lewis 2017, 3 for an alternative view on the role of alt-right in Trump's presidential win).

There are a number of other factors which contributed to the growth of the alt-
right, including Breitbart's alignment with alt-right ideology, a move spearheaded by
executive chairman Steven Bannon, Breitbart's support of Trump's presidential bid,
and Bannon's subsequent appointment as Trump's White House Chief Strategist.
The promotion of the alt-right also relied on the media profile of Milo Yiannopoulos,
cultivated on news shows, conferences, and campus tours (from 2015, his public
appearances were marketed as the 'Dangerous Faggot Tour', with all the pomp and
circumstance that celebdom entails). As the charismatic, attractive, well-spoken, confident, and provocative mouth piece of Breitbart and the wider alt-right movement,
Yiannopoulos promoted many of the alt-right's key ideas, including criticisms of
liberalism, cultural Marxism, the 'regressive left', 'snowflake' culture, man-bashing,
offense culture, trigger warnings, safe spaces, political correctness, feminism, identity politics, and multiculturalism, all under the banner of supporting free speech
and provoking the liberal left. Yiannopoulos' position as a gay man in a relationship with a black man also gave some defense to the claim that the alt-right was not
(simply) a White nationalist movement, with Yiannopoulos issuing a statement in
2017 stating, "I disavow white nationalism and I disavow racism and I always have"
(Yiannopoulos, in Bernstein 2017). By mid-2017, Yiannopoulos' stock was flying
high, with a $250,000 book deal, an invitation to speak at the Conservative Political
Action Conference, and widespread public recognition, until his fall from right-
wing grace following the release of past comments where he appeared to condone
hebephilia (see Bernstein 2017 for an in-depth history of Yiannopoulos' relationship
with Breitbart and the alt-right).

While the alt-right may have lost ground in terms of membership and media coverage since 2017 (Bhattarai 2017; Farhi 2019), it maintains some influence in the public sphere among young, heterosexual, predominantly White, Anglo men, particularly for its defense of men and (supposed) masculine and Western values and as a locus for sexism, misogyny, and a call-to-arms for the defense of (White) masculinity. In doing so, it continues a long line of historical paradigms at the intersection of masculinity, White supremacism, and nationalism. For example, Mosse (1996, 7) argues that "modern masculinity from the very first was co-opted by the new nationalist movements of the nineteenth century," while Nagel (1998, 244) notes that "State power, citizenship, nationalism, militarism, revolution, political violence, dictatorship, and democracy . . . are all best understood as masculinist projects, involving masculine institutions, masculine processes and masculine activities." Indeed, the nation state is perhaps best thought of as a masculine institution, a point also made by Enloe (2014, 93), who sees nationalism as "typically sprung from masculinized memory, masculinized humiliation and masculinized hope," or, as Banerjee (2012, 6) puts it, "masculinized imaginations construct the dominant view of nation" (see also Mulholland, Montagna, and Sanders-McDonagh 2018 and Slootmaeckers 2019 for more recent discussions of masculinities and nationalism). Arguably, the alt-right is just another entry in the catalog of male nationalist projects.

In a White nationalist/supremacist context, White masculinity becomes a prerequisite for protecting the 'homeland' from the threats of multiculturalism and diversity, where only 'real men' can defend against the cultural degradation represented by outsiders and immigrants (Williams 2018, 8; see also Fjordman 2006 for an example of antifeminist and antimigration discourse in action). As Wodak (2015, 2) notes, "all right-wing populist parties instrumentalize some kind of ethnic/religious/linguistic political minority as a scapegoat for most if not all current woes and subsequently construe the respective group as dangerous and a threat 'to us', to 'our' nation." Thus, White masculinity becomes operationalized as a moral, national, and civic good, since "patriotism is a siren call that few men can resist, particularly in the midst of a political 'crisis'" (Nagel 1998, 252).

Both the alt-right and the wider White nationalist movement are also predicated on an antifeminist orientation, a belief that the status of men is somehow under threat, and a concern with what they consider to be the ongoing emasculation of men (Burns 2017; Kelly 2017; Mudde 2018; Williams 2018, 9). Again, this is nothing new. Writing nearly 30 years ago, Ferber (1998, 136) cites an excerpt from the White supremacist magazine *Northern Vanguard* about the decline of Western masculinity:

> As Northern males have continued to become more wimpish, the result of the media-created image of the "new male"—more pacifist, less authoritarian, more "sensitive," less competitive, more androgynous, less possessive—the controlled media, the homosexual lobby and the feminist movement have cheered . . . [T]he number of effeminate males has increased greatly . . . legions of sissies and weaklings, of flabby, limp-wristed, non-aggressive, non-physical, indecisive, slack-jawed, fearful

males who, while still heterosexual in theory and practice, have not even a vestige of the old macho spirit, so deprecated today, left in them.

Similarly, in their discussion of *Loaded*, *Nuts*, and *Zoo* (UK men's magazines located at the nexus of heteronormativity, homophobia, and stereotypical 'lads' interests such as drinking, football/soccer, and sex), García-Favaro and Gill (2016) show how men draw on a repertoire to position themselves as a hated, demonized, and attacked social group whose social rights, freedoms, and biological imperatives are being constrained by a self-serving and tyrannical group of feminists. Moreover, men offer a repeated articulation of themselves as "victims of relentless and on-going vilification, attack and bullying by feminists" (García-Favaro and Gill 2016, 389), as part of an ongoing discursive formation they call the "emasculation nation." Of particular interest to García-Favaro and Gill is how heterosexual, White, Anglo men come to view feminism as a conspiracy to strip men of all social power. Such discourses abound in the alt-right, as well as in the general space of the manosphere (see also Marwick 2022).

Ultimately, the attraction of the alt-right (and other extremist movements) comes down to three factors. The first is that these movements offer a space for disaffected young men who feel marginalized by the current trends of contemporary politics, giving them a sense that their actions are, in even a minor way, changing the world.

Second, this positioning is amplified by a sense of victimization, what Kimmel (2018, 15) calls aggrieved entitlement, or "a gendered sense of entitlement thwarted by larger economic and political shifts, their ambitions choked, their masculinity lost . . . Their manhood had been taken away from them by unseen conspiratorial forces, and their recruitment was seen as a way to reclaim their manhood and restore that sense of entitlement." Railing against a shadowy global conspiracy, the alt-right provides an outlet for this discontent and sets up a figure of the 'Other' responsible for the problems, frustrations, and troubles men face. This framing of 'us' versus 'them' can be a powerful in-group motivator (Tajfel et al. 1979; see also Carian 2022).

The explicit articulation of 'us' versus 'them' affords a third attraction, that men who occupy the 'other' are positioned as lacking the essential characteristics of masculinity, as effeminate, amoral, animalistic, or deviant and thus not worthy of being called 'real' men. Reflecting on interviews conducted with former neo-Nazis and White supremacists, Kimmel (2018, 15) notes that these men "developed a worldview that constantly shored up their own sense of masculinity through the emasculation of the 'others' against whom they were fighting: feminist women, immigrants, Jews, gays – all depicted as not 'real men', but unqualified poseurs who've taken over the government and turned it against its authentic native sons." As Mudde (2018) suggests, "many radical right parties espouse a strongly gendered discourse in which they appeal to a frail masculinity, threatened by emasculating feminists, effeminate liberals, and overly virile 'Others'. By defending their nation, and protecting their fragile women and children, men will not only regain their masculinity vis-à-vis 'Other' men (e.g. black men, immigrants, Muslims) but also vis-à-vis their women."

Finally, this all coalesces as a perfect storm of circumstances for recruitment purposes. By convincing young men that their problems are the result of external forces hell-bent on disassembling their current way of life, that these 'others' are the reason behind their woes, and that by reclaiming a sense of primal masculinity is it possible to fight back, you have a potent form of in-group rhetoric which can be difficult to resist (see also Boise 2019, 148). Add in a sense of belonging, purpose, and community (see also O'Malley and Helm 2022), it is easy to see how masculinities can become a rallying point for extremist organizations. But while Kimmel (2018) argues attention to masculinities is missing from contemporary accounts of radicalization, we know surprisingly little about the intersection of linguistic practice and masculinities in extremist spaces (although see Christensen and Jensen 2010; Haider 2016; Burns 2017; Pearson 2019; Roose et al. 2022 for some notable exceptions; Christensen 2010 also provides an interesting discussion of masculinities in far-left and antifascist organization).

REDDIT, THE ALT-RIGHT, AND /R/THE_DONALD

Reddit is one of the world's largest content aggregator sites and social media platforms, with over 330 million monthly active users, 21 billion monthly page views, and 138,000 active communities (Archibald 2019; Stout 2019). Founded in 2005, Reddit is now worth $10 billion and is the third most visited site in America, after Google and YouTube (Isaac 2021). One of the attractive aspects of Reddit is its 'subreddits', user-created communities dedicated to almost every hobby, activity, sport, event, political party, and profession under the sun. Facilitated by a site-wide 'up-vote/down-vote' system used to promote relevant content, subreddits have the advantage of curating content specifically with a community's interests in mind, ensuring a stream of fresh content to attract (and keep) users (see Chandrasekharan et al. 2017 for an overview of the site's mechanics). Users do not have to sign up for an account to read threads, and although an account is needed to submit content, post comments, and to engage with other members, there is no expectation for a user to interact with others on the site. Since user accounts are anonymous, Reddit has a reputation as a haven for trolling, hostility, and harassment, although community and site moderation plays a major role in tackling antisocial behavior (see Kilgo et al. 2018 for a discussion of anonymity on Reddit, and LaViolette 2017; Massanari 2015, 2017; Ging 2017 for discussions of toxic technocultures and technological governance on Reddit, particularly as they relate to networked misogyny).

As previously mentioned, subreddits (identified with an /r/ prefix) are organized around specific interests and can be about almost any topic imaginable. Although there is very much an 'anything goes' philosophy which underpins subreddit creation, there is active policing of content to ensure that only appropriate and legal subreddits are created. Reddit's policies state that content is prohibited if it is "is illegal; is involuntary pornography; is sexual or suggestive content involving minors; encourages or incites violence; threatens, harasses, or bullies or encourages others to do so; is personal and confidential information; impersonates someone in a misleading or deceptive manner; uses Reddit to solicit or facilitate any transaction or gift involving certain goods and services; is spam" (Reddit Inc. 2019; see also Reddit Inc. 2020). Over the years, subreddits promoting hate speech, racism, violent content, illegal pornography, selling drugs, and other 'dark market' activities have all been banned (see Chandrasekharan et al. 2017; Breland 2019; Habib et al. 2019 for discussions of the effect of Reddit's content policy on tackling hate speech and harassment).

It is these more insalubrious parts of Reddit culture which often make their way to media coverage of the site. Over the years, the site has hosted a variety of controversial content, including a thread where innocent people were accused of being the perpetrators of the 2013 Boston Marathon bombing (Shontell 2013); the celebrity photo hacking scandal in 2014 known as 'The Fappening' (Carroll 2014); and the 'pizzagate conspiracy' in 2016 which claimed a human trafficking and child sex ring was operating from a pizza restaurant in Washington, DC (Aisch, Huang, and Kang 2016), among other examples of racism, trolling, misogyny, and harassment (Quinn 2017; Robertson 2019; Schroeder 2020; see also Marantz 2019 for a discussion of mass-media propaganda and online radicalization on Reddit, Twitter, Facebook, and other social media sites).

On the other hand, there are subreddits which are more progressive, promoting inclusivity and positive social action, including /r/random_acts_of_pizza (dedicated to anonymously buying pizza for people facing personal difficulties) and /r/personalfinance (about helping people address their financial problems). Friendships have been forged, help offered, and connections made among people who sometimes live thousands of miles from one another. Consequently, Reddit captures both the best and the worst of human nature, reflecting the reach the site has as the "front page of the Internet."

To examine the intersection of nationalism and masculinities in 'alt-right' spaces, this chapter analyzes data collected from /r/The_Donald, a community originally meant for supporters of Trump's presidential bid in 2015, but quickly co-opted by 'alt-right' posters, becoming the "epicentre of Trump fervor on the internet" (Martin 2017). With nearly 800,000 subscribers at the time of data collection, /r/The_Donald was active during Trump's original election campaign, sharing memes, tweets, and news stories about Trump and his policies, while promoting conspiracy theories, fake news, and disinformation which sought to undermine Hillary Clinton, the Democratic party presidential nominee (Brandom 2018; see also Zimmer et al. 2019 for a discussion of how different subreddits engage with fake news).

Combining 'shitposting' (that is, deliberately provocative or offensive content), 'edgy' humor, memes, ironic racism, and a general attitude of 'fuck your feelings', the subreddit also became a site for criticizing feminism, liberalism, identity politics, multiculturalism, mainstream media, political correctness, diversity, globalism, social justice warriors, safe spaces, and trigger warnings, while simultaneously advocating and promoting racist, sexist, misogynistic, antisemitic, and Islamophobic content (see Martin 2017). As Cole (2018, 71) argues, "The_Donald epitomizes *par excellence* an established and growing public pedagogy of hate," acting as a locus of symbolic (and sometimes physical) violence against others.

Of course, many members of /r/The_Donald did not agree with the characterization of themselves as sexist, racist, or promoters of hate speech, with one poster claiming that members of /r/The_Donald "love Hispanics, we love Middle Easterners, we love women and gays and religious freedom. This fight is not, and never has been, about hating people from other countries. Our only problem is with behavior and ideology that threatens the safety and prosperity of the American people."

A number of analyses have, however, challenged this. For example, Squirrell (2017) found that while the language of White supremacism was relatively uncommon in /r/The_Donald, this was because explicit racism was banned, while implicit or coded racism was common, including "displaying Islamophobic sentiment and passing it off as criticizing Islamism or claiming that 'Islam is not compatible with Western culture'" (Squirrel 2017; see also Sonnad and Squirrell 2017). Similarly, Martin (2017) analyzes over 50,000 active subreddits and 1.4 billion comments to quantify how similar one subreddit is to another. His findings showed that /r/The_Donald was more similar to /r/kiketown, /r/fatpeoplehate, r/TheRedPill, and /r/coontown, all controversial subreddits which promoted misogyny, racism, and hate speech (and all of which, bar /r/TheRedPill, have since been banned,).

In June 2019, /r/The_Donald was quarantined, effectively placing it in a state of "digital detention" (Stewart 2019). This meant that subreddit content could no longer be promoted to Reddit's front page, limiting the community's potential reach. New users to the site also had to choose to enter the subreddit and were faced with a 'Are you certain you want to continue?' warning before being granted access. In late February 2020, Reddit updated their conduct code to state that the site does "not tolerate the harassment, threatening, or bullying of people on our site; nor do we tolerate communities dedicated to this behavior." At the same time, Reddit administration removed several /r/The_Donald moderators, claiming that they were approving content which contravened Reddit's content policy. New moderators were then appointed by Reddit's admin team and the subreddit was placed in 'restricted mode', at which point, no new threads were approved and community members moved all activity to a site outside Reddit's control. All of these decisions were viewed by members of /r/The_Donald as attempts to stifle open discussion, with accusations of censorship leveled at Reddit and CEO Steve Huffman (Vigdor and Chokshi 2019), alongside claims of hypocrisy and double-standards. The subreddit was formally banned in June 2020 for violating Reddit's rules against harassment and the promotion of hate speech (Allyn 2020).

/r/The_Donald, along with other alt-right spaces, has also been accused as being a site for the radicalization and indoctrination of young, predominately White, men (Holmes 2016; Cornelisse 2018; Grover and Mark 2019). As Squirrell (2017) argues, "we're witnessing the radicalization of young white men through the medium of frog memes." Tracing the radicalization journey, Evans (2018) shows how a self-confessed 'red-piller' moves from "arguments in comment sections to far-right YouTube personalities to 'the_donald' subreddit to 4chan's /pol/ board and eventually to fascist Discord servers" (see also Ribeiro et al's. 2019 discussion of YouTube algorithms in driving a "radicalization pipeline"). In a comprehensive discussion, Munn (2019) argues that radicalization follows a progression from normalization to acclimation to dehumanization through hundreds of different nudges, pushes, and prods (see also Marwick 2022). At this end point, the "dehumanizing rhetoric transforms rights-bearing subjects into apolitical objects. It clears the way for its targets to be mistreated, as in rape threats, or managed by others, as in the deportation schemes of racial utopias. Through this cognitive shift, alt-right individuals can support such activities while retaining their moral superiority" (Munn 2019). Thus, these media outlets not only shape an individual's views, perspectives, and opinions, they also recalibrate an individual's belief system and moral compass.

MEN AND MASCULINITIES IN /r/The_Donald

While one of the most common characterizations of /r/The_Donald is that it is a meeting place for "disaffected white men from all walks of life to share a communal hatred" (Squirrell 2017), what also emerges as a recurrent trend is how specific configurations of masculinity become a community rallying point. Trump's politics of domination, competition, and hierarchy, coupled with his articulation of misogyny, populism, and American exceptionalism (Mendoza-Denton 2017), clearly resonate with his supporters, even as he implicitly sanctions hate crimes and other morally questionable activity (Edwards and Rushin 2018). As Wade (2018) points out, Trump "threw emasculating barbs at supposedly lesser men, spewed sexist insults at uppity women, sexually objectified underage girls, and coveted the totalitarian power of dictators. He bragged about pussies and penis size and how he'd never rape an ugly woman. Instead of cratering, his campaign soared" (see also Prasad 2019 for a discussion of Trump and gendered insults and Banet-Weiser 2018, 111 about how Trump's misogyny bolstered his campaign). Trump embodies an authoritarian, conservative, and patriarchal form of masculinity celebrated by his supporters. The fact that his nicknames among /r/The_Donald members include *daddy* and *god-emperor* points to the elevated status he enjoys.

Charting the link between Trumpian masculinity and radicalization, Mohutsiwa observes that "college educated young men were then ripe enough to be sold [the] idea that Trump represented a return to Men Being Real Men" (in Holmes 2016). The evocation of 'Men Being Real Men' is an important one, since it relies on the notion that Trump represents a form of 'ideal' masculinity based on power and marginalization of the 'other', where only men like him can defend America from the threat of immigration, globalization, and liberal propaganda in order to "Make America Great Again" (what McMillen 2018 calls "MAGA masculinity").

Some of these ideas have been previously explored. For example, in his investigation of different user groups on /r/The_Donald, Squirrell (2017) develops a "taxonomy of trolls," including 4chan shitposters (an online forum infamous for posting racist, sexist, and antisemitic content), antiprogressive gamers, men's rights activists, antiglobalists, and White supremacists (see also Cole 2018, 68–69). While these groups have slightly different linguistic patterns, Squirrell argues that /r/The_Donald is a space where men coalesce around a common hatred of liberalism and a love of Donald Trump, while developing a shared vocabulary which is simultaneously jocular and subversive.

Discussing Trump's argumentative strategies, Lakoff (2016) examines morality, power, and the ideal hierarchical social structure championed by Trump and his supporters, with specific reference to Trump's characterization as a dominant and authoritarian 'father figure'. The naturalization of dominance is based on the strong male trope, one who leverages his physical and societal power to enforce his worldview. As such, Trump and his supporters tap into a long-standing ideology of male superiority. It is joined, however, with an explicit comparison with other groups which are taken to be emblematic of moral degradation, even if this means essentializing the entire group (see the collected chapters in McIntosh and Mendoza-Denton 2020 for more work on the language of Donald Trump).

While this body of research has contributed to our understandings of the patterns of usage which characterize particular subcommunities on /r/The_Donald, we know very little about how specific substantiations of masculinity are deployed on the subreddit. How are 'White men' discursively positioned in relation to other substantiations of ethnic masculinities? What are the circulating discourses related to 'black men', especially given their historically subordinated position in American society? And what are the dominant associations of 'Muslim men' in an era of sustained Islamophobia and anti-Muslim sentiment?

DATA AND CORPUS CONSTRUCTION

The data for this chapter are taken from the /r/The_Donald subreddit, collected in November 2019 using the Python Reddit API Wrapper (PRAW, Boe 2019). PRAW is a Python package which allows a user to access Reddit's API (Application Programming Interface) to carry out a variety of operations, including upvoting/downvoting content and comments, responding to comments, subscribing to subreddits, and more. PRAW was used to search for particular words and phrases, download the top results of this search, and output them to a .csv file. For the purposes of the analysis, the following search terms were selected—*men, black men, muslim men,* and *white men*[4]—reflecting some of the broader sociopolitical concerns which dominate discussion on the subreddit. One point worth making is that Reddit's search system returns different results for multi-word phrases depending on whether the phrase is placed in quote marks or not. Thus, *"white men"* matches thread titles and comments which contain both *white* **and** *man* together, while *white men* matches thread titles and comments which contain *white* **or** *men*, although not necessarily together. For the corpus construction, quote searches were utilized, although some overlap across the search terms occurred. Finally, the search parameters were set to return the top-voted thread of all time.

While PRAW is a useful tool for downloading threads, a number of steps are required in order to prepare and clean the data, including removing all links (e.g. Imgur, YouTube, Wikipedia), bot comments,[5] usernames, ASCII art, comments consisting

4. Lowercase search terms were used but the results returned both uppercase and lowercase tokens.

5. Bots are automated programs triggered by specific user requests and/or commands. For example, /u/RemindMeBot lets users set reminders, while /u/stabbot stabilizes gifs, html5 videos, and other video formats. Bots are usually identified through self-post

Table 5.1. BREAKDOWN OF /R/THE_DONALD CORPUS (RANKED BY TOTAL
NUMBER OF WORDS)

	Number of threads	Number of comments	Number of words
men	74	22,122	439,698
White men	92	16,071	377,450
Black men	99	5,544	146,874
Muslim men	102	4,350	108,690
Totals	**367**	**48,087**	**1,072,712**

of only emoji, and quotes taken verbatim from other sources (e.g. one thread had excerpts from the Declaration of Independence, while others contained quotes from news reports). Since the data collection process retrieves everything included in a thread, it was also necessary to manually remove comments which had been flagged as deleted or removed. Consequently, the number of comments in Table 5.1 does not necessarily reflect the number of comments on a particular thread, since the online comment count is the sum of actual, removed, and deleted comments. Only minimal meta-data was collected, including thread title, thread ID, thread URL, date of thread creation, and number of reply comments. Since this chapter does not focus on interactional aspects, usernames were not collected. After preparation, the data were exported using a script to separate each thread into the original thread and replies into individual.txt files. The final corpus comprises 1.13 million words and over 50,000 replies across 467 threads (Table 5.1).

ANALYSIS

In the following analysis, I manually review the topic focus of the top threads in each subcorpus (covering thread titles and thread replies), along with the main collocates, n-grams,[6] and concordance lines relating to each of the search categories, starting from the general category of *men* and working through each **men* phrase individually (all examples are unedited and retain the original spelling and punctuation). The collocation analysis was conducted in #LancsBox, using the same parameters as Chapter 5. Because the initial results for modified *men* variants were inconclusive and/or low in number, the collocate analysis instead searched for collocates of

comments like 'This bot was created by /username' or 'I am a bot, and this action was performed automatically'.

6. N-grams are "combination[s] of words that appears with regularity in a corpus" (Collins 2019, 180), where *n* refers to the number of words in the phrase. In this chapter, 3-grams are examined in each subcorpus.

men within each of the subcorpora. High frequency function words were also deleted after review.

MEN

For the *men* subcorpus, thread titles included variant phrases of *men* which were not part of the overall search parameters (e.g. *dutch men, hispanic men, swedish men,* and *syrian men*).

(1) "Non-Western migrants" (i.e. Muslims) make up MORE THAN 50% of the people receiving government benefits in the Netherlands. DUTCH MEN AND WOMEN, UNCUCK YOUR COUNTRY! VOTE GEERS WILDER!
(2) Germany has flooded their country with unskilled, violent young men raised to hate Western culture. Who'd have guessed THAT wouldn't work?
(3) ***CALLING ALL 'PEDES*** Two Hispanic Men Video Themselves Violently Beating White Woman On Her Front Yard, Protecting Trump Sign. SPREAD LIKE FIRE

In these examples, national identities are typically deployed to highlight the (apparent) growing threat of multi-culturalism, both in Europe and America (although the juxtaposition of *violent men* and *Western culture* makes this implicit rather than explicit). Nationality becomes a rallying point for demarcating the lines of 'us' versus 'them', where 'they' become simultaneously associated with violent, criminal, and immoral acts (see also Bernard 2021, 78–94 for a thematic analysis of 'us' versus 'them' posts in /r/The_Donald). The threads also highlight anti-Muslim sentiment and Islamophobia, usually centering around sexual assault, rape, and abuse (examples 4 and 5).

(4) Syrian men, posing as "teenagers," enrolled in a Canadian High School and sexually assaulted a 14-year-old girl.
(5) Pakistan: Girl kidnapped when 12 and sold into sex slavery finally found and returned to her family . . . only to be honor killed by her brother because she had been with men. This is Islam!

On the other hand, a thread concerning the murder of Indian man Srinivas Kuchibhotla[7] appears to highlight a surprising antiracist sentiment:

(6) PIECE OF SHIT SHOOTS 3 INDIAN MEN, KILLING 1. as he yells "GET THE FUCK OUT OF MY COUNTRY" redacted pushing narratives already.

---

7. Kuchibhotla was murdered by Adam Purinton in a bar in Kansas in 2017. Two other men, Alok Madasani and Ian Grillot, were also wounded in the attack. Purinton pleaded guilty to federal hate-crime charges and received three consecutive life sentences.

The evaluative phrase *piece of shit* continues through the thread, with the top-voted replies also describing the shooter as a *racist deadbeat drunk*, alongside other negative evaluations such as *asshole*, *bastard*, *crazy*, *fucking idiot*, *loser*, and *scum*. The negative reaction to this shooting is predicated on the fact that Kuchibhotla and Madasani represented the 'right' kind of immigrant (examples 7–9):

(7) Indian guys are usually great guys. They absorb American culture instantly. They promote our values. They don't push their religion

(8) I love Indian Americans. Good people; intelligent, entrepreneurial, family oriented. You know, the type of people you WANT in your country.

(9) Indian immigration are some of the best type Western countries can get. They cause no harm, assimilate wonderfully, most intelligent people out there, also the most richest ethnic group in the US per capita.

These examples present a positive evaluation of Indian men, primarily because they are considered to assimilate, adopt American culture, and have characteristics which make them desirable migrants (e.g. work ethic, intelligence, entrepreneurial spirit). Other groups, on the other hand, do not and are thus presumed to be unfit candidates for migration. This point is also echoed by Baker and Levon (2015, 123), who note that "implicit in [these newspaper articles] is the notion that Asian men who abandon their 'foreign' values and norms can achieve gendered normativity."

Beyond the racialized dimension of the threads, a number of other topics emerge as important. The top-voted thread, for example, concerns Piers Morgan and his calls to establish a "Men's March" as a counter-protest to feminism.

(10) Piers Morgan: "I'm planning a "Men's March" to protest at the creeping global emasculation of my gender by rabid feminists. Who's with me?"

Here, we see some of the issues mentioned previously, including the view of men as emasculated and feminism as a social ill (the use of *rabid* denotes an uncontrollable, virulent, and fanatical belief in something). Morgan taps into the general victimization discourses, mobilized within a sympathetic audience.

The concept of a "men's march" is also co-opted as shorthand for the Allies' fight against Germany, drawing on a (since deleted) Twitter post by tech entrepreneur and businessman Andy Swan, which included a picture of the Allied beach landings in Normandy (Figure 5.1). Three other top-voted threads in this subcorpus are copies of the same Twitter post which, collectively, have over 900 comments and nearly 40,000 upvotes, suggesting a high level of community engagement (the same tweet was published on January 24, 2018 by Ryan Fournier, cofounder and chairman of the American youth group *Students for Trump*).

As Williams (2018, 50) notes, paramilitary discourses are often deployed in nationalist rhetoric because "paramilitaries [represent] masculinity, power and discipline, all features that young men [are] looking to attain and display." Drawing on imagery of conflict, patriotism, and heroism, some of the replies in these threads explicitly criticize feminism, with parallels being drawn between feminism and

Andy Swan @
@AndySwan

The Men's March Against Fascism didn't have
nearly as many signs.

RETWEETS 9,458   LIKES 14,378

7:03 AM - 23 Jan 2017

461   9.5K   14K

Figure 5.1. Andy Swan's tweet, posted January 23, 2017

Nazism, most explicitly through the portmanteau *feminazi*. While this framing allows men in /r/The_Donald to buy into a narrative where they are the noble heroes defending Western culture from the claimed horrors of feminism, it also has the effect of trivializing feminism—'real' men go to war against 'real' enemies and feminism is not worth their attention, as examples 11–13 suggest.

(11) Men's March usually is a march toward the battlefield and death.
(12) The real march against fascism was a hard fought, bloody victory by good men who had no other choice but to prevail. If they did not, evil would have. If they did not win, there would be no entitled flabby feminist. If they did not, there would be no bleeding heart, Kraut loving liberals. If they did not, there would be no Xir sipping its chai. If they did not, there would be no entitled little shits screeching for their own segregation
(13) I would say we shouldn't compare the two, one was a march against fascism and the other was ladies making shit up to be upset about.

Other thread topics include supportive commentary about law enforcement and critical discussions about celebrities, usually framed in terms of their supposed hypocrisy or because of their view on Trump and/or his supporters. As might also be

Table 5.2. TOP 20 COLLOCATES FOR "MEN" IN THE *MEN* SUBCORPUS
(RANKED BY FREQUENCY)

Subcorpus	Frequency	Collocates
men	203	times (43), create (26), trans (23), weak (19), oppressive (8), 70% (8), beta (6), capable (6), disproportionately (6), 30% (6), 50% (6), international (6), assaulted (5), breed (5), forgotten (5), raises (5), sacrifices (5), sacrificed (5), secretary (5), worthless (5)

expected, a number of threads relate to politicians and politics (e.g. Donald Trump, Melania Trump, Eric Trump, Elizabeth Warren), as well journalists and political commentators (e.g. Tomi Lahren, Milo Yiannopoulos, Bill Maher, Kurt Schlichter).

For the top collocates in the *men* subcorpus, some relate to current affairs, including International Men's Day, the gender pay gap (*raises, 30%,* and *70%* are all used to talk about salary rates), and debates about transgender men and women in professional sports (Table 5.2). Others are more obscure. For example, the collocate of *secretary* is in reference to comments made by DC Public Schools Spokesperson Hillary Tone in 2016, who posted on her Facebook page that "if wanting to get rid of something qualifies you to run it, I want to be Secretary of White Men" (see Chasmar 2016). Similarly, *create, time,* and *weak* are all returned as collocates because of a quote by G. Michael Hopf[8] from his novel *Those Who Remain* (2016, 20): "Hard times create strong men, strong men create good times, good times create weak men, and weak men create hard times" (*breed* is sometimes used in place of *create*).

Beyond these examples, we can tease out other prevalent discourses related to men. These include disagreement that men are *oppressive* and *worthless*, that men are *capable* individuals who *sacrifice* themselves for the greater good, and that more men are sexually assaulted than women in America, while undesirable men are characterized as *beta* and *weak*.

For the concordance analysis (Table 5.3), the phrase "men are" was selected in order to examine how men were generally positioned in the subcorpus, with three main discourses emerging. The first is about broader social treatments of men, usually as a pastiche or caricature where men are described in negative categorical terms—*evil, scum, sexist, bad guys, incompetent.* This typically appears as a 'tongue-in-cheek' commentary and a critique of how /r/The_Donald believes men are viewed in wider society and how men are represented in media outputs. Second, men are positioned as victims—*emasculated, disposable, disrespected, discarded, totally forgotten, worth much less.*

The third theme relates to *liberal men,* who come in for particular criticism, being described as *pigs, cucks, false,* and at an *evolutionary dead-end.* Liberal men are

---

8. Hopf notes (2016, 330), however, that "even though I get attributed to it, I did not originate this quote."

Table 5.3. SELECTED CONCORDANCE LINES FOR "MEN ARE" IN THE *MEN* SUBCORPUS (VARIABLE L/R SPAN)

1	feminists insisting that all	men are	evil oppressive rapists
2	in a room with her, therefore all	men are	evil
3	because your group believes all	men are	scum. THATS SEXISM YOU IDIOT
4	All	men are	sexist, all whites are racist
5	Yeah like I said,	men are	always the bad guys and women are
6	all goes back to single mothers.	Men are	being emasculated by the
7	looking at the warmongering,	men are	disposable
8	That's really true, and actually sad.	Men are	so disrespected and I worry that it's
9	are strong and courageous and the	men are	either evil or incompetent
10	equality on both sides and RN,	Men are	just being fucked over and turned into
11	they'll be protesting how Western	men are	misogynistic for having a penis
12	even human to begin with? Because	men are	to be discarded like a piece of
13	Boys and	men are	totally forgotten in American society
14	In general	men are	worth much less to society and are

Table 5.4. SELECTED CONCORDANCE LINES FOR "LIBERAL MEN ARE" IN THE *MEN* SUBCORPUS (VARIABLE L/R SPAN)

1	portion of this current crop of	liberal men are	at an evolutionary/biological dead-end
2	have saved a few letters	"Liberal men are	Cucks"
3	Likewise,	liberal men are	just a false image of what a man
4	If	liberal men are	pigs, how can they ever hope to
5		Liberal men are	pigs who masquerade as feminists
6		Liberal men are	so unattractive to me it's crazy

those men who fail to meet community standards of masculinity (this stance is also encapsulated in the word *cuck*, discussed in more detail in Chapter 6).

Closer attention to specific threads about liberal men also highlight the range of negative evaluations directed toward them (examples 17 and 18):[9]

(14) Liberal men are so unattractive to me it's crazy. They don't even look like men to me, they don't act it to say the least. It's not even because I am self-loathing like the REEEEdacted[10] crew thinks, I just like men.

9. As far as it is possible to be confident about online gender identities, these two comments appear to be posted by female members of /r/The_Donald.
10. The use of 'REEEEdacted' here is a play on 'REEEEE', which has since come to be both a meme and an onomatopoeic expression of rage or frustration. It is also potentially a statement about left-wing liberal outrage for communities like /r/The_Donald.

Table 5.5. TOP 15 3-GRAMS IN THE *MEN*
SUBCORPUS (RANKED BY FREQUENCY)

Rank	Frequency	3-gram
1	365	i do n't
2	205	a lot of
3	159	i 'm not
4	152	it 's a
5	147	they do n't
6	141	it 's not
7	139	one of the
8	126	to be a
9	120	you do n't
10	102	do n't know
11	101	this is the
12	101	i ca n't
13	92	i did n't
14	91	i 'm a
15	85	a bunch of

(15) Liberal men I've met have come off as phoney, non-committal, people pleasing,
self-serving pariahs with zero self-respect. I live in California and a lot of the
men here are riddled with these huge character flaws, no one taught them to
respect themselves or women. I used to accept this until I met my SO which
made me respect more conservative values.

Thus, liberal men are considered to be sexually and physically unattractive,
amoral, phoney, self-serving and flawed, and to lack self-respect. Liberalism ultimately comes to be bound up with negative traits from which 'real men' should distance themselves.

Finally, the most common 3-grams[11] (that is, three-word lexical bundles) are
presented in Table 5.5. The top 15 3-grams tend to have negative valence (*I don't,
I'm not, they don't, it's not, you don't, I can't* and so on), suggesting that comparative
discourses are common (e.g. *x* group does or does not do *y*).

Reviewing collocates of the top 3-gram *I don't*, this phrase typically co-occurs
with mental processes such as *agree, believe, care, know, see, think,* and *understand*, a
finding which makes sense in light of the fact that /r/The_Donald markets itself as a
space for discussion and debate (Table 5.6).

11. In the case of n-grams, particles like -*'ve*, -*n't*, -*'m*, -*'ll*, and -*'re* are counted separate
from the stem to which they are attached. For example, *don't* is counted as two words
do + *n't*.

Table 5.6. SELECTED CONCORDANCE LINES FOR "I DON'T" IN THE *MEN* SUBCORPUS (VARIABLE L/R SPAN)

1	Piers, while	I don't	agree with you on lots of things
2	Yes	I don't	agree with her saying women are the
3	And just because	I don't	believe homosexuality is moral
4	In any case though,	I don't	believe tougher law enforcement and
5	the total because	I don't	care, to me it's not MINE
6	This is easily defined as sexist but	I don't	care
7	Well	I don't	know about you
8	To be fair	I don't	know for sure
9	men should keep theirs as well.	I don't	see any reason to concede that
11	Fair enough, but	I don't	see harm in trying to reduce the
12	Well,	I don't	think I've ever heard Alabama called
13	and you know what,	I don't	think I would either
14	That is also weird and	I don't	understand it
15		I don't	understand your point, care to expand

Two 3-grams stand out as somewhat different to the others—"a lot of" and "a bunch of." In terms of co-occurrence, *a lot of* appears with *people* 15% of the time[12] and tended to be somewhat neutral in valence (e.g. *a lot of people here in Canada*, *a lot of people in this country*, *a lot of people upset*). On the other hand, the phrase "a bunch of" is most often used to refer to the 'opposition', typically in a negative or derogative sense (Table 5.7).

Again, one of the effects here is to contrast these groups (*angry lesbians*, *cucked Germans*, *delusional retards*, *fat feminists*, *fucking traitors*, *spoiled children*, *Islamist savages*, *male feminists*, *roided up women*, and so on) against the calm, rational, and 'non-cucked' community membership of men on /r/The_Donald. By positioning these groups as different, deviant, and 'other', /r/The_Donald can construct an identity as standing up for masculine moral values.

WHITE MEN

In terms of size, the *White men* subcorpus is the second largest by number of thread replies and number of words, reflecting, in some respects, the overall demographics of /r/The_Donald. This contrasts with Baker and Levon (2015, 118), who found that black men were most frequently referenced in British newspaper articles, suggesting that "this identity is the marked 'other' (the prototypical man is not black in other words)." This difference is potentially because /r/The_Donald serves a dialogic

---

12. There were 205 occurrences of *a lot of* and 30 of these co-occur with *people*.

Table 5.7. CONCORDANCE LINES FOR "A BUNCH OF" IN THE *MEN* SUBCORPUS (VARIABLE L/R SPAN)

1	a woman, could care less about	a bunch of	angry lesbians and feminist
2	French are just	a bunch of	baguetty kebab munching surrender
3	Right and now we're left with	a bunch of	cucked Germans, and Jews using
4	What	a bunch of	delusional retards
5	taught that the founders were just	a bunch of	dirty racists
6	that want guns in the hands of	a bunch of	drunkasses, most pro gun people
7	Riff Raff is just a goofster all	a bunch of	fat feminist tanks and no one that
8	Time magazine is run by	a bunch of	fools
9	I'm supposed to be sad that	a bunch of	freakazoids and third world savages
10	country are being thrown away by	a bunch of	fucking traitors
11	a trip to a local store. Then	a bunch of	Islamist savages jumped on him and
12	can someone link me some shit with	a bunch of	male feminists vindicating this
13	in at 19, the people are	a bunch of	pussies not all, but close to ZERO
14	on 'birth sex'. So now you have	a bunch of	roided up 'women' who are now
15	had abandoned Christianity as	a bunch of	sanctimonious moralizing for old
16	Just	a bunch of	skull fucked Nazis Like Hillary said
17	It's all	a bunch of	socialist Skittles
18	and certainly not at the hands of	a bunch of	soft pussies like you
19	the ones that pass won't be	a bunch of	soft-headed, weak-willed, entitled
20	want rid of them because they are	a bunch of	soy pussies that are scared of
21	in the name of Islam. They are	a bunch of	spoiled children who virtue sign just
22	My grandfather didn't kill	a bunch of	tojos in the pacific for the children
23	Fuck the media. They're	a bunch of	traitorous pigs
24	That "woman's march" is really just	a bunch of	triggered tumblr twats on parade
25	revolution we cant take/don't need	a bunch of	uneducated Somali workers
26	and convey an image. Now we have	a bunch of	washed up musicians trying to
27	to be one. Or something. They're	a bunch of	whack-jobs

function, rather than the reporting function which characterizes newspapers, where user discussion coalesces around specific topics related to the predominant user group.

By examining the thread titles, we can see the main preoccupations within the subcorpus, such as the social status and position of White men, both in America and further afield (examples 16–24).

(16) The last acceptable form of racism & sexism is the hatred of white men - legitimized by the culture and the media.

(17) "Treating straight white men like the scum of the Earth doesn't make you 'woke'. It makes you racist, sorry."

(18) Gillette put out a new far-left ad attacking White men & 'Toxic Masculinity' but the people are waking up and rejecting this leftist propaganda, just look at those down votes.

(19) Our 'tolerant liberal' Lauren Duca proclaims on Twitter that "straight, white men are generally trash" - Even sadder, she has totally cucked white male followers kissing her ass in reply

(20) It's considered a good thing to openly discriminate against White men. Imagine the outrage if this was said about any other group. Wake up.

(21) [DAILY REMINDER: CIS WHITE MALES ARE DEMONS!] University equality lectures bans straight, white men

(22) /pol/: White Men are increasingly being written out of classic roles in entertainment franchises. It seems minor, but it's actually very telling.

(23) White men being harassed for walking down the street by liberals.

(24) White men would literally get booed for showing up to meetings at Google. Can't make this shit up.

The primary discourses in these examples relate to White men as victims of hate speech, discrimination, and racism. This is part of a process of making space for "overt celebrations of white pride in mainstream public discourse by disarticulating whiteness from its position of domination to reimagine white U.S. Americans as disadvantaged and disenfranchised" (Hartzell 2018, 11; see also Bucholtz 2019). This is not unexpected given a similar finding in the *men* subcorpus. In this subcorpus, however, the threads develop a more explicit racial character, where whiteness is mobilized as a precarious identity. This covers a variety of ground, from the idea that there is a leftist agenda of emasculation facilitated by complicit media companies (examples 16, 18, 22), to the claim that there is regular and open discrimination against White men (examples 20, 21, 23, 24).

For the top collocates (Table 5.8), we see a similar picture of victim positioning (*attacking, rid, banning, ban*), although other aspects are also worth discussing. For example, *white men* are described in terms of their sexuality (*straight*), their age (*young, old*), and their social status (*rich*), although there are also debates around their intelligence (*uneducated*), their contribution to society (*built*), how they are presented in the media (*portrayed*), and limited discussion about *radicalization, profiling* and

Table 5.8. TOP 20 COLLOCATES FOR "MEN" IN THE *WHITE MEN* SUBCORPUS (RANKED BY FREQUENCY)

Subcorpus	Frequency	Collocates
White men	972	white (685), women (83), straight (33), old (32), young (18), rich (17), built (14), uneducated (12), paying (9), threat (9), radicalization (6), rid (8), ban (7), banning (6), claiming (6), complain (6), fought (6), attacking (5), profiling (5), portrayed (5)

the *threat* of White men (these latter three are usually in the context of discounting these issues).

By examining concordance lines, we can develop a better picture of exactly how these discourses are realized. To that end, two general trends are discussed: conceptualizations of victimhood; and cultural superiority and contributions to the world.

As previously discussed, a common discourse in the *White men* subcorpus is that of victimhood. More specifically, a concordance analysis of the phrase "White men are" highlights how members of /r/The_Donald believe White men are evaluated in almost exclusively in negative terms.

> White men are . . . *bad, criminals, demons, racist, uneducated, the devil, the problem, the villain, the worst, literally Hitler, the most dangerous, the new juden, the cause of evil, oppressing everyone else, prohibited from organizing, ruining the world, preventing women to reach the top, the biggest threat to this country, the cause of all the world's problems, the only people who do bad things*

Again, it is important to note that these are the broader evaluations /r/The_Donald members believe circulate in mass media and social commentary more generally, rather than a statement of opinion about their own group. As such, most of the discussion about the negative positioning of White men tends to be critical and disbelieving. We see a similar deployment of victimhood in Table 5.9, which presents the results of the concordance lines for "hate white men."

The groups most strongly associated with negative sentiment toward White men are women, the 'left', 'liberals', and representatives of these group (e.g. comedian Lena Dunham and American Democratic party politician Alexandria Ocasio-Cortez), although there is also a sense of incredulity that people would ever have a negative view of White men (e.g. line 5). Some of these concordance lines also raise the issue

---

Table 5.9. CONCORDANCE LINES FOR "HATE WHITE MEN" IN THE *WHITE MEN* SUBCORPUS (VARIABLE L/R SPAN)

1	Seriously, if "the lefties"	hate white men	so much why don't they go
2	People really	hate white men	for no reason other than Twitter
3	by a group of people that ,	hate white men	it will continue to turn our
4	These people claim to	hate white men	but they use things the white
5	Why do all these white women	hate white men	so much? Lena Dunham is
6	The real reason you	hate white men	is because they out achieve you
7	worried she only	hated white *men*	It's interesting to see people fight
8	AOC hates	hates white men	so much she only wants them
9	This man obviously hates	hates white men	what a racist and sexist bigot
10	She hates	hates white men	Can we please let this dumbshit
11	neoliberal White Culture that	hates white men	so much. Neoliberals are eaten

---

Table 5.10. CONCORDANCE LINES FOR "WHITE MEN" IN THE *WHITE MEN* SUBCORPUS (VARIABLE L/R SPAN)

1	go live in a country built by	white men	then complains about White men?
2	working in a company created by	white men	who owes her freedom to white men
3	in a language created by	white men	Talk about cultural appropriation
4	on social media invented by	white men	and her profile picture is her in
5	uphold a constitution made by	white men	then why don't they push their
6	you're living in a country run by	white men	Notice how it's a superpower?
7	white men to continue to do what	white men	have always done, work hard and pay
9	because	white men	have created the most prosperous and
8	Dependent on the wealth	white men	have created
10	she understand white men are	white men	are responsible for the modern world?
12		white men	are by and large responsible for much today's society
14		white men	are the reason why slavery has come to an end
15		white men	are the reason why you enjoy most of your electronic gadgets and science
16		white men	are the reason why there is a democracy

of cultural contributions. For example, line 4 states that while people *claim to hate white men*, they are happy to use things this group invented.

This touches on the second discourse prevalent in the subcorpus, that of the cultural contributions made by White men and consequent claims of cultural superiority. One of the surprising findings was how often extensive lists of inventions and technological developments were posted by community members, often as a way of foregrounding White men's contributions to the world. This explication draws on lexis associated with creativity and invention, including *built*, *create*, *invented*, and *constructed* (Table 5.10).

A closer look at 'invented' offers further support regarding the cultural contributions of White men promoted in /r/The_Donald (Table 5.11). Here, discourses of cultural superiority are more implicit, usually through a conflation of identities where "white people" is equivalent to "white men," or where "we" acts as a stand-in for White men more generally. Nevertheless, such discussions elide the contributions of other groups, while simultaneously holding up White masculinity as the pinnacle of cultural advancement (see also Ferber 2007, 17). In some cases, such White male exceptionalism is also bound up with antiwomen positions (example 25).

(25) Oh yeah. White men are the reason why there are so many problems in the world. I guess you'd prefer to live in Zimbabwe or Congo or China or Venezuela. Fucking bitch.

Table 5.11. CONCORDANCE LINES FOR "INVENTED" IN THE *WHITE MEN* SUBCORPUS (VARIABLE L/R SPAN)

1	good things they have were also	invented	in mostly white nations
2	We basically	invented	everything except paper
3	how much stuff would still not be	invented	if white people were deleted
4	white men . . .	invented	all the greatest things
5	take back everything we've ever	invented	. . . see how these hate-filled bitches
6	the computer mouse. This guy	invented	all kinds of stuff including steroids
7	not being the inventor. And he	invented	the computer mouse
9	Donald Knuth	invented	LaTeX, the industry computer
8	she's posting on social media	invented	by white men and her profile picture
10	You know, white men	invented	computers and the internet so maybe
11	white men who pretty much	invented	everything we use today
12	to find a basic technology not	invented	by a white guy
13	Actually white people	invented	peanut butter
14	White people	invented	everything except peanut butter
15	white people	invented	the vote
16	Stuff white people	invented	aerosol can, air conditioning
17	and concepts that white people	invented	like voting, democracy or the Rights
19	Yea, fuck all those white guys that	invented	the printing press, lightbulb, airplane
20	This is why they	invented	70+ of them
21	She should try boycotting things	invented	constructed and maintained by white
22	proud of my people because we	invented	peanut butter or the traffic light
23	Not only did we end slavery, we	invented	every single liberal ideal that led to
24	white people? on a computer? that	invented	with electricity? that we invented?
25	but the vast majority were	invented	by whites
26	Those guys who	invented	the modern world and run it for
27	was going to be US men who	invented	transistors, swivel chairs, light bulbs

Taking all of this together, there are a number of things to emerge from reviewing the *White men* subcorpus. The first is that there is deep-seated rejection of the idea that White men are responsible for the existence of inequalities and structural hierarchies, regardless of whether these are tied to race, ethnicity, or gender. On the contrary, members of /r/The_Donald advocate a position of victimhood based on an assumed attack on White men from a number of quarters. Not only does this position ignore the relative degree of sociocultural privilege which most men have enjoyed over the course of history (and continue to enjoy), this sense of aggrieved entitlement is also a continuation of established narratives of supposed male persecution. Second, there is an implicit argument that *because* White men have contributed so much to society, this excuses them from criticism or denunciation, particularly as it relates to sexism, racism, or misogyny. The insidious nature of this argument is concerning because it essentially reframes negative behavior as the social 'cost' of cultural and scientific progress. Third, the comments can be seen as a way of reframing White male contributions where potential associations with White supremacism are erased or minimized. As Hartzell (2018, 24) points out, "these formations of pro-white rhetoric attempt to reason that open affirmations of white pride and pro-white political positions are not necessarily white supremacist but, rather, are justifiable expressions of white racial consciousness."

MUSLIM MEN

The *Muslim men* subcorpus presents a rather different conceptualization of men and masculinity which concentrates on three discursive areas—moral deviancy, rape, and child sexual abuse (what is surprising is the relatively paucity of threads about terrorism). A review of the thread titles provides a stark illustration of this discursive positioning. For instance, examples 26–31 highlight issues of moral deviancy, violence, and lack of assimilation into American culture. In doing so, the intent is to show how Muslim men are incompatible with White Western values and how their morals are diametrically opposed to American morals. Furthermore, many of these threads are charged with an emotional intensity and a call-to-arms stance (see Papacharissi's 2015 discussion about the role of anger in digital publics), particularly through the use of all caps (26, 28, 31) and the evocation of a complicit media (26). Finally, the events discussed in the threads are seen as part of an Islamic threat to American cultural identity. There is a clear policing of borders, nation, and behavior, brought together under the umbrella of moral outrage and religious criticism, which sets out who belongs and who does not, who meets the standards of masculinity and who does not, and who the 'good' men and the 'bad' men are.

(26) Woman forced to change her airline seat because two muslim men seated next to her "have cultural beliefs that prevent them for sitting next to, or talking to or communicating with females." Feminists, Mainstream Media, and Liberals are SILENT!

(27) India: 4 Muslim men hack atheist man to death because he posted "anti-Muslim" messages on Facebook. #ReligionOfPeace!

(28) IMPORTANT AND NEEDS ATTENTION: In Dearborn Michigan Muslim Men are practicing polygamy illegally and use their wives to each claim separate welfare from the state as 'fatherless' moms!

(29) Two Muslim men with a bag of knives run down pedestrians in Melbourne. Nope. It was drugs. Not the Religion of Peace™.

(30) Death due to dancing. Hindu Youth Stabbed to Death by Six Muslims in Delhi Mall. Singh accidentally brushed his elbow against one of the six Muslim men who then stabbed him.

(31) Swedish TV Chef Violently Assaulted By 'Muslim Men' Because He 'LOOKS LIKE TRUMP' . . . NOTE TO EUROPE – BETTER SEND THEM BACK BEFORE IT'S TOO LATE!

In the second subset of threads, we see a focus on illegal and violent social practices, including rape and sexual assault. Here, White women are most often identified as the target of aggression by Muslim men. As Keskinen (2011, 109) argues, "rape of an individual woman turns into a symbol of an attack on the whole ethnic group or nation and becomes interpreted as a violation of the honour of its men" (see also Nagel 1998, 252–253). Thus, rape becomes a symbol of a broader cultural invasion led by Muslim men, a problem to be solved though force or exclusion (Gill and Harrison 2015, 37). Moreover, Muslim men are typically viewed as a homogenous and essentialized group, while women are characterized as a resource to be exploited, arguably by both White men and Muslim men, albeit for different reasons.

(32) 2 American Women Assaulted by Muslim Men in Paris for Refusing to Sleep With Them. SPREAD THIS LIKE WILDFIRE AND USE IT AS AMMO FOR LE PEN. #NotMyParis

(33) Recently, 90 Muslim men attacked a Christian church in Uganda. These savages murdered the pastor, beat the Christian men, and raped the Christian women. Such atrocities happen every single day in Muslim counties. Fake News will never report the truth.

(34) (Disturbing video 0:21) Muslim men are enforcing Sharia Law which says non-Muslim women can be raped, stolen from, beaten, etc. But we get called islamophobe for stating the facts?

(35) PROSECUTORS: MIGRANT SEX ATTACK MEANS 'JUST INTERESTED IN YOU' – 2 German women repeatedly assaulted by Muslim men (Cucks are just as dangerous as Islamic Jihadists)

The positioning of Muslim men as criminal, morally deviant, and sexually violent becomes even more pronounced in the final subset of threads, which focus on child sexual abuse by British Muslim men (example 37 is one of the few exceptions to this pattern in discussing America). These threads are the result of a number of cases where Muslim men were found to be operating grooming gangs in different cities across the UK, including Bradford, Rotherham, and Rochdale (see Tufail 2015). As such, many of the threads discuss media coverage of the cases, the police response, and criminal sentencing, while foregrounding the Muslim aspect of the perpetrators' identities.

(36) WAKE UP: 27 Muslim men 2 Muslim women charge with child sex trafficking – leave U.K. court shouting "Allah Akbar"

(37) MUSLIM RAPE GANG IN LOS ANGELES – 15-year-old girl was brutally and viciously raped by five Muslim men while walking home from school

(38) Muslim Men Yell 'Allahu Akbar' In Court As They Are Sentenced For Raping 11 Year Old Girl – NEVER ISLAM!

(39) Muslim men are statistically 200 times more likely to be child rapists than non-muslims.

(40) Rotherham child abuse trial hears how girl was passed around and raped by 100 (Muslim) men

Table 5.12. TOP COLLOCATES OF "MUSLIM" IN THE *MUSLIM MEN*
SUBCORPUS (RANKED BY FREQUENCY)

Subcorpus	Frequency	Collocates
Muslim men	248	muslim (51), women (44), two (16), rape (15), know (12), charge (10), koran (10), white (10), keep (9), making (8), slave (8), dress (7), slaves (7), asian (6), 4:34 (5), buy (5), decide (5), markets (5), real (5), uk (5), Western (5)

(41) London police chief Cressida Dick says grooming gangs "have been part of our society for centuries and centuries and centuries" and declines to accept that mostly white girls are being targeted by mostly Muslim men of South Asian origin. Proves authorities are still in denial.

(42) 12 Muslim men arrested in the wake of the Rotherham scandal face 45 sex offence charges against underage girls between 1998 and 2003

(43) Sexual exploitation of British Sikh girls by Muslim men has been 'ignored' by police due to 'political correctness'

Collectively, the characterization of Muslim men is wholly negative, where "The Arab (and now Muslim) Other is portrayed as animal, barbaric, uncivilized, inhuman and the 'essence of evil'" (Noble 2012, 218), a perspective advanced in how Muslim men are named (e.g. *koranimals*, *mooslims*, and *muslimes*).

These discourses are also expressed in the collocates of "Muslim" (Table 5.12).[13] More specifically, a variety of negative valence collocates are returned, including *rape* and *slave(s)*, while religious collocates also emerge, including *koran* and *4:34* (the latter referring to a passage in the Qur'an about traditional gender roles, particularly in the context of marriage).

Concordance lines for the phrase "muslims are" (Table 5.13) also reveals a general picture of negative evaluation, with Muslims framed as *terrorists*, *extremists*, *utter psychopaths*, and *pedophiles*, while even superficially positive descriptions (e.g. *peaceful*, line 13) are actually sarcastic.

It is notable in the *Muslim men* subcorpus the extent to which the /r/The_Donald community is content with essentializing an external group while being critical of attempts to do the same to White men. Essentializing the 'other' appears to be an acceptable tactic, but it becomes unfair, divisive, and unrepresentative when applied to White men, suggesting again a sense of White male exceptionalism which

13. Although the initial plan was to examine collocates of *men* in the sub-corpus, in line with the previous analyses, only one collocate was returned. Consequently, collocates of *muslim* were searched for instead, since the majority of the threads tended to use *muslim* as a stand-in for 'muslim men'.

Table 5.13. SELECTED CONCORDANCE LINES "MUSLIMS ARE" IN THE *MUSLIM MEN* SUBCORPUS (VARIABLE L/R SPAN)

1		Muslims are	all potential terrorists and should be
2	hundreds of millions of	Muslims are	extremist. thats a fact
3	The only thing	Muslims are	good for is enriching the grounds with their dead bodies
4	The lesson is that	Muslims are	incompatible with any other society
5	Fucking hell,	muslims are	literally going to take over the fucking
6	But . . .	muslims are	literally the most inbred people on the
7	Which means	Muslims are	n't peaceful whatsoever
8	safety just because a minority of	Muslims are	n't utter psychopaths
9	All	Muslims are	pedophiles
10	who still believes that not all	Muslims are	terrorists needs to wake the fuck up
11	b-but huffington post told me	Muslims are	the "true feminists"!
12	But	Muslims are	the [true feminists] so it's cool
13	Don't you love how peaceful	Muslims are.	They just focus on themselves and
14	was talking about how violent	Muslims are	

underpins the discursive positioning of self and other on the subreddit. This is also part of a strategy of dehumanization, which serves as a key element in extremist radicalization.

Second, the prevalence of Islamophobic sentiment aligns with the discursive representations of Muslim men in other media contexts (see Gill and Harrison 2015; Tufail 2015, 2018; Baker and Levon 2016; Morgan 2016; Ahmed and Matthes 2017), forming what Goldberg (2009, 165) calls "the *idea* of the Muslim," or "a singularity which manages to represent the 'threat of death', fanaticism, female oppression, [and] irrationality" (Noble 2012, 218). This moral panic is well-established in the armory of public opinion, where an external group is positioned as a 'folk devil' organized along moral contours and boundaries (Cohen 1972). For members of this subreddit, only do Muslim men fail to observe a number of legal and moral parameters, but this failure is subsequently extended to an entire religion. The comments of Noble (2012, 225) here are instructive, where he highlights how the strategic deployment of the 'other' serves to relocate the 'face of evil' as external to White Western contexts:

The 'face of evil' works in several, contradictory, ways. It allows us to identify evil, to recognize it as a material entity. It provides us with a physiognomy of evil where a face is a reflection of the character of evil, personified in particular humans but representative of a certain moral universality, much like phrenology. This allows us to recognize types as evil—uncaring, sadistic, animalistic, violent, unemotional. Yet this type is grounded in the abhorrent behavior attributed to particular groups—Middle Eastern, Lebanese or Muslim. The face becomes the metonym for the cultural pathology of evil, while evil becomes the pathology of a 'culture'. This allows us to fix in our sights a sense of evil as both present and removed—it is near, but it is someone else.

Third, these threads highlight a lack of criticality that what might be driving the prevalence of sexual criminality is not so much religion as it is gender, riven through with misogyny, hostile sexism, male exceptionalism, status, and power. Since a perspective which problematizes gender, and more specifically masculinity, is undesirable in terms of the positive presentation of men, the alternative strategy is to shift to other aspects of identity which can be more conveniently politicized within an antiimmigration stance. While these threads are part of broader discourses of 'cultural incompatibility', they overlook the commonalities which underpin sexual abuse and assault, namely that most instances of rape, sexual abuse, and sexual assault are carried out by men, regardless of their ethnicity, social class, or religious background (Wells 2003, 8). As Ging (2017, 10) points out, "This perversion of intersectionality not only appeals to the Islamophobic sensibilities underpinning both atheist and Christian elements of the manosphere but it is also routinely used as a strategy to deny the existence of rape culture in the west and thus to recuperate the virtue of white Western masculinity."

Finally, the focus on Muslim men in relation to rape, sexual violence, and child exploitation ignores the intersection of other forms of inequality among other groups. As Gill and Harrison (2015, 45) argue, "Over-reporting cases of South Asian men as perpetrators of grooming and sexual exploitation of white girls overlooks broader statistics and socioeconomic factors such as poverty and neglect, which often lie at the root of sexual exploitation." To that end, it could be argued that the principal intent in /r/The_Donald is not to highlight cases of sexual abuse and to advocate for improved police response, social care, and institutional interventions, but rather to position Muslim men as an external 'evil' against which White masculinity can be valorized and celebrated as the 'best' form of masculinity.

BLACK MEN

The final subcorpus concerns Black men, which presents yet another conceptualization of masculinity in /r/The_Donald. Reviewing the thread titles, we can see a number of themes emerge, particularly around violence, the Black Lives Matter campaign and the intersection of race and politics.

Similar to Muslim men, Black men are framed in terms of violent and criminal practices, although the threads tend to be about assault and battery rather than rape (that said, the latter is an element in examples 45 and 52). Overall, examples 47–55 are emblematic of an association of Black men with violence and criminality, building on a common stereotype of Black men as hyper-physical, hyper-aggressive, and criminal sexual predators (Welch 2007; Baker and Levon 2015).

Threads about Black violence are also inflected with political commentary, usually highlighting anti-Trump sentiment and attacks against Trump supporters (examples 44, 46, and 48). This is taken as evidence of discrimination against pro-Trump members and a way to mobilize sympathy within the community that they are on the right moral side. Finally, these threads reveal again a belief in a media conspiracy against covering attacks on Trump supporters and revealing the truth of violence perpetrated against White people (examples 44, 48, 49, and 51). This further solidifies the community position as one under siege from an external 'other', reinforcing the us vs. them divide.

(44) White special needs man, gagged and tortured by several black men, black thugs force him to say, "f**k Donald Trump" and "f**k white people"

(45) Two black men 'rape a white women while yelling racial slurs' outside of a Colorado mall

(46) Trump supporter beaten and carjacked by 4 black men accusing him of voting for Trump. MEDIA SILENCE.

(47) Trans Black Women Killed By Other Black Men. Where's the Media Outrage? Black Lives Matter? LGBT?

(48) This is not the first attack where black men kidnap and torture a white man because he was a Trump supported. The same thing happened four months ago but MSM covered it up. It is up to us to expose the truth!

(49) Media silent after fake 'hate crime' involving the murder of a little girl, exposed. The murder of Jazmine Barnes, supposedly done by a 'white terrorist', was committed by two black men.

(50) Hate Crime: Four black men who violently assaulted a white teen, leaving him in the ICU in critical condition, because he posted 'I back the blue' on a BLM social media post have been indicted.

(51) Four black men assault a lone white man on a train for the crime of being white – media? SILENT!

(52) BLM caused these: White woman raped as revenge for 400 Years Of Slavery. Blacks Burn White Woman Alive. Black men brutally murder 2 white teenagers. Black man enters home of white family, tortures 10-year-old to death in front of his parents, then kills the whole family

Threads about violence among Black men also relate to threads concerning the Black Lives Matter campaign. In the examples below, the BLM campaign is evaluated almost exclusively negative terms, including claims that the campaign has no basis in reality (examples 55, 57, 58), that it is part of a leftist political agenda (example 56), or that reports of police brutality against Black men are exaggerated (example 58).

(53) The 131 Black Men Murdered by Black Lives Matter

(54) Someone call Black Lives Matter! Nine black men have been murdered in Baltimore in the last week! Systematic oppression detected!

(55) New study of racial bias in police shootings finds trained police officers have no racial bias but unarmed black men are more likely to be shot by . . . college students!

(56) MAJOR RED PILL "AHA" MOMENT! In 2016 MSM pushed 'white cops shooting unarmed black men' stories. BLM vanished after Nov. 8. BLM was created as nothing more than a 'get out the vote' campaign because they new Hillary would lose without the black votes that Obama got.

(57) In a year with 200-plus slayings, most St. Louis victims are black men in unsolved cases (BLM doesn't give a fuck)

(58) 21,500,000 black men live in the USA. In 2015 104 black men were killed by police. That makes up .00047% of the population. Call me crazy, but that doesn't warrant riots, citing: "HERP DERP POLICE BRUTALITY OPPRESSION." This is cultural Marxism. Trump is the only one that can stop it.

Concerns among the Black community in relation to police brutality, misconduct, and discrimination are minimized, rejected, or dismissed (see also Carney 2016; Rickford 2016), even when existing research has shown otherwise (see, for example, Voigt et al. 2017 for a discussion of police respect toward White and Black community members, and Chaney and Robertson 2013 for an overview of racialized police violence). Instead, violence *among* Black men is framed as the more pressing problem (examples 57, 58), one which reduces violence to an interpersonal problem rather than a structural one.

The BLM coverage contrasts with threads about Ed Buck, a Democratic party donor who was arrested after two Black men were found dead in his apartment following an overdose of methamphetamine (see John et al. 2019 for an overview of the case).

(59) This is Democrat Donor Ed Buck. He has killed more black men than any single cop in America. #BLM

(60) The family of the 1st man killed by Ed Buck filed a wrongful death suit against him because the Los Angeles District Attorney's office declined to file criminal charges. Ed Buck has killed 2 black men. Where is Al Sharpton? Black Lives Matter? Where are the riots?? Where is the 24hr media coverage??

(61) Just some pictures of Adam Schiff, Ted Lieu, and Hillary Clinton with major Democratic donor Ed Buck who enjoyed getting black men hooked on meth. 2 of them died in his West Hollywood apt.

(62) Just a picture of Side o Beef with Ed Buck . . . "He has been soliciting young, gay black men . . . He has them wear these long white under-johns. He takes pictures of them. He hits them up with meth. The more meth that they smoke and inject, the more money that he gives them . . . ." WILL SHE DISAVOW?!?!

(63) Just a picture of California Democrat Congressman Ted Lieu and a Serial Killer of Black Men

(64) Ed Buck, Mega Donor to Hillary Clinton and Gavin Newsom, arrested for drugging Gay Black men, 2 have died

What is salient in these threads is not necessarily sympathy toward the Black men who died, but rather how the event encapsulates a claimed hypocrisy among Democratic party politicians and voters regarding their support for minority communities. Thus, the focus on Black men in these threads becomes a locus for undermining claims of racial tolerance and equality in the Democratic party, further weakening any assertion of moral authority. Black men become reframed as a weapon with which to attack politicians like Adam Schiff, Ted Lieu, and Hillary Clinton, where their association with Buck is taken as evidence of their moral improbity.

This sense of hypocrisy is also picked up in threads about a 2018 incident in Philadelphia, where a Starbucks' manager refused two Black men (Donte Robinson and Rashon Nelson) access to the bathroom because they had not purchased anything (see Gayle 2018 for further background on the story). Citing a lack of cooperation by the two men, the manager called the police to escort them off the premises. Public opinion quickly went against Starbucks and their disproportionate response, leading to a formal apology from CEO Kevin Johnson and the arrest being expunged from Robinson and Nelson's records.

In many ways, the case becomes operationalized as a way of highlighting inconsistency among left-wing voters regarding discrimination, as well as critiquing how identity politics has somehow infected common-sense discourse (examples 66, 67). Furthermore, the lack of media balance and their failure to cover anti-Trump sentiment is also evoked (examples 65, 71).

(65) Two black men loitered in a starbucks and demanded to use bathrooms without being customers. Management called police. Left lost its shit calling starbucks racist. Black man went to cheesecake factory and was physically threatened by employees and called a stupid n*****. Left is silent. Difference?

(66) Two black men arrested for no reason at all at a Starbucks in a hick Republican town--oh wait, it was in LEFTIST PHILLY!

(67) The LEFT eating their own: Calls grow to boycott STARBUCKS after arrest of black men.

(68) Starbucks manager who called police on two black men has left the company

(69) Starbucks CEO Blames White People For Black Men Being Arrested At Philadelphia Starbucks

(70) SJW Starbucks has two black men arrested for trespassing since they wanted to use the bathroom, during a business meeting, without buying anything.

(71) How many people heard about two black men being removed from a Starbucks? How many people heard about 2 police officers being assassinated? WHY!?!?!

The collocates for this subcorpus (Table 5.14) are not especially numerous, but they do converge on discourses of criminality and violence, through collocates such as *police*, *killed*, and *rape*, alongside verbs like *asked, leave, call*, and *refused*, all typical terms in crime reporting. Identifiers such as *two*, *three*, and *young* are also returned (the use of numbers in relation to groups of Black men also accords with Baker and Levon 2015).

In summary, the range of discourses for Black men are wider than those related to Muslim men, but they similarly tend to coalesce around negative prosodies. There are some exceptions in cases where Black men announced support for Trump, or

Table 5.14. TOP COLLOCATES OF "BLACK" IN THE *BLACK MEN* SUBCORPUS (RANKED BY FREQUENCY)

Subcorpus	Frequency	Collocates
black men	321	black (129), white (31), two (31), men (22), police (10), women (10), killed (9), gay (8), man (8), unarmed (8), asked (7), leave (7), bernie (6), rape (5), refused (5), call (5), called (5), interested (5), three (5), young (5),

where Black men are seen to 'break free' from the control of the liberal, left-wing media, while several threads argued that Democratic policy decisions under Clinton and Obama were responsible for the criminalization and mass incarceration of Black men, the break-up of Black families, and the number of gun-related deaths in cities like Chicago. Generally speaking, however, these threads were in the minority and had an ulterior motive of characterizing Black men as victims of Democratic policy failures (see Yglesias 2019 for a discussion of this point in relation to the 2020 presidential election).

CONCLUSIONS

This chapter has provided a comprehensive analysis of discourses of masculinities in /r/The_Donald. Through the analysis of thread titles, collocates, and concordance lines, I have shown how these discourses are bound up with White nationalist stances, uncovering how constellations of the 'other' are constructed and how particular masculine identities are evaluated as undesirable, deviant, or morally unacceptable.

The analysis revealed that White men in /r/The_Donald are generally conceived as victims of oppression and marginalization, advancing an agenda of aggrieved entitlement where the position of White men is viewed as under threat, that their contributions and social value to the world are not recognized, and that they are unfairly discriminated against. At the same time, however, a number of threads lay claim to White men as exemplars of cultural superiority and intellectual rationality, usually with reference to technological innovation. Taking these two discourses together, a narrative which positions White men simultaneously as cultural victims *and* cultural saviors is advanced.

White men are also contrasted with other groups of men, most particularly Muslim men and Black men. The overarching narrative is that these groups are violent, sexually abusive, and criminal, with an implicit framing of them failing to uphold morally and legally normative standards of masculinity. That said, these failings are generally subsumed under racial or religious explanations, with limited criticality about masculinity as a locus of violent or criminal social action. The consequent hierarchy of masculinity, then, places White men at the top and Muslim men at the bottom, with Black men being afforded an ambivalent position depending on the strategic and political aims of the thread and the commentators.

By providing a clearly defined 'other' against which community members' conceptualization of masculinity can be compared, establishing a sympathetic and supportive community which valorizes and celebrates aligned contributions and calls out common 'enemies', and framing this as a defense of American identity and cultural purity, it is easy to see how the promotion of White masculinity in /r/The_Donald becomes a seductive part of the alt-right armory. Couple this with the mobilization of antifeminist, antiliberal, and antidiversity viewpoints, and the subreddit represents a perfect storm of circumstances for the engagement and recruitment of men who feel as though they have been consigned to the margins of society and left behind by the current trends of contemporary politics.

But /r/The_Donald does not exist in isolation to other online communities with a predominantly male membership. Instead, it exists as part of a broader system of male-centric and male-authored websites, blogs, and social media spaces known as the 'manosphere'. Indeed, the manosphere has been catapulted into the public consciousness in recent years for its promotion of sexist, racist, and misogynistic discourses and the advocacy of traditional heteronormative masculinity as the gold standard of male behavior. While /r/The_Donald has important commonalities with other manosphere outlets, it is also marked out by a number of significant differences. Thus, Chapter 6 examines the kinds of masculine identities which exist outside the political sphere of /r/The_Donald.

CHAPTER 6

"Alphas Get Treated Like Bygone Emperors and Betas Live Lives of Quiet Desperation"

Toxic Masculinity and Discourses of Gender in the Manosphere

INTRODUCTION

The previous chapter examined the intersection of language and masculinities, with reference to /r/The_Donald and the alt-right movement. As I noted in the conclusion, the alt-right also overlaps with the 'manosphere', a male-centric collection of male-authored websites, blogs and social media spaces (see also Southern Poverty Law Center 2012; Marwick and Caplan 2018, 12). These manosphere outlets ostensibly promote topics related to men's concerns, from men's rights (particularly in the context of marriage, divorce, and child custody) to self-improvement, relationships, dating, fitness, physical health, and more. In some ways, these sites act as a digital equivalent of the established men's movement 'retreats', where men would engage in discussion with one another about their lives, their worries, and their concerns, learning from one another through mentoring and reflection (see Bliss 1987, 57).

That said, the manosphere has been routinely criticized for promoting sexist, racist, and misogynistic content and advocating for traditional heteronormative masculinity as the gold standard of male behavior (Ging 2017). Moreover, there are calls within the manosphere to end feminism and to reestablish traditional gender roles, with many blaming feminism for rises in immigration, declining birth rates in the West, the increasing number of divorces, dating and relationship problems, and the destructive effects of capitalism and consumerism.

A number of scholars have consequently examined how the manosphere can act as a site for the radicalization of men who feel disenfranchised by contemporary

Language and Mediated Masculinities. Robert Lawson, Oxford University Press. © Oxford University Press 2023.
DOI: 10.1093/oso/9780190081041.003.0006

social politics (see Bratich and Banet-Weiser 2019). Writing about the intersection between the alt-right and the manosphere, Futrelle (2017) observes that,

> There are good reasons why men's rights activism has served for so many as a gateway drug to the alt-right: Both movements appeal to men with fantasies of violent, sometimes apocalyptic redemption . . . And both movements are based on a bizarro-world ideology in which those with the most power in contemporary society are the true victims of oppression.

Futrelle's comments highlight the pipeline between the manosphere and the alt-right, where members who might join for the purposes of self-improvement become radicalized into the more extreme elements of manosphere philosophy, adopting a variety of misogynistic and sexist viewpoints (Beekmans et al. 2018; see also Chapter 5).

Thus, the manosphere operates as a complex assemblage of advocating for male improvement and betterment, while promoting antifeminist and sexist positions and a heteronormative masculinity bound up with traditional notions of manhood, including compulsory heterosexuality, claimed rationality and intelligence, psychological strength, and a 'no-nonsense' mindset. To that end, the manosphere has been cited as a key locus for expressions of 'toxic masculinity',[1] a phrase which has dominated discussions about men in recent years, particularly in relation to masculinities in the public sphere.

Drawing on data collected from four manosphere communities on Reddit, this chapter sets out a comprehensive treatment of the 'manosphere' and 'toxic masculinity', two concepts which have been relatively underexamined in the context of language and masculinities studies. The chapter then analyzes how gender is represented in these communities, focusing on noun referents related to gender (e.g. *man*, *woman*). In doing so, the chapter unpacks the discursive frames surrounding men and women in manosphere spaces, providing an insight into the nature of gender politics in the manosphere and how sexist and misogynistic discourses are maintained and promoted by community members.

WHAT IS 'TOXIC MASCULINITY'?

One of the ideas tackled in this chapter is 'toxic masculinity', a thorny concept which has dominated headlines in recent years. Commentators, journalists, and academics have raised concerns about toxic masculinity as a public health concern (Solnit 2017; Warraich and Califf 2017), while others have cited it as a contributory factor in men's depression, poor mental health, and negative self-image (Kupers 2005; Parent, Gobble, and Rochlen 2019). Even established bastions of men's consumer goods

---

1. Although quote marks used here, for general ease of reading, most instances of the term 'toxic masculinity' are not placed in quote marks.

have weighed in on the debate. For example, shaving company Gillette released a short film in 2019 titled 'Believe' which tackled a range of issues commonly associated with expressions of toxic masculinity, including bullying, sexual harassment, and male aggression. The video was meant to encourage men to intervene when they encountered other men engaging in 'toxic' social practices, recasting its well-known slogan of "The Best a Man Can Get" to "is this the best a man can get?" While the film may have been well meaning, its reception was far from positive. For example, on Gillette's official YouTube page, the film has almost 1.6 million downvotes, compared with only 840,000 upvotes, while the comments section is replete with negative views about the company, its advertising strategy, supposed censorship, and claims about its 'man bashing' stance (see Trott 2020 and Formato and Iveson 2022 for analyses of YouTube comments about the advert).

Despite media attention on 'toxic masculinities', however, there exists very little academic research on the concept, from a linguistic perspective or otherwise, partly because the term has only recently come into wider public consciousness and partly because it remains a contentious term with no clear definitional boundary. Before going any further, it is worthwhile discussing what is meant by the term and how it has been operationalized in academic and lay accounts.

Although 'toxic masculinity' appears to be a relatively new addition to the masculinities vocabulary, it has a long history which can be traced back to the work of Shepherd Bliss and the mythopoetic men's movement in the 1980s (Snyder 2017; Sculos 2019, p.c.). As noted in Chapter 1, one of the main aims of the men's movement was to promote a 'primal' or 'deep' masculinity rooted in nature, connection, and community. To that end, toxic masculinity was viewed as a character type which should be rejected by men, in favor of "a return to some a priori 'eternal masculine', founded on care and compassion, as well as 'strength'" (Boise 2019, 147, although as he goes on to note, this framing was very much based on traditional gender roles and the idea of the benevolent patriarchal defender).

The term stayed more or less under the radar in the 1990s and the early 2000s, but it came to social prominence from around 2010 onward, partly in lock step with the growing profile of the manosphere and partly due to increasing media coverage about men and masculinities more generally. But what does 'toxic masculinity' actually mean? To what extent is it a useful way of thinking about men and the kinds of practices in which some men engage? And how has the term become a site of contestation among different communities?

Exploring the militarization of men, the 'warrior' code, and the shift in traditional masculinity among Vietnam war veterans, Karner (1996, 77) offers one of the first academic treatments of toxic masculinity, characterizing it as "excessive drinking, almost compulsive fighting and violent competition with other men or male authority figures, dangerous thrill seeking, and reliving or reenacting combat behavior in their stateside environments." She goes on to argue that the adoption of toxic masculinity by Vietnam war veterans was partly influenced by their inability to align themselves with culturally dominant modes of masculinity available in America at the time, noting that "traditional patterns of achieving manhood created emasculating situations, replicating and reifying the disappointment of Vietnam. This left only the more destructive, less socially acceptable, toxic behaviors for seeking the status of male adulthood" (Karner 1996, 90).

Later work further explored the nexus of masculinity and extreme or destructive social practice. For example, Kupers (2005, 714) defines toxic masculinity as "the constellation of socially regressive male traits that serve to foster domination, the devaluation of women, homophobia, and wanton violence." In a similar vein, Barr (2019) defines it as the "harmful behavior and attitudes commonly associated with some men, such as the need to repress emotions during stressful situations, and to act in an aggressively dominant way." While these are useful starting points, they overlook how such domination might be fostered or how women might be devalued. In a more wide-ranging definition, Sculos (2017b, 3) suggests that toxic masculinity is,

> hyper-competitiveness, individualistic self-sufficiency (often to the point of isola-
> tion nowadays, but still, and more commonly in the pre-Internet days, in a paro-
> chial patriarchal sense of the male role as breadwinner and autocrat of the family),
> tendency towards or glorification of violence (real or digital, directed at people or
> any living or non-living things), chauvinism (paternalism towards women), sexism
> (male superiority), misogyny (hatred of women), rigid conceptions of sexual/
> gender identity and roles, heteronormativity (belief in the naturalness and supe-
> riority of heterosexuality and cis-genderness), entitlement to (sexual) attention
> from women, (sexual) objectification of women, and the infantilization of women
> (treating women as immature and lacking awareness or agency and desiring meek-
> ness and "youthful" appearance).

In all of these definitions, toxic masculinity involves the promotion of male dominance, the devaluation and sexual objectification of women, suppression and denial of emotions (especially those which portray weakness), the celebration of sexual
promiscuity, the rejection of long-term relationships, alongside advocating violence,
misogyny, and masculine supremacy. In this way, toxic masculinity can be seen as an
extreme manifestation of practices associated with traditional or hegemonic masculinity, to the point where these practices cause harm to oneself or to others. For
example, competitiveness is not necessarily toxic, in and of itself, but adopting a
'win at all costs' mentality which ignores the potential cost of success arguably is.
Similarly, heteronormativity is not 'bad', but positioning heteronormativity as the
best or most 'natural' expression of sexual identity devalues and marginalizes other
sexual identities (see also Englar-Carlson and Kiselica 2013, 402 for a discussion of
(mal)adaptive traits).

For some men, the pursuit of normative ideas about masculinity leads to overcompensation amid fears that they are not living up to abstract or idealized standards of
what it is to be a man (Vinopal 2018). Thus, engagement in violent, extreme, or
abusive practices is driven by a desire to be read as prototypically 'manly'. It is here
we see the effects of toxic masculinity on men's self-image, where harmful social
practices are adopted in an attempt to shore up a sense of masculinity, what Vandello
and Bosson (2013) term 'precarious manhood'. In this framework, masculinity is

conceptualized as something which has to constantly fought for and protected, a position which draws on Gilmore's (1990) treatment of masculinity as an earned social status. And this pursuit of social status vis-à-vis toxic masculinity not only affects men, but also women, children, and others who might be caught in the crossfire of men actively pursuing toxic masculine practices, whether that be through domestic violence, physical assault, or sexual abuse (Snyder 2017; Elliott 2018; Wright 2018).

As might be expected, questions have been raised concerning the utility of 'toxic masculinity' as a concept (see Flood 2019 and the associated comments on the article contents for some sense of this debate). Before examining these questions, it is worthwhile asking why some people challenge the claim that toxic masculinity even exists and why men become defensive about certain practices being labeled as toxic. As O'Malley (2017) argues, one reason is that challenges to our own self-image of 'goodness' are face-threatening (see also Bola 2019, 7):

One of the issues with being a 'good' man is that it's definitional. Because we see ourselves *as* good, we assume that, by default, what we *do* is good . . . Once you've defined yourself as being 'one of the good ones', it's *very* hard to want to look around and admit that maybe you *aren't* as good as you could be. Very, very few people like to believe that they might *not* be the good guy, and so they're invested in not asking too many questions. This is why so many men get their backs up when someone points out that they could be doing better. Criticism, even *mild* criticism, gets taken as a deeply personal attack because hey: you're one of the *good* ones.

Self-reflection and self-critique are difficult since they force us to confront the less savory aspects of our personhood. When recounting narratives, for example, we typically foreground the best version of ourselves, what Ochs, Smith, and Taylor (1989) term the 'looking good' constraint. While the recent evocation of toxic masculinity has encouraged men to think about the kinds of practices in which they engage and how these practices might negatively affect themselves or others, it is perhaps understandable that doing so can be a challenge to men's self-conceptualization as one of the 'good guys'.

One of the most common critiques against 'toxic masculinity' as a definitional or descriptive label is the term becomes conflated with masculinity more generally (see also Banet-Weiser and Miltner 2016; Marcotte 2016; O'Malley 2016; Boise 2019). For example, Russell (2017) argues that "the term implies there's a problem with masculinity, and teaching our boys and men that their innate wiring is wrong, stupid, and even toxic creates far worse problems." We also see this stance in much of the negative reaction toward the Gillette advert, where toxic masculinity is taken as an identity which covers all men. Critics of the term usually reframe it as 'toxic behavior' unconnected to specific expressions of gendered identity, or suggest that if 'toxic masculinity' exists, then we have to talk about 'toxic femininity' (see Veissière 2018 for one interesting discussion of toxic femininity).

A related claim is that the critique of toxic masculinity is part of a liberal/leftist agenda to disempower men, where the perceived emasculation of men is interpreted as a broader strategy of 'man-shaming'. In an editorial published in the *National*

Review, for example, Ben Shapiro (2017) makes the following point about what he terms the "toxic masculinity smear":

> It's indicative of a general belief among members of the Left that masculinity itself is toxic and must be quashed. Hillary Clinton spoke last month at a Planned Parenthood gala where drinks called "toxic masculinity" were served; she explained that men are "doing everything they can to roll back the rights and progress we've fought so hard for over the last century." Men, you see, are the problem. Men make war; men commit crimes; men rape; men infuse their aggression into everything.

Shapiro goes on to make a series of claims about the 'essence' of men, including their 'innate drive for aggression' and their need to build, create, and defend, contending that the rally against toxic masculinity is a rally against masculinity itself. As he puts it, "the Left's dichotomous choice between emasculation and toxic masculinity leaves men out in the cold – and leaves them searching for meaning." For Shapiro, this sense of masculine purpose is intimately bound up with family, fatherhood, and a role as a provider. Strip these away and men's lives have no meaning—they become, in Shapiro's words, "nonentities" or even "societal tumors."

Shapiro's forced choice between 'emasculation' and 'toxic masculinity' misses the point, though, that toxic masculinity is not something men *are*, but rather, it is one particular performance of masculinity, where extreme social practices become normalized as a desirable aspect of masculine identity, either through the enforcement of norms from other people or as a form of self-inflicted pressure (Hess and Flores 2016, 1088). It is entirely possible, however, for men to refute destructive behaviors and to embrace socially harmonious practices without compromising who they are as men (I explore some of these discourses in Chapter 7; see also Pinkett and Roberts 2019, 4 for their alternative term of 'non-tender masculinity').

In response, several high-profile scholars have attempted to frame toxic masculinity as something positive. For example, evolutionary psychologist Gad Saad (2018) argues that:

> In no culture ever studied have women repeatedly preferred to mate with pear-shaped, low-status, tepid men possessing high-pitched, nasal voices. In no documented culture do women's sexual fantasies revolve around granting sexual access to unemployed, unambitious men who occupy the lowest stratum of the social hierarchy. Instead, women are attracted to "toxic masculine" male phenotypes that correlate with testosterone, and they are desirous of men who are socially dominant, who are strategically risk-taking in their behaviors, and who exhibit patterns of behaviors that will allow them to ascend the social hierarchy and defend their positions from encroachers.

Overlooking the problems of evolutionary biology as an explanation for human behavior (as discussed in Chapter 2), Saad forwards an essentialized view of 'ideal' masculinity, one rooted in sexual domination, aggression, and risk-taking. As such, it is easy to see how men who feel they do not measure up to these standards might view themselves as failed men, or that even men who reject "toxic masculine phenotypes" might wonder if they are real men. It is at this point that spaces like the manosphere come into play as a source for the reclamation of a masculinity that has been lost, stolen, or taken away, where toxic and destructive notions of what it is to be a man are promoted and celebrated.

THE MANOSPHERE

While the first use of the term 'manosphere' occurred in November 2009 with the publication of themanosphere.blogspot.com, the beginnings of the manosphere as a focused assemblage of male-authored and male-focused articles, blogs, forums, and social media sites can be traced back to 2001 and the founding of the blog *No Ma'am*[2] (although there are, of course, other websites predating this blog which focus on men's issues; for example, Hermansson et al. 2020 suggest that the manosphere's beginnings go back to the emergent 'pick-up artists' community in the early 1990s). In the first post published on the blog, something akin to a 'call-to-arms' was issued, listing the following aims and objectives.

> The goal is to instil [sic] masculinity in men, femininity in women, and work toward limited government!
>
> By instilling masculinity in men, we make men self-reliant, proud, and independent. By instilling femininity in women, we make them nurturing, supporting, and responsible.
>
> By working for a limited government, we are working for freedom and justice. Women having 'other qualities' is not interesting to men because we don't need them! Femininity will be the price women pay for enjoying masculinity in men!

Although not explicitly named as a manosphere site, the blog represents one of the first articulations of online gender relations that would come to develop over the intervening 20 years, including the valorization of traditional gender roles and essentialized gender characteristics, the promotion of a conservative political outlook, and an antifeminist stance (although the manifesto has since been the target of criticism by established MGTOWers; see Barbarossaa 2015; ThePlagueDoctor0 2015).

In 2007, *No Ma'am* was joined by *Chateau Heartiste*, a blog run by James C. Weidmann under the pseudonym 'Roissy in DC'.[3] Building on the growing 'seduction' community, the site styled itself as a 'pick-up artist' (PUA) space,

---

2. This blog is available from http://no-maam.blogspot.com/2001/02/mgtow-manifesto.html.

3. Both 'Chateau Heartiste' and 'Roissy' come from Anne Cécile Desclos' erotic novel *The Story of O* (1954), which has been variously criticized for its depiction of violence against women and its main themes of female subjugation, objectification, and sexual humiliation (see Musser 2015).

offering advice for men seeking sexual relationships with women and charting an array of strategies, hints, and tips, usually based on evolutionary psychological models and 'scientific' approaches to attraction, social roles, and relationships. As the blog grew in popularity, Weidmann started to promote White nationalist, antifeminist, and antileftist content, establishing it as a radical outlet for right-wing rhetoric (in 2019, WordPress banned *Chateau Heartiste* for violations of its terms of service).

A number of other manosphere sites have been founded over the years, variously uniting MRAs, PUAs, MGTOWs, involuntary celibates, father's rights activists, and members of the alt-right (see X-man 2019 for an 'insider's perspective' on the aims and objectives of different manosphere outlets). As noted previously, these outlets ostensibly focus on male improvement and "men's issues," including dating, relationships, marriage, divorce, child custody, fathers' rights, child maintenance, and alimony, as well as discussions about male incarceration rates, male suicide and depression, media bias against men, and false rape allegations.

These manosphere sites also typically promote an idealized masculinity characterized by sexual promiscuity, physical strength and fitness, unyielding confidence, financial security, and prototypical attractiveness. The following example, taken from the Membership Page for the blog of Charles Sledge (n.d.), demonstrates one such configuration:

> I want you to take a second and imagine something with me. I want to imagine yourself a year into the future. Except it's not you as you are now but the dream version of you. Imagine this. You wake up and roll out of bed. You look over at the smoking hot naked girl you took home the night before laying next to you. You smile and then check your phone and look at three more wanting to hang out with you that day. You chuckle glad she didn't take a peek herself. You go into the bathroom and look at yourself in the mirror. You smile pleasantly. You've lost just about any trace of fat and are sporting a heavily muscled strong physique. One that performs just as well as it looks. After getting ready for the day you usher the girl out who says she can't wait to see you again and that you were the best lover of her life. A compliment that is commonplace now. You laugh and give her a smack on the behind while sending her on her way as she giggles happily. Going back inside you flip open your computer and take a look at your bank account. You shake your head smiling 'When did all those 0's get there' you wonder. You sit back and sigh happily. While you were busy testing the limits of your bed restraints last night you made more money than the average guy makes in a week.

The rest of the entry continues in much the same vein, promoting a 'Hollywood' version of masculinity, one which is all show and glamor and representing an arguably unrealistic and narrow conceptualization of what it is to be a 'masculine' man. Here, the route to masculinity is framed as a commodity which can be purchased, all for the low price of $9.99 per month (it is perhaps no surprise that paid courses, e-books, and online seminars are commonplace in the manosphere, particularly among the PUA community; see Bonnar 2019).

Beyond the scope of male self-improvement, daily coaching, and life advice, perhaps the most obvious hallmark which unites the various strands of the manosphere is an explicitly misogynistic and antifeminist stance (although the intensity of this position varies depending on the outlet). A cursory review of comments posted in the manosphere gives some sense of how women and feminism are viewed. Not only is there a strong conspiracy theory component (i.e. control of mass media for the purposes of feminist propaganda; feminism is a cult; men are losing their rights; see also Marwick and Lewis 2017, 17–19; HOPE Not Hate 2020 for discussions of online conspiracy theorists and their beliefs), the explicit marginalization and denigration of women and feminism is a common theme (see Hardaker and McGlashan 2016 and Ging and Siapera 2018, 2019 for more in-depth discussions of networked misogyny; Farrell et al. 2019 also examine the linguistic dimension of misogyny, with a specific focus on Reddit). The following excerpts are typical of these positions:

(1) Feminism is "a cult that is destroying society. You cannot reason with members of the cult any more than you can reason with the soldiers of ISIS or Boko Haram. Instead they are either to be mocked, fought, or ignored.

(2) If feminism was just another stupid cult saying stupid things on Twitter that would be ok. The problem is that feminism owns the government, the mass media, has totally owned the public opinion and they are successfully removing constitutional rights from men.

In a *Return of Kings* post about Lt. Kara Hultgreen (see Yader 2014), one of the first female naval pilots, one commentator argues that:

(3) Women are a nuisance in the office, in the warehouse, in the shop, in the barracks, on the base, near the base, in your house, and so on. They are a liability, a weak link, a pain in the ass. In many places their presence is simply offensive to men. Women would be offended by men being on their teams or in their bathrooms. Men are offended at women being in their squad or in their [Marine Expeditionary Unit]. Leave them home in the kitchen where they belong until the enemy is on the doorstep, and THEN she can get the rifle and protect the ranch. Until then, women are a nuisance.

At the most extreme edges, commentators suggest that women should be sidelined from all public activities, stripped of their decision-making powers, and have their right to vote taken away. As notorious manosphere author, blogger, and self-styled PUA Daryush Valizadeh (2015) claims, women "have shown to consistently fail in making the right decisions that prevent their own harm and the harm of others. Systems must now be put in place where a woman's behavior is monitored and her decisions subject to approval of a male relative or guardian who understands what's in her best interests better than she does herself."

Similarly, the MGTOW mission statement presents a negative characterization of women, drawing on common tropes about their sexual promiscuity, superficiality, and exploitative nature (see also the excerpt from Cooper 2020, entitled "20 Red

Flags You NEED to Avoid with Women," as an example of the antiwomen stances adopted in the manosphere).

(4) The women [men] encounter demand attention, loyalty, resources and undue privilege, while offering very little in return. The natural hypergamous nature that once served them well in their quest to secure the best possible mate is now a sustained lifestyle bringing an endless pursuit of bigger and better. The average young woman today is less concerned about the number of quality men who would commit to her than she is about the number of men who retweet a photo of her breasts (from 'The manosphere', MGTOW n.d.)

The manosphere, then, offers a space for men to pursue some degree of self-improvement, against a backdrop of antifeminist and misogynistic discourses, leading the Southern Poverty Law Center (2012) to note that while "some [manosphere] sites make an attempt at civility and try to back their arguments with facts, they are almost all thick with misogynistic attacks that can be astounding for the guttural hatred they express." In the remainder of this chapter, I examine how these discourses manifest and the constructions of gender which emerge across different manosphere outlets.

MANOSPHERE SPACES ON REDDIT

Although the manosphere is a relatively broad church, I discuss four subreddits which broadly map on to the schema set out in Ging (2017)—/r/MensRights, /r/TheRedPill, /r/Incels, and /r/MGTOW (see also Figure 6.1,[4] which sets out how the claimed intersections of 'activism' and 'desire of women' are refracted within different manosphere communities).

Before moving to the analysis, I discuss each subreddit's composition and their main philosophical and ideological underpinnings. As I demonstrate, each community has its own concerns, but they tend to be united by an antifeminist stance, with varying degrees of male-oriented positivity. As such, the manosphere is not necessarily a homogenous or uniform community, but rather one where different outlets advocate varying 'solutions' to what they see as the problem of feminism.

/r/MensRights

As Marwick and Caplan (2018) discuss, the development of Men's Rights Activists (MRA) was due to a split between the mythopoetic Men's Liberation and the Men's Rights movements of the 1970s and 80s. While the mythopoetic men's movement suggested that men had to recapture a sense of primal masculinity and homosocial

4. This grid was created by a redditor in 2019 and shared via the /r/MGTOW subreddit.

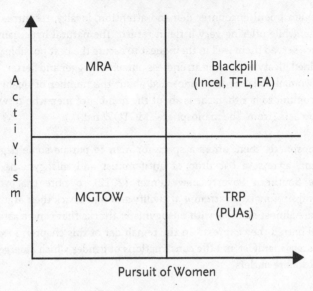

Figure 6.1. The 'Manogrid'

solidarity, the belief among MRAs was that White men were in crisis and that this crisis could be attributed to the growing influence of feminism in American culture. In their overview of the MRA movement, Marwick and Caplan (2018, 547) note that "The contemporary men's rights movement is thus a reaction to diminishing social status of cisgender white men, and the emergence of feminist and multicultural activism as a mainstream political force. It is thus defined as much *against* feminism as it is *for* men's rights" (emphasis in original).

Nevertheless, the /r/MensRights subreddit refutes claims of any antifeminist stance, describing itself as a pro-equality community which focuses on the "often neglected needs of men, boys, and their children" (/r/MensRights FAQs n.d.). Advocating for more social, institutional, and political intervention for issues which disproportionately affect men, /r/MensRights markets itself as a space for men to discuss topics related to men's rights, including (but not limited to) compulsory military service, divorce, child custody, child support/child maintenance, alimony arrangements, single fatherhood, workplace death rates, incarceration rates, male suicide rates, male mental health, false rape allegations/accusations, legal and educational discrimination, reproductive rights, and male genital mutilation (i.e. circumcision). As the sidebar description states, "At the most basic level, men's rights are the legal rights that are granted to men. However, any issue that pertains to men's relationship to society is also a topic suitable for this subreddit." But as Gotell and Dutton (2016, 71) note, very few MRAs actively engage with public policy or grassroots direct action, preferring instead to concentrate on "shifting attitudes through cyberactivism rather than by influencing law." Similarly, Banet-Weiser (2018, 172) notes how MRA groups coopt the discourses of victimization, suggesting that feminist logics are being "rerouted" by misogyny and using "these logics to center men as discriminated against" (see also Rensin 2015).

Examining antifeminist stances in MRA communities, LaViolette and Hogan (2019) found in their analysis of lexical variation in /r/MensRights and /r/MensLib that the top-voted /r/MensRights comments use the term *men* less frequently than other /r/MensRights comments and that the terms *she* and *her* are used more frequently in /r/MensRights compared to /r/MensLib. Taking these findings together, they observe that "very successful /r/MensRights discourses are less likely to make reference to the actions of men" and that the "advanced use of *she* and *her* points to an androcentric discourse which places more attention on the actions of women than of men" (LaViolette and Hogan 2019, 330–331). These results lead LaViolette and Hogan (2019, 331) to argue that /r/MensRights is "more accurately described as an antifeminist movement than a pro-men movement."

In a similar vein, Schmitz and Kazyak (2016) found a range of antifeminist sentiment across 12 MRA websites, noting that "MRAs construct over-simplified cultural models of the social world, such as by obfuscating the multiple goals of equality inherent to feminism and reducing it to a concept that only seeks to derogate men and masculinity" (Schmitz and Kazyak 2016, 18). In their review of the male supremacist movement, the Southern Poverty Law Center (2021) notes that "While some corners of the men's rights movement [focus] on legitimate grievances (male homelessness and rates of suicide, male conscription, lack of male shelters for domestic violence victims or some discrepancies in the family court system around the issue of child custody and alimony) to draw in followers, it then [orients] those followers to who they believed was the root cause of all these issues: women, aided by a large feminist conspiracy." Like the broader scope of the manosphere, MRA sites occupy a liminal zone, offering support and advice to those who may be in genuine need, while simultaneously acting as a space for antiwomen and antifeminist sentiment to flourish.

/r/TheRedPill

Briefly discussed in Chapter 2, /r/TheRedPill is one of Reddit's more notorious communities, resulting in it being quarantined in 2019 for repeated breaches of Reddit's community guidelines (although many within the community viewed the quarantining as ideologically-motivated censorship). Founded in 2012 and drawing on the symbology of the 'red pill' from *The Matrix* movie as a marker of social emancipation (see also Taylor 2021), the subreddit had nearly 1,700,000 subscribers at the time of writing, describing itself as a place for the "discussion of sexual strategy in a culture increasingly lacking a positive identity for men." To that end, /r/TheRedPill positions itself as a community where men learn to use 'game' in order to attract women, usually for sexual purposes, drawing on evolutionary psychology approaches to establish a 'strong frame' and an 'alpha mindset'. Such approaches have been criticized for being manipulative, exploitative, dehumanizing, and controlling, where women are viewed as simple automatons conditioned to respond to specific interactional tricks and misdirection (Zuckerberg 2018, 39).

In general terms, 'red pilled' men are the only ones rational enough to see through the apparent veil and bluster of social norms which underpin gendered interactions. Thus, a very specific form of masculinity is promoted within the community, one which is sexually active, physically fit, confident, forthright, and stoic, but also one which sees the world for what it is, which adopts a 'facts not feelings' mindset, and which values a scientific truth based on empirical evidence, pragmatism, and observation (Van Valkenburgh 2018). Those who do not measure up to these community ideals are failed men—*white knights*, *Social Justice Warriors*, *betas*, or *cucks*, unworthy of attention or value.

Consequently, discussion topics on /r/TheRedPill range from strategies on seducing women, through to mindfulness, self-improvement, physical exercise, stoicism, relationships, marriage, divorce, life lessons, teachable moments, and stories of 'transformation'. And, like most of the manosphere, a core ideology of /r/TheRedPill is that the world is controlled by feminism as part of a conspiracy theory to get rid of men. As such, comments which defend women or feminism are often policed by downvoting, brigading, or 'dogpiling' (see Massanari 2017 for a discussion of these strategies of silencing and how Reddit's technological features facilitate the development of what she calls 'toxic technocultures').

While this is an overt continuation of the aggrieved entitlement discourse observed in Chapter 5, there is more of a central focus that feminism has had a negative impact on Western sexual politics, leading to inequal opportunities for dating, relationships, and sex, all of which are now weighted in favor of women (Cornelisse 2018, 21; Dishy 2018). The following quote is indicative of how the nexus of feminism, sex, and power is characterized by some members of /r/TheRedPill:

(5) The last dozen or so girls I've dated and fucked, eight have told me they don't like what they see in modern feminism and that they're tired of it. And I've had several female colleagues and friends say the same thing—one even went so far as to say: "don't call me a feminist—those bitches are crazy." Basically, to sum up what these women told me: "I just want to be girly and pretty and have someone take control and make decisions so I don't have to." And the one girl who claimed to be a feminist and wanted to talk about it? Yeah, she's the one who wanted me to shove her face in the bed and spank her "harder, HARDER!" while I was behind her and choke her when I was on top, telling me to "destroy that little pussy"

Thus, /r/TheRedPill has shifted beyond its original confines of self-improvement, dating advice, and seduction techniques, toward a more critical stance on feminism and purported 'equality' discourses, with the subreddit often seen as one of the key entry points into the broader manosphere culture (Tait 2017).

A portmanteau of 'involuntary celibates', the term incels refers to men who desire relationships with women but who believe that, due to physical or personal shortcomings, they are overlooked as potential partners. Men who identify as incels also believe that the 'sexual marketplace' is weighted in favor of women and that there is a systematic bias toward prototypically attractive men, regardless of their personality or how they treat women.[5] In many ways, incels see themselves as substandard or failed men, arguing that society rewards looks over character and discriminates against men who do not measure up to superficial standards of attractiveness (excerpt 6). This 'failure' of masculinity can be predicated along the dimensions of ethnicity, height, physical appearance, and mental health, where those who identify as incel feel humiliated, rejected, and worthless in relation to what they see as a monolithic relationship context based on a series of rules, regulations, and edicts about what 'works' and what does not. All of this coalesces as a specific type of victim positioning centered on sexual privilege, a caustic and misogynistic attitude toward women as superficial, manipulative, and duplicitous, and a dominant view of a hegemonically masculine identity as an unobtainable gold standard (Beauchamp 2018; Sisley 2019).

(6) Wake up normans. We're not delusional, we're decent fucking men who understand that in this world looks take precedence over everything. If you are a sub-7 male you are a slave. You're worthless. Nothing you do or say matters. Women will never love you for you, and you will forever be a disposable utility in the eyes of a woman. Get this through your thick skulls. Cough up the blue pill, walk outside and observe life for how it is. Look at how attractive people are treated and compare that to how you yourself are treated. Look at how men with full heads of hair, 6ft+ and fantastic bone structure are treated and compare that to how you yourself are treated. Wake the fuck up. Unless you're physically desirable, you're worthless.

First coined in 1993 on a support website for those who wanted to discuss their sexual inactivity (Ling et al. 2018), incels came to media prominence following the 2014 Isla Vista shooting, perpetrated by Elliot Rodger who killed four men and two women before taking his own life. Rodger came to be heralded as an idol of the incel community, both for his actions and the publication of his 'manifesto' about his crisis of masculinity, his 'war on women', and insecurities about his virginity (see Myketiak 2016 and Blommaert 2018 for critical analyses of Rodger's manifesto).

5. One practice within the incel community is known as 'Chadfishing' (or the 'Chad experiment'), where a dating profile of an attractive man is created, alongside an invented history of disturbing behavior (e.g. domestic abuse). The aim of 'Chadfishing' is to show that regardless of how terrible a man is, women will still be prepared to sleep with him because of how good-looking he is (see also Klee 2019).

Rodger subsequently inspired a number of other attacks by self-identified incel members. For example, Alek Minassian posted on his Facebook page, "The Incel Rebellion has already begun! We will overthrow all the Chads and Stacys! All hail the Supreme Gentleman Elliot Rodger!" before killing ten and injuring another 16 in a vehicle-ramming attack in Toronto in April 2018. Less than six months later, Scott P. Beierle shot six women and killed two in an attack in Tallahassee, with investigations discovering pro-incel videos he had posted to YouTube in 2014 (Riley 2018), while Jake Davison, later found to have participated in incel communities on Reddit, carried out a shooting in Plymouth, England which claimed the lives of five people in 2021 (see also Hoffman, Ware, and Shapiro 2020 for a discussion of the incel movement and attacks committed by self-identified incels).

In their discussion of masculinity, violence, and mass shootings, Vito, Admire, and Hughes (2018, 91) argue that "Violent behavior is particularly salient for men who feel entitled to certain social privileges. When these expected privileges are thwarted and/or their position of authority threatened, these men often respond with frustration and hatred." In the aforementioned cases, violence was utilized as a destructive way of responding to a sense of marginalization and perceived power-lessness and as a way of compensating for a supposed loss of masculinity (see also Kalish and Kimmel 2010; Dragiewicz and Mann 2016; Nicholas and Agius 2018). This ideology has led to calls to investigate violence committed by incels as a public health concern (Riley 2018; Baele, Brace, and Coan 2019, 1) and as an emerging domestic terrorism threat (Brigham 2020; Hoffman, Ware, and Shapiro 2020; Texas Department of Public Safety 2020; Lewis 2021).

One of the largest online incel communities until 2017, /r/Incels was banned following an update to Reddit's guidelines prohibiting content which "encourages, glorifies, incites or calls for violence or physical harm against an individual or group of people." Given that much of the content on /r/Incels promoted explicit misogyny and violence against women, Reddit's decision was unsurprising, although several other subreddits emerged to take its place, including /r/Braincels (banned in 2019) and /r/Communitycels (banned in 2020). The subreddit, and the wider incel community, has been variously described as a poisonous, hostile, and toxic echo chamber which advocates and celebrates gendered violence as part of a sociopolitical agenda against the 'normies' (Janik 2018). As Robertson (2019) points out,

> A highly visible subset of incels take their complaints to surreal and uniquely nihilistic extremes. Instead of simply complaining that lots of women won't date them, they posit that literally all women are viscerally disgusted by all men who don't meet an objective, universal, and ridiculously high standard of male beauty. They're monomaniacally focused on romantic relationships as the only worthwhile goal in life, and they resist basically any solution except forcible revolution.

Linguistic research on incel communities is relatively sparse. In their analysis of incel.me, an online forum founded after /r/Incels was banned, Baele, Brace, and Coan (2019) reveal a community worldview dominated by biological determinism (where one's biology and genetics determine one's future) and radical dualism (where in-group and outgroup members are characterized along a cline of positive to negative respectively). A similar study by Jaki et al. (2019) on the same forum found a range of keywords associated with gender, physical traits, and sex, with a number of negative characterizations for women. Moreover, their analysis revealed that approximately 30 percent of the threads were misogynistic, 15 percent were homophobic, and 3 percent were racist, suggesting that content on incel.me is more likely to contain hate speech compared to, for example, a random selection of Twitter posts. At the narrative level, Høiland (2019) discusses how the incel community promotes a 'looks over personality' mindset in relation to romantic and sexual partnerships, reinforcing a sense of aggrieved entitlement and a perceived powerlessness in the face of contemporary dating pressures, a similar conclusion reached by Heritage and Koller (2020). Alongside a discussion of how hegemonic masculinity is deployed as a desirable character trope within the incel community, Høiland (2019, 73–81) examines how women are positioned as shallow, irrational, and ignorant. A consequent view within the community is that since women choose a partner on the basis of looks rather than character, personality, or disposition, they are thus deserving victims of any subsequent domestic abuse, misogyny, or sexual violence directed toward them. As such, the prevailing discourse across the incel community is one of violence, sexual privilege, male supremacy, and explicit misogyny (Tolentino 2018; Sugiura 2021; Halpin 2022).

/r/MGTOW

Briefly introduced earlier, MGTOW is the acronym for the 'Men Going Their Own Way' movement, first attested in late-2001 with the launch of the *No Ma'am* website (the website mgtow.com was later registered in 2012). A space for men who want to break away from romantic relationships with women, the MGTOW movement advocates a philosophy of male separatism and a "neo-individualistic dogma to live on one's own terms at all costs" (Lin 2017, 78). As the sidebar description for /r/MGTOW claims, "This subreddit is for men going their own way, forging their own identities and paths to self-defined success" (the subreddit was quarantined in early 2020). In this sense, the hallmarks of traditional masculinity, including "self-sufficiency, activity, mastery, courage, toughness, autonomy, rationality, competitiveness, technological skill, stoicism, and emotional detachment" (Harrison 2008, 56), are respected and prized.

Positioning themselves as victims of 'gynocentrism', those who identify as MGTOWers believe that the rejection of women and romantic relationships and, in extreme cases, economic and social disengagement, is necessary for male self-preservation. The prevailing ideology for many MGTOWers includes a disavowal of romantic and sexual attachment,[6] an antimarriage stance, a suspicion of government,

6. Sex is a point of contention within the MGTOW community. Some MTGOWers advocate complete sexual abstinence, viewing sex as another system of female control; others

and antifeminist views. In the eyes of MGTOWers, women are manipulative, parasitical, controlling, and devious, content to exploit men for their financial resources until a better provider comes along, at which point the incumbent man will be cast aside in favor of the newer, fitter, richer, more sexually appealing one. In some cases, these antiwomen views emerge because /r/MGTOW becomes a haven for divorced men who believe they have been the victims of an unfair system which is biased against men, whether that be in relation to child custody, alimony arrangements, or division of property and financial resources. Communities like /r/MGTOW market themselves as a space for men to vent their feelings of anger, betrayal, and resentment following divorce proceedings and any subsequent fallout, usually encouraged, supported, and amplified by other men. The following excerpt, in response to a redditor sharing the news that he was getting divorced, is just one illustrative example of the kind of antiwoman diatribes in /r/MGTOW:

(7) Congratulations you realize that no women will ever make you happy, I am 47 and sadly realize this at 44 after dating so many cunts, never been married my last girlfriend refused my marriage proposal and cheated on me. Women are trash and they will ruin your life, they have no passions whatsoever except eat and get fat trash other be jealous, whine all the time, and shame their better part.

In her discussion of online antifeminism, Lin (2017, 89) summarizes this position as follows:

MGTOW believe modern women have been "brainwashed" by feminism to believe "they are right no matter what." She will "ride the cock carousel" with as many men as possible, most of whom will mistreat her and valorize her feminist claims of victimhood. When women do decide to settle for a man, he will be a passive "beta-type," whom she will boss around and target for his "utility value"—financial assets and stability. The "beta" may be a Purple Piller18 who is aware of the risks of marriage, but tries to hold out for a "Disney-ending." However, divorce proceedings will inevitably sway in a woman's favor, due to institutionalized female privilege.

In its most extreme incarnation, MGTOWers advocate a complete break from society, living away from towns and cities in a form of homesteading, complete with hunting, growing their own food, and an 'off-the-grid' lifestyle. Although this final stage represents the ultimate rejection of women, society, and government,

support sexual, but not romantic, relationships with women; and yet others treat sex as a commodity that can be purchased, as in the case of escorts and prostitutes. In some cases, marriage is acceptable provided the wife adopts a relatively traditional gender role and sex occurs as often as the husband wants it, as the following comment from /r/MGTOW demonstrates—"Imagine a whole woman in your bed and you don't even get to smash. Sex in marriage is an entitled because otherwise what's the point in even calling yourself husband and wife? What separated you from strangers? This society is completely fucked. Our grandfather's would look down on us so much. Their grandsons have become pussies."

most MGTOWers maintain some degree of connection with their everyday lives (Lamoureux 2015).

Although it is difficult to determine why the MGTOW movement has grown, we can suggest a number of possibilities. The first is that, like other manosphere outlets, MGTOWers believe the social privileges of men are under attack, with men now 'second-class citizens' relegated to the side-lines. The 'History of MGTOW' page, for example, makes the following point:

(8) Men are no longer revered or respected on a most basic level for their contributions and past sacrifices, and are now reduced to 'idiots' for that. The recent cultural explosion of MGTOW should have long been expected in the face of this kind of nonsense which is force-fed to the sheeple who will buy it by the trough (MGTOW 2020).

By joining a community like /r/MGTOW, men are provided with a space where they believe they can reclaim this lost sense of 'reverence' and rally against what they perceive to be a growing threat to their position in society, shoring up their identities as men and their own sense of self-value and superiority.

The second reason is that the movement taps into prevalent discourses about men as victims of a range of pro-women systems which privilege women over men. Rather than challenge these systems, as members of /r/MensRights claim to do, MGTOWers believe the 'game' to be rigged in favor of women and refuse to participate in it. By recognizing what they believe to be an inherent social unfairness toward men, identifying as MGTOW allows men to claim a 'win' of sorts against society more broadly.

Finally, movements like MGTOW are attractive because they offer a sense of belonging and a welcoming space for men in lieu of offline forms of alliance and homosocial bonding. Since one precondition of belonging to almost any group is the observance of a set of fundamental beliefs which undergird the group, it is possible to leverage the desire to be validated through explicit acts of loyalty. In their discussion of passive harassment by MGTOW members on Twitter, Jones, Trott, and Wright (2019, 15) note that "the need to perform their rejection of women leads to expressions of sexism, antifeminism, and more broadly, misogyny in order for individuals to prove their allegiance and belonging among their male peers." Thus, a prerequisite for membership access, and all the comforts that this bestows in terms of acceptance, validation, and community approval, is contingent on explicit demonstrations of antiwoman and antifeminist sentiment (see also Vivenzi, de la Vega, and Driessen 2017; Wright, Trott, and Jones 2020).

DATA AND CORPUS CONSTRUCTION

Data for this chapter were collected from /r/MensRights, /r/TheRedPill, and /r/MGTOW using the Python Reddit API Wrapper (PRAW, Boe 2019), while data for /r/Incels were collected using the online repository pushshift.io, primarily because the

Table 6.1. BREAKDOWN OF THE MANOSPHERE CORPUS (RANKED BY TOTAL NUMBER OF WORDS)

	Number of threads	Number of comments	Number of words
/r/MensRights	100	69,515	1,668,499
/r/TheRedPill	100	33,541	1,573,254
/r/Incels	100	16,737	496,593
/r/MGTOW	100	15,680	490,042
Totals	**400**	**135,473**	**4,246,509**

subreddit was banned in 2017 and was no longer inaccessible via Reddit. The constitution of the Manosphere Corpus is presented in Table 6.1.

ANALYSIS

The analysis examines gendered lexis across four manosphere subcorpora (see also (Koller et al. 2019) for an approach based on appraisal theory and a broader keyword analysis which covers other lexical categories and Krendel 2020 for a focus on the terms *woman*, *girl*, *man* and *guy*). More specifically, the analysis focuses on three main categories of gendered noun referents—positive referent terms (e.g. *bro*, *princess*), neutral referent terms (e.g. *man*, *woman*), and negative referent terms (e.g. *dick*, *bitch*). Positive terms were classified as having an affirmative discourse function, either in terms of an in-group identifier (e.g. *bro*, *dude*, *guys*) or as an evaluatory statement (e.g. *alpha*), while negative terms were classified as an insult term (e.g. *pussy*, *faggot*) or having a derogatory function (e.g. *white knight*, *beta*). Neutral terms included items that had some sort of generic gendered reference (e.g. *male*, *female*, *man*, *woman*) or a relational function (e.g. *father*, *mother*, *son*, *daughter*, *husband*, *wife*). As might be expected, however, positive and neutral terms can be used with a negative valence (e.g. "*Dude*, stop being such a dick"), and as Cameron (1994, 32) notes, "Many instances of sexism are manifested not in single words or specific constructions but through an accumulation of discursive or textual choices." The analysis, then, is further augmented through the use of concordance lines to illustrate terms in context.

The terms for each category were created by generating a word list in #LancsBox for each subcorpus and then identifying every lexical item which had a specific gendered or sexed referent. Not every term was used in every subcorpus, so once the top twenty terms in each category were identified, these terms were matched across the other subcorpora. For example, because *roastie* was one of the top twenty terms in the /r/Incels subreddit, this term was also searched for in the other three subreddits.

Only noun forms were considered (variant spellings such as *bruv*, *womyn*, *phaggot* etc. were ignored), while verb forms (e.g. 'Are we supposed to *bitch* when the odds are against us?"), certain premodifying adjectival forms ("That was such a *dick* move"), formalized insult terms ("Karma is a *bitch*"), metonyms ("No *pussy* is worth that trouble"), nominal forms relating to body parts ("Don't stick your *dick* in crazy"), and false positives (e.g. mis-spellings) were not included. Furthermore, instances where a term was used as an illustrative example or as meta-commentary (e.g. "I grew up in the UK where the word 'cunt' has all the weight of a comma"), or where a term was part of a copy/pasted or quoted comment, were excluded. In a minority of cases, terms commonly associated with women were used in reference to men (e.g. "He's a giant *cunt*"),[7] while the converse was also true (e.g. "I prefer calling rude women a *dick*"). These 'reverse-slurs', however, did not occur frequently enough to justify separating out individual instances and were thus retained as part of the analysis. Ultimately, the analysis uncovers how these lexical choices perpetuate a particular set of gender ideologies, showing how these terms become rallying points for men to police acceptable forms of masculinity and femininity and to critique those who fall outside narrowly defined parameters.

MALE TERMS

In the analysis which follows, positive terms, neutral terms, and negative terms are presented for each group. Terms are organized alphabetically, including singular and plural forms, rather than by rate of use, while concordance lines are provided to illustrate patterns of usage.

Male Positive Terms

The first part of the analysis examines the use of positive reference terms for men (Figure 6.2), covering seven terms—alpha*(s)*, bro*(s)*, brother*(s)*, dude, guys, you guys, and *man*.[8]

Given that the data are from mainly Anglosphere speakers, some of the results are somewhat predictable. For example, *man* as a colloquial gendered interjective (e.g. "Hey *man*, I'm pretty new to Reddit") is common across all four subreddits, although it is lowest in /r/MensRights and highest in /r/Incels. This pattern potentially reflects the age demographics of each community, with MGTOW members

7. A number of posters claimed that *cunt* is not gendered, arguing that it can be used in reference to men, that the taboo valence of the term is overstated, or that there is coequivalence between *cunt* and *dick/cock/prick*. While insult terms of all kinds are problematic, these claims overlook the fact that *cunt* in reference to men can be positive in evaluation ("He's a good cunt") but is generally negative when used to talk about women. Furthermore, *cunt* tends to be rated as among the most offensive swearwords by both men and women, compared to *dick/cock/prick* which tend to be further down the taboo scale.

8. In the case of *man*, this has been categorized as positive if used as a vocative or interactional function (e.g. "Hey *man*, this is what I think" and neutral if it is used in a more generic sense (e.g. "That man is funny").

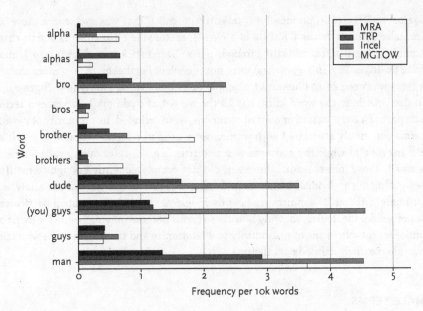

Figure 6.2. Positive male gendered terms across the manosphere corpus

generally older than those who identify as incel or red pillers. This is supported by the fact that references to 'marriage' and 'divorce' are almost three times higher in /r/MGTOW than in /r/Incels, which might be expected for those in later life stages, as well as by self-reported demographic data for each community.

With the exception of *guys* and *you guys* (discussed later), singular forms are almost always preferred over plural forms, suggesting that interactions in the subreddits are generally unidirectional (i.e. one redditor directing their contribution to another redditor) rather than multi-directional (i.e. one redditor directing their contribution to many redditors). To that end, many of these terms are vocative in function—"*Dude*, what are you talking about?" and "Tell me about it, *bro*." Generally speaking, these terms are positive in valence across each subreddit, building a supportive and mutually encouraging environment or mitigating face threats (Tables 6.2 and 6.3).

Both *bro* and *dude* are also emblematic of what Kiesling (2004) calls 'cool solidarity', indexing a "complex and somewhat indeterminate combination of distance, casualness, camaraderie, and equality" (Kiesling 2004, 288; see also Kiesling 2018 on 'masculine ease'). As such, it is perhaps surprising that /r/Incels leads the use of both *bro* and *dude,* given the relative degree of angst in this subreddit about masculine status. For example, Heritage and Koller (2020, 152) note that incels "view themselves as nonnormative within broader society and see women and societal standards of masculinity as the cause of their problems."

There are other notable findings. For example, the use of *brother(s)* is marked within /r/MGTOW (Table 6.4), where they are not only strategies for building a

Table 6.2. SELECTED CONCORDANCE LINES FOR "BRO" IN THE MANOSPHERE CORPUS (VARIABLE L/R SPAN)

	Subreddit			
1	MRA	pretty insensitive comment	bro	like you don't even care about
2	MRA	I dunno	bro	Sounds like a bunch of insecure
3	TRP	Thanks for the advice	bro	much appreciated
4	TRP	YOU MY HERO,	bro	FUCK YA!
5	Incels	Good on you,	bro	
6	Incels	Just try,	bro	If nothing happens, try harder
7	MGTOW	Well done,	bro	Maybe throw some of that
8	MGTOW	Whatever makes you happy	bro	it's about going your OWN way

Table 6.3. SELECTED CONCORDANCE LINES FOR "DUDE" IN THE MANOSPHERE CORPUS (VARIABLE L/R SPAN)

	Subreddit			
1	MRA	Preaching to the choir	dude	I think the best way to go
2	MRA	Calm down	dude	Swearing and random caps are unnecessary
3	TRP	You need psychiatric help	dude	
4	TRP	OP you are a real ass	dude	Always remember it's not what
5	Incels	It's your attitude	dude	You seem stubborn as a mule too
6	Incels	This isn't complicated	dude	I'm not going to keep arguing
7	MGTOW	congrats	dude	keep it up
8	MGTOW	This should be pinned here	dude	

Table 6.4. SELECTED CONCORDANCE LINES FOR "BROTHER" IN THE /R/ MGTOW SUBCORPUS (VARIABLE L/R SPAN)

1	Yes you can	brother	You can define masculinity for **yourself**
2	Godspeed,	brother	Hope you feel better soon!
3	Keep at it	brother	I'm rooting for you!
4	You speak the truth, my	brother	my ex literally got into slingshots
5	Keep your head up	brother	Document everything
6	Live as you want to live	brother	i dress well keep fit, i do
7	Will do, my	brother	And it will be dedicated to all my brothers
8	Great job my	brother	You understand and value true freedom

communal sense of comradeship and solidarity, but they also encode close fraternal relationships through their association with religious orders and the military (e.g. *band of brothers, brothers in arms*).

By virtue of its philosophy of male separatism, MGTOW is perhaps the best example of a 'monastic' and isolationist worldview, so the use of *brother* is understandable when the subreddit is viewed in this light (interestingly, references to *monk* and *monk-mode* are highest in /r/MGTOW). Of course, *brother(s)* is not exclusive to /r/MGTOW, but if we view the other subreddits as online/virtual examples of male bonding (or Männerbund) spaces (see also Hermansson et al. 2020, 183), then we can make sense of how the use of *brother* is one way affiliation, closeness, and connection are discursively constructed in these male-only (or at least male-dominant) spaces. This also becomes part of the management of homosociability within these spaces, demonstrating closeness but within a recognized and culturally approved framework of male relations.

The other interesting positive evaluation term is *alpha/alphas*, used almost exclusively in /r/TheRedPill. Originally popularized in David Mech's work on wolf packs (Mech 1970), the term 'alpha' found purchase in a variety of zoology and primatology research (e.g. de Waal 1986; Nishida et al. 1992) to refer to the most socially dominant male among pack animals. The term was eventually co-opted into the discourse of the seduction community through the publication of *The Game* (Strauss 2005). Part autobiography and part handbook, *The Game* narrates the author's experience of becoming a PUA through acquiring 'alpha' traits, including being "well groomed, possessing a sense of humor, connecting with people, and being seen as the social center of a room" (Strauss 2005, 24). Being 'alpha' has come to be associated with normative ideas of hegemonic masculinity—power, confidence, success, strength, bravery, and (sexual) attractiveness (see the excerpt from Charles Sledge's website earlier in the chapter for an example of the 'alpha' male, and Russell 2021 for an examination of alpha masculinities).

Although the term has been criticized in the literature on men (e.g. Kaufman 2014), 'alpha' holds significant sway in the manosphere context, particularly in 'seduction' communities like /r/TheRedPill (see also Singal 2016). Part of its attraction rests on the fact that 'alpha' is often couched in evolutionary biological and psychological terms. And as noted in Chapter 2, such accounts are very attractive in the context of thinking about masculinity, even though they are very often replete with "misinterpretations and hysterical overextrapolations of our 'natural' gender roles" (Singal 2016), as well as ignoring the complex and contextual nature of human interactions and social structures.

Of all the subreddits, /r/TheRedPill has the most 'how to' posts on developing 'alpha male' qualities. Since these posts claim to distill complex human behaviors and interactions into easy-to-learn heuristics that will facilitate dating and seduction success, they are especially popular in /r/TheRedPill. Some of these posts evoke the primacy of science (e.g. "How to bag a bitch with SCIENCE: Psychological mechanisms for the alpha male" and "Article: Scientists discover brain's neural switch for becoming an alpha male"), while others are guides to alpha behavior (e.g. "Alpha male strategies: 10 dating commandments," "The six traits of an alpha male," or "29 mistakes the typical alpha male makes"). Furthermore, the writers of these posts can claim community cachet for their contributions to knowledge, alongside promoting their status as self-proclaimed 'alpha' exemplars (see also Coates 2003, 46 on the role of 'technical knowledge' in relation to men's talk).

Consequently, /r/TheRedPill is very much invested in the concept of the 'alpha male', and any suggestion that it does not exist is roundly rejected by most TRPers. For example, one thread discusses a video by comedian and social commentator Adam Conover about alpha males, as part of his series *Adam Ruins Everything* (2017). In the segment, Conover discusses some of the early research on alpha males (mainly from zoology) and argues that this cannot be taken as evidence for the existence of alpha males in human societies. The resounding evaluation of Conover's video is, however, wholly negative, arguing that it advances a strawman argument based on a flawed premise. But perhaps more interesting is how the video becomes reconfigured as part of a claimed global assault on men, furthering the narrative of a persecuted masculinity spearheaded by left-wing media outputs. A comment by the OP ('original poster') which accompanies the thread is a good example of this worldview.

(9) As someone who works in the media myself I can attest first-hand that the media and establishment structures doing all they can to attack real men is not by accident. It is by design. The goal is to weaken men and make them effeminate losers who are easy to walk over. Strong, masculine men are the #1 enemy to the global establishment . . . These videos are good for the individual male who is looking to climb the ladder in the male hierarchy. Unfortunately its bad for men and society as a whole. The weaker men get, the easier it will be for oppressive establishment operatives to trample our rights and walk all over us with more tyranny and freedom/liberty stripping actions.

Here, we see the deployment of the victimhood discourses examined in Chapter 5, alongside the evocation of a shadowy and all-powerful 'global establishment' hellbent on stripping men of their rights and privileges and a call-to-arms for 'masculine men' to fight back. Other redditors respond in much the same way, framing 'alpha' males as necessary retaliation to the ever-encroaching state apparatus.

Regardless of whether the alpha male exists as a concept, it has a great deal of influence within /r/TheRedPill as a benchmark or aspirational target. A closer look at concordance lines and collocations demonstrates how the term is deployed across the subreddit, including the notion of 'alpha-ness' as an ongoing process (Table 6.5). For example, of the nearly 100 instances of *an alpha* in the /r/TheRedPill subcorpus, approximately 20 percent collocate with a conjugated form of the verb 'to be', including *be an alpha* (11 tokens) and *being an alpha* (10 tokens). Other concordance lines show the kinds of positive associations linked to 'alpha' status, including *genuine*, *natural*, *sexy*, *strong*, *true*, and *ultimate* (Table 6.6).

In terms of collocational analysis, one of the strongest collocates of *alpha* is the related term *beta*. In this alpha/beta binary, *alphas* are viewed to be the sexually confident and successful exemplars of masculinity, while *betas* fail to measure up to community standards of what it is to be a man (interestingly enough, what constitutes

Table 6.5. SELECTED CONCORDANCE LINES FOR "AN ALPHA" IN THE /R/
THEREDPILL SUBCORPUS (VARIABLE L/R SPAN)

1	but if you are	an alpha	and beta males in the manosphere
2	You can be	an alpha	and still want a monogamous long term
3	Not everyone can be	an alpha	right?
4	if you are incompetent, you cannot be	an alpha	you are just a phony
5	the psychological effect being	an alpha	had on him
6	Being	an alpha	is at the top, that could be
7	Being an	an alpha	isn't something you can become by
8	Being	an alpha	is not always seeking what other alphas

Table 6.6. SELECTED CONCORDANCE LINES FOR "ALPHA(S)" IN THE /R/
THEREDPILL SUBCORPUS (VARIABLE L/R SPAN)

1	no different from a genuine	alpha	in the eyes of a woman
2	She wants a strong	alpha	not a fat sick Beta with roses
3	A true	alpha	leads from the front with competence
4	loving yourself makes you the ULTIMATE	alpha	trust me
5	a queen gets fucked by the baddest	alphas	in the world and commands an army
6	Barbarian	alphas	can always conquer civilized betas
7	plenty of examples of legit	alphas	who wouldn't put up with that
8	flocking to 22-25 year old ripped	alphas	They are grossed out by over 30s

an 'alpha' appears to be the topic of contestation within /r/TheRedPill; see also Ging 2017, 13). Indeed, one of the most common refrains across /r/TheRedPill is 'Alpha fucks, beta bucks' (alternative spellings include *fux/bux*)—that is, alphas provide women with sexual satisfaction, while betas are only useful insofar as they are exploited by women for their financial resources. This sense of 'alpha exceptionalism' is part of the hierarchy of masculinity prevalent throughout /r/TheRedPill, although as I go on to discuss later in this chapter, the 'alpha' is not always universally well-received across the manosphere.

The final terms in the positive category are *guys* and *you guys*, which function in slightly different ways across each subreddit. The use of *guys* is relatively straightforward, acting as a generic group address term, usually accompanied by a plural pronoun form *we* or *us* (Table 6.7).

While *you guys* may initially appear to be the same as *guys*, it has quite a different function. More specifically, the term *guys* introduces positive (or occasionally neutral) statements or questions, while *you guys* is almost exclusively used to introduce negative statements from redditors outside the subreddit community (Table 6.8).

Table 6.7. SELECTED CONCORDANCE LINES FOR "GUYS" IN THE MANOSPHERE CORPUS (VARIABLE L/R SPAN)

	Subreddit			
1	MRA		guys	regardless of the message, can we all
2	MRA	Jeez	guys	how often do we have to see
3	TRP		guys	red flags are real . . . we should always
4	TRP	Guys	guys	we all know OP fucked up more
5	Incels	ok	guys	whats more important looks, money or status?
6	Incels		guys	please tell me theres a tutorial on
7	MGTOW	Be careful,	guys	I fell for this "double edge"
8	MGTOW	Come on	guys	Let's be fair now. The only reason

Table 6.8. SELECTED CONCORDANCE LINES FOR "YOU GUYS" IN THE MANOSPHERE CORPUS (VARIABLE L/R SPAN)

	Subreddit			
1	MRA		you guys	are a hate sub though
2	MRA		you guys	are living a fabricated world
3	MRA	Whether	you guys	are actually sexist, you sure *act* like sexists
4	MRA		you guys	are all miserable fucks, aren't you?
5*	TRP	Idk about	you guys	but I'm getting a concealed carry
6*	TRP	This subreddit and	you guys	helped and keep helping my growth journey
7*	TRP	How much effort do	you guys	put in toward sexual success
8*	TRP	I can't begin to tell	you guys	all how much this means to me
9	Incels		you guys	are freaks. Some creepy ass motherfuckers
10	Incels		you guys	are proof that autistic retards have no
11	Incels	But	you guys	all have such a fucking victim complex
12	Incels	Jesus Christ, you	you guys	even have bots that protect you from
13	MGTOW	Holy cow you	you guys	are sick lol "Her tits sag"
14	MGTOW		you guys	couldn't organize your way out of
15	MGTOW		you guys	claim that it's some social propaganda
16	MGTOW	Ridiculous, you	you guys	are pathetic

Here, we have several examples of how *you guys* establishes a combative or confrontational evaluative stance, where members of three of the four subreddits are criticized for their views, philosophy, or behavior, usually by redditors who do not claim membership of the individual subreddits. In this frame, members of /r/MensRights, /r/Incels, and /r/MGTOW are positioned as deviant or nonnormative (*creepy ass, miserable, sick, pathetic, freaks, retards* etc.). Interestingly enough, however, this pattern does not hold in /r/TheRedPill (starred in the examples in Table 6.8), where *you guys* seems to be part of generally positive statements (in that sense, it patterns more closely with the findings for *guys*).

Male Neutral Terms (Generic)

For the neutral category, terms were divided into two groups—those terms which encoded a generic male referent (e.g. *man, male, boy*) and those which encoded a relational meaning (e.g. *husband, father, dad*). Beginning with the generic male referents (Figure 6.3), we can see that the terms with the highest rate of use are *men* and *man*, although /r/MGTOW and /r/Incels seem to prefer *guy(s)* as a more informal term. Both generic *dude(s)* and more age-specific *boy(s)* are used at a lower rate, although *boy(s)* is used more in /r/MensRights, partly reflecting the broader interest within this subreddit concerning, for example, violence against young men and boys, male

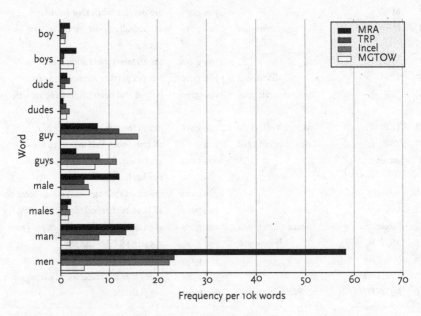

Figure 6.3. Neutral male gendered terms (generic) across the manosphere corpus

genital mutilation (circumcision), boys' education, and other topics connected to the men's rights movement.

In the collocational analysis of *men* we see the broader community foci which characterize each subreddit (collocates were generated using AntConc and the log-likelihood score, which takes into account the absolute frequency of each collocate). For example, while *women* is one of the main collocates of *men* in each subreddit, there are other collocates which highlight the different kinds of terms typically associated with men (Table 6.9).

In /r/MensRights, these collocates include *rights, issues, victims, violence, feminism, feminists, movement,* and *problems,* suggesting a more politically engaged program of discourse (although as Gottel and Dutton 2016, 71 note, such discourse is most concerned with cyberactivism rather than influencing policy).

In /r/TheRedPill, on the other hand, collocates of *men* are mainly concerned with appearance and character traits, particularly the hierarchy of *weak* versus *strong,* alongside references to age (*young*), ethnicity (*white*), and region (*Western*),

Table 6.9. TOP TWENTY COLLOCATES FOR "MEN" IN THE MANOSPHERE CORPUS (RANKED BY LOG-LIKELIHOOD SCORE)

MRA	TRP	Incel	MGTOW
women	women	women	women
rights	men	men	men
issues	weak	attractive	want
men	times	get	good
victims	white	attracted	white
just	create	top	society
equal	young	short	think
violence	strong	ugly	just
same	rights	just	way
boys	just	percent	work
feminism	want	same	young
feminists	get	laid	sex
white	society	average	strong
day	gay	want	attractive
rape	sex	way	same
work	pill	benefit	blame
problems	good	desperate	asian
movement	same	lot	know
get	western	physically	built
society	red	unattractive	black

a constellation which supports the general primacy of the 'alpha male' figure within this subreddit. It is also no surprise that *sex* is a strong collocate, given the focus of the subreddit on pursuing sexual relations, as well as verbs of desire (e.g. *want*).

In /r/Incels, we are presented with a rather different image of men and masculinity, with *men* collocating with a series of negative terms, particularly related to physical and sexual attractiveness (or lack thereof), including *desperate*, *short*, *ugly*, and *unattractive* (see also Heritage and Koller 2020). Sex also emerges as a concern through the euphemism *laid*, although this is exclusively part of the passive construction *get laid*. Sex, then, is conceptualized as an event that happens *to* men, rather than as something actively pursued, unlike in a subreddit like /r/TheRedPill, subverting the typical cultural narrative of men as sexually active.

Last, /r/MGTOW appears to be something of a blended set of collocates, sharing discourses to do with dating and relationships common in /r/TheRedPill (*attractive*, *sex*), but also an apparent concern with ethnicity (*asian*, *black*, *white*), men's contribution to contemporary society (*built*, *society*, *work*), age and naivety (*young*), and idealized masculinity (*strong*).

Male Neutral Terms (Relational)

Like the positive terms, the singular forms of relational terms are preferred almost categorically in every subreddit (Figure 6.4). Of these singular terms, *father* is the predominant term in at least three of the subreddits, alongside the related term *dad*. Use of these terms is highest in /r/MensRights and /r/MGTOW, reflecting broader

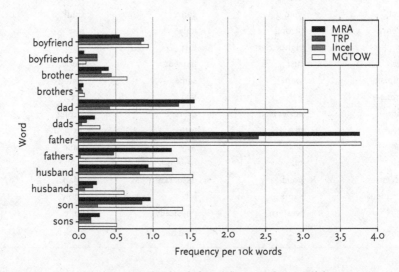

Figure 6.4. Neutral male gendered terms (relational) across the manosphere corpus

Table 6.10. SELECTED CONCORDANCE LINES FOR "BOYFRIEND" AND "HUSBAND" IN THE /R/MGTOW SUBCORPUS (VARIABLE L/R SPAN)

1	talk about with her next victim, errr	boyfriend	
2	So basically her	boyfriend	was supporting her with the bills
3	Now that her	boyfriend	went MGTOW she doesn't have anyone to pay her bills
4	working, and basically leeching of her then	boyfriend	all while attending school that he was most likely paying for
5	no surprise she cheated on her	husband	several times and we have a bet
6	her life by her cheating on her	husband	
7	She cheated on her loyal	husband	and now she lays in the bed she made
8	the bitches straight up cheating. Their	husband	/boyfriend knows nothing about it

Table 6.11. SELECTED CONCORDANCE LINES FOR "BOYFRIEND" IN THE /R/ THEREDPILL SUBCORPUS (VARIABLE L/R SPAN)

1	Common 'brush off' lines like telling you she has a	boyfriend,	saying you're a nice guy, telling you let's just be friends
2	to ever take the "I have a	boyfriend"	shit-test at face value. You'll be surprised
3	the types of girls who have a	"boyfriend"	who she met in class waiting for
4	Oh and	"boyfriend."	Lol. That word means nothing to prewall
5	rejections are a test. And with the	boyfriend	excuse, is it best to just abandon
6	fuck him and go back to their	"boyfriend"	for free pizza. I'm not certain

community interest in issues to do with visitation and custody rights, child support, single fatherhood, and false paternity claims.

Romantic relationships between men and women are also marked through the terms *boyfriend(s)* and *husband(s)*. In some subreddits (e.g. /r/MGTOW), discussions are usually concerned with the negative effects of relationships, including infidelity and financial exploitation (Table 6.10), while others highlight women's use of existing partners as a strategy for rejecting romantic advances (Table 6.11).

/r/Incels, on the other hand, very rarely discusses men in relational terms, with this subreddit ranked lowest for almost every item (the only exception is *boyfriend*, where it is joint highest with /r/TheRedPill). When such topics are discussed, they tend to be fairly negative representations, as concordance lines for *father* demonstrate (Table 6.12).

Table 6.12. SELECTED CONCORDANCE LINES FOR "FATHER" IN THE /R/ INCELS SUBCORPUS (VARIABLE L/R SPAN)

1	gray-ish hair. But then again, my	father	was a giga-Chad, so I obviously do
2	a child and regularly beaten by my	father	But I am a man about it
3	worthless piece of shit that is my	father	who used to beat her and me
4	you end up in jail like my	father	
5	Last time I spent time with my own	father	for fuck sakes was when I was 10

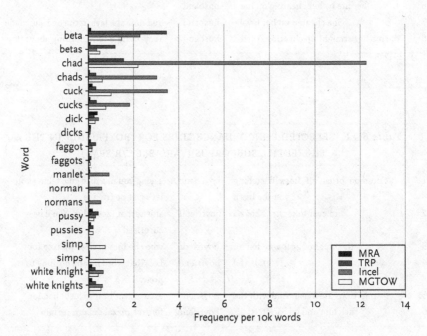

Figure 6.5. Negative male gendered terms across the manosphere corpus

Male Negative Terms

For the male negative terms, these broadly fall into three groups—body parts (e.g. *dick*), homophobic terms (e.g. *faggot*), and innovative coinages (e.g. *simp*, *manlet*). There are, however, some differences in usage across the four subreddits (Figure 6.5).

For example, /r/Incels has a much wider pool of negative referent terms, outstripping every other subreddit in terms of rate of use. Some of these terms are exclusive to /r/Incels, like *manlet* (a short man who is unable to attract women because of his height) and *norman* (a term for 'normies', or nonincels), while others are used elsewhere in the corpus but are used most in /r/Incels. Perhaps the most notable of these is *chad(s)*, which is used almost five times more compared to /r/ MGTOW, the next highest subreddit.

Defined in the Incel Wiki (2020) as "[a man who is] . . . usually good looking, wealthy, muscular or has otherwise high status," a 'Chad' is typically conceived as the epitome of masculinity and meets (or excels) what are assumed to be normative standards for male attractiveness, with the summary of physical characteristics which mark out a 'Chad' reaching an almost pathological level of detail (see Squirrell 2018 and Tranchese 2019 for discussions of Incels' use of pseudoscientific discourse):

> Common characteristics for a Chad born from looks often include: Above manlet height, large frame, broad shoulders, 0-1 on the Norwood scale, hunter eyes with little to no upper eyelid exposure, positively or neutrally tilted eyes, prominent high cheekbones, thick eyebrows, a large skull, compact midface, killer long chin, defined squarish jawline, long vertical ramus, gonial angle of approx. 120 degrees, forward growth of the mandible and the maxilla, a short straight nose, an ideal philtrum to chin ratio (with the philtrum being shorter), clean exotic skin, healthy bite with white teeth, and last, low body fat (below 15%).

The status of the 'Chad' in /r/Incels is complex, held up as an exemplar of 'alpha maleness' and the object of women's sexual desire, while simultaneously being the target of scorn, resentment, and envy. For members of /r/Incels, 'Chads' represent the top of the dating (and masculine) hierarchy, but they also serve as an explicit reminder of their own (self-claimed) inadequacies in terms of looks, personality, and character and their perceived failures as men. Chads do not, however, stand alone and are usually discussed in relation to women through the lens of dating and sex (Table 6.13).

Table 6.13. SELECTED CONCORDANCE LINES FOR "CHAD" IN THE /R/INCELS SUBCORPUS (VARIABLE L/R SPAN)

1		Chad	could fuck her right in her cubicle
2		Chad	doesn't respect femloids but he gets laid
3	He is a	Chad	and would get sex anyway
4	Go be at	Chad	's dick and leave us
5	. THEY ONLY LOOK AT	Chad	THIS WAY
6	SMV roasties begging for	Chad	and was ready to settle
7	I live in Australia and femoids go crazy for	Chad	
8	[women] exploit betas and then they fuck	Chad	afterward
9	you are a beta. She will fuck	Chad	ten times over while you stare at
10	Knowing females she probably fucked	Chad	to get baby

These concordances also highlight some of the misogynistic views incels have of women, as superficial, shallow, and manipulative, interested only in men for their looks and not for their personality, their behavior, or their personal history, establishing a nihilistic worldview where looks are everything and character means nothing.

After *chad*, the next most common negative referent term is *beta*. Like *alpha*, *beta* has the highest rate of use in /r/TheRedPill and is practically nonexistent in /r/MensRights. The concordance lines (Table 6.14) demonstrate the kinds of undesirable behaviors and characteristics associated with 'beta males', highlighting the low regard in which they are held. This evaluation is further supported through collocation analysis. For example, although *bucks* is the second strongest collocate of *beta* in /r/TheRedPill (after *alpha*), other frequent collocates tend to be almost wholly negative, including *autist*, *bitch*, *chump*, *cowards*, *cuck*, *faggot*, *loser*, *orbiter*, *provider*, *schlub*, *simp*, and *wimp*.

Other negative terms highlight general failures of masculinity, including *cuck* (short for 'cuckold' and used to refer to a man who agrees to their partner having sex with other men; see Squirrell 2017 and Kosse 2022 for discussions of the racial and political dimension of *cuck* in the alt-right), *faggot* (taboo term for a gay man), *simp* (meaning either a 'simpleton' or a **S**ucker who **I**dolizes **M**ediocre **P**ussy; see Taylor 2019), and *white knight* (a man who defends women from sexist attacks).

While it might be expected that these terms be used exclusively as types of 'outgroup' identifiers, what is surprising is the extent to which they police masculinity *within* and *across* the different subreddits. Tables 6.16–6.18 demonstrate these evaluative stances, highlighting how masculine status is a precarious one.

Table 6.14. SELECTED CONCORDANCE LINES FOR "BETA" IN THE MANOSPHERE CORPUS (VARIABLE L/R SPAN)

	Subreddit			
1	MRA	All	beta	must die. They ruin the world with
2	MRA	Alphas get treated like bygone emperors and	beta	live lives of quiet desperation
3	MRA	too old for the SMP are dying,	beta	are getting cucked divorce raped and locked
4	TRP	is a perfect example of what a	beta	looks like . . . gets cucked and then loses
5	TRP	It's pussy ass	beta	fags who make themselves a bitch
6	TRP	I was the biggest	beta	cuck loser you can imagine
7	Incels	Yes, you are a	beta	She will fuck chad ten times over
8	Incels	Go and become a	beta	orbiter cuck yourself
9	Incels	Blue pilled	beta	cuck idealism
10	MGTOW	Thirsty men and	beta	simps taught girls to behave this way
11	MGTOW	Women love money from	beta	males
12	MGTOW	Most men today are soy	beta	wimps

Table 6.15. SELECTED CONCORDANCE LINES FOR "SIMP," "CUCK," "WHITE KNIGHT," AND "FAGGOT" IN THE MANOSPHERE CORPUS (VARIABLE L/R SPAN)

	Subreddit			
1	MRA	Weak, stupid, opportunistic, beta	simp	idiots who are lazy to kick themselves
2	TRP	Any normal bluepill beta	cuck	would shower them with sympathy and say
3	Incels	But i believe some	white knight	blue pilled beta males are all in this thread
4	MGTOW	Some black cock loving	faggot	once said feminism is cancer

Table 6.16. SELECTED CONCORDANCE LINES FOR "CUCK" IN THE MANOSPHERE CORPUS (VARIABLE L/R SPAN)

	Subreddit			
1	MRA	I'm not some green haired liberal	cuck	just trying to have a civil discussion
2	TRP	You fucking	cuck	losers jesus christ you are so pathetic
3	Incels	That's a	cuck	brah
4	MGTOW	So Stop being a	cuck	and instead of coming all angry at me

Table 6.17. SELECTED CONCORDANCE LINES FOR "FAGGOT(S)" IN THE MANOSPHERE CORPUS (VARIABLE L/R SPAN)

	Subreddit			
1	MRA	haha I knew you were a	faggot	
2	TRP	MGTOW are	faggots	There, I said it
3	Incels	Stop saying it like a	faggot	and actually do it
4	MGTOW	Lrn2 history	faggot	This isn't an incel sub

Taking all of this together, we can see the complex hierarchies of masculinity which exist across the manosphere, where masculine status is debated, contentious, and ephemeral and claims to being 'manly' are fraught (see also Connell 2005, 79 for a discussion of the lexical means some heterosexual men and boys are expelled from the circle of masculine legitimacy).

Table 6.18. SELECTED CONCORDANCE LINES FOR "WHITE KNIGHT"
IN THE MANOSPHERE CORPUS (VARIABLE L/R SPAN)

	Subreddit			
1	MRA	one may call him a	white knight	, parasite, soyboy, low T
2	TRP	he was very much a	white knight	beta bordering on martyrdom
3	Incels	The typical	white knight	beta cuck
4	MGTOW	You realize you are the neckbeard	white knight	right?

FEMALE TERMS

The analysis now examines how women are represented in the manosphere corpus, focusing on the use of different terms of reference and how these index evaluative stances about women and femininity.

Female Positive Terms

Explicitly positive identifiers for women are rare, with only a few instances attested in the corpus, including *unicorn*, *princess*, and the acronym *NAWALT* ('not all women are like that'). Nevertheless, these terms are almost always framed negatively. For example, *unicorn* (an attractive, perfect yet nonexistent woman) is characterized as a duplicitous or unfaithful woman, as a fiction or fantasy, or as an unrealistic vision of femininity (Table 6.19).

Princess acts in much the same way, although this term is more likely to collocate with other negative descriptive terms (e.g. *immature*, *worst*, *narcissistic*, *selfish*). These female archetypes are also regularly framed as something to avoid, to blame, or to reject (Table 6.20).

The last term is *NAWALT* ('Not All Women Are Like That'; not attested in /r/ MensRights), usually used in contrast with *AWALT* ('All Women Are Like That'). While this term suggests at least a recognition of heterogeneity and difference among women as a group, the actual usage reflects a very different worldview (Table 6.21).

Like *unicorns*, *NAWALTs* are fictions entertained by men who have yet to see the 'real truth' of women as manipulative, deceitful, and duplicitous. In that sense, *NAWALTs* represent another entry in the dictionary of terms which highlight the prevalence of misogyny within the manosphere.

As the discussion suggests, women are very rarely referred to in positive terms, and even those women who might tick the boxes for acceptable expressions of femininity are typically framed as a naïve and unrepresentative fantasy. To that end, these 'positive' terms are anything but, used primarily to highlight the perception

Table 6.19. SELECTED CONCORDANCE LINES FOR "UNICORN" IN THE MANOSPHERE CORPUS (VARIABLE L/R SPAN)

	Subreddit			
1	MRA	advise men to risk their whole lives based off of a special	unicorn	woman that is unlikely to exist
2	TRP	Their perfect little	unicorn	Turned out to be a donkey
3	TRP	No fucking idea what their	unicorn	gf is doing behind their back
4	Incels	You find a	unicorn	marry it then she fucks your bro
5	Incels	You really think you've found a	unicorn	mate?
6	MGTOW	Stop searching for that	unicorn	bruddah. No such animal exists
7	MGTOW	Any	unicorn	can turn into a viper extremely quickly

Table 6.20. SELECTED CONCORDANCE LINES FOR "PRINCESS" IN THE MANOSPHERE CORPUS (VARIABLE L/R SPAN)

	Subreddit			
1	MRA	these Disney Princess types for years	princess	They're immature and the absolute worst
2	MRA	Yes and those women with	princess	complex are to blame for that
3	TRP	social media is her only life, daddy's little	princess	narcissistic, rude to people lower than her
4	TRP	holding out for their perfect	princess	who'll complete them is staggering
5	Incels	blue pill is the fantasy that every woman is a perfect	princess	and the red pill is the fantasy that every woman is a computer
6	Incels	people like the insecure types or the	princess	that insists on being pampered
7	MGTOW	woman that has those standards has some daddy	princess	complex issues, avoid
8	MGTOW	these worthless lazy selfish unethical	princess	snowflake slut queen bitch whores

that women are never able to meet the unrealistic standards set up for them within the manosphere.

Female Neutral Terms (Generic)

Moving now to the generic neutral terms (Figure 6.6), the first thing to note is that across all four subreddits, *women* is the most common term of reference, followed

Table 6.21. SELECTED CONCORDANCE LINES FOR "NAWALT" IN THE MANOSPHERE CORPUS (VARIABLE L/R SPAN)

	Subreddit			
1	TRP	Stable woman is a	NAWALT	fantasy. Their "instability" is built in and driven by her biology
2	Incels	Keep pushing your	NAWALT	fairy land around in your head
3	MGTOW	the only place where those mythical	NAWALT	unicorns actually exist

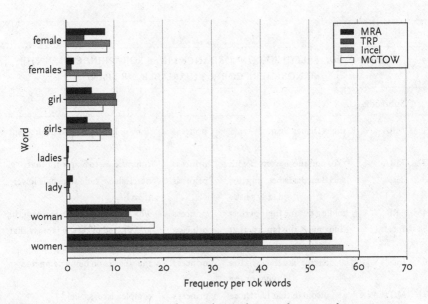

Figure 6.6. Neutral female gendered terms (generic) across the manosphere corpus

by the singular form *woman* at roughly a third of the rate. Other generic terms, such as *female(s)* and *girl(s)*, are used at similar rates, although *girl(s)* is more likely across all of the subreddits, while *females* is primarily used in /r/Incels (a finding discussed later).

One implication is that the widespread use of this noun characterizes women as a collective group rather than as individuals, underlining the notion of women's assumed homogeneity. This ties in with the meanings encoded in *AWALT* and *NAWALT* and their associated philosophies, where women's autonomy and individualism are subordinated to service a worldview of women as mindless drones.

The collocation analysis of *women* also highlights some interesting semantic associations (Table 6.22). In /r/MensRights, for example, the main collocates for *women* include the vocabulary of equal rights (*equal, oppressed, problems, issues, equality*; see also LaViolette and Hogan 2019, 331), *rape* and sexual or physical *violence* toward women (usually dismissing claims of rape prevalence or framing domestic violence as a nongendered issue), the family unit (*children*, although this term also forms part of the phrase 'women are children', itself a negative characterization), and homelessness among women. In /r/TheRedPill, the framing is more directed toward sex and relationships, evidenced though collocates such as *attractive, attracted, fuck,* and *sex*, while women are described as *whores* or *children*. *Hate* also emerges as a collocate, usually as part of challenging claims of misogyny and sexism leveled at members of the subreddit.

In /r/Incels, we see the vocabulary of desirability deployed through terms like *sex, attractive,* and *attracted*, with the last two terms speaking to the view within /r/Incels of a presumed inequity of attraction between men and women. This is further supported by the term *want*, often used in the phrase "Women don't want to sleep/have sex/have anything to do with you." Women are also described as *shallow* who

---

Table 6.22. TOP TWENTY COLLOCATES FOR "WOMEN" IN THE MANOSPHERE CORPUS (RANKED BY LOG-LIKELIHOOD SCORE)

MRA	TRP	Incel	MGTOW
men	men	men	men
rights	women	want	women
women	attractive	just	hate
violence	want	sex	want
equal	just	get	just
just	whores	attractive	get
get	sex	women	think
same	get	talk	good
children	attracted	attracted	know
oppressed	hate	treat	white
victims	say	hate	man
issues	value	shallow	even
feminism	fuck	know	shit
want	love	say	modern
likely	know	think	love
problems	children	different	society
rape	even	actually	same
equality	fucking	man	rights
work	think	care	fuck
homeless	lot	same	western

only *care* about looks or money and do not *care* about personality or character, with /r/Incels members viewing themselves as lacking in the former but enriched by the latter. This culminates in explicit expressions of misogyny through the term *hate* (examples 10–12).

(10) I've seen subhuman women who are literal 3's turn into 6+ with make-up. I fucking hate women and I fucking hate make-up. They shit on men who want to have plastic surgery done, yet they're fucking fake themselves.

(11) I only hate women with the degenerate Western "progressive" mindset.

(12) I use this account to blow off steam on /r/Incels because I hate women and sympathize with those that truly can't improve themselves due to biological problems.

Finally, some discussions in /r/MGTOW are concerned with a general idea of *good women*, while others focus on the negative traits of *white women*, *Western women*, and *modern women* as *sluts*, *selfish*, *silly*, *entitled*, *disgusting*, *brainwashed*, *bitchy*, and *privileged*. As in /r/Incels, *hate* is a main collocate in this subreddit, but here it tends to be used in a similar way as /r/TheRedPill (i.e. rejecting accusations of misogyny), although with an added dimension of indifference.

(13) They don't have to . . . It's like hating babies for crapping their pants. I don't hate women, I'm simply indifferent. I don't bother them or care about them, so why should I hate them?

(14) I hate feminism but I don't hate women. I just don't need them around.

(15) But we don't hate women. The fact is, we don't *care* enough about them to hate them. They're a non-issue as long as we remain unattached (unmarried, no kids) to them.

(16) Most of us don't hate women. We simply do not like what women have to offer in a relationship. We also discuss pitfalls that are common with women. Its part of going our own way.

Taking all of this together, the semantic prosody related to women within each subreddit tends to be primarily negative, with women as the objects of sexual desire, as the target of hate, or portrayed as harmful or damaging (or some combination of these discourses).

Female Neutral Terms (Relational)

For the relational terms (Figure 6.7), women are most likely to be discussed as someone's *mother*, *mom*, or *wife*, with each of these terms being led by /r/MGTOW (in fact, this subreddit leads in use for almost every item, with the exception of *girlfriend(s)*).

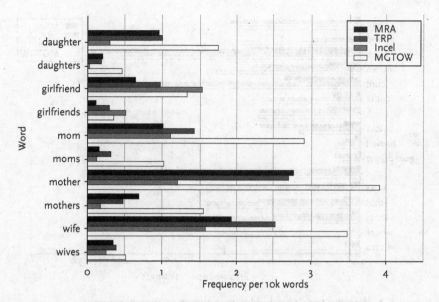

Figure 6.7. Neutral female gendered terms (relational) across the manosphere corpus

For *mother* and *mom*, the most common adjectival premodifier is *single*, reflecting a concern with (a claimed) negative social impact on children (and society more generally) of single motherhood, as well as explicit moralizing about monogamy, the nuclear family, and heteronormativity. The following excerpts from /r/MensRights and /r/TheRedPill are good summaries of these views.

(17) Being raised by a single mother is the single-worst risk factor in the upbringing of a child.

(18) Having 1 dad and mom is optimal for the child to be successful which is why monogamy was established thousands of years ago into culture/society and has worked. Having a single mother raise a child, especially male can result in a feminine man.

The lowest rate of use for each of the relational terms is in /r/Incels, although this subreddit curiously leads in rates of use for *girlfriend(s)*, beating even /r/TheRedPill, where this kind of social positioning might be more expected.

Female Negative Terms

Unlike the negative male terms, negative female terms tend to have a wider distribution across more items and a larger number of terms are likely to be used in each subreddit (Figure 6.8). By way of comparison, negative male terms tend to have more

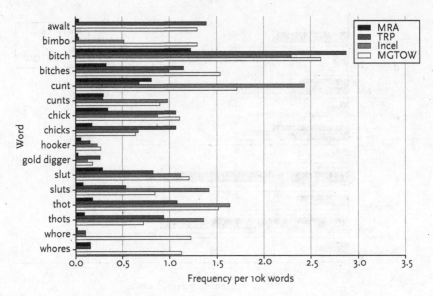

Figure 6.8. Negative female gendered terms across the manosphere corpus

restricted use in specific subreddits (e.g. *beta(s)* in /r/TheRedPill, *chad(s)* and *cuck(s)* in /r/Incels, and *simp(s)* in /r/MGTOW), while more general terms occur at a rate of 0.5 words per 10,000, compared to nearly double the rate for negative female terms (between 1.0 and 1.5 words per 10,000).

Regardless of the rate of use, it is with the negative terms that we see a much more explicit articulation of misogyny and sexism. For example, the most common negative referent in three of the four subreddits is *bitch* (Table 6.23), often premodified with *crazy*, *dumb*, *fat*, *stupid*, and *ugly* (this contrasts with Rüdiger and Dayter's analysis of PUA forum posts, which found a relatively low rate for *bitch*; see Rüdiger and Dayter 2020). Use of *bitch* also tends to be part of a moralistic evaluation of women (usually in relation to committing crimes, false claims of rape, or seeking alimony/spousal maintenance), alongside advocating the use of physical or sexual violence against such women (this is particularly notable in /r/Incels; see also Squirrell 2018).

As Table 6.24 shows, *cunt* follows much the same pattern, while other negative terms play out in much the same way, including well-established insult terms like *bimbo*, *gold digger*, *hooker*, *slut*, and *whore*, which highlight the assumption of women's lack of intelligence, their naivety, their sexual promiscuity, or their interest in men purely for financial gain. Others are relatively newer coinages, such as *thot* ('that hoe over there') or *AWALT* ('All Women Are Like That'), as in examples (19) and (20).

Table 6.23. SELECTED CONCORDANCE LINES FOR "BITCH" IN THE MANOSPHERE CORPUS (VARIABLE L/R SPAN)

	Subreddit			
1	MRA	She was always a crazy	bitch	
2	MRA	I would rather physically destroy a	bitch	than pay her way through life and be dead broke
3	MRA	Dumb fucking fat	bitch	
4	TRP	Even if this worthless	bitch	understood this she'd probably still be ok with it
5	TRP	Chase a check, never chase a	bitch	
6	TRP	If you give a	bitch	an inch, she'll take the whole damn house and everything in it
7	Incels	i don't think so. the	bitch	deserves the rope
8	Incels	That fucking	bitch	deserves to have her head stomped in
9	Incels	give me ONE reason why this fucking	bitch	does not deserve to be gangr4ped
10	MGTOW	my ex cunt	bitch	told me after her last xmas party
11	MGTOW	Dumb	bitch	spread her legs to another man and thinks she has the right to tell him what to do
12	MGTOW	What a cancerous	bitch	she is!

(19) Asian cunts like herself who whore out on instagram would be nothing without their **thot** fakeup and streetwear bullshit and white worship. She even published a book of poems of her thoughts of being a fucking stupid teenager.

(20) **AWALT** doesn't mean that EVERY SINGLE WOMAN is a carbon copy of one another; though there's plenty of basic bitches who are interchangeable for the most part. It does, however, mean that women are governed by a common set of instincts and desires which one can freely observe once he's taken them off the pedestal. Hypergamy, solipsism, lack of accountability, feelz over realz, etc.

These examples also highlight the prevailing view within the manosphere of women as vapid, superficial, unintelligent, insincere, sexually promiscuous, driven by emotions, and lacking in individuality, in contrast to men who are framed as rational, moral, intelligent, distinctive, loyal, and honorable (see also McCrea 2019 for a discussion of the deployment of 'logic' discourse by men). While there is a hierarchy of men and masculinity, there is also a belief that women fall well below the status of men.

As Figure 6.9 shows, some subreddits use unique referential terms. For example, /r/MensRights talks about *feminazis* (a portmanteau of *feminist* and *nazi*) while

Table 6.24. SELECTED CONCORDANCE LINES FOR "CUNT" IN THE MANOSPHERE CORPUS (VARIABLE L/R SPAN)

	Subreddit			
1	MRA	Just means the stupid	cunt	will have less battery to send Instagram and snap chat of her precious little face crying about how it's raining
2	MRA	I hoped that	cunt	is removed from your phone and life
3	MRA	Fuck any cunt	cunt	bitch who complains about only getting 50% custody
4	TRP	Current day, my son being raised by a mentally unstable	cunt	I'm getting calls from the school every other week
5	TRP	waiting for a reply I msg her on FB and called her a	cunt	and to go fuck herself and then blocked her
6	TRP	Forget *her*; one less entitled, dishonest	cunt	in the world is doing all American *men* a favor!
7	Incels	You did the world a favor, showing a	cunt	that her cunt is worthless and ain't getting her shit
8	Incels	Shut up, degenerate	cunt	Go back to tumblr. Your vagina is your only asset and we aren't interested. Women are shit and you're the worst kind
9	Incels	Fucking slut	cunt	with her peace symbol hand gestures
10	MGTOW	you are a feminist	cunt	your opinions about MGTOW are mute
11	MGTOW	Any woman says she loves children she is a lying	cunt	
12	MGTOW	now she is playing the victim poor little	cunt	ass bitch

/r/TheRedPill talks about women as *hamsters* or having *hamsters* (or "the thought processes used by women to turn bad behavior and bad decisions into acceptable ones to herself and her friends," Hansen 2011).

The concordance lines (Table 6.25) further demonstrate the kind of harmful and sexist perspectives bound up with these terms. It is in /r/Incels, however, where we see another level of malice through its insult terms, including *femoid*[9] (a portmanteau of *female* and *humanoid*), *roastie* (a term for a sexually active woman

9. *Fem** is a productive stem in /r/Incels, generating other insult terms such as *femloids*, *femorrhoid*, *femshits*, and *femgremlin*.

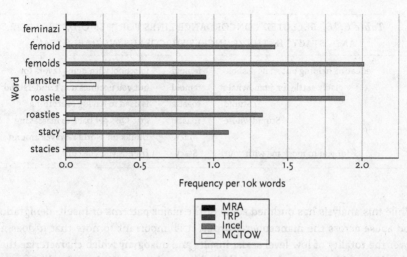

Figure 6.9. Negative female gendered terms across the manosphere corpus used in fewer than three subreddits

---

Table 6.25. SELECTED CONCORDANCE LINES FOR "FEMINAZI" AND "HAMSTER" IN THE /R/MENSRIGHTS AND /R/THEREDPILL SUBCORPORA (VARIABLE L/R SPAN)

	Subreddit			
1	MRA	Go back to 2xchromasomes	feminazi	
2	MRA	If you research them even a little and aren't a	feminazi	shill, you'll reach the same conclusion
3	MRA	you will never see your average idiotic	feminazi	say that despite claiming they want equality for both men and women
4	TRP	I always enjoy it when a	hamster	thinks she can hop back on the cock carousel as a 30+ single mother living off hubby's income
5	TRP	it still makes you, and every other feminist a hypocritical	hamster	bitch
6	TRP	kind of bullshit did her	hamster	come up with

---

whose vagina resembles roast beef; see Squirrell 2018) and *stacy/ies* (a proto-typically sexually attractive, yet superficial, woman; see Jennings 2018). As might be expected, all of these terms are exclusively negative, with the primary effect of dehumanizing women. This also explains the higher use of *females* in this subreddit, where women are discussed in almost a detached and technical manner, furthering this dehumanizing effect (Table 6.26).

Table 6.26. SELECTED CONCORDANCE LINES FOR "FEMOID," "ROASTIE," AND "STACY" IN THE /R/INCELS SUBCORPUS (VARIABLE SPAN)

1	equating helping out some asshole	femoid	in school with doing favors for
2	gladly settle for a landwhale	femoid	but you normies don't understand
3	Stupid	roastie	is used to having everything
4	Stupid whore	roastie	gtfo QB's get back to massaging
5		Stacy	thinks the world revolves around
6	for you to mock me with your	Stacy	friends you vile cunt

While this analysis has outlined some of the major patterns of insult, denigration, and abuse across the manosphere corpus, it is important to note that it does not cover the totality of low-level sexist insults and misogyny which characterize these subreddits. Additional analyses would highlight other means through which women are negatively represented and evaluated, all of which work together to foster an undercurrent of aggression, hostility, and antagonism. Nor does the analysis examine how feminism and feminists are represented and evaluated, although as might be expected, it treads much the same path as the antiwomen sentiment outlined so far. Ultimately, what is constructed in these negative terms is an unfavorable view of women, replete with stereotypes about women as sexually promiscuous, morally damaged, manipulative, and untrustworthy.

CONCLUSION

As the analysis has shown, gender is incredibly salient in the manosphere. But perhaps more important is that members of the manosphere are more likely to center their discussions on women than on men, with the general pattern that *women* are talked about more than *men* in almost every subreddit (Figure 6.10). The same pattern holds for other pairs of gendered referents, including *woman/man*, *female(s)/male(s)*, and *female/male*. In fact, /r/MensRights is the only subreddit which does not follow this pattern.

In their comparison of /r/MensRights and /r/MensLib, LaViolette and Hogan (2019, 330–331) suggest that the "advanced use of *she* and *her* [in /r/MensRights] points to an androcentric discourse which places more attention on the actions of women than of men." My analysis in this chapter suggests that such a claim could potentially be expanded to other subreddits within the scope of the manosphere. One corollary of this is that the manosphere (or at least the subreddits considered in this analysis) is less a space for talk *about* men and more a space for men to express their anger, misogyny, and sexism toward women. As much as these spaces might claim to be nonmisogynistic, it is difficult to reconcile this with the analysis presented.

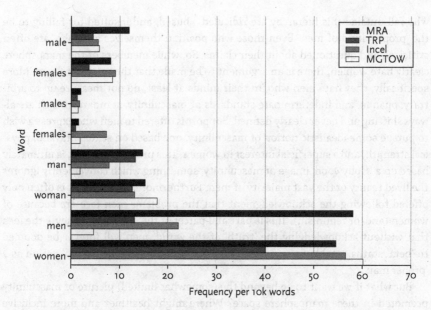

Figure 6.10. Comparison of male and female referents across the manosphere corpus

In addition to reflecting general antiwomen sentiment, this communal denigration of women also facilitates homosocial male bonding (Sedgwick 1985; Bird 1996; Kiesling 2005). As noted previously, one precondition of belonging to a group is the observance of a set of communal beliefs. The use of positive in-group markers such as *brother* suggest that men value this sense of communal belonging (Marche 2016), but the use of negative referent terms for women clearly demonstrates an alignment with the dominant manosphere ideologies. Moreover, the policing of men who do not follow this antiwomen agenda, marked through terms like *white knight*, *simp* and so on, suggests that men who do not abide by these common values, even if those values are marked by sexism and misogyny, are censured and held up for public criticism (Jones, Trott, and Wright 2019, 1916). This kind of masculine policing consequently has implications for broader gender relations and how men can act as allies in combating online sexist discourse. For example, Ging (2017, 653) notes that if women cannot "articulate gender-political opinion online without fear of hate speech or harassment, the outlook for gender equality and democracy generally is bleak" (see also Siapera 2019, 21). I would suggest that we can go even further to argue that the manosphere (and other toxic technocultures) also exerts a "chilling effect" on men, since attempts at challenging sexist and misogynistic behavior in these spaces are often met with vitriolic resistance.

Additionally, although the manosphere claims to be a space where men support, advise, and guide one another, particularly for specific 'male-related' problems, there is evidence to suggest that there is only a small margin of 'acceptable' constellations of masculinity. Not only are masculinities viewed in a hierarchical way, but men who fall outside this hierarchy are ridiculed, abused, and insulted for failing to be the 'proper' kind of men. Even those who position themselves as 'alpha' are often criticized and questioned about their claims. So, while members of the manosphere clearly hate women, there is an argument to be made that they also hate men. More specifically, they hate men who, in their minds at least, do not measure up to arbitrary, opaque, and indeterminate standards of masculinity, standards which are always shifting and never clearly defined. Support is offered to men who express a wish to pursue some idealistic notion of masculinity, one based on sexual bravado, physical strength, and a superficial interest in women. This project, however, is ultimately based on a 'Hollywood' image of masculinity, something which conveniently ignores the lived reality of the vast majority of men. Furthermore, this support is often only offered following the acknowledgment that the problems men face are because of women (and/or feminism). This is part and parcel of the 'red pill' journey—the idea that without acknowledging the 'truth' of the world, men will forever be doomed to 'beta' status, unable to enjoy the riches which come with self-actualization as a 'proper man'.

But what if we want to go beyond the (somewhat limited) picture of masculinity promoted in these manosphere space? Where might healthier and more inclusive ideas about masculinity be found? What do these masculinities look like? And what role does language play in such configurations? To date, there has been limited attention in language and masculinities studies on what might be more broadly termed 'positive masculinities', so it is to these issues the next chapter turns.

CHAPTER 7

Positive Masculinity and *Brooklyn Nine-Nine*

Reconfiguring Dominant Gender Tropes in Television Comedy

INTRODUCTION

The chapters so far have concentrated on how language is implicated in the construction, promotion, and maintenance of problematic, extreme, and toxic masculinities. While these have been useful in sketching out underlying discourses of exclusion and marginalization, they overlook how hegemonic ideas of 'being a man' are reconfigured and challenged in contemporary society.

To that end, this chapter focuses on 'positive masculinities' and explores how men are being encouraged to pursue healthier conceptualizations of masculinity, where the kinds of 'toxic' practices discussed in previous chapters are not framed as desirable or attractive. Given the negative implications of toxic and extreme substantiations of masculine practice, in terms of health, self-image, and the potential harm to others, opening up a space for a more positive and inclusive sense of masculine identity based on emotional vulnerability, empathy, cooperation, compassion, and a disavowal of violence, is an important social justice project (see also Winton 2018).

The first part of the chapter reviews the concept of 'positive masculinity', examining how a range of organizations encourage men to reflect on, and challenge, traditional notions of masculinity. Indeed, there appears to be more willingness to expand the definitions of what 'being a man' entails, with charities like *A Band of Brothers*, *Good Lad Workshop*, *Beyond Equality*, and *MenCare* part of a growing movement to engage more men (especially young men) in questioning hegemonic conceptualizations of masculinity (Yogachandra 2014; Allegretti 2021). Similarly, the *Campaign Against Living Miserably* (CALM) and *Movember*[1] projects promote advocacy for men's health

---

1. Founded in 2003 by Travis Garone and Luke Slattery, *Movember* raises money for men's health, including testicular cancer, mental health, and suicide prevention, based on

Language and Mediated Masculinities. Robert Lawson, Oxford University Press. © Oxford University Press 2023.
DOI: 10.1093/oso/9780190081041.003.0007

issues, including male depression, anxiety, suicide, prostate/testicular cancer, and more. In doing so, these charities facilitate conversations about what it is to be a man and how a more positive way of enacting a masculine identity might be fostered, one less reliant on domination, hierarchy, violence, and control.

Since the media plays a key part in setting out cultural scripts and expectations of masculinity (and of gender more broadly; Stamou, Maroniti, and Dinas 2012; Queen 2012; Fägersten and Sveen 2016; Lawson and Lutzky 2016; Bednarek 2018), the second part of the chapter presents an analysis of the television comedy show *Brooklyn Nine-Nine* to examine how men use language to connect with others, build relationships, and demonstrate affiliation with friends and loved ones, subsequently subverting and destabilizing hegemonic forms of masculinity. Given that the intersection of language, masculinity, and television is a somewhat unexplored area, this chapter is important in improving our understanding of the role the media plays in promoting alternative constructions of masculinity.

WHAT IS POSITIVE MASCULINITY?

Although the first attempt at formalizing 'positive masculinity' can be traced back to the field of psychology and the introduction of Bem's Sex-Role Inventory (Bem 1974), the use of the term in this chapter has more in common with the approach set out in the early stages of the mythopoetic men's movement. In this framework, Bliss and his contemporaries advocated for men to engage in a range of male-positive behaviors, with Bliss (1987) arguing that "if men were to place greater value on their relationships with other men, spend more time with children, have a better connection to nature, work with women for equality, and take better care of their bodies, society as a whole would almost certainly be transformed for the better." As Boise (2019, 147) points out, however, the mythopoetic men's movement was rooted in a strong antifeminist position and the fact that "rather than seeking transformation, they adopted strongly antifeminist politics and overtly reactionary notions of a return [of] gender roles through promoting a vision of the 'benevolent patriarch' as the (nuclear) family's economic and spiritual provider." In a similar vein, Cross (2008, 140) argues that "The mythopoetic men's movement looked for liberation from 'toxic' masculinity not in gender equality but in replacing the bourgeois man of constraint and competition with a myth of the male war band." Thus, the pursuit of positive masculinity, at least in mythopoetic terms, was at the expense of broader systems of gender equality and inclusion.

As noted in previous chapters, the mythopoetic men's movement stalled somewhat in the 1990s, but interest in gender roles and men's psychology kept the idea of positive masculinity forefront in the minds of researchers and activists. O'Neil (2010) offers a useful summary of the crossover between the psychology of masculinity, mental health, and some of the hallmarks of the mythopoetic men's movement,

the 'challenge' of growing a moustache in November (hence the name of the charity).

noting that "operationalized aspects of masculinity constructs predict the hazards of being male. The male gender role is dangerous to men's emotional and interpersonal health" (O'Neil 2010, 102; see also O'Neil 2012; Gerdes and Levant 2018). Making much the same argument, Englar-Carlson and Kiselica (2013, 400) draw attention to the fact that a "consistent [research] finding has been a strong association between rigid and restrictive adherence to traditional masculinity and negative health outcomes among men, such as a decreased ability to express emotions and to seek help for both physical and mental health concern." They go on to observe that while much of the extant research on men and masculinities argues that rigid gender norms underlie many of the negative practices associated with men, such as violence, detached fathering, homophobia, and misogyny, there has been limited attention paid to male strengths and empowerment. Advancing what they term the "Positive Psychology/Positive Masculinity Model" (PPPM), Englar-Carlson and Kiselica (2013, 401) define positive masculinity as "the adaptive character strengths, emotions, and virtues of men that promote well-being and resiliency in self and others," moving away from "solely what is wrong with men to identifying the qualities that empower men to improve themselves and society."

In the course of their article (as well as in previous work, e.g. Kiselica and Englar-Carlson 2010), they outline ten "traditionally orientated strengths of men"—male relational style, male ways of caring, self-reliance, generative fathering, fraternal organizations of service, worker-provider tradition, male courage, daring and risk-taking, humor, and heroism (Englar-Carlson and Kiselica 2013, 402; see also Vinopal 2019). While it is worthwhile questioning the extent to which these traits are specifically 'masculine' (a point I return to later), they nevertheless underpin many of the existing cultural discourses about positive practices related to masculinity. Englar-Carlson, Kiselica, O'Neil and others take the view that the development of PPPM, rooted as it is in a strength-based approach, is an important step in moving away from a narrative that men and boys are "defective and damaged, need to be fixed, and are at fault for the problems they bring to counseling" (Englar-Carlson and Kiselica 2013, 401). Proponents of positive masculinity ultimately argue for an approach which encourages men to be emotionally open, self-reflective, and willing to discuss their problems in order to change behavior (see also Davies, Shen-Miller, and Isacco 2010, and Lomas et al. 2016 for discussions of 'possible masculinities' and the therapeutic applications of the model in the psychological treatment of men).

The importance of fostering a sense of positive masculinity has also been of concern to those working outside psychology and the social sciences. Since the early 2000s, a number of charities and organizations have attempted to put into practice some of the insights drawn from psychology and studies about healthier substantiations of masculinity.[2] CALM's mission statement, for example, notes that

---

2. It is important to note that several organizations which claim to represent men's issues operate as part of the MRA movement. For example, A Voice for Men (founded by Paul Elam in 2009) states in its mission statement that it aims to "provide education and encouragement to men and boys; to lift them above the din of misandry, to reject the unhealthy demands of gynocentrism in all its forms, and to promote their mental,

"We challenge boring male stereotypes and encourage positive behavioural change and help-seeking behaviour, using cultural touch points like art, music, sport and comedy" (CALM n.d.). In recent years, the charity has organized campaigns focused on male mental health and suicide prevention, including #Project84 and #DontBottleItUp (see Jordan 2019 for a discussion of gender ideologies on the *CALM* website). Similarly, charities such as *A Call to Men, A Band of Brothers, The Good Men Project, ManKind, MenCare, Beyond Equality, The ManCave Project*, and *The Good Lad Initiative* all advocate for forms of masculinity which reject toxic, problematic, or violent practices and encourage men to adopt a different set of masculine gender norms based on openness, connection, and inclusion (see Godwin 2018 and Wade 2018 for discussions of the "Men's Movement 2.0" and men's health charities respectively). Not only do these programmes offer help to men who might suffer from self-destructive behavior, they also facilitate violence reduction against women and girls, overwhelmingly the target of male sexual, physical, and domestic abuse (Connell 2003; Pease 2008; Flood 2008; Baird 2012; Hoang, Quach, and Tran 2013; Hall 2019). As O'Neil (2010, 105) suggests,

> Positive masculinity is about changing the dialogue to what men can strive for that transcends the sexist socialization they have experienced. Many men remain confused about who they are or who they should become in terms of gender roles. Therefore, positive-healthy masculinity can be a vehicle to mediate the essentialist and destructive stereotypes that cause much unnecessary suffering for men, women, and children.

At the heart of many of the charities which promote positive masculinities is how other men can act as constructive role models for one another, sharing their experiences and working as agents of change (Kohn 2018; Ruiz 2018). While this taps into some of the processes previously explored in the mythopoetic men's movement, a number of scholars have argued that men acting as role models for other men and boys is an important aspect of cultural learning. For example, Veissière (2018) suggests that while the importance of same-sex role models has been recognized for women and girls (e.g. Lockwood 2006; Young et al. 2013), the same cannot be said for men and boys. He goes on to argue that instead, "Rites of boyhood and manhood, such as the ones cultivated in fraternities and athletic cultures, are now overly associated with the 'toxic' archetypes. Those who promote the importance of initiation into manhood . . . are typically dismissed as quack mystics, misogynists or 'ALT right' conservatives." Positive masculinity charities, on the other hand, believe that rites of initiation can be affirming experiences and that they do not need to rely on ritual humiliation, degradation, or physical risk (see Bohler 2013; Poling 2013).

physical and financial well-being without compromise or apology" (Elam 2010). Perhaps best known for declaring October to be 'Bash a Violent Bitch month', *AVFM* has since been categorized as a male supremacist hate group by the Southern Poverty Law Center (Southern Poverty Law Center 2021; see also Gotell and Dutton 2016; White 2019).

The importance of role models is also reflected in the fact that some prominent male celebrities are now promoting positive masculinity as something to which men should aspire (cf. Baldoni 2017; Entenmen 2017; Howes 2017; Webb 2017). Similarly, businesses like Harry's Barbers (New York) share positive examples of male behavior through their social media outlets (e.g. Harry's 2018), while even online comics are starting to highlight how men can act as positive role models, with the work of artist Christopher Grady a good example (Figure 7.1; see also Bologna 2017).

Grady's comic, replete with the stereotypical imagery of tough masculinity (folded arms, no smiling), provides a light-hearted subversion of the well-worn cultural tropes of the male gaze and objectification of women, showing how fathers can be better teachers and role models for their sons.

Taking all of this together, there appears to be a willingness to challenge some of the dominant, destructive, and stereotypical notions of masculinity and manhood, opening up a critical space for alternative conceptualizations of what it is to be a man

Figure 7.1. 'Real'. Reproduced by permission from: Christopher O'Grady, *Lunarbaboon*, http://www.lunarbaboon.com/comics/real.html

(see Deschenes 2016; Gilpin and Proulx 2018 for examples of teaching resources about positive masculinity). As O'Neil (2010, 105) argues, "Positive-healthy masculinity is needed if men are truly going to be able [to] deconstruct their gender roles, understand essentialism, regain their human potential, and understand how sexism is the real form of violence that causes their pain and sucks out their passion for living."

That said, there exists a degree of criticality toward the term 'positive masculinity' and what it encompasses. The first issue is that there is, of course, nothing inherently 'male' about characteristics such as courage, humor, or self-reliance, so the evocation of positively masculine traits could be considered something of a misnomer. As Englar-Carlson and Kiselica (2013, 402) point out, however, "Boys and men. . . are socialized to develop and demonstrate these positive qualities and behaviors, which are then modeled and then passed down in male-particular ways." Thus, it is important to acknowledge that even though positive masculine traits are not exclusively masculine, they are often coded as masculine by wider society. The second concern with a focus on positive masculinity is the danger that it minimizes the negative dimensions of hierarchy, dominance, and inequality. While this is certainly an issue, Hall (2019, 109) argues that examining both the positive and the negative sides of masculinity is necessary to develop a comprehensive understanding of what masculinity entails in the twenty-first century (see also Seager and Barry 2019).

LANGUAGE, MASCULINITIES, AND TELEVISION

As noted previously, the media plays a key part in setting out cultural scripts and expectations of masculinity, with televised media arguably one of the most pervasive formats for the reproduction, maintenance, and reconfiguration of masculinities. To date, however, very few researchers examining mediated masculinities have integrated linguistic approaches into their analytical accounts. Given that linguistic practice is one of the primary means through which gender identity is constructed, this is a surprising gap in the literature. To that end, the chapter now turns to discuss why television shows are useful sites for investigating masculinities from a linguistic perspective (see also Bednarek 2018, 5 for a discussion of the broader importance of television shows in linguistics).

First, there are a number of practical reasons why linguists might use television as a source of language data. For instance, the overall quality of the data is (normally) excellent, removing the disfluencies of overlaps, interruptions, and false starts which typify everyday talk (although television data has its limitations and cannot be taken as representative of everyday speech). Fägersten (2016, 3) proposes that television dialogue represents "a communicative ideal: all participants have, potentially, equal opportunity to speak; conversational contributions are well formed, smoothly delivered, and (usually) impeccably timed; there are rarely any pauses, hesitations, interruptions, or even external disruptions; and instances of misspeaking, mishearing, or misunderstanding are unusual." Television shows are also readily available through either live streaming or 'on-demand' services (BBC iPlayer, Netflix, Amazon Prime, Hulu, YouTube), meaning that data is (relatively) easy to access. In terms of data preparation, a number of sites host transcripts, eliminating the time and expense needed for transcription. And because television shows are in the public domain, there are usually no ethical issues in working with such data.

Second, although linguists tend to prioritize the language dimension, television shows are inherently multimodal, combining both audio and visual resources for the purposes of characterization, world-building, and storytelling. Since communication is not simply based on the spoken (or written) channel, attending to the multilayered semiotics of television allows us to develop a more comprehensive picture of how meaning-making happens (van Leeuwen 2014, 288; see also van Leeuwen 2004).

Third, television shows are not static reflections of society, but are part of its ideological fabric. Discussing the social role of movies, Giroux (2001, 6) notes that "A far cry from simple entertainment. . . films function as public pedagogies by articulating knowledge to effects, purposely attempting to influence how and what knowledge and identities can be produced within a limited range of social relations." It is not difficult to extend Giroux's point to the broader scope of televised media, where documentaries, news reports, comedy shows, dramas, and adverts present a particular picture of the world and the characters who inhabit it. Television is not value neutral but instead simultaneously shapes (and is shaped by) the world. As Bednarek (2018, 1) points out, "We can speak of a culture-media dialectic, where TV dialogue both constructs and reflects cultures and their ideologies. Dialogue is hence an important source of information about language and society" (see also Kellner 2011; Holtzman and Sharpe 2014). Holtzman and Sharpe (2014, xx) make an astute observation when they say that "much of our sense of personal and group identity, our beliefs about what is 'normal', and our understanding of individuals and groups that are different from us is created and/or reinforced by the pervasive entertainment media culture'. Or, as Kellner (2020, 7) puts it, "radio, television, film, and other products of the cultural industries provide the models of what it means to be male or female, successful or a failure, powerful or powerless. Media culture helps shape the prevalent view of the world and deepest values: it defines what is good or bad, positive or negative, moral or evil."

Four, analyzing television shows can uncover implicit gender ideologies, revealing how contemporary substantiations of masculinity (and femininity) are promoted and normalized. As Connell (2005, 252) points out, "Heterosexuality, masculine authority and feminine nurturance are made normative by the dominant media story-lines and entertainment genres, providing reassurance both for the alienated wage-earner and the bored housewife with children." In one of the earliest analyses of television and the policing of masculinity, Buckingham (1993) discusses how television shows become a proxy for 'doing' masculinity for the boys in his fieldwork, from stated preferences and dislikes of particular television characters and shows to the development of male banter and homosocial bonding (see also Craig 1992 for one of the first edited volumes on masculinities and the media, including comic books, music, movies, and sports).

A variety of recent work in media studies has examined how masculinities are represented in television shows and movies (see Hansen-Miller and Gill 2011; Shary 2012; Scharrer and Blackburn 2018; Cuklanz and Erol 2021). For example, Feasey (2008) argues that the investigation of "[televised] masculinities is crucial, not because such representations are an accurate reflection of reality, but rather, because they have the power and scope to foreground culturally accepted social relations, define sexual norms and provide 'common-sense' understandings about male identity for the contemporary audience." Similarly, Lotz (2014) discusses how men and masculinities are presented in a variety of American television shows, including *Scrubs*, *Entourage*, *Nip/Tuck*, *The Sopranos*, *Breaking Bad*, *Dexter*, and many more, asking "what characteristics do these series that mediate on the contemporary condition of being a man attribute to 'good' men?" (Lotz 2014, 5). As Lotz (2014, 8) goes on to remind us, "television storytelling has . . . performed significant ideological work by consistently supporting some behaviors, traits, and beliefs among the male characters it constructs as heroic or admirable, while denigrating others." Moss (2012, x) makes a similar point that "the media is enormously powerful in conveying accepted and acceptable models of masculinity." Taking all of these factors together, then, television comes to be a useful locale for examining the nexus of language and masculinity.

MASCULINITIES IN *BROOKLYN NINE-NINE*

Brooklyn Nine-Nine is a police procedural comedy television show which premiered on 17th September 2013 and finished its eighth and final season in September 2021.[3] The show follows Detective Jake Peralta (played by Andy Samberg) and the day-to-day goings-on of Brooklyn's (fictional) 99th police precinct, featuring a recurring cast of characters, including Captain Raymond Holt (Andre Braugher), Detective Charles Boyle (Joe Lo Truglio), Sergeant Terry Jeffords (Terry Crews), Detective Michael Hitchcock (Dirk Blocker), Detective Norm Scully (Joel McKinnon Miller), Sergeant Amy Santiago (Melissa Fumero), Detective Rosa Diaz (Stephanie Beatriz), and administrator Gina Linetti (Chelsea Peretti). *Brooklyn Nine-Nine* has been acclaimed[4] by critics and viewers for its diverse cast (Samberg and Truglio are White, Braugher and Jeffords are Black, and Beatriz and Fumero are Latina; see Scharrer 2012 for a discussion of ethnic diversity in police television shows), its humor and its representation of serious issues, including parenthood, workplace sexism, family dynamics,

---

3. Each episode is written by different people over the course of the show, including Dan Goor, Justin Noble, Laura McCreary, and Tricia McAlpin, so there may be individual stylistic idiosyncrasies in the dialogue as a result of this. This is an avenue for future research and is not considered here.

4. It is also worthwhile adding that there have also been a number of criticisms leveled at the show, particularly in terms of it being cop propaganda (or 'copaganda') and presenting police officers and the criminal justice system in a positive light (Jackson 2020; Martin 2020).

institutional racism, representations of LGBTQ + people, friendship, dating, and the pressures of police work, leading to a series of Golden Globe Awards, Emmy Awards, and Critics' Choice Awards (Johnson 2015; Jacobsen 2018).

Perhaps one of the show's most notable features is its representation of contemporary masculinities and how it subverts many of the cultural tropes of police masculinity popularized in movies like *Die Hard*, *Rush Hour*, *Lethal Weapon*, and *Bad Boys*, as well as shows like *NCIS*, *The Wire*, and *The Shield*. Briefly, these tropes include physical strength, toughness, emotional stoicism, quick wit, inventiveness, risk-taking, and macho posturing. In *Brooklyn Nine-Nine*, Peralta, in particular, venerates these tropes and regularly positions himself as the prototypically tough police detective. As VanArendonk (2018) notes,

> Peralta loves the idea of the bad-boy lone wolf, the masculine superhero who saves his friends by being his own man. He loves John McClane and the *Rush Hour* movies. He loves wearing leather jackets, and code names, and impressive cases, and he begins the series as a dude who would love nothing more than to prove his colleagues wrong while also saving the day.

As the show unfolds, however, Peralta and the other male characters deconstruct these tropes and engage with a broader conceptualization of masculinity, one which is more closely aligned with the positive masculinities framework. This reconfiguration of masculinity has been regularly cited as one of the more progressive characteristics of the show. Gor (2018) argues that "the show [manages] to address poignant issues such as toxic masculinity and queer representation," while Johnson (2015) suggests that a major strength of the show is its ability to break stereotypes based on ethnicity, gender, and sexuality. The character of Sergeant Terry Jeffords, for example, has "all the qualities of the traditional 'Alpha-male'. He's strong, built out of pure muscle, is a high-ranking leader, and has no problem raising his voice to get a job done when the time calls for it. On the surface, he's a walking definition of masculinity" (Ziegler 2019). Nevertheless, he also displays emotional vulnerability, openness, and a caring side to his friends and his family, while also unashamedly sharing his love for fashion and dealing with serious topics such as his experiences of racial profiling. Similarly, Captain Holt is a gay Black man working in the staunchly heteronormative world of policing who has to fight against institutionalized racism and homophobia over the course of his career. But he is also a character who remains a strong, positive, and charismatic leader secure in his own sense of masculine identity (see Simpson 2015; Stolworthy 2017; VanArendonk 2018).

This more nuanced representation of masculinities also holds true for the characters Peralta and Boyle, both of whom demonstrate empathy, caring, and sensitivity throughout the show, but are also able to be tough and decisive when needed. Peralta, for example, is down-to-earth, approachable, kind, and in touch with his emotions, yet he also has his flaws and struggles with the fact that his father abandoned him as a child (an inversion of the absent Black father narrative device; Gor 2018).

Boyle also subverts a number of hegemonic masculine stereotypes, through his regular displays of affection for his friends, the importance of his family, his interest in unconventional cooking, and his sometimes overly familiar gifts to others. But he also demonstrates bravery (taking a bullet for one of his coworkers), loyalty, and commitment to his job. Importantly, none of these alternative representations of masculinity are ever the target of cheap jokes at the characters' expense. For example, Boyle's loyalty to (and occasional hero worship of) Peralta is never framed as pathological, deficient, or unseemly, while the struggles of Jeffords and Holt are never belittled. Ultimately, the male characters of *Brooklyn Nine-Nine* are arguably more rounded than many of the representations of police masculinities found elsewhere on television (see Scharrer 2012). As Ari (2018) notes, "It seems television is on a trajectory toward progressive and healthy depictions of men, exemplified by *Brooklyn Nine-Nine*" (see also George 2016; Leighton-Dore 2019).

Since friendship is an important aspect in men's emotional stability and overall mental health (hooks 2004; Magrath and Scoats 2019), it is perhaps no surprise that *Brooklyn Nine-Nine* also explores how men establish homosocial relationships. As Gor (2018) puts it, "The men of *Brooklyn Nine-Nine* are friends all through the mundane to the life-shifting things. We see it in Jake babysitting Terry's twins or Jake offering to spend time with Holt when he's feeling lonely because his husband is out of the country. And Charles, Jake's best friend, would do anything for Jake. Anything. Especially if it's embarrassing." The friendship between Peralta and Boyle, which has been described as a 'bromance' (that is, a personal relationship between heterosexual male friends which is usually intimate, nonsexual, and emotionally expressive; Robinson, White, and Anderson 2017) deconstructs many of the tropes surrounding the depiction of male friendships on television. Their willingness to build a relationship based on emotional disclosure and mutual affection, rather than disparaging banter, put-downs, and taboo insults, has been commended as a progressive representation of male friendship (although see Cahuasqui 2020 for an alternative view).

Even the actors themselves have talked about the ways in which masculinity has been reconfigured on *Brooklyn Nine-Nine*. For example, speaking about his character Boyle, Joe Lo Truglio commented that "it's important to show that adoration does not have to be a weakness, especially with straight men to other straight men. And I love that. The characters have never shied away from Boyle's enthusiasm for friendship and connection and it's a testament to their courage" (in Mullen 2019), while Crews[5] has praised the show for opening up different kinds of masculinity to a wider audience (Bandyopadhyay 2019). The show moves past the representation of men as violent, angry, hapless, bumbling, foolish, inept, and emotionally bereft, a caricature most often captured in older television sitcoms and police/cop shows.

5. Terry Crews is a vocal critic of toxic masculinity and has spoken out against male and female sexual abuse, testifying before the Senate Judiciary Committee in 2018 for the Sexual Assault Survivors' Bill of Rights (Parker 2018; Giorgis 2018; Vagianos 2018). He has also written about positive masculinity and has been an advocate for sexual abuse survivors (Crews 2014).

This more inclusive representation of masculinities has also been recognized by viewers, as the following quotes from the *Brooklyn Nine-Nine* fans' subreddit suggest:

(1) Think back to 2005–2008 ish. Who was the face of sitcoms then, the person that men were looking up to whether they realized it or not? Barney Stinson— a disgusting character who romanticized degrading women, toxic masculinity, etc. He was so engrained into bro culture for so many years. Who's the face of them now? Jake fucking Peralta, who's pretty much the opposite. He still manages to be cool and likeable, but without being sexist and horrible. In fact, he goes so far in the other direction. Kids who grow up watching Brooklyn 99 are gonna be so much better off tbh, I love the examples it sets.

(2) The show proves to young boys that they can still be a man, and not be overly aggressive, possessive, entitled, never-compromising—these are the trademarks of toxic masculinity. It's the natural and positive traits of masculinity—emotional strength and solidarity, generosity toward the fellow man with what one could spare, commitment to principles, introspective thought on the self to better improve, supportive without stifling.

While the present discussion does not seek to measure the directionality of influence on viewers in terms of gender norms and conventions, a variety of work has argued that such an influence does exist. For example, Scharrer and Blackburn (2018, 170) point out that "there is evidence that the cultural environment provided by television storytelling within particular genres is associated with emerging adult viewers' conceptions of what masculine gender roles should entail," ultimately suggesting that television has the potential to shape viewers' understandings of gender stereotypes and masculine gender roles. Whether or not television shows have an effect on how viewers think about gender is, to some extent, beside the point. Representation matters and writing characters who embody a wider scope of positive masculine traits and practices can only be a good thing.

DATA AND CORPUS CONSTRUCTION

For this chapter, six seasons of *Brooklyn Nine-Nine* (totaling 130 episodes or approximately 3,000 minutes) were manually collected from an online script repository. For each script, only the actual text for each character was included, with no information about which character was saying which line. Consequently, it was necessary to review each episode and include line-by-line attribution. Following this, all scripts were checked for accuracy, although features such as overlap, interruption, in/out-breath, and so on were not included since they were not relevant to the analysis.

All the scripts were transformed into eXtensible Markup Language (XML) format, using the XTranscript tool (Gee 2020), which converts transcripts into a machine-readable hierarchical network structure, making "XML documents exhaustively searchable and therefore useful for linguistic research" (Rüehlemann and Gee 2017, 276). To that end, XML transcripts contain 'tags' with content between them, indicating a variety of metadata about the transcribed text that can be queried using specific software tools (outlined in more detail in the next section). For example, in Excerpt 7.1, the element <u> contains more information about each turn through the attributes "who" and "n," which refer to the speaker of the turn and the cumulative number of turns in the transcript respectively.

<u who="JAKE" n="1">

This job is eating me alive. I can't breathe anymore. I spent all these years trying to be the good guy, the man in the white hat. I'm not becoming like them. I am them. </u>

<u who="AMY" n="2">

Hey! What are you doing, weirdo? </u>

<u who="JAKE" n="3">

I'm doing the best speech from Donnie Brasco. Or actually, ten of me are doing the best speech from Donnie Brasco. What's up?

Excerpt 7.1. Example of XML transcript from Season 1, Episode 1

XML offers a number of advantages for the quantitative analyses of transcribed data. For example, while it is possible to quantify by hand the number of words a speaker produces in a conversation, this is time-consuming and error prone, especially for larger corpora. In contrast, XML tags allow for much quicker analysis compared to conventional approaches. In the context of 'big data' frameworks, the speed, reliability, and replicability of XML methods are major benefits. Furthermore, XML tags can be extended to include features such as overlap, latching, pauses, speed, intonation, and more that might be of analytical interest.

Table 7.1 describes the *Brooklyn Nine-Nine* corpus (*B99* corpus hereafter), detailing the number of episodes in each season, when each season first aired, each season's overall word count, and the total number of words in the corpus. As can be seen from this overview, the word count gets progressively larger season-by-season and reduces significantly in Season 6. This is because FOX canceled the show after

Table 7.1. OVERVIEW OF *BROOKLYN NINE-NINE* CORPUS BY SEASON

	Number of episodes	First aired	Number of words
Season 1	22	September 17th 2013	86,538
Season 2	23	September 28th 2014	93,306
Season 3	23	September 27th 2015	94,325
Season 4	22	September 20th 2016	97,542
Season 5	22	September 26th 2017	103,099
Season 6	18	January 10th 2019	87,115
			561,925

Season 5, only for NBC to pick it up in 2018. This deal was originally for a thirteen episode run, but NBC expanded the season to eighteen episodes, with a view to developing a business case for the release of Season 7 (Maas 2019).

ANALYSIS

The *B99* corpus was explored using AntConc (Anthony 2020) and #LancsBox (Brezina, Timperley, and McEnery 2018), both described in earlier chapters, as well as a software program called ConcXML.[6] This last program uses XPath to query the XML annotations, providing a summary of the number of words and turns produced by a specific speaker. For example, to query the contributions made by a particular speaker, entering the command //u[@who="Name"] into ConcXML (where "Name" is replaced by a character name) brings up all the lines annotated with a specific speaker code. Thus, the query //u[@who="Peralta"] returns all lines annotated with the <u who="Peralta"> tag in the corpus, along with a summary of the number of words and turns.

The analysis which follows first presents a quantitative analysis which charts the overall distribution of speech across each of the nine recurring characters, both by number of words and number of turns (this distinction has been made because a character could produce a lot of words but few turns, or vice versa).

Following this, I outline a keyword analysis of the four main male characters (Peralta, Holt, Boyle, and Jeffords), showing the differences in their linguistic practice and what this might tell us about the kinds of identity projects the characters pursue. After presenting the quantitative results, the analysis considers a more qualitative dimension, showing how closer attention to specific excerpts can tell us more about heterosexual friendships, male vulnerability, and the development of a positive masculinity agenda in the show.

AMOUNT OF SPEECH

The first part of the analysis presents the number of words and turns produced by each speaker in each season of the show (Figures 7.2 and 7.3). As the principal character, it is perhaps no surprise that Peralta produces both the highest number of words (171,348) and the highest number of turns (11,162), while Scully and Hitchcock produce the lowest numbers of each (this is primarily due to their roles as supporting characters). This pattern holds across all six seasons, with Peralta having more than triple the number of contributions compared to Holt, the next most prolific speaker, followed by Boyle and Jeffords. As captain responsible for the Nine-Nine precinct, Holt plays a central role in all six seasons, first as a disciplinarian intent on improving the squad, and in later seasons as a confidant and mentor for those

6. ConcXML is an experimental software program currently being developed by the Research and Development Team (RDUES) at Birmingham City University.

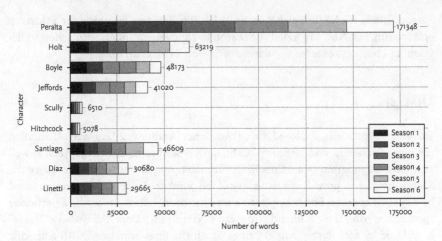

Figure 7.2. Number of words by speaker across six seasons of *Brooklyn Nine-Nine*

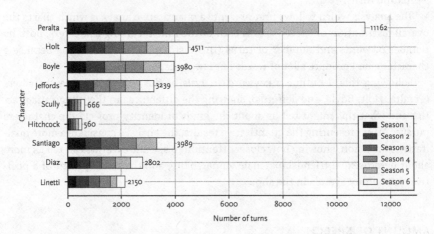

Figure 7.3. Number of turns by speaker across six seasons of *Brooklyn Nine-Nine*

under his charge. Moreover, Holt acts as one of the main narrative foci throughout the show, both for his position as a gay Black man navigating a primarily White and heterosexual industry and for his career goal of being promoted to the role of Police Commissioner.

Of the female characters (Santiago, Diaz, and Linetti), Santiago has the highest number of words and turns, gradually increasing both over the course of the six seasons. Furthermore, not only does Santiago have the fourth highest word count (only marginally less than Boyle), and the third highest turn count overall, she is third in both these categories in Season 5 and Season 6, reflecting her more central involvement in later plot lines and her growing relationship with Peralta (this culminates at the end of Season 5 with their wedding).

With the exception of Peralta, the quantitative analysis suggests that contributions are equitably distributed among the rest of the cast, with the top four positions occupied by two White characters (Peralta and Boyle), a Black character (Holt), and a Latina character (Santiago). While three of these characters are men, partially reflecting the male-dominated nature of contemporary policing, these findings nevertheless suggest that Black and Minority Ethnic characters are given substantial parts, supporting claims about the show's commitment to diversity and inclusion (Baldwin 2018; Park 2018; Scott 2019).

KEYWORDS

Looking more specifically at the four main male characters (Peralta, Holt, Boyle, and Jeffords), the keyword analysis tells us more about the kinds of linguistic practice typical of each character (the keyword analysis was conducted in AntConc). Broadly speaking, these keywords can be divided into fourteen main categories, from work names and titles through to specific linguistic features such as exclamations and degree adverbs. As can be seen, there is some variation in the keywords across each of the four speakers, although certain patterns can be highlighted (Table 7.2).

For example, terms related to family life are more likely to be used by Boyle and Jeffords, with each of them talking about their children (NIKOLAJ, AVA, CAGNEY, LACEY), their partners (GENEVIEVE, VIVIAN, SHARON), or their extended family (ZEKE, MILTON). Both men also use a number of other 'family' terms, such as GIRLS, KIDS, and COUSINS. For Boyle and Jeffords, family and personal relationships dominate their vocabulary, while the world of work appears to be less of a concern. The keywords for Peralta, on the other hand, tend not to be family oriented and instead center on work names (AMES, CHARLES, HOYTSMAN, JUDY), evaluatives (AWESOME, COOL, SUPER, WEIRD), and exclamations (HEY, OH, OKAY, RIGHT, WOW).

There are also strategies which are specific to individual characters. For instance, Jeffords often refers to himself in the third person (e.g. "Terry loves answering the hard questions," "Terry feels like a king," and "Terry fumbled the task"), while work is almost exclusively the domain of Holt, who uses the highest number of work names, titles, and work-related terms. As an openly gay character, it is no surprise to see that Holt also has GAY as one of his character keywords.

These findings can also be shown graphically using a radar chart (Figure 7.4), which makes the dispersion of keywords by topic clearer and highlights the range (or lack thereof) of keywords across each speaker. For this analysis, the individual keywords for each category were counted (derived from Table 7.2), converted to a percentage score, and then plotted to one of ten categories (for ease of interpretation, some of the original categories were merged—(i) work names, work terms, and titles; (ii) family names and family terms; and (iii) food and character terms).

Table 7.2. TOP TWENTY KEYWORDS FOR PERALTA, HOLT, BOYLE, AND JEFFORDS

	Peralta	Holt	Boyle	Jeffords
Work names	AMES, CHARLES, HOYTSMAN, JUDY	DIAZ, JEFFORDS, KEVIN, LARRY, MADELINE, PERALTA, SANTIAGO, WUNTCH	JAKE, JAKEY, RO	JAKE
Titles	SARGE	COMMISSIONER, DETECTIVE, DETECTIVES, OFFICER, SERGEANT		SIR
Work terms		DISMISSED, OFFICE, PRECINCT		
Family names			BOYLES, GENEVIEVE, JASON, MILTON, NIKOLAJ, VIVIAN	AVA, CAGNEY, LACEY, SHARON, ZEKE
Family terms			COUSIN, COUSINS, PAPA	GIRLS, KIDS
Evaluatives	AWESOME, COOL, SUPER, WEIRD		BEST	
Exclamations	HEY, OH, OKAY, RIGHT, WOW		MM, OH	DAMN, MAN
Degree adverbs	DEFINITELY, TOTALLY			
Character terms		CUMMERBUND, GAY	TRUCK, GOBBLE	LEAK, MOO, PARLOV
Gendered referents	GUY		GUYS	
3rd person referents				TERRY
Hedges		PERHAPS, SUPPOSE		
Food			BUTTER, MUFFINS	CANTALOUPE, YOGURT
Miscellaneous	ANYWAYS, CAUSE, WAIT			DENIAL, GOT, TICK

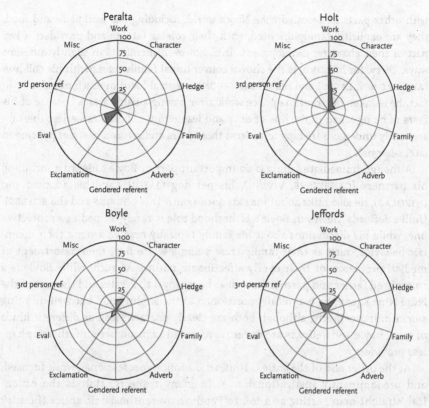

Figure 7.4. Radar chart of main keyword categories for Peralta, Holt, Boyle, and Jeffords

As has already been mentioned, Holt has the narrowest dispersion across the different categories, with his keywords only covering work, hedges, and character terms. Moreover, the largest category for Holt is work-related terms (80 percent), with only Peralta coming close to this rate (25 percent). Conversely, both Boyle and Jeffords have the highest number of family-related terms (45 percent and 35 percent respectively), food items (e.g. MUFFINS, YOGURT), and more specific character terms, many of which relate to particular plot devices (e.g. PARLOV is an idol of Jeffords' and an author who receives a number of death threats in Season 4, while TRUCK refers to a food truck Boyle purchases in Season 5). Peralta is something of an anomaly in that he has the highest rate of evaluatives (AWE-SOME, COOL, SUPER, WEIRD), exclamations (HEY, OH, OKAY, RIGHT, WOW), and degree adverbs (DEFINITELY, TOTALLY), whereas use of these strategies by other characters is almost nonexistent.

So, what might these results tell us about the characters' identities and how broader notions of masculinity are implicated in their characterizations? First and foremost, Boyle and Jeffords have the most varied keyword coverage, covering eight and nine of the original fourteen categories, respectively (compared to only seven for Peralta and five for Holt). Although both Boyle and Jeffords show engagement with other parts of *Brooklyn Nine-Nine*'s world, including the workplace and food, they are explicitly family-oriented, with their role as fathers and providers a key part of their character development. This, however, manifests in slightly different ways. Terry, for instance, is the show's conventional family man,[7] with his children (AVA, CAGNEY, LACEY) and his wife (SHARON) a central focus in much of his talk. In fact, he is taken off frontline police work after having a panic attack because of his fears of being killed in the line of duty and leaving his children fatherless (he subsequently undergoes therapy to address these fears and returns to street policing in later seasons).

Although immediate family is an important part of Boyle's identity, including his partners (GENEVIEVE, VIVIAN), his pet dog (JASON), and his adopted son (NIKOLAJ), he also talks about his extended family (his COUSINS and the BOYLES). Unlike Jeffords, however, Boyle's fatherhood role is rarely framed as a protective one, while his discussions about his family typically revolve around their eccentric behavior, such as their family crest being a white flag, their assortment of medical problems, or their overly affectionate nature. As such, while Boyle is a committed father and partner, as well as being loyal to Peralta and the rest of the Nine-Nine squad, he is typically positioned as the slightly odd but well-meaning sidekick. Importantly, although both are clearly characterized as different kinds of men, Boyle and Jeffords are never represented as incompetent fathers or hapless providers.

At the other end of the scale is Holt, who adopts a professional, work-focused, and predominantly institutional role. In many respects, Holt is the canonical 'straight man', acting as a foil to Peralta's overenthusiastic antics (Rodrick 2014), as well as being the precinct's disciplinarian. Furthermore, Holt embodies a number of hegemonically masculine traits, including stoicism, gravitas, and discipline, all of which contribute to his role as father figure and leader of the squad (Simpson 2015). These aspects of Holt's characterization are compounded by his almost complete lack of emotional disclosure, his deadpan expression, and his low baritone voice.[8] This is also reflected in the very limited distribution of his keywords which almost exclusively center on the workplace. For example, the fact that many of his keywords are last names (e.g. DIAZ, JEFFORDS, PERALTA, SANTIAGO, WUNTCH) specify not only with whom he has his primary interactions, but also the social distance and lack of personal intimacy he has with his colleagues (although as the seasons progress, he becomes more open with his coworkers).

Compared to the other three male characters, Peralta's keywords are different in that the majority of them are not referential nouns, but instead are adjectives and exclamations. While Peralta is frequently reprimanded by his colleagues for being immature, reckless, and irresponsible, he is also an enthusiastic and eager

---

7. The official *Brooklyn Nine-Nine* YouTube channel even includes a ten-minute promotional video titled "Terry Jeffords: The Family Man."

8. In Season 1, Episode 1 ("Pilot"), Peralta refers to Holt as the 'robot captain' on account of his lack of emotional expressiveness and observance of workplace rules.

detective. Arguably, Peralta's keywords reflect this element of his characterization, where he regularly evaluates different cases and events in animated and excited terms. Since traditional forms of hegemonic masculinity tend to disavow explicit demonstrations of enthusiasm in favor of what Kiesling (2018) calls "masculine ease," or "a stancetaking practice in which the masculine speaker displays unconcern [or] comfort" (Kiesling 2018, 2), Peralta's linguistic practice here subtly subverts the typical representation of police officers as detached and emotionally uninvolved.

BROMANCE AND HETEROSEXUAL FRIENDSHIPS: THE CASE OF PERALTA AND BOYLE

Having set out some of the quantitative aspects of the *B99* corpus, the analysis now considers how more fine-grained qualitative analyses can help us uncover how the male characters deal with a range of issues, including homosociality and emotional vulnerability, and what these might tell us about the integration of a positive masculinity perspective. In addition to drawing on some of the insights developed previously, this analysis also uses conversation analysis methods to highlight the turn-by-turn ways the characters attend to issues of identity and representation.

The first of these analyses focuses on the friendship between Peralta and Boyle, which is regularly cited as one of main comedic elements of the show (Keim 2017). As noted earlier, this relationship is based on mutual affection, trust, and loyalty. In a discussion in the *Brooklyn Nine-Nine* fan subreddit, for example, one commentator makes the following observation:

(1) Charles is a stand-up guy that Jake can always depend on to stick by his side, not lie to him or screw him over, or really do that to anyone—with Charles, what you see is what you get. With Jake's daddy issues, that's one of the best qualities he can find in a person, so yeah he finds Charles weird and stuff, but I think he likes him. He definitely loves him.

More specifically, I am interested in how homosociability is deployed in the show and how these two characters manage the tension between the demands of traditional male behavior and what could be termed more intimate 'bromance' interactional strategies. This analysis thus provides more linguistic detail to answer the question of "how might same-sex friendships and intimacies with other men now be subtly, but meaningfully, supported in popular television? (Lotz 2014, 5).

First and foremost, we can look at how naming practices index particular attitudinal and relational positions. The keyword analysis, for example, showed that both Peralta and Boyle have a reciprocal naming pattern (each of their names are key for the other), although a closer look reveals some asymmetry. For example, while Peralta uses the formal name CHARLES, Boyle uses both the full name JAKE, as well as the diminutive form JAKEY. As Schneider (2012, 2) notes, diminutives can express positive speaker attitudes, including endearment and affection, a finding supported in the following concordance lines (Table 7.3).

While a number of Boyle's utterances are straightforward statements (examples 4, 13, 14, 15, 16), others cover a variety of interpersonal functions, including being supportive of Peralta (examples 1, 2, 5, 7, 8), demonstrating knowledge of Peralta's personal life (examples 10, 11), boosting Boyle's own standing (examples 3, 9, 12), or mitigating the impact of imperatives (examples 6, 12). These examples show how the diminutive form helps establish Boyle's close relationship with Peralta, generating affiliation and alignment. In comparison, Peralta never uses the diminutives *Chuck* or *Chucky/Chuckie*, preferring exclusively to use *Charles* (interestingly enough, however, Boyle is called *Chuck* by a number of other characters, including the slightly unhinged undercover cop Adrian Pimento).

That said, there are other notable address terms used between Peralta and Boyle, including *dude* and *buddy*, although there are some differences in their overall distribution. For example, *dude* is only ever used by Peralta twice in the show to censure Boyle, and it is never used by Boyle, while *buddy*, on the other hand, is used eighteen times by Peralta and only four times by Boyle. Table 7.4 sets out Peralta's use of *buddy*, showing how it is integrated into strategies of questioning (examples 1, 6, 18), encouraging (examples 2, 7, 9, 13), apologizing (examples 10, 14), or as a preemptory strategy in mitigating criticism (examples 3, 8, 11, 17).

Table 7.3. SELECTED CONCORDANCE LINES FOR "JAKEY" IN THE *B99* CORPUS (VARIABLE L/R SPAN)

	Season	Episode			
1	1	7	Way to go,	Jakey	
2	1	13	No,	Jakey	, no! That car is your superpower
3	1	17	I got this,	Jakey	
4	1	17	Gotta go,	Jakey	
5	1	17		Jakey	, you're the best
6	1	21	Dance with me,	Jakey	
7	2	4	What's the playbook,	Jakey	?
8	2	7	Succulent bossing,	Jakey	. I'm gonna go home and
9	2	13	On it,	Jakey	
10	2	14	your type, isn't it,	Jakey	? Like Sophia and Sa-
11	3	1	no free soda refills,	Jakey	is going on a date.
12	3	11	Don't worry,	Jakey	. I got it.
13	3	11		Jakey	!
14	5	9	She's gone,	Jakey	. She's creeping her
15	6	11		Jakey	, I've got a hot case
16	6	14	I was fooled,	Jakey	. You're my computer

Table 7.4. SELECTED CONCORDANCE LINES FOR "BUDDY" IN THE *B99* CORPUS (VARIABLE L/R SPAN)

	Season	Episode			
1	1	12	What're you wearing, there,	buddy	?
2	1	13	Congrats again,	buddy.	I really am proud of you.
3	1	17	I've seen this before,	buddy,	and it is bad.
4	1	17	Hey,	buddy.	Got you that fancy coffee
5	1	17		Buddy,	I honestly don't know, but
6	1	19	What are you talking about,	buddy?	
7	1	19	We love you,	buddy.	Warts and all.
8	1	20	Okay,	buddy.	We have got some great opening lines
9	1	20	Great idea,	buddy!	
10	1	22	I'm so sorry,	buddy.	
11	2	11	And I hear you,	buddy.	I really do. It's just it's pretty
12	3	3	Hey,	buddy.	Got you some of those fish donuts
13	3	3	I've got to hand it to you,	buddy	whatever you're putting down, she is
14	3	3	Hey,	buddy.	Sorry about Genevieve.
15	3	6	All right,	buddy,	don't worry.
16	3	10	Merry Christmas,	buddy.	
17	3	15	Hey,	buddy.	Look, I'm not gonna waste your time
18	3	18	What's going on there,	buddy?	

There are other things which contribute to the development of Peralta and Boyle's homosocial relationship. For example, they have a range of inside jokes and shared songs, while overlaps, usually avoided in scripted television shows, are strategically used to generate affiliation. Excerpt 7.2 is a good example of how these strategies combine to create interactional closeness between Peralta and Boyle.

1	PERALTA	Okay, I'm thinking classic us.
		I'm thinking old times.
		I'm thinking...
	PERALTA	[[Rigity-rigity-role playas!
5	BOYLE	[[Rigity-rigity-role playas!

Excerpt 7.2. Season 4, Episode 4 – "The Night Shift"

Not only does this excerpt draws on a preexisting frame of affiliation through reference to 'classic us' (line 1) and 'old times' (line 2), these two lines help set up the delivery of the simultaneous utterance in lines 4 and 5, highlighting the characters' shared repertoires and mutual alignment. As van Leeuwen (2017, 121) observes, "'Being in sync' is not just a figure of speech, but a real sign of affiliation in spoken dialogue."

While these elements of Peralta and Boyle's relationship contribute to an overarching sense of camaraderie, there are instances in the show where explicit disclosure becomes a point of contestation, particularly when such disclosures threaten masculine homosociality. For example, in "M.E. Time," Boyle is assigned to a new case alongside Diaz and Peralta, leading to the following interaction (Excerpt 7.3).

1	BOYLE	I just got a DOA on Bessimer street.
	JEFFORDS	You're the primary, you're in charge.
		Take Diaz and Peralta.
	BOYLE	Yes.
5		My fantasy threesome.

[Confused looks from Diaz and Peralta]

| | BOYLE | Of cops on a case. |

Excerpt 7.3. Season 1, Episode 4 ("M.E. Time")

This is a good example of how overstepping the accepted bounds of interactional closeness is managed by Boyle, as well as how such breaches are policed by other characters. More specifically, the contested element of this interaction is Boyle's statement in line 5, where he responds to Jeffords' instruction to take Diaz and Peralta onto the investigation as his "fantasy threesome." This is, obviously, the punchline of the joke and fits in with Boyle's generally unwitting use of double entendres (for example, he refers to his 'Save the Date' cards for his wedding as STDs, while his team nicknames are typically sexualized in nature, such as 'The Night Boys' or 'The Dark Stallions').

What is interesting here is how Boyle's statement is problematized by the other characters. Following Boyle's utterance, the camera zooms in to Diaz and Peralta's confused faces, a typical means of indicating disapproval (see Figure 7.5 and 7.6), leading Boyle to produce a self-initiated repair (line 7) which clarifies his initial statement. While Boyle's original intent had nothing to do with sexual desire, in offering this repair he distances himself from this subtext, explicitly framing his relationship with Peralta (and Diaz) as a professional one in front of their colleagues. Through this repair, Boyle upholds the homosocial contract of distance and detachment (see also Kiesling 2005), limiting the possible damage to both his own reputation, as well as that of Diaz and Peralta.

At other times, it falls to Peralta to manage the interactional closeness between the two characters. For instance, following the revelation that Peralta and Santiago are in a relationship (Season 3), Boyle and Peralta have the following conversation (Excerpt 7.4).

Figure 7.5. Wide shot of Diaz and Peralta's reaction to Boyle's 'threesome' statement

Figure 7.6. Close up shot of Diaz and Peralta's reaction to Boyle's 'threesome' statement

1	BOYLE	Hey, guys.
		I just discovered a new drug too.
		It's called "your relationship,"
		and I'm high on it.
5	PERALTA	Charles, I'm gonna need you to back off, man.
	BOYLE	Roger that.
	PERALTA	Yeah.

Excerpt 7.4. Season 3, Episode 7 ("The Mattress")

Although Boyle offers a positive evaluation of Peralta's new relationship (line 2–4), his disclosure leads Peralta to produce a bald on-record reprimand (line 5), partly mitigated by the use of the address term *man*, indicating that Boyle has overstepped a personal boundary. Thus, Boyle's moments of overintimacy are often identified as problematic by Peralta.

Similarly, although Peralta and Boyle's shared songs indicate a degree of interactional closeness, there is also a recognition of how these moments contravene typically accepted norms of interaction between men (Excerpt 7.5).

1	BOYLE	Yeah, it was.
		My hunch, my hunch, my lovely case-y hunch.
		Come on, Jake, sing with me.
	PERALTA	That's not gonna happen.
5		I will literally never-
		Whatcha gonna do with all that hunch,
		all that hunch inside your brain
	BOTH	We're gonna solve, solve, solve this case,
		solve this case right in your face
10	PERALTA	We should probably leave this prison.
	BOYLE	Yep.

Excerpt 7.5. Season 3, Episode 3 ("Boyle's Hunch")

This episode centers on Genevieve, an art gallery owner accused of robbing her own gallery in order to claim the insurance policy held on it. Although she is the prime suspect, Boyle believes that she has been framed by an ex-partner. Following up on this line of inquiry, Peralta and Boyle visit Genevieve in prison to ask who might have a grudge against her, leading Genevieve to suggest that an ex-boyfriend might have a motive to steal paintings from her gallery. After the interview, Peralta and Boyle learn that this ex-boyfriend has opened a new art gallery in another city, ultimately supporting Boyle's hunch.

Celebrating his instincts, Boyle extends an invitation to Peralta (line 3) to join him in singing an improvised song (based on 'My Humps' by Black Eyed Peas). Although Peralta initially rejects this invitation (line 4), and even upgrades his rejection (line 5), he ultimately joins Boyle in a moment of shared talk (or rather, shared singing), complete with simultaneous finger pointing and choreographed dance moves (Figure 7.7).

As upbeat as this incident is, Peralta states at the end that they should "probably leave this prison" (line 10), indicating at least some degree of embarrassment in their public performance. All of this is to suggest that even moments of levity between the two characters are shot through with the recognition that hegemonic norms are being broken.

The same issue presents itself in relation to displays of emotionality and vulnerability. One instance of this is in "The Last Ride." Monitoring a potential drugs base, Boyle and Peralta are under the looming threat of the Nine-Nine being closed down

both: ♪ We're gonna solve, solve, solve this case ♪

Figure 7.7. Wide shot of Peralta and Boyle performing "My Hunch"

and this stakeout being their last case together before they are reassigned new partners (Excerpt 7.6).

1	BOYLE	Yes, you're right.
		It's gonna be fine.
		I'm gonna be totally fine without you.
		I'm gonna check the distance on the warehouse
5		there.
	JAKE	Copy.
	BOYLE	Yep, the building hasn't moved.
		It's still .1524 kilometers away.
	JAKE	Wait, are you just holding up the binoculars
10		so I can't see you cry?
	BOYLE	No!
	JAKE	Yeah, I didn't think so.
		Come to think of it, I'm gonna double-check our building
		distance as well.

Excerpt 7.6. Season 4, Episode 15 ("The Last Ride")

Initially, Boyle gives a positive appraisal of the upcoming closure in a three-part list (line 1–3; Jefferson 1990), before stating that he is going to check the distance to a nearby warehouse (line 4). Peralta's technical utterance of "copy" (line 6) and

Boyle's overspecified description (line 8) frames this as a professional interaction. In line 9, however, the tone of the interaction shifts as Peralta opens with the first part of a question and answer adjacency pair (Stokoe 2008). This leads Boyle to produces what Pomerantz (1984) calls an unmarked 'preferred response', one which upholds the homosocial contract of avoiding emotional disclosure. That said, his response is also marked in that it violates the maxim of quality. This attempt at deception is picked up by Peralta (line 9), who then joins in with the pretense of using the binoculars to mask his own grief at their partnership being dissolved, a moment carried on in the next sequence (Excerpt 7.7).

1	PERALTA	See anything?
	BOYLE	Nope.
		You?
	PERALTA	No, I just love these binoculars so much.
5		I don't wanna put them down, you know?
	BOYLE	Oh, man, when this case is over, I'm gonna miss these binoculars.
	PERALTA	Me too.
	OFFICER	It's almost 8:30.
10		We're gonna get into position.
	PERALTA	Okay, thanks, Marv.
	OFFICER	Are you guys crying?
	PERALTA	I said thanks, Marv!
		That means move on.

Excerpt 7.7. Season 4, Episode 15 ("The Last Ride")

Again, both Boyle and Peralta continue to deny their own emotions, covering up their crying by pretending to use the binoculars to monitor the warehouse. Distancing themselves from the primary object of their emotions, both characters project their feelings of loss onto the binoculars (lines 4 and 6), allowing them to develop plausible deniability regarding their emotional disclosure. Finally, Peralta refuses to engage with the police officer who informs them that the warehouse is about to be raided, side-stepping his direct question whether they are both crying (lines 12–14). In the context of an institutional setting where crying is seen as a weakness, their responses make sense, but this also shows how expectations of hegemonic masculinity carry weight in even fictional spaces.

Taken together, these two excerpts illustrate the progressive aspects of positive masculinity in the show and its willingness to present moments of emotional disclosure. But it is also clear how such representations are wrapped up in normative scripts of tough masculinity. While humor is generated by exploring this tension, the fact that both Boyle and Peralta are ultimately reduced to foregoing their emotional realities in favor of the stereotypically impassive male character suggests that a positive masculinities perspective only goes so far.

MASCULINITY AND VULNERABILITY: THE CASE OF SERGEANT TERRY JEFFORDS

In the last section, I discuss the intersection of masculinity and vulnerability, focusing on Sergeant Terry Jeffords, a focus motivated by three factors. The first is that of all the male characters on *Brooklyn Nine-Nine*, Jeffords is open about his mental health difficulties and how these affect his ability to do his job. For example, at the start of the show we find out he has recently become a father, but due to a series of panic attacks and his fear of being killed in the line of duty and leaving his newborn daughters fatherless, he is not allowed to undertake street policing until he has had therapy (Excerpt 7.8).

1	TERRY	A year ago, my wife and I had twin baby girls.
		Cagney and Lacey.
		[shows picture of them to Holt]
	HOLT	They have adorable chubby cheeks.
5	TERRY	Ever since, I kinda got scared of getting hurt.
		Lost my edge.

Excerpt 7.8. Season 1, Episode 1 ("Pilot")

Jeffords' disclosure of being scared of injury and even death, especially to a superior officer, underpins Houbrick's (2019) observation that,

> Terry is an emotional man. He does not keep things bottled up like Jake, Rosa, or Holt. He's also more in tune with his emotions than Amy and Boyle, knowing how to process and move on with his feelings. As a father, he teaches his children it's ok to cry. And as a Sergeant, he teaches the detectives how to understand what they're feeling and how to deal with it appropriately.

Second, this emotional vulnerability is juxtaposed against Jeffords' extreme size and muscularity (Figure 7.8), disrupting conventional tropes of the strong and emotionally stoic character type, particularly at the intersection of race and physicality. This subversion is particularly important given how Black (hyper-)masculinity is normatively associated with inexpressiveness and unemotionality. For example, in her discussion of Black masculinity and emotional sensitivity, Chaney (2016, 106) notes that the pursuit of hypermasculinity "forces black men to suppress psychologically, emotionally, and spiritually painful experiences." While this juxtaposition is one way the show creates humor, it nevertheless helps dispel the notion that physical strength does not always entail psychological resilience.

Finally, the analysis in this section addresses Zafimehy's (2019, 6) contention that "the study of Black masculinity representation in sitcoms remains a largely ignored topic in Feminist media studies and other related-academic fields." Although scholarship has examined the construction of Black masculinity in a number of

Figure 7.8. Jeffords in Season 1, Episode 3 ("The Slump")

media contexts, including music (Alim, Lee, and Mason 2011; Williams and Stroud 2014) and sports (Lavelle 2010; Merullo et al. 2019), there has been limited attention to Black masculinities in television shows, especially from a language and gender perspective.

This section of analysis concentrates on two elements. The first is a discussion of one of Jeffords' verbal idiosyncrasies, also noted in the keyword analysis, which is that he often refers to himself in the third person, an act known as *illeism* (originally coined by Samuel Taylor Coleridge in 1809; Wordsworth 2019). Not only is this something commented on by other colleagues, Jeffords' motivations for doing this have also been the focus of a number of fan theories, including one that Jeffords is actually referring to Terry Crews, the actor who plays him, in a sort of self-referential metacommentary.

Zatychies (2020), on the other hand, suggests that "Terry talks to Terry in third-person when the subject is his emotions, as a way to detach." As recent research has suggested (e.g. Grossmann et al. 2021), however, individuals who regularly refer to themselves in the third person have more humility, empathy, and improved emotional regulation, a perspective which would make sense in terms of Jeffords' character. And a collocational analysis lends some credence to this claim, revealing that two of the strongest collocates for *Terry* are *love* and *hate*, both verbs of affect which encode a strong emotional response (Table 7.5).

It is, of course, entirely possible that Jeffords' self-referential verbal tic is simply a strategy to make his character stand out through a catchphrase. Given what we know, however, about his willingness to be emotionally open and his protective nature over the Nine-Nine, it is difficult to reconcile this with a claim that Jeffords is 'detached'. Instead, the analysis shows that Jeffords is not only able to articulate his feelings to the rest of the squad, but he does so with some degree of regularity (indeed, more than any other character in either first or third person), ultimately destabilizing the idea of the unemotional Black man working in the unsympathetic and indifferent industry of law enforcement.

Table 7.5. SELECTED CONCORDANCE LINES FOR "LOVE" AND "HATE" BY JEFFORDS IN THE *B99* CORPUS (VARIABLE L/R SPAN)

	Season	Episode				
1	2	14	You know	Terry	loves	love. I'm in.
2	2	9		Terry	loves	kreplach.
3	2	21		Terry	loves	walls.
4	2	21	That's lavender.	Terry	loves	lavender.
5	3	1		Terry	loves	love, but
6	3	1		Terry also	loves	maintaining a professional work environment.
7	3	4		Terry	loves	responsible agricultural practices.
8	5	3		Terry	loves	women!
9	5	3		Terry	loves	tea!
12	5	13		Terry	loves	answering the hard questions
13	5	6	You were right.	Terry	loves	to be loved!
14	3	3		Terry	hates	creepy crawlers.
15	3	7		Terry	hates	bathroom talk
16	3	14		Terry	hates	windchill.
17	4	12		Terry	hates	hospitals. They reek of death.
18	4	16		Terry	hates	birds.
19	5	10	This is nasty.	Terry	hates	bugs.
20	5	16	It's true.	Terry	hates	tests!

We see a similar process of destabilization in the second analysis, which concentrates on "Moo Moo," the sixteenth episode of Season 4.[9] In this episode, the main plot point is Jeffords' arrest by a White police officer (Officer Maldack) while out searching for his daughter's comfort blanket (the 'Moo Moo' of the episode's title) in the affluent New York neighborhood where he and his family live. As one of the few moments in the show to directly tackle issues of police racism, discrimination, and institutional harassment, the episode was praised by viewers and commentators for confronting more serious social problems (Crump 2017; Viruet 2017; McCarthy 2019).

In response to being racially profiled, Jeffords decides to seek an apology from Maldack, who tells him that the only reason he stopped Jeffords was because he looked out of place in the neighborhood, alluding to Jeffords' skin color (Excerpt 7.9).

1	MALDACK	Okay, but you and I both know that you don't
		exactly look like you belong in that neighborhood.
	JEFFORDS	I live there.
	MALDACK	Look, nine out of ten times I get called to
5		that neighborhood, it's about a guy that
		looks like you.

Excerpt 7.9. Season 4, Episode 16 ("Moo Moo")

Following this, Jeffords decides to raise a complaint against Maldack, but Holt suggests that this is the wrong course of action and will lead to Jeffords being unable to climb the promotion ladder. He advises Jeffords to keep pushing forward in his career and to change the system from the inside once he is in a position of influence. As Crump (2017) notes in his episode review, "consider. . . that black Americans are criticized in the media, whether mainstream or social, for protesting against police violence. Your choices are limited: Either you put up and shut up, and nothing gets better, or you speak your piece and take your licks for it."

1	JEFFORDS	Sir, I can't get why you don't want me to file
		the complaint.
		I thought you of all people would support me.
	HOLT	First of all, let me say, what that officer did
5		to you was wrong, deeply wrong, and I'm furious
		about it.
	JEFFORDS	Okay.
		So why don't you back me up?
	HOLT	Because that complaint could backfire.
10		Cops who blow the whistle on other cops almost
		always face a backlash.

Excerpt 7.10. Season 4, Episode 16 ("Moo Moo")

9. "Moo Moo" garnered further attention following the death of George Floyd in 2020 while he was in police custody, leading to four episodes of Season 8 being scraped in order

It is at the climax of this disagreement where Jeffords opens up about his race, fatherhood, and his children. Jeffords' reflection on being reduced to the cultural stereotype of the violent Black offender (lines 1–13), his recognition of the potential dangers his daughters might face in an interaction with a 'bad cop' (lines 14–20), and his decision to take a course of action which might jeopardize his career (lines 23–25), all coalesce in a powerful moment of vulnerability and emotional disclosure.

1	JEFFORDS	You know why I became a cop?
		[Flashback to Jeffords' childhood where a cop saves him from some local bullies]
5	JEFFORDS	I wanted to help people like that cop helped me.
		But right now, I don't feel like a superhero.
		I feel the opposite.
		When I got stopped the other day, I wasn't a cop.
10		I wasn't a guy who lived in a neighborhood
		looking for his daughter's toy.
		I was a Black man, a dangerous Black man.
		That's all he could see: a threat.
		And I couldn't stop thinking about my daughters.
15		And their future.
		And how years from now, they could be walking down
		the street, looking for their kids' Moo Moo, and get
		stopped by a bad cop.
		And they probably won't get to play the police card to get
20		out of trouble.
		I don't like that thought,
		and I'm gonna do something about it.
		So I don't care if it might hurt my career.
		I'm filing that report.
25		Even if I have to go over your head to do it.

Excerpt 7.11. Season 4, Episode 16 ("Moo Moo")

Jeffords' frankness during this sequence again subverts the 'strong but silent' male character type (see Moss 2012, 24). This moment, along with the scope of Jeffords' linguistic practice, suggests a concerted attempt to promote emotionality and vulnerability and to show that these are not necessarily incompatible with dominant scripts of being a man.

to tackle the subject of police brutality and the Black Lives Matter protests (Howard 2020; LeBlanc 2020), while the cast of the show donated $100,000 to the National Bail Fund Network (Lord 2020).

CONCLUSION

This chapter has set out one of the first attempts at integrating a positive masculinities framework with an analysis of television media data, drawing on corpus linguistic methods, conversation analysis, and multimodal semiotics to explore characterization in *Brooklyn Nine-Nine*. A key argument has been how media representations of men and masculinities can be powerful agents of change, promoting a broader picture of what constitutes masculinity. For example, the four main male characters in the show all engage with behaviors which present a varied picture of masculinity, from the calm and stoic character of Holt to the enthusiastic charm of Peralta and the family man images of Boyle and Jeffords. These characters are very much removed from the typical representations of police masculinity, suggesting that content creators are willing to push the boundaries of traditional masculine exemplars.

At the same time, however, the analysis has demonstrated how hegemonic expectations of manhood and masculinity occasionally overshadow this positive masculinity perspective, particularly as they relate to constructions of homosociality and male friendship. Nevertheless, the show represents an important step in diversifying the range of mediated masculine performances. As Diviney (2019, citing Moss 2012, 127) argues, "In a society where 'young men and men in general never learn to deal with intimacy and fear, doubt, and genuine emotion', *Brooklyn Nine-Nine* is proving that you can have all of those things and still be a man."

CHAPTER 8

The Language of Fatherhood 2.0

Discourses of Caring Masculinities on an Online Fathers' Forum

INTRODUCTION

Fatherhood,[1] what Scheibling (2020, 6) defines as a "gendered term used to describe the parental status and practices of men," is arguably one of the most significant moments in a man's life, and over the past 100 years we have seen fatherhood shift from the traditional breadwinner and aloof patriarchal protector to an identity that is more caring, involved, and hands-on. This shift has been, in part, prompted by a structural need to reframe childcare responsibilities as no longer exclusively a "women's issue," as well as promoting parenting as an aspect of gender equality, encouraging fathers to take a more active role in the lives of their children, and contributing to improvements in health outcomes for fathers, mothers, and children (see also Edwards, Doucet, and Furstenberg 2009). For example, in their report on recommendations on health promotion interventions for maternal and newborn health, the World Health Organization (2015, 3) note that,

> Interventions to promote the involvement of men during pregnancy, childbirth and after birth are recommended to facilitate and support improved self-care of women, improved home care practices for women and newborns, improved use of

1. Following McKeown, Ferguson, and Dermot (1997), it is important to acknowledge that the term 'father' has a range of meanings, including biological father, symbolic father, or a person who engages in the practical act of fathering (see also Edwards, Doucet, and Fustenberg 2009: 8). McKeown, Ferguson, and Rooney (1997: 9) go on to note that "All of these may be different people and are usually men; however, it is symptomatic of the changing ground of fatherhood in our time that the father figure in some 'fatherless' families may not always be a man." While the scope of fatherhood has undoubtedly expanded, this chapter adopts a similar perspective to McKeown, Ferguson, and Rooney (1997) in its focus on men as fathers.

Language and Mediated Masculinities. Robert Lawson, Oxford University Press. © Oxford University Press 2023.
DOI: 10.1093/oso/9780190081041.003.0008

skilled care during pregnancy, childbirth and the postnatal period for women and newborns, and to increase the timely use of facility care for obstetric and newborn complications.

These interventions include shared parental/paternity leave schemes (Chemin 2011; Addati, Cassirer, and Gilchrist 2014), workshops targeted at expectant fathers (e.g. the Birmingham Women's Hospital offers "Dads Only" workshops, while the UK charity *Future Men* runs one-day sessions for new dads), and positive advertising campaigns about fatherhood and fathers. Similarly, healthcare providers are paying more attention to men's involvement (or sometimes lack thereof) in healthcare appointments, ultrasound scans, antenatal health screening, and antenatal education sessions, as well as the impact fathers have on infant health and their long-term social and educational outcomes.

The market for 'dad books' is also expanding, including many which adopt an inclusive and hands-on approach to fatherhood, from *Dads Don't Babysit: Towards Equal Parenting* (Freed and Millar 2018) to *Pregnancy for Men: The Whole 9 Months* (Woods 2018), while others tackle the historical and cultural side of fatherhood (e.g. Machin 2018). That said, a number of publications continue to draw on canonical 'male' activities as an overarching theme, simultaneously appealing to the assumed interests of future fathers and recasting fatherhood into specific gendered metaphorical frames. For example, Sinclair's (2012) *Commando Dad: Basic Training* constructs fatherhood as a military operation, with the father in the role of commanding officer responsible for the pastoral care of his "Baby Trooper" (rendered as a military-style abbreviation "BT" throughout the book). Others exploit the 'survival and bushcraft' genre, including *The New Dad's Survival Guide: Man-to-Man Advice for First-Time Fathers* (Mactavish 2005), *The New Dad's Survival Guide* (Kemp 2014), and *The Goodfather: Expectant Dad Survival Guide* (Price 2018), while others draw on stereotypical 'dad' hobbies like sports (*The First Season of Fatherhood*, Goss 2016) or cars (e.g. *Haynes Explains Babies: Owners' Workshop Manual*, Starling 2016).

Media representations of fathers and fatherhood are also far more positive than at any time in the past. Although the image of the bumbling and clueless father still abides in some movies, television shows, and adverts (Steward 2015; Wyles 2018; Scheibling 2020, 8–9; see also Scharrer 2001 for a discussion of American sit-com fathers between 1950 and 1990), content creators are now pursuing more nuanced and realistic portrayals of fathers which go beyond the domestically incompetent, overbearing, or domineering patriarchal figure (Smith et al. 2018; see also Podnieks 2016a, 9 for a discussion of media representations of fathers).

Taking all of this together, it would be reasonable to say that the contemporary image of the father is one who is involved and actively contributes to parenting and supporting their partner throughout the pre-, inter-, and postlabor process (this, of course, is not to suggest that all fathers follow this kind of script; see Flood 2010, 330). In their comprehensive discussion of fathers in the UK, for example, Burgess and Goldman (2018, 28–31) note that a sizable proportion of fathers attend NHS antenatal appointments and 'parentcraft' classes compared to previous decades, although they suggest that constraints such as cost, scheduling, job flexibility, wording of invitations/appointment letters, and lack of knowledge about up-coming appointments can have a detrimental effect on uptake among fathers and that fathers are sometimes excluded by healthcare professionals at different points during the pregnancy (Burgess and Goldman 2018, 35; Cossletts 2022). They end by remarking that the "great majority [of fathers] are keen to participate, and do participate, in important aspects of antenatal and neonatal care, as well as in labor and birth; and that this benefits their partner" (Burgess and Goldman 2018, 45). This suggests a broader process of inclusion for fathers in what has historically been viewed as solely the domain of women. As Hilton (2010) puts it,

> Modern dads are different. We read books about fatherhood, we talk to our friends about fatherhood, we seek emotional engagement and we make educational sock puppets. We practise breathing exercises with our pregnant partners, we feel per-manently guilty and inadequate, and we're in an unspoken Dad of the Year competi-tion every time we set foot in a park or playground. We are not simply being fathers; we have turned fatherhood into a cult. We have bumbled unwittingly into the age of the superdad.

While fatherhood has been well-researched in the context of masculinities studies (Pleck 2010), as well as sociology (Lupton and Barclay 1997), media studies (Prinsloo 2006), law (Collier and Sheldon 2008), economics (Sigle-Rushton 2005), and psy-chology (Genesoni and Tallandini 2009), there has been much less attention within language, gender, and sexuality studies (although some notable exceptions exist, such as Sunderland 2000; SturtzSreetharan 2017a, 2017b; Pichler 2021). This is sur-prising given the scope of language and masculinities research, but it also speaks to how the linguistic dimension of fatherhood has been relatively unproblematized in the scholarship.

To that end, this chapter examines the online construction of fatherhood, dovetailing with an emergent research agenda which is broadly concerned with the intersection of fatherhood and digital technologies, especially social media spaces, in a framework termed 'Fatherhood 2.0' (Scheibling 2019a, 2019b). The chapter does three things. The first is that it sketches out some of the background literature on fa-therhood and masculinities, including the framework of caring masculinities (Elliott 2016). Second, it discusses existing work in language and gender studies which focuses on parenting, tracing the main concerns of this research as they relate to motherhood and fatherhood. And third, building on the caring masculinities approach, the chapter presents an analysis of data collected from a fatherhood forum. This analysis is one of the first attempts to unite a critical analysis of fatherhood and masculinities with close attention to the linguistic practice deployed by fathers in online spaces.

FATHERHOOD AND MASCULINITY

As noted in the introduction to this chapter, the critical analysis of fatherhood has a long lineage which goes back to the work of Russell (1978), Barker (1994), Lupton and

Barclay (1997), Pleck and Pleck (1997), Pleck (1998), Duindam (1999), and others. Much of this work has integrated a hegemonic masculinities perspective, where fathers are understood in relation to dominant constructions of men's identities—as protector, as patriarch, as provider, and as disciplinarian. In their review of fatherhood in the 1990s, Lupton and Barclay (1997, 2) note that "Men are generally still expected to participate fully in the economic sphere, to act as providers for their families, and are encouraged to construct their self-identities as masculine through their work role." Of course, while Lupton and Barclay's point here has a ring of truth to it, fatherhood was in a state of flux even at that time. For example, discussing changing practices of fatherhood in the Republic of Ireland, McKeown, Ferguson, and Rooney (1998, 8) observe that "Good fathers are increasingly expected to be emotionally involved with their children. They are expected to share housework and take an interest in the children's schooling. It is no longer presumed that the father is the sole breadwinner or that his role is simply to supply the weekly wage packet."

Other work has examined the cultural representation of men and fatherhood across a range of media outputs, focusing on how such representations have changed over time (Furstenberg 1988; Scharrer 2001; Caesar 2008; Steward 2015; Wyles 2018). For example, older media representations of fathers have tended to promote them as the patriarchal defender of the family or as an incompetent buffoon, while contemporary content creators are engaging with more nuanced characterizations (Doucet 2016, xi). The collected papers in Podnieks (2016b) go further to examine fatherhood in blogs, fiction and nonfiction books, stand-up comedy routines, video games, and newspaper articles, ultimately "advancing the assessment of these representations in terms of their aesthetic, economic, and ideological influences, and according to how they intersect with the lived experiences and personhoods of real men and their families" (Podnieks 2016a, 9).

Other trends in the fatherhood literature have analyzed the discourse of fathers' rights activists, particularly as it pertains to antiwomen sentiment. Dragiewicz (2008), for instance, discusses backlash sentiment among fathers' rights activists in America and their negative reactions to the Violence against Women Act introduced in 1994 (VAWA), while Flood (2010) examines efforts by the fathers' rights movement in Australia to discredit female and child victims of family violence, and how their activism has influenced changes in family law which privilege fathers' contact with their children over their safety. Both Dragiewicz and Flood conclude that the motivating factors for fathers' rights activists are primarily to do with exercising familial power and imposing the authority of patriarchy. Indeed, one of the questions raised in this body of work is the extent to which fathers' rights groups actively engage with changing the socio-political landscape of fatherhood and parenting, particularly as it pertains to equal rights. Dermott (2008, 123), for instance, suggests that "It is certainly true that fathers' groups are rather less concerned with challenging the ongoing inequalities that exist with respect to childcare within couple relationships (for example, there has been little focus on promoting flexible forms of working among fathers or encouraging men to take on a greater proportion of childcare tasks) than they have been with asserting men's rights after the breakdown of relationships." In this way, we see some overlap with the broader men's rights movement in terms of limited engagement with socio-political activism (Gotell and Dutton 2016).

As much as this work has advanced our knowledge of how men understand their lived realities of fatherhood and how fatherhood engages with wider issues of gender (in)equality, it has only been in recent years that an overarching theoretical framework has come to the fore which places caregiving at the center. This framework, known as 'caring masculinities', forms the focus of the next section.

CARING MASCULINITIES

Initially introduced in Boyle (2002) and further developed in Gärtner (2007), Dermott (2008), Hanlon (2008, 2009, 2012), Ranson (2015), Elliott (2016), Jordan (2020), Joshi (2021) and elsewhere, caring masculinities are organized around the "rejection of domination and [the] integration of values of care, such as positive emotion, interdependence, and relationality, into masculine identities" (Elliot 2016, 241). Caring masculinities are concerned with how men enact caring behaviors and how men orient themselves toward the characteristics and values of care. This framework has been subsequently useful in charting how men come to conceptualize caring roles in their everyday lives and how these roles are integrated into their sense of self.

One of the key questions in caring masculinities is how caring becomes evaluated as a nonhegemonic practice which threatens traditional masculine status (Elliot 2016, 254). Drawing on interview data collected from a group of men based in Ireland, Hanlon (2012) explores men's narratives of care and their responsibilities for either adult or child dependents. One of the points to emerge in his analysis is how caring masculinities can be seen as antithetical (or at least antagonistic) to expressions of hegemonic masculinity (Dragiewicz 2008; Hanlon 2012; Rice-Oxley 2017; Bonner-Thompson and McDowell 2020). This tension arises, in part, because the act of caring for others is stereotypically coded as a 'feminine' activity rather than as a 'masculine' one (see also Maxwell 2018, 39–42 for a discussion of similar points in relation to working-class and economically disadvantaged fathers in Scotland). This is not, however, a new tension. In his best-selling book *The Common Sense Book of Baby and Child Care* (originally published in 1946), American pediatrician Benjamin Spock stated that "some fathers have been brought up to think that the care of babies and children is the mother's job entirely. But a man can be a warm father and a real man at the same time" (Spock 2013, 26–27; see also LaRossa 1988, 451 for a discussion of the changing historical position of fathers).

While there appears to have been at least some shift in contemporary public attitudes, many men still feel obliged to adopt stereotypically 'manly' behavior as fathers, acting as a strict disciplinarian who upholds particular standards of behavior for his children (note, for instance, the maternal warning of "Just wait till your father comes home!"; see also Friedman 2016, 88; Cook 2018). Reflecting on his parenting style, McCammon (2019) admits that "when my son was born, I began to unconsciously adopt 'manly' postures: stoicism, discipline, courage." In her discussion of American men attending fatherhood classes, Randles (2018a, 2018b) similarly observes how many of the participants in her study struggled to reconcile 'manly' fathering with taking an equal role in childcare and household duties. Indeed, many of the fathers adopted the language of 'helping' in relation to parenting and other domestic responsibilities (helping to cook dinner, helping with chores, helping with homework etc.). Randles (2018c) goes on to suggests that "casting men as masculine playmates and helpers reinforces gender inequality in families by obscuring that women still do the majority of household labor." As Burgess and Goldman (2018, 34) argue, however, caring masculinities can become a productive way in which men can pursue more positive constructions of masculinity.

> Since it seems likely that expectant and new fathers may fear that expressing or seeking help for their own support needs will detract from their partner's, it has been suggested that resources to encourage them to make their own needs visible should be framed around caring fatherhood, and should align men's self-care with their role as supporter and protector.

Thus, caring masculinities can be a useful framework for thinking through how men come to understand their positionality as caring individuals and what this means in their everyday lives (see also Jordan 2020). Before considering how such caring masculinities might emerge through online discourse, the discussion examines previous work within the scope of language, gender, and parenting.

LANGUAGE, GENDER, AND PARENTING

Although the linguistic analysis of parenting is a relatively new addition to language and gender studies, this majority of work thus far has tended to focus on motherhood specifically, or parenthood at a more generic level. In one of the earliest studies, Marshall (1991) sets out an analysis of childcare and parenting manuals, identifying three main discourses which cover the idea of motherhood as an 'Ultimate Fulfillment', as well as discourses of compulsory heterosexuality and equality of parenting. Other work on the textual representation of parenting includes McGlashan (2015) and Sunderland and McGlashan (2012, 2015), which offer analyses of same-sex parent family picture books. In the realm of spoken discourse, Coates (1997) discusses how a group of women negotiate dominant and subversive notions of motherhood, suggesting that criticism of their own children "directly challenges the idea of women as loving, caring, nurturing beings for whom having children is the ultimate experience of their lives" (Coates 1997, 294).

McKenzie's ethnography of *Mumsnet* (Mackenzie 2017, 2018, 2019), the world's largest online parenting site, represents one of the first studies to bring together the themes of language, gender, and parenthood through the lens of digital interaction, investigating "what kind of social norms and expectations are relevant to parents, and especially mothers, in a contemporary British context" (Mackenzie 2019, 3–4). In her work on the same community, Jaworska (2018) examines mothers' narratives of postnatal depression. She concludes that "the participatory nature and the opportunity of immediate response that [*Mumsnet*] affords is another technosocial feature which facilitate telling and sharing trouble stories" (Jaworksa 2018, 31), highlighting the positive interactional benefits online support forums afford users.

Although there has been limited interest in the discursive construction of fatherhood, especially as it relates to masculinities, there have been a few attempts at tackling this subject. In their discussion of fatherhood and domestic life among young British men, Edley and Wetherell (1999, 184) note that for many participants, "a good father was constructed as being highly involved in the care of his offspring." Drawing on Van Leeuwen's social actor theory, Sunderland (2000) presents an analysis of a corpus of parenting texts, identifying three main discourses relating to fatherhood—'father as baby entertainer', 'father as bumbling assistant', and 'father as line manager' (see also Chapter 5 in Sunderland 2004).

Similarly, Lazar's (2000) analysis of a family advertising campaign in Singapore discusses the tensions between the "Discourse of Conservative Gender Relations" and the "Discourse of Egalitarian Gender Relations." Under the scope of egalitarian gender relations, she notes that the advertising campaign deploys the cultural image of the 'New Man', where "men are very comfortable with infants and very young children, and are expressive of care and emotion" (Lazar 2000, 380; see also Baker and Levon 2016). Although the 'New Man' is ostensibly oriented toward breaking down gendered stereotypes, Lazar argues that such egalitarianism is based on the feminization of men and, crucially, that there is limited evidence within the advertising campaigns of an egalitarian sharing of parental responsibilities between fathers and mothers. Lazar (2000, 396) ultimately concludes that the image of the 'New Man' can be viewed as, "a hybridized form of masculinity that gets the best of both worlds with little significant cost to men."

The image of the 'New Man' also underpins SturtzSreetharan's (2017a, 2017b) work on fatherhood and the use of the Osaka dialect in Japanese movies. She notes that this form of "affective fatherhood," as a combination of masculinity, intimacy and informality expressed through use of the Osaka dialect rather than standard Japanese, renders a "style of fatherhood that embraces hands-on participation in child rearing, engaging in play with children and general rapport within the family" (SturtzSreetharan 2017b, 555; see also Ren 2019 and King 2020 for complementary analyses of the Osaka dialect and fatherhood). Finally, Pichler (2021) is one of the few studies to examine Black men's conversations about race, fathering, and fatherhood.

FATHERHOOD 2.0

Beyond the mediated representation of fathers, a growing area of research is what has been broadly termed 'Fatherhood 2.0', or the examination of fatherhood in different online media spaces. As might be obvious from the name, Fatherhood 2.0 is concerned with how fatherhood is constructed in online and digital spaces, including how fathers use social media to share their experiences of fatherhood, how they seek advice from others (including other fathers, but also counselors, social workers, psychologists, and healthcare professionals), and how they present themselves to the world as fathers. In some of the earliest work on Fatherhood 2.0, the importance of online spaces designed exclusively for fathers was highlighted. For example, Fletcher and St George (2011, 1103) note that "there are few online venues that are specifically created for the benefit of new fathers, and even fewer research studies or evaluations of these sites," ultimately encouraging a range of research to engage with the critical analysis of online spaces dedicated to fathers.

Some of this work has investigated fathers' use of social media indirectly. Ammari and Schoenebeck (2015), for instance, interviewed fathers about their use of social media and found that they tend to use it to archive their experiences of fatherhood, access social support from others, and learn more about how to be father. Similarly, Eriksson and Salzmann-Erikson (2013, 64) observe in their discussion of forum use by Scandinavian fathers that "online support groups for fathers are quickly becoming a frequently accessed resource on the Internet, making them an important tool for fathers who want to discuss their experiences" (see also Salzmann-Erikson and Eriksson 2013; Makhija 2019).

Most work in Fatherhood 2.0 research, however, has examined 'dad blogs'— that is, blogs authored by fathers, usually with a focus on their everyday lives with their children and their parental responsibilities (see Osborn 2019 for an overview of dad blogs). In one of the first studies in this sphere, Johansson and Hammarén (2014) analyze several blogs which chart the lives of young fathers in Sweden, while Åsenhed et al. (2014) discuss the blogs of first-time fathers, outlining how they voice their fears and worries about the health of their partners and their babies, as well as their feelings of exclusion in antenatal sessions (see also Friedman 2016; Johansson and Andreasson 2017; Lee 2018 for more work on dad blogs).

Adopting a cyber-ethnographic approach, Scheibling (2019b, 2020) offers a comprehensive analysis of both the offline world of dad bloggers, via his attendance at the Dad 2.0 Summit (an annual gathering of prominent fatherhood bloggers, media personalities, and commercial interests), as well as a qualitative analysis of dad blogs. He argues that blogs serve a number of functions for fathers, from building communities between fathers from different backgrounds, to helping reframe the mediatized representation of fathers and engaging fathers in advocacy and activism, particularly around paid parental leave, access to baby changing tables in men's public bathrooms, and broader processes of gender equality and inclusivity (see also Podnieks 2016a, 5). Scheibling (2019b, 12) concludes that "dad bloggers are producing 'counter-discourse' by challenging stereotypical images and narratives that paint fathers as absent or incompetent parents." Similarly, Friedman (2016, 87) suggests that "Daddyblogs . . . subtly shift the inherent sexism and heterosexism of patriarchal parenthood and narrate caregiving tales."

As useful as this body of work has been, however, much of the research within Fatherhood 2.0 has a number of limitations. The first is that such work tends to adopt primarily thematic analyses, where the categories and themes are developed through a 'top-down' iterative analytical process. Carter et al. (2021) evaluate the utility of such thematic approaches against corpus linguistic methods, arguing that the latter benefits from wider coverage of data and a more objective 'bottom-up' starting point, as well as being replicable by other researchers (see also Dragiewicz 2008, 138).

Second, data is collected somewhat indiscriminately in the majority of Fatherhood 2.0 work, normally using the Google search function, copying/pasting blog content, and setting arbitrary limits on the number of blogs included in a sample. This can be both time consuming and potentially prone to error. Although Scheibling (2020, 6) argues that "when dealing with a potentially massive amount of online data, it is necessary to set some informed limits," data scraping programs coupled with corpus methods can permit a significantly larger amount of data to be analyzed (see, for example, Lutzky and Kehoe's 2017 analysis of 630 million words of blog posts and comments from 2000 to 2010). Not only does the analysis of more data mean a fuller account of communicative practices within a particular community, but it also offers the opportunity to see how widespread certain concerns are and what linguistic strategies are (un)common across different users.

Finally, the focus on dad blogs in Fatherhood 2.0 research has meant correspondingly less attention on other media, such as online forums. Since these forums are arguably more interactional than blogs, they are not constrained by the perspective of one blogger, thus allowing for a wider range of voices and experiences.

The remainder of this chapter, then, sets out an analysis of an online support forum for fathers, showing how corpus linguistic methods, coupled with close qualitative analysis, can help us better understand how men construct different aspects of fatherhood.

DATA

One of the challenges for this chapter was finding an online space where fathers regularly engaged in discussion and conversation with one another. *Mumsnet* was, of course, one option, but although the site advertises itself as a site "by parents for parents," the majority of users, perhaps unsurprisingly, self-identify as mothers. Moreover, the dedicated father subforums tend not to be active, with the majority of posts receiving fewer than ten responses. Fatherhood forums are also not especially widely advertised, nor do they have a massive uptake by fathers (Friedman 2016, 87). Although anecdotal, even within the small friendship network of fathers I met through a local NCT (National Childbirth Trust) class, none of them had ever visited, posted, or engaged with online forums, either before or after their children were born.

There are, however, a number of forums explicitly dedicated to fathers, including *TheDadsNet*, *Separated Dads*, and *Families Need Fathers*. Perhaps the most active forum for fathers is dad.info (*DadInfo* hereafter), a UK-based website and forum founded in 2008 and administered by the nonprofit families' charity Fegans. The site has since developed into Europe's largest advice and support website for fathers, offering a range of help, advice, and guidance, "[celebrating] the changing role of Dads with engaging, helpful, practical, entertaining resources and content for every stage of their journey" (from the dad.info "About Us" page, dad.info 2008). Organized into subforums around both parenting issues and more general concerns (e.g. child safety, education, and families, as well as entertainment and current affairs), the forum has nearly 40,000 signed up members and monthly traffic of approximately 50,000 visitors, plus a team of moderators, support staff, and content creators. The forum is, like most online forums, an asynchronous mode of communication, where users post comments and threads and receive time-delayed replies. Content can be edited by users, either to add more detail, to correct information, or sometimes to delete submissions (posts cannot be deleted by a user, but submissions can be edited to remove all post content). At its core, however, the site is primarily an advice and support-giving space, rather than an explicitly community-focused site, a point I return to later in the chapter.

For the purposes of this study, I contacted Fegans directly via email to explain my interests in masculinities and fatherhood, requesting permission from the CEO to include *DadInfo* as the focus of this chapter. Following a discussion regarding ethics, anonymity, and data protection (see Chapter 3 for details), permission was granted to collect text data and reproduce parts of it for the purposes of this chapter, subject to a number of conditions, including anonymizing usernames, deleting any personally identifying information, and aggregating post submissions in the analysis. Consent was also obtained from one poster to analyze a thread on new fatherhood, a point dealt with in more detail later.

THE DAD.INFO CORPUS

Data for the analysis were scraped from the site using Selenium run via Python which allows forum posts, titles, authors, dates of publication, and other associated metadata to be collected from websites. Since the main *DadInfo* site contains 26 subforums, a decision was taken to concentrate on the top-four most used subforums (Table 8.1) containing over 400 posts (this excludes the 'Welcome to the forum' subforum, which is almost exclusively used by new members to introduce themselves to the *DadInfo* community). These four subforums represent approximately 65% of the total amount of content posted to the site, with the remaining 35% divided across 22 other subforums (nb. the number of replies and total word count in Table 8.1 are approximate).

DAD.INFO ANALYSIS

In the first part of the analysis, I present an overview of the *DadInfo* corpus, focusing on the top keywords in each of the four subforums, before setting out the main collocates of *father*. Given that many fathers use online forums to seek legal advice, particularly relating to child custody, divorce proceedings, dealing with court proceedings, self-representation, and other family court issues, it is perhaps no surprise that the largest subforum on the site is *Legal Eagle*. This is followed by *Child*

Table 8.1. OVERVIEW OF *DADINFO* CORPUS (RANKED BY NUMBER OF TOPICS)

Forum	Number of topics	Number of replies	Total word count
Legal Eagle	7628	42,800	6,900,000
Child Maintenance	2552	9352	1,600,000
Families	487	2214	435,000
Relationships	462	2577	500,000
Totals	11,129	56,943	9,435,000

Maintenance, a more specialized subforum which deals with questions related to child maintenance (also known as 'child support' in the USA). *Families* and *Relationships* are somewhat smaller, each focusing on issues to do with family life and personal relationships respectively. A keyword analysis shows the main concerns which typify each subforum (Table 8.2).

As might be expected, the keywords are very specific to each subforum. For example, in the *Legal Eagle* subforum, a range of legal terminology is common, including titles (JUDGE, SOLICITOR), institutions and legal organizations (POLICE, COURT(S), CAFCASS), procedural elements (STATEMENT, MEDIATION, HEARING, ORDER), and the principal individuals involved in family court proceedings (MOTHER, CHILDREN, SON). In contrast, the *Child Maintenance* subforum is more concerned with issues related to finances and child support payments (PAY, PAYMENTS, AMOUNT, MONEY), financial health (INCOME, ARREARS, ARRANGEMENTS, BENEFIT), advice websites (CMOPTIONS, GOV), and governmental agencies (CSA, CMS, SERVICE). These two forums ultimately fulfill an instrumental role, helping fathers navigate the complex arena of family law and the financial dimension of supporting their children. There are, however, a number of posts in these two forums which complain about a perceived lack of fairness, either in terms of the conditions laid out in family court proceedings or material changes in the other parent's circumstances which affect, for example, visitation rights (Table 8.3). These statements are also concerned with how such decisions might affect their children, demonstrating a broader process of parental worry, as well as garnering sympathy and support from other forum members.

Both *Relationships* and *Families* are, on the other hand, substantively different from the first two subforums, particularly in their focus on the inter-personal rather than the institutional and instrumental. More specifically, the *Relationships* subforum tends to focus more on the general vocabulary of relationships (TOGETHER, RELATE), marriage (WIFE), and relationship interventions (COUNSELLING, TALKING), as well as verbs of affect (LOVE, FEEL), the impact of a new BABY on a relationship, and concurrent issues to do with SEX and SLEEP (usually a claimed lack of each), while the *Families* subforum focuses on family members (KIDS, WIFE, MUM, GRANNY, MIL/MOTHER-IN-LAW), verbs of affect (LOVE, FEEL(ING), WANT), and relational talk (RELATIONSHIP, TOGETHER). Taking these two forums together, we can

Table 8.2. TOP 20 KEYWORDS IN THE *DADINFO* CORPUS

Legal Eagle	Child Maintenance	Families	Relationships
COURT	CSA[b]	LOVE	RELATIONSHIP
CONTACT	PAY	FEEL	THINGS
ORDER	CMS [c]	KIDS	COUNSELLING
HEARING	PAYMENTS	WIFE	WIFE
EX	INCOME	RELATIONSHIP	FEEL
CAFCASS[a]	AMOUNT	USER	RELATE
JUDGE	BASED	MUM	LOVE
SOLICITOR	SERVICE	LIFE	LIFE
GET	ARRANGEMENT	BABY	TOGETHER
MEDIATION	BENEFIT	FEELING	SEX
SEE	PAYMENT	THINGS	BABY
POLICE	CONSULTANT	BLOCKED	FEELING
JUST	PAID	TOGETHER	FRIENDS
SON	CMOPTIONS	GRANNY	REALLY
CHILDREN	MONEY	RELATE	JUST
REPORT	ARREARS	REALLY	TALKING
COURTS	OPTIONS	TIME	SLEEP
MOTHER	GOV	MIL	WORK
STATEMENT	EDUCATION	GREAT	MAYBE
SAID	TAX	LITTLE	HARD

[a] CAFCASS (Children and Family Court Advisory and Support Service) is an English nondepartmental public body founded in 2001 which promotes and advocates for the welfare of children and families involved in family court issues, such as custody proceedings, child arrangement orders, and adoption cases.
[b] The CSA (Child Support Agency) was the Governmental department responsible for calculating how much child maintenance the nonresident parent should pay the resident parent, as well as the enforcement of such payments.
[c] The Child Maintenance Service (CMS) was introduced in 2012 to replace the CSA, following a series of criticisms about the CSA's efficiency and management.

see the development of a very male-centric, heteronormative, and heterosexual space, but one where men are at least willing to share their personal difficulties and to seek out help from other fathers and forum members. Indeed, many posts subvert the stereotypical image of the strong father and family provider, with members admitting to a variety of personal difficulties in relation to their financial situations, their children, or their partners.

Although members very rarely post threads talking about the positive aspects of their lives, the fact that many of them are new fathers is often highlighted as something worth celebrating, even if this change has led to major personal difficulties. For example, one commonly occurring pattern is that posters responding to a thread often attempt to constructively reframe a problem by offering their congratulations about the arrival of a new baby. This was usually part of a formulaic structure of 1) the statement of a problem by a poster, typically connected to home life and relationship

Table 8.3. SELECTED CONCORDANCE LINES FOR "NOT FAIR ON" IN THE *DADINFO* CORPUS (VARIABLE L/R SPAN)

1	on travelling costs, and also	not fair on	me or my daughter to spend
2	him home, twice a week, is	not fair on	me or my son.
3	a step back and thought its	not fair on	my child having to be interviewed
4	It's	not fair on	my daughter
5	Your right, it's	not fair on	my daughter and it annoys me that
6	never fully stopped but	not fair on	my daughter or me, as well as
7	Whatever it is, it's	not fair on	my daughter.
8	to start straight away as this is	not fair on	my son as he will take time
9	I have said it's	not fair on	my son to be in a room
10	and its not fair on me and	not fair on	the children who are now asking
11	I can swallow that, but it is	not fair on	the kids.
12	on being treated like this it's	not fair on	you or your little one

issues, followed by 2) the issuance of a congratulatory message about the new arrival from posters responding to the thread (Table 8.4).

Congratulatory exclamations were also appended with specific advice about the original poster's (OP hereafter) situation. In celebrating new father status, the refocalizing appears to the first part of an overarching problem-solving sequence which juxtaposes the difficulties of fatherhood against its benefits and advantages, reminding posters about what they have gained in becoming a father. In many ways, congratulating on the arrival of a new child is a socially normative script, but seen against the larger context of support-giving, it is arguably a useful strategy in helping positively reframe fatherhood for someone who is struggling.

Looking more specifically at the collocates of *father* (with a five-word span left and right), a number of interesting patterns emerge (Table 8.5). Although it does not appear in the *Relationships* subforum, *biological* is the strongest collocate in the three other subforums. Importantly, the prevalence of this collocate, especially in the *Legal Eagle* and *Child Maintenance* subforums, highlights the weight the status of 'biological father' carries in family court proceedings, specifically in terms of a biological father's legal duty to pay toward the child's upbringing. This obligation applies even if the biological father is not named as having parental responsibility.[2] As such, the other main collocates in *Legal Eagle* and *Child Maintenance* are generally to do with the legal status of fatherhood, the type of relationship the father has

2. Biological fathers in the UK gain parental responsibility only if specific conditions are met. These include being legally married to the mother either at the time of the birth, or after; if they are on the child's birth certificate, but only if the registration took place after December 2003; if both the mother and father have signed an agreement that gives the father parental responsibility; or if a court awards the father parental responsibility.

Table 8.4. SELECTED CONCORDANCE LINES FOR "CONGRATULATIONS" IN THE RELATIONSHIPS SUBFORUM (VARIABLE L/R SPAN)

1	able to deal with it together.	Congratulations	on the baby daughter.
2	Hi there	Congratulations	on your new arrival.
3	oh and	congratulations	on your imminent new arrival!
4	you must be a dad by now.	congratulations.	has anything changed?
5	not to take things to heart.	Congratulations	btw.
6	First of all	congratulations	on the birth of your daughter
7	Firstly big	congratulations	on the arrival of your baby girl!
8	First of all	congratulations	on how far you have come with
9	hi there and welcome	Congratulations	on becoming a Dad,
10		Congratulations	and the very best wishes for a
11	through a very difficult time.	Congratulations	on having a son

Table 8.5. TOP TEN COLLOCATES FOR "FATHER" IN THE *DADINFO* CORPUS

Legal Eagle	Child Maintenance	Families	Relationships
biological	biological	biological	figure
mother	birth	role	husband
step	certificate	mother	loving
relationship	mother	boxing	step
loving	step	law	role
named	absent	named	bad
bio	rights	children	deserves
see	proved	figure	great
birth	named	son	real
rights	responsibility	relationship	alcoholic

with the mother, the rights a father might have in relation to his children, and the financial responsibilities which go along with fatherhood. In the *Families* subforum, *father* collocates with specific family members (*father-in-law*, *mother*, *son*, *children*) or fatherhood status (*biological*, *named*, *role*, *figure*), while the appearance of *boxing* as a collocate is because of one thread which discussed the OP's father visiting during Boxing Day. Similarly, the focus in the *Relationship* tends to center on a general relational discourse, covering positive and negative behavioral characteristics (e.g. *great*, *loving*, *bad*, *alcoholic*), complicating familial factors (e.g. *step*-father), or marital status (*husband*).

To complement the analysis presented in the preceding section, the next part of the chapter outlines a close qualitative analysis of a narrative thread about becoming a new father. While this thread was chosen because it deals with a major aspect of fatherhood beyond the financial or legal dimensions, there was also a more practical reason for this choice. More specifically, my wish to uphold the ethical standards set out in Chapter 3, particularly in terms of informed consent in this community, was at odds with the stark reality that many of the threads I was interested in were posted by members of *DadInfo* who contributed only once or twice in total, in some cases many years ago, and who were no longer active users of the site. Although this original data was interesting from an analytical standpoint, tracking down specific individuals for consent purposes was ultimately unsuccessful, to the extent that I was only able to secure the consent of one poster. This was, of course, a disappointing outcome, but it supports my claim that the site primarily serves a transactional support-giving function, rather than a community-building function. Fathers use it when they need it, typically in moments of significant personal distress and difficulty, and once they have received the support they are looking for, they appear to have only limited ongoing engagement, if any at all (in fact, four of the top five posters to the site were moderators rather than regular members).

While I could have used Markham's notion of *composite accounts*, or the "straightforward activity of selecting representative elements from the data set and composing a new original that is not traceable back to the originals" (Markham 2012, 340) to analyze a wider pool of nonconsented data, this did not satisfy either my own ethical standards, nor that of Fegans (see also Livingstone and Locatelli 2012 for a critique of Markham's approach). Consequently, the only solution was to use as best I could the data for which I had been able to acquire consent. Nevertheless, the thread I discuss below is a fairly indicative example of the kinds of worries and concerns that many 'new dad' posters share, highlighting their shift into a caring masculinities frame.

BECOMING A NEW DAD: CHALLENGES, REFLECTIONS, AND WORRIES

Before setting out the analysis, it is worthwhile noting that narratives of personal experience are important because they are an "attempt to convey simply and seriously the most important experiences of their own lives" (Labov 1997, 397). Becoming a new father is, for many men, one of the most notable moments of their lives. Not only does it mean taking responsibility for the health, safety, and welfare of a new child, but it also entails significant changes to home life, relationships with partners, and a host of other personal matters. In terms of formal features, the narrative follows the structure set out in Labov and Waletzky (1967), comprising an abstract (the clause which briefly sets out what the narrative is about), an orientation clause (information concerning the time, place, and participants in the narrative), a series of complicating actions (specifically, the notable events in the narrative), an evaluation (why the story is important, interesting, or unusual), a resolution (what finally happened), and a coda (the shift back to the present conversation).

In the analysis, I discuss how the OP positions himself as a husband and new father in a narrative about labor, childbirth, and worries about the health and wellbeing of his wife and new child. I also show how implicit evaluations of hegemonic masculinity are embedded in OP's account and how these evaluations sit alongside some of the characteristics of caring masculinities. The full thread is divided into four parts in the discussion below, reflecting the different stages of the labor, the birth, the aftermath of the event, and the link the OP makes back to the forum.

Brand New Dad—Tuesday 16th December

1 I am a brand new Dad. My wife gave birth to a baby boy on Wednesday morning
2 two days ago. The birth itself was far worse than I could have imagined, It turned
3 out alright but I just wasn't prepared for the two days of induction and then a full
4 and long labour. She was induced Monday morning and didn't give birth until
5 Wednesday at 3am. It ended up in surgery where I nearly passed out and she had
6 to have a spinal block. I watched her sitting on the bed in agony as the by this time
7 crazy strong induced contractions were kicking in, with an anaesthetist trying to
8 stick a needle in her spine and telling her to sit still. She then had the suction cup
9 thing. After all this there was a brief moment of joy as he was lifted out and placed
10 on her chest for five seconds. He was then taken away. We looked at each other
11 exhausted but excited. We then started to realise we weren't going to get him back
12 any time soon. I basically broke down, I know I'm kind of weak i guess. It was
13 all a bit much.

Excerpt 8.1. Father_of_1—"I'm kind of weak I guess"

To start with, lines 1 and 2 set out both the overarching narrative abstract ("I am a brand new dad"), as well as the main orientation clause ("My wife gave birth to a baby boy on Wednesday morning two days ago"), before offering the first complicating action in the rest of line 2—more specifically, that the birth was far from straightforward (although this statement is minimized almost immediately with the phrase "It turned out alright" in line 3). The OP then provides further details about the length of his wife's labor and that the labor had to be induced, framing the event as nonnormative or unusual and thus worthy of sharing.

The focus on his wife continues in lines 4–9 with further complicating actions, each arguably more serious that the next. This sequence moves from actions carried out on his wife (the induction, the contractions, the spinal block, and the application of a suction cup, or ventouse, which is designed to aid delivery of the baby), through to actions carried out on his son in line 9, where he is eventually delivered. This section of the narrative ends with the OP revealing that although his son was born safely, he had to be transferred to Special Care, although the specific reason for this is not disclosed.

While the focus in this opening sequence is mainly on the OP's wife and child, we see repeated calls back to the OP's physical and mental state, including that he almost fainted during the labor (line 5). But it is in line 12 where the full emotional impact of his son's move to Special Care is revealed. On realizing what is happening with his son, the OP shares that he "basically broke down." The change in perspective from first person plural *we* in the preceding sentences (lines 10–11) to first person singular *I* (line 12) is important, as it signifies a shift in what he considers to be communal reactions (e.g. *exhausted*, *excited*, *realised* in line 11) to something more personal and private. Although willing to disclose this emotional breakdown, this disclosure is complicated by his claim that he is "kind of weak I guess." This acts as a recognition that his behavior is at odds with normative expectations—to wit, there is an implicit evaluation that being weak is an undesirable state of being, especially for a husband and new father. Given the circumstances, it is entirely understandable why he should react in the way that he has, but his admission of supposed weakness suggests he is ashamed or embarrassed by his behavior.

The next excerpt continues with another series of complicating actions, this time focused on his son and his care.

1 Basically they took him into special care, where he stayed until this afternoon.
2 So for 2 1/2 days we didn't have him with us. We could only see him by looking
3 through a plastic incubator, to be honest right from the start this messed with my
4 head. Because they had taken him away almost immediately I hadn't had a proper
5 chance to really see his face. So I then started to think maybe they got the wrong
6 baby. Maybe this plastic box I'm looking into isn't even my baby, I think I
7 experienced a massive disconnect from him.

Excerpt 8.2. Father_of_1—"They took him into special care"

Again, we have further emotional disclosure and a glimpse into the psychological difficulties the OP is facing (line 3) and the confession of his worry that his son might not be his (line 5). This is an interesting subversion of the usual trope of a child being fathered by another man. In this case, the OP's worry is that the hospital has placed a different child in the incubator, a worry predicated on the fact that the OP and his wife only had a short time with their son before he was taken away. As such, neither of them had that initial opportunity to bond with their son, leading to the OP having a "massive disconnect from him," although his statement here is hedged through the use of *I think*.

It is the final section of the thread (Excerpt 8.3) where the eventual resolution of the narrative is revealed and we discover that his son was returned to the OP and his wife, along with a series of positive evaluative statements about his son (lines 2–3). Having finished the main narrative (middle of line 5), we then arrive at a transition point where the OP explicitly shifts back to his main purpose of sharing the story with the forum, using the discourse marker *so* to introduce a topic shift (line 5). This shift also contains an upgraded evaluative statement ("I'm finding it *really hard*"), alongside an admission that the 'normal' feelings which should accompany the birth of a new child were absent.

1 It was then all about getting him back to us, thats all we wanted. To cut a long
2 story short he came back today, initially I was extremely happy. He was asleep
3 and beautiful. I do love him fully. Then he started to cry and basically to be a
4 normal baby. This was the first time we had, had to look after him. Special care
5 had been doing it for two days. So the reason I am writing on here is because I'm
6 finding it really hard. Just having a new baby. Everyone says you get such an
7 overwhelming sense of love and all you want to do is care for him, but for me not
8 having the normal birth and instant hug with him. I am mostly feeling stress and
9 worry.

Excerpt 8.3. Father_of_1—"I do love him fully"

The narrative finishes with a coda linking the thread back to the forum through a series of direct questions, each of which is framed as an appeal for support and the seeking of common ground with other fathers (Excerpt 8.4.).

1 I know it's early days and that this is the hard bit but does it get easier?
2 Did anyone else out there have a similar experience? or feel any of the things I am?

Excerpt 8.4. Father_of_1—"Does it get any easier?"

This attempt at normalizing his thoughts and feelings through comparing himself to other fathers is a common one on the forum, since other fathers talked of similar worries about their self-perceived lack of physical and emotional strength, their difficulties in adjusting to a new family context, and their struggles in dealing with the changes that being a father brings about. Later posts from the OP further cement this emotional disclosure (Excerpt 8.5, line 1), as well offering his own advice to fathers who might be in the same position (line 4–6).

1 Thanks for the reply. It does indeed get easier. I cried for the first 3 days pretty much.
2 Just needed a good nights sleep and my whole perspective shifted.
3 I think it's important for some people to know who may be reading this,
4 if you have a disturbing or disjointed start to your babies life,
5 you don't have to feel ashamed that you don't have this extreme wave of emotion
6 and loving for your baby

Excerpt 8.5. Father_of_1—"It does indeed get easier"

In subsequent email exchanges with Father_of_1, he shared that this event discouraged him and his wife from having another child, highlighting the long-term impact that traumatic experiences of childbirth and labor can have, for both mothers and fathers.

Reviewing this narrative, we can make a number of observations. The first is that while this account is mainly about Father_of_1's positionality, it also outlines a number of other concerns, principally to do with the health of his wife and child. In this account, we see a manifestation of Held's (2006, 10) point that "the ethics of care values emotion rather than rejects it . . . such emotions as sympathy, empathy, sensitivity, and responsiveness are seen as the kind of moral emotions that need to be cultivated."

Additionally, the thread gives us an insight into how dominant discourses of masculinity are subverted by Father_of_1, particularly through his moments of emotional disclosure and his worries about his wife and his son. And the over-riding pressure of hegemonic masculinity is certainly something Father_of_1 recognizes. For example, in a follow up post, he notes that he is "not exactly your stereotypical John Wayne type man. I'm not completely weak but I do have feelings too." This evocation of John Wayne, one of the normative exemplars of movie masculinity and the embodiment of the strong, silent, and stoic type, suggests a lack of identification with this as a model of manhood. Even so, there are some qualifiers in his statement, since he goes on to state that he even though he has feelings, he is not "completely weak." This management of image suggests that even those men who are willing to divulge their inner emotional turmoil are still mindful of demonstrating some degree of alignment with what they consider to be desirable masculine traits.

CONCLUSION

Although fatherhood is one of the key domains where men care for others, to date there have been limited efforts to examine caring masculinities from a language and gender perspective. This chapter has attempted to address this gap by offering one of the first accounts to analyze the linguistic dimension of caring masculinities, drawing on both quantitative corpus linguistic methods and fine-grained discourse analysis.

As this chapter has discussed, online spaces provide fathers with the opportunity to share their experiences with one another in a communal and supportive environment, and *DadInfo* is no exception. While the issue of financial support was clearly forefront in the minds of many fathers, especially in the *Legal Eagle* and *Child Maintenance* subforums, other subforums afforded men the opportunity to talk about the range of personal difficulties they faced, as well as highlighting the relational aspect of fatherhood. Taking these points together, we can suggest that although the image of the traditional male provider role persists, fathers, in this community at least, are seeking out support and help with interpersonal issues and engaging more fully with their roles as fathers and caregivers.

The qualitative analysis also sheds light on how a new father manages emotional disclosure and the tension between aligning with caring masculinity and other, more traditional, expectations of masculinity. The account highlights the beginnings of an identity which fit squarely within the caring masculinities framework through the way that it "exclude[s] domination and embrace[s] the affective, relational, emotional, and inter-dependent qualities of care" (Elliot 2016, 252). While there is clearly more work to be done in this area, particularly in examining a wider range of data from a qualitative perspective, this chapter has demonstrated some of the productive ways the analysis of caring and fatherhood can be brought under the umbrella of language and masculinities studies.

CHAPTER 9
Conclusion

Where Next for Language and Masculinities Studies?

INTRODUCTION

In the final chapter, I talk about what the book tells us about masculinities in the twenty-first century, situating the discussion against a backdrop of Western gender politics, online culture wars, and contemporary gender relations. In doing so, my aim is to trace the connections the book makes to wider social issues and to explore some of the implications of the book's findings.

In the first part of the chapter, I discuss the "Don't we already know this?" problem, a particularly prevalent issue in language studies. More specifically, a common trend among the general public is to question what linguistics adds to the world in terms of social relevance or cultural utility (see Lawson and Sayers 2016a). Related to this, I reflect on why we should bother investigating language use in the first place and how linguistics can help us uncover implicit ideological systems related to gender.

The chapter then considers how the findings relate to the broader scope of men and masculinities, contextualizing the book in relation to five key areas. The first is what the book might tell us about how men and boys 'learn' to do gender, particularly in terms of digital literacies. This is a growing area of interest in digital humanities scholarship and has implications for how we understand the kinds of identity projects boys and men pursue in online spaces (see also the collected papers in Ging and Siapera 2019).

Second, I examine the intersection of masculinities and radicalization, focusing on how the analyses in the book can help us better understand the role masculinities play in attracting men to extremist movements and what they might offer us in terms of shifting men away from those movements.

The third part of the discussion centers on the deployment of 'victimhood' discourses as they relate to men. By unpacking the role these discourses play in the manosphere and beyond, I show how they continue a long line of historical precepts

Language and Mediated Masculinities. Robert Lawson, Oxford University Press. © Oxford University Press 2023.
DOI: 10.1093/oso/9780190081041.003.0009

from early masculinist movements, albeit reconfigured for a twenty-first century context.

Fourth, I explore how the book might tell us more about contemporary (Western) gender relations, particularly in terms of feminism, social justice, and gender equality. This relates to the fifth discussion point concerning the role of mediated masculinities and their potential for enacting social change.

The penultimate section sketches out some of the possible trajectories for language and masculinities studies, charting how the field might develop over the course of the next five to ten years. Finally, I end the book with some thoughts about the contribution of the book to masculinities research generally and language and masculinities work specifically.

DON'T WE KNOW ALL THIS ALREADY?

Language occupies a curious liminal zone by virtue of being both the subject of scientific inquiry *and* something people use on a day-to-day basis. In practical terms, most people believe that they have a good understanding of how language works. But familiarity with a language does not mean a concordant understanding of how, for example, language might be connected to broader ideological systems. One of the challenges of teaching students new to linguistics is that there is a whole vocabulary for talking about language in a systematic way and that their assumptions and intuitions about how language works (and what language does) might not necessarily hold up in the light of empirical review.

This is not, of course, to denigrate speaker intuition or speaker knowledge. Linguists do not have all the answers (see, for example, the discussion in Cameron 1997, 48 about how a researcher's gender bias can influence their interpretation of linguistic data) and speaker knowledge is often crucial in uncovering issues of accent discrimination, language attitudes, or ongoing language change (see Bauer and Trudgill 1998 on language myths; Niedzielski and Preston 2010 for a discussion of the importance of folk linguistics; and Rymes 2020 on 'citizen sociolinguistics'). As Wolfram (2016) argues, however, there is value in educating people about the systematic nature of language and how it hides just as much as it reveals.

Nevertheless, the fact that speakers have an intuitive knowledge about how language works can sometimes lead to questions from outside of linguistics about its intellectual or social utility. Why have a discipline dedicated to investigating language when how it works is (apparently) self-evident? Indeed, a common criticism of (socio)linguistic research is that research findings are obvious or that even a cursory examination of the data would illuminate what was going on in a particular context. In her analysis of discourses of unemployability, for example, Mautner (2009, 128) observes that:

> Detractors of corpus-based methods could argue, of course, that one hardly needs a huge database of text and sophisticated software to 'prove' that being unemployed is not a pleasant thing. On the other hand, we should not forget [...] that a fair

proportion of any empirical work is devoted, precisely, to finding evidence for the intuitively obvious.

But as Mautner goes on to argue, we cannot rely on intuition to investigate language use, especially since what seems 'intuitive' is only intuitive after the fact. Language is an everyday phenomenon that, for most, seems unremarkable. It is this 'taken-for-granted' nature which makes language such a powerful entity in the first place. As van Dijk (1993, 254) reminds us, "dominance may be enacted and reproduced by subtle, routine, everyday forms of text and talk that appear 'natural' and quite 'acceptable'." It can be difficult to *de*-naturalize language use to see what is happening under the surface, but linguistics at least gives us the tools to attempt to do so. Chafe (1994, 38) makes an excellent observation about the nature of linguistics training:

> I find it helpful to think of linguistic form as if it were located in a pane of glass through which ideas are transmitted from speaker to listener. Under ordinary circumstances language users are not conscious of the glass itself, but only of the ideas that pass through it. The form of language is transparent, and it takes a special act of will to focus on the glass and not the ideas. Linguists undergo a training that teaches them how to focus on the glass, but fluent users of a language focus their consciousness only on what they are saying. People use language to organise and communicate ideas without being at all conscious of how their language does it. It is undoubtedly this transparency of language that makes it so difficult for most people to understand why language should have a science devoted to it. Still, there are many aspects of language a person can learn to be conscious of. Linguists do that professionally, and the experience of becoming conscious of previously unconscious phenomena is one of the principal joys of linguistic work.

Linguistics, then, brings to light the hidden and the implicit, showing the inner workings of a resource many of us take for granted. While some of the findings presented in the book might seem obvious, developing an empirical and evidential basis is a necessary and important step in unpacking the routine and the inconspicuous ways in which language is bound up with masculinities and gender ideologies.

THE 'SO WHAT?' QUESTION

One of the big questions arts and humanities research has to contend with is the 'so what?' question. Books about Romantic literary culture, the rock art of Mongolia, the Anglo-Norman historical canon, the history of bassoon reed making, or even the analysis of language and masculinities, can seem disconnected from the realities of everyday life. The evocation of the 'ivory tower' often brings to mind idle academics writing about their pet interests, head in the clouds and oblivious to what is 'really important'.

STEM subjects (Science, Technology, Engineering, Maths), on the other hand, historically have not faced the same level of scrutiny about their social value. Not only do many of the outputs from these fields have a tangible reality, from decoding DNA to developing new climate change models, discovering new materials, or building bridges, cars, and houses, they are usually about issues which have a direct effect on people's lives. Consequently, STEM subjects are generally afforded a positive social status, with the concomitant funding and prestige this brings. Very rarely are those working in STEM asked to justify their existence.

The same cannot be said for scholars in arts and humanities subjects, who have come under increasing pressure to narrate their social relevance and value, usually in economic terms (Belfiore and Upchurch 2013). This push toward the social relevance of academic research is now formalized in the concept of 'impact', defined as "an effect on, change or benefit to the economy, society, culture, public policy or services, health, the environment or quality of life, beyond academia as the result of excellent research" (HEFCE 2011, 26). Impact is now a major component of the UK's Research Excellence Framework[1] and a key part of articulating the wider application of academic research.

Although many linguists are now, and have been for some time, on board with the impact agenda (see, for example, the collected papers in Lawson and Sayers 2016b; Mearns and Corrigan 2016; McIntyre and Price 2018), an occasional view among the general public is that linguistics research is a waste of money, where funding and resources would be better directed to more 'important' social issues. For example, public responses to my own PhD research were particularly unflattering (see Lawson 2011 for an overview), while other colleagues have shared similar experiences, where members of the general public have treated linguistics as a triviality or would prefer linguists to 'stay in their lane' (see English 2020).

Work at the interface of language, gender and society is often highlighted as one of these 'soft' subjects which does not add much to society or to knowledge. Increasingly, however, it is also framed as part of a left-wing feminist attack on the 'realities' of sex and gender. For example, Friberg (2017) makes the following observation:

> The very latest innovation is the ridiculous pseudoscience of 'gender studies', the sole and express purpose of which is to deconstruct gender roles. It all amounts to a sheer attack against all forms of traditional gender roles which, under the cover of 'justice' and 'equality', aims to create an atrophied human being who is dependent on neutered academics for his or her value system. The result of all this is confused gender identities; a society where young men achieve less and less in education, suffer from completely irrational insecurities and even have reduced testosterone levels—far lower than have been normal since they began to be measured.

1. The Research Excellence Framework is a program of evaluation which measures the research capacity of UK higher education institutions (see Lawson and Sayers 2016a for a history of UK research evaluation schemes).

Overlooking the claim that 'gender studies' is responsible for men's lower testosterone levels, views like this are commonplace in conservative, far-right, alt-right, and manosphere communities, where anything to do with the critical study of gender is delegitimized (see also Sculos 2017b, 5), unless, of course, such work supports the status quo. The prevailing view for some on the right is that challenging bigotry, racism, sexism, and misogyny, or advocating for minority rights and equal treatment is less about addressing social injustices and more about promoting a normatively 'good' and 'moral' character. This mischaracterization of social activist work seeks to divert attention away from the embedded structural problems in society, in a form of linguistic misdirection. The negative reconfiguration of phrases like *social justice warrior* or the term *woke* is just one strategy of trivializing a commitment to equality and inclusivity (see also Ohlheiser 2015; Waterson 2020; Smith 2021; Cammaerts 2022), with Davies (2020) noting that "a bogey-ideology known as 'wokeness', constructed by conservative commentators and 'free speech' advocates, now serves as an all-purpose bin into which any form of activism, complaint or critical theory can be thrown" (we see a similar history with the term *politically correct*; see Messer-Davidow 1993 and Wilson 1995).

For scholars working in language and gender (as well as disciplines like critical discourse analysis and other arts and humanities subjects), their interest is in examining "the complexity of contemporary society, thus trying to make a positive contribution in untangling live ethical, practical, and scholarly challenges" (Belfiore and Upchurch 2013, 4). By this point in the book, it should hopefully be clear how language and masculinities studies fall under this remit. We know, for example, that men and masculinities vary over time and that gender relations are intimately bound up with broader social and structural changes brought about by technology, politics, migration, demography, economics, and more. We also know that language is a key part of how we present ourselves to the world and one of the means through which we evaluate others, for better or for worse. Language is inherently political and cannot be divorced from the social context in which it exists. To that end, the critical examination of language and masculinities in contemporary contexts is vital in terms of mapping out how gender relations are organized in the twenty-first century.

For those readers working in the field of language and gender (or in allied subjects), my comments here might seem to be preaching to the converted. For those readers who are coming to this book from a different background and who might wonder why someone would bother to write a book about language and masculinities, I hope that the discussion here and elsewhere goes some way to articulate the social value of such an endeavor.

SOME BROADER IMPLICATIONS

Having set out some of the underpinning epistemological issues related to linguistics and its social and intellectual contribution, the next section of the chapter considers the implications of the book in terms of its connections with men and masculinities research. My aim here is to think about how the book sits alongside ongoing debates about men in the twenty-first century and what attention to linguistic practice adds to our analytical accounts.

DIGITAL LITERACIES AND LEARNING TO DO GENDER

One of the main contexts for the book has been online spaces, particularly alt-right and 'manosphere' outlets. My focus on these communities has been motivated by an interest in how men 'do' gender in these spaces and how they acquire normative ideas about what it is to be masculine. In their discussion of 'new literacies', Lankshear and Knobel (2011, 13) suggest that "People read and write differently out of different social practices, and these different ways with words are part of different ways of being persons and different ways and facets of doing life." Thus, community membership is predicated on learning specific rules which align with the dominant ideologies of that group (or, more broadly, individuals must become literate in the group's communicative norms), usually policed by more experienced members of the group. This thinking is influenced by Lave and Wenger's (1991) idea of the Community of Practice, where newcomers to a community gradually learn the practices which underpin group identity, as well as Gee's (2007) notion of 'affinity spaces', where the primary orienting factor is the underlying group interest, rather than the people who constitute the group.

In his discussion of learning and video games, Gee (2007, 98) notes that "In an affinity space people relate with each other primarily in terms of common interests, endeavours, goals, or practices, not primarily in terms of race, gender, age, disability, or social class." The discussion of /r/The_Donald, /r/TheRedPill and other manosphere spaces, however, suggests that affinity spaces can also be predicated on social categories like race and gender and that these aspects of identity can have a substantial impact on the depth of engagement, and sense of belonging, one can achieve. It is, of course, impossible to know with any certainty that members of these manosphere communities are (white) men, but since these outlets are designed for, and promoted to, this group, it would seem odd if they were not the dominant users.

In the context of the manosphere (and online spaces more generally), digital literacies go beyond the basics of textual comprehension—being able to read and write—and are instead interwoven with competency in a range of ideological, technical, and modal affordances. In order to participate in manosphere outlets, for example, users need to learn not only the technical vocabulary and norms specific to each space, but also the underpinning values, principles, and beliefs and how to talk about these ideas, usually in a way that elicits community approval. To be 'literate' in the manosphere means not only knowing what the normative scripts of masculinity are, but also to enact them in online interactions and to demonstrate an alignment with the dominant ideologies which form the foundation of the community, integrating these practices into a constructed sense of self (Mundy and Denny 2020, 4). This includes the promotion of male superiority, the marginalization of women, the denigration of feminism, and a host of other practices as discussed in Chapters 5 and 6. Furthermore, user contributions are policed through a variety of technical affordances (e.g. upvotes/downvotes on Reddit, mass brigading), enforcing dominant ideologies and preventing alternative or opposing viewpoints from being expressed (Tait 2017; Jacobson 2019, 169). In other spaces, such as fatherhood forums, it means knowing about parenting, engaging with broader discourses of responsibility and caring, and supporting other fathers through their difficulties and struggles, all while drawing on a communal set of cultural reference points and linguistic practices.

So, what does all of this mean in terms of literacies more broadly? While there has been a great deal of research on how boys engage in literacy education, very little is known about how young men are socialized into gendered literacy practices in informal digital spaces. As Jacobson (2019, 171) argues, "One important aspect of sociocultural analyses of literacy is how individuals come to be members of communities that engage in distinct reading and writing practices. . . [Much] of what individuals learn to do with literacy happens outside of school and in association with members of particular groups and networks." Understanding these processes is not only important in terms of charting the pathways of recruitment, but also for recognizing the motivations young men might have for engaging with manosphere communities and giving students the analytical tools to be able to challenge some of the gendered discourses circulating in the manosphere and beyond (Orenstein 2020, 233). This call is also taken up by Jacobson (2019, 180), who notes that "Formal education can play a role in students' productive use of these out-of-school spaces by helping students develop the analytical language needed to recognize and resist discourses of toxic masculinity, particularly when these discourses utilize coded language (i.e. words that appear uncontroversial but that are meant to serve as an implicit signal to those who share the speaker's or writer's ideological beliefs)" (see also Lawson 2021).

MASCULINITIES AND (DE)RADICALIZATION

The intersections of literacy, participation theory, and gendered digital practices also has implications for our understanding of how masculinity is connected to the radicalization of young men and their recruitment to extremist organizations. As Brown and Saeed (2015) and Kimmel (2018) have argued, there has been a paucity of research on the role gender plays in radicalization, a surprising gap in the literature given that membership of radical, supremist, extremist, and terrorist organizations is almost exclusively male (Möller-Leimkühler 2018; Coffé 2019; Roose et al. 2022). Furthermore, masculinity is often evoked in nationalist and supremacist contexts as part of a discourse of protectionism, where 'real' men defend their countries against claimed external threats. On /r/The_Donald (as discussed in Chapter 5), this framing also helps reify a desirable formulation of 'White' masculinity, where masculine strength, moral courage, resolve, and inventiveness are contrasted with an amorphous 'other' lacking in these qualities, as well as setting up internal masculine hierarchies (for example, the positioning of 'liberal men' as lesser substantiations of manliness).

Although the book has not examined the processes of radicalization, its focus on charting some of the dominant discourses of masculinity within the alt-right and the manosphere is an important contribution, showing how particular conceptualizations of manhood are promoted as ideal and desirable. By identifying what kinds of normative scripts of masculinity are mobilized within these spaces, we can start to unpack how these configurations become rallying points for recruitment to nationalist and supremacist causes, as well as hate groups, far-right/-left extremist groups, male supremacy groups, and terrorist organizations (see Wilkinson 2016; Magdy et al. 2016; Proctor and Mazurana 2019; Roose, Flood, and Alfano 2020; Roose et al. 2022).

We also need to understand the social and psychological factors related to masculinity which underpin radicalization if we are to have any hope of developing effective de-radicalization interventions. By exploring what draws men into these movements, how idealizations of masculinity are promoted in extremist organizations, and the linguistic means used to do so, we are better placed to educate young men about persuasive language, manipulation, and exploitation, giving teachers and educators the tools to recognize (and intervene) in emergent and ongoing processes of radicalization (Lawson 2022; Weale 2022). Discussing her work on incels and extremist behavior, Ging (cited in Sisley 2019) observes that "There are young men becoming radicalised because they are confused, because they don't live up to idealised masculinity, because they feel humiliated and rejected." Since male adolescence is often characterized by worries about meeting arbitrary standards of masculinity (Martino 1999; Oransky and Marecek 2009; Reigeluth and Addis 2016), conversations about alternative masculinities and healthier ways of being a man are crucial in preventing extremist organizations from exploiting young men's insecurities about their masculine status (see also Ezekilov 2017; Dignam and Rohlinger 2019, 594). Indeed, this idealism of masculinity can have profound effects on the mental health of boys and men (see also Plowright 2020). Better provisions for men to talk about these pressures would go some way toward addressing the growing numbers engaging with extremist movements, both online and offline.

The focus on masculinity in relation to extremism opens up other research directions around desistance, violence prevention, and anti-radicalization (see Horgan 2008 for a discussion of deradicalization interventions). For example, the role of fathers in combating radicalization is hugely under-investigated (Moore 2019), as is how male mentors, coaches, friends, and counselors can model positive behaviors (Orenstein 2020). Some research has suggested that such interventions can be successful in terms of changing behavior and encouraging nonengagement with extremist ideologies. For example, Garfinkel (2007, 1) notes that "change often hinges on a relationship with a mentor or friend who supports and affirms peaceful behavior" (although see Brown 2019 for a more critical reflection on mentorship within the UK Government's Prevent strategy, as well as Pinkett and Roberts 2019 concerning role models in educational settings). Given the limited effectiveness of deradicalization programs (Koehler 2019; Ward 2019), there is an urgency to consider how we can augment existing approaches in desistance and rehabilitation by paying closer attention to masculinities (see Pearson 2019 for an excellent analysis of masculinities and class in the English Defence League, a radical far-right movement based in the UK).

One of the prevailing trends uncovered in the book is the mobilization of a 'victimhood' discourse, particularly within manosphere outlets, which frames men (and White men, especially) as being the substantive losers in a global culture war. For example, in a Fox News interview, Gavin McInnes (2016) argues that "by every metric, men have it worse," while Jolivet (2019, 1) suggests in his book *Society Kills Men: Feminism Loses When Half Are Held Back* that "male suffering is manifesting in many ways and is brought about by the way of the many norms, institutions, and government policies and laws that have existed for decades." This claimed 'war on men' is not new. In his book *The Myth of Male Power*, for example, Farrell (1993, 355) claims that "the wound that unifies all men is the wound of their disposability," citing suicide rates, incarceration rates, workplace death rates, the existence of the draft and compulsory military service as evidence for how men are treated as the 'disposable sex'.

While Farrell falls foul of selective interpretation and hyperbole (see Winder 1994; Robinson 2000; Van Valkenburgh 2019), he occasionally touches on the very real problems faced by men. As discussed elsewhere, for instance, men are overwhelmingly represented across a number of indices of poor health outcomes, including suicide, homelessness, addiction, and incarceration. Furthermore, men's life expectancy is lower and they are more often the victims of violent crime, up to and including murder. Summarizing some of the issues men face, Connell (2005, 248) observes that "the effects of the current gender order on men collectively include: higher level of injury (including industrial accidents, road injuries), higher exposure to many forms of toxicity and stress, [and] higher levels of drug dependency (most commonly, alcoholism)." It would be folly to argue that academic, social, and governmental attention should not be directed at intervening in areas where men are doing demonstrably less well than women. In the face of these disadvantages, the idea goes, how can men be so powerful? Nevertheless, there are a number of issues worth discussing in relation to this 'victim' positioning.

The first is how parts of the manosphere draw on the language of contemporary identity politics to construct a 'discourse of oppression'. In their discussion of what they call the 'emasculation nation', García-Favaro and Gill (2016, 394) note that "far from gender inequality being disavowed, repudiated or rendered unspeakable, it is repeatedly formulated, exemplified and forensically deconstructed–but this gender inequality is focussed exclusively on men." In a similar vein, Marwick and Caplan (2018, 12) suggest that "By saying 'You're not the victim, I'm the victim!' the [Men's Rights Activist], whether he be Sargon of Akkad or a poster on soc.men, is able to adopt a defensible position as the suffering victim, turning feminist (or queer, or anti-racist) activism on its head and re-framing it as oppressive." This strategy ultimately leads to a rerouting of feminist logics, where these logics are used to "center men as discriminated against and in need of recuperation and reparation" (Banet-Weiser 2018, 172). Co-opting these logics of victimization and oppression serves to justify networked misogyny and online harassment in the face of claimed persecution by feminists and women more generally, where symbolic violence is seen as a necessary component in the backlash against the dangers of feminism. Additionally, it acts as a situated tactic to reclaim 'power' over others and to subvert the narrative of men as holding all the cards.

Again, these strategies are not new. For example, in her review of the cultural and literary expression of white masculinity in crisis, Robinson (2000, 209) observes that "the appropriation of 'victimism' by the socially privileged represents an attempt to hold on to a slipping symbolic power which is no longer vested in the white man as 'universal'." A similar point is made by Brown (1995), who argues that access to political power is increasingly defined by the ability to define oneself as injured (see also Ferber 1998; Dragiewicz 2008, 127; Bloch, Taylor, and Martinez 2020). In the contemporary context of the manosphere, we are seeing a rearticulation of a male victimism which is bound up with an increasingly precarious sociopolitical environment wrought by Trumpism, online culture wars, right-wing nationalism, anti-diversity sentiment, and more. We need to unpack these discourses and place them in their particular sociocultural context in order to deconstruct and challenge them.

Second, claiming 'victimism', either real or imagined, does not erase the benefits and advantages that men accrue by virtue of being male, what Connell (2005, 79) calls the "patriarchal dividend," or the "advantage men in general gain from the overall subordination of women." Of course, being male does not automatically mean that life will be easy. A man who is unemployed or in precarious employment, living in an unstable home, lacking important social support systems, potentially surrounded by street violence, drugs, and crime, and who has to make choices between heating or eating may find it hard to see exactly where his privilege lies, as might men undergoing difficult divorce proceedings, who are given limited access to their children, who are living with long-term work-related illnesses, or who are suffering from intimate partner violence (see also Rhymes 2014; Stemple, Flores, and Meyer 2017; Lien and Lorentzen 2019; Taylor, Keeling, and Mottershead 2019 for discussions about the prevalence of domestic violence committed by women). As Connell (2005, 249) reminds us, the advantages and costs of gender relations are spread unevenly and there are dangers of ignoring the diversity within the category of 'men'. That said, claiming universal hardship on account of being a man is a difficult position to sustain given the general scope of benefits afforded to men in terms of their economic, political, and social power (see also Pease 2008, 10 who reminds us that "we must avoid the simplicity of the view that men are oppressed by the male sex role").

Third, the victim discourse tends to overlook the structural contexts which give rise to inequality and unequal distribution of resources, as it applies to both men and women. As Ging (2019, 48) notes, "this mancession rhetoric, which has been widely propagated by the mainstream media, evades economic and structural analysis, encouraging men to blame their disempowerment on women, LGBT people, people of colour and identity politics more generally" (see also Robinson 2000, 8; Sculos 2017b, 7; Van Valkenburgh 2018, 17). Thus, socioeconomic issues tend not to figure in victimism accounts, where instead the specters of feminism, diversity, liberalism, and 'leftist' ideology predominate. In his discussion of educational provision for young white men in Britain, for example, Marcus (2020) argues that such boys are, "more likely to be the victims and perpetrators of crime, join gangs, suffer from substance abuse, and develop mental illness." In searching for the underlying reasons for these problems, however, Marcus ultimately blames the 'left' and 'identity politics', conveniently ignoring the damage caused by a decade of austerity, cuts to police numbers, social workers, and social care budgets, and a lack of investment in schools, education, youth services, youth clubs, and after-school provision (see Messner 2016; Densley, Deuchar, and Harding 2020 for discussions of the causal factors underpinning youth violence and male social disengagement).

The role that other men play in maintaining systems of male inequality is also often overlooked in manosphere spaces. Discussing this point in his article on toxic masculinities, Boise (2019, 148) contends that "antifeminist and right-wing activists often conveniently ignore the fact that men are often the ones who send other men to war, kill and imprison other men, are quantitatively more likely to be embroiled in both the drug trade as well as the 'war' against it at all levels and are overrepresented as executives in the very industries which fuel drug addiction." Similarly, critical accounts of how the structures of late capitalism, and the relentless focus on profit at the expense of people, are implicated in unequal outcomes for men are conspicuous by their absence. While O'Neil (2010, 104) notes that "Human qualities of both men and women have absolutely been subordinated to distorted masculine and feminine stereotypes in our capitalist society to make money and sway public opinion," criticisms of how capitalism exploits and alienates men tend to be thin on the ground. Van Valkenburgh (2019, 9) even goes as far as to suggest that parts of the manosphere simply perpetuate the late capitalist agenda, arguing that "faced with accumulating evidence of late capitalism's negative economic outcomes—such as economic crises, alienation, exploitation, and unemployment—yet evidently unable to question capitalism's supposed benevolence, the sidebar discourse [of The Red Pill subreddit] enables men to divert hostility away from their surrounding economic system and redirect it onto women."

Rather than casting a critical eye on these issues and arguing for a reconfiguration of the socioeconomic structures which underpin contemporary Western society, 'identity politics', and the disciplines which examine such issues, become convenient scapegoats for the current narrative surrounding the disempowerment of men. In something of a prophetic observation, Messner (2016, 14) suggests that "if current industrial nations continue to lack the will to address the many ways in which a huge strata of young men are being treated as dispensable by the economy and the criminal justice system, it is possible that some of these men will find resonance with Internet-based anti-feminist men's rights discourse that blames women and the liberal state for men's woes." As the discussion presented in this book has demonstrated, we are clearly in this moment, but as Boise (2019, 148) argues, unpacking how a victimism discourse is deployed across the various elements of the manosphere and beyond can help us better understand how the 'war on men' framing facilitates recruitment efforts to masculinist movements and on to subsequently more extreme political viewpoints (see also Kelly 2017).

A book like this naturally raises questions to do with gender relations in the twenty-first century. In each of the chapters, there is a consideration of how masculinities are framed as ideal, desirable, deviant, subversive, normative, and so on, but beyond this, the book has also engaged with how women, femininities, and feminism are positioned. Much of this evaluation has been explicitly negative, misogynistic, sexist, and violent, alongside the promotion of a 'backlash' sentiment against feminism. Although this backlash has a long history (see Faludi 1992; Hawkesworth 1999; Dragiewicz 2008), it is now an integral part of the politics of the alt-right and the manosphere. For example, Jolivet (2019, 3) argues that "gynocentrism, feminism, and especially radical feminists are killing men—literally, spiritually, and mentally, by making life that much tougher, less fulfilling, more depressive, and with less hope and reason to live for." We do not need to look far back to see similar claims. For example, writing almost thirty years ago, social critic Camille Paglia made the point that "men have sacrificed and crippled themselves physically and emotionally to feed, house and protect women and children. None of their pain or achievement is registered in feminist rhetoric, which portrays men as oppressive and callous exploiters" (Paglia 1993; see also Blake 2014 for a discussion of women's participation in the Men's Rights Movement). Indeed, the dominant view within alt-right and manosphere spaces is that feminism is a man-hating ideology about female empowerment rather than equality, that the world is too feminized, that women no longer face discrimination and disadvantage, and that feminism is a 'cancer' (see discussions in Archer 2018; Bakar 2019; Orchard 2019; Wong 2019 about ongoing challenges to women's equality in the West and beyond).

This backlash is also often predicated on the claim that if women are 'winning' then men must be 'losing'. In her discussion of an MRA meeting held in London in 2018, Whyte (2018) makes the following point—"that men are disenfranchised by women was accepted as fact by all of the delegates and speakers I listened to. Their fury and frustration were palpable, at times distressing." But as a number of scholars have pointed out, at length, gender equality is not a zero-sum game; there are no 'winners' or 'losers' (Connell 2003; Pease 2008; García-Favaro and Gill 2016; Veiszadeh 2018; Deckers 2019). The same point is made by social psychologist Joseph Vandello (cited in Vinopal 2018), who observes that "Some men see [gender equality] as a zero-sum game. That women's advancement must come at a cost for men. That's not the reality, but it's the perception."

Again, Connell's work on masculinities is instructive here. Presenting a cost-analysis of men's advantages and disadvantages, Connell (2005, 246–248) shows how men both 'win' and 'lose' in relation to power, the labor market, emotional support, sexuality, and cultural institutions. For example, while men have higher levels of economic participation, they are also overrepresented in dangerous and risky occupations. Similarly, men have almost complete control of institutions such as the military and the police force, but they are also the main targets of military violence, conscription, criminal assault and more. Connell (2005, 248), nevertheless, suggests that "this 'balance sheet' is not like a corporate accounting exercise where there is a bottom line, subtracting costs from income. That is the error made by backlash polemicists who try to refute feminism by reciting men's disadvantages." Of course, the reality is that inequalities exist for both men and women, but questions of "who has it worse?" do little to change material contexts and lived realities.

One related argument is that the pursuit of gender equality is more likely to happen when men are involved as active agents of change (Connell 1997; Pease 2000; Flood 2005; Pleasants 2011; Flood 2015), challenging issues at a systemic level and engaging with broader policy agendas. Involving men in gender equality efforts is, of course, no silver bullet, and some writers have set out thoughtful discussions regarding the difficulties such an endeavor can potentially bring about, from reducing funding for women's services to devaluing the contribution of women (Pease 2008). As Gary Barker[2] (cited in Edwards 2017) suggests, "It's easy to become the trendy new way to do gender equality and assume engaging men will solve it all, and that any man showing up to work on this is coming on his white horse." Nevertheless, there has been growing attention on how men and boys can contribute to addressing gender inequalities. Edwards (2017), for example, goes on to note that "development groups are increasingly arguing that with patriarchal culture norms standing as the key barrier to women's empowerment, projects must target changing attitudes among men and boys in order to create lasting improvements for women and girls." Similarly, Okun (2018) argues that men play a critical role as partners and allies, something which has become even more important in the context of the #metoo movement, digital harassment, increasing physical and sexual violence toward women, and the growing prominence of online misogyny. This process must involve a reflection of male entitlement and privilege, as well a critique of the role men play in sustaining cultures of inequality and oppression.[3]

Beyond this, given the ways in which certain substantiations of 'traditional' masculinity are associated with a range of negative health outcomes, including suicide (Wyllie et al. 2012; Coleman 2015), drug and alcohol abuse (de Visser and Smith 2007; Willott and Lyons 2012; Wilton, DeVerteuil, and Evans 2014), and interpersonal violence (Connell 2002; DeKeseredy and Schwartz 2005; Dumas et al. 2015), pushing against dominant ideas of patriarchal and hegemonically masculine behavior can also have benefits for men, improving overall mental and physical health and life expectancy.

Public education programs, improving critical media literacy in schools, mentoring, and other approaches should be woven into long-term interventions related to promoting gender equality of all kinds (Flood 2005, 461). Perhaps even a "progressive manosphere" and a retooled men's movement could be part of this,

2. Gary Barker is the founder of global charity Promundo, which focuses on advancing gender equality and violence prevention.
3. Kelly, DiBranco, and DeCook (2021) also set out a number of recommendations for reducing rates of misogynistic violence and male supremacism, including improving access to mental health services, integrating into early years education discussions of consent, boundaries, and mutual respect, and avoiding interventions that reinforce boys' and men's entitlement.

one which is nonracist, nonsexist, diverse, and positive in orientation, following the lead set by organizations such as *Huddle Up* program (developed by the National Consortium for Academics and Sports) and the *ManKind* project (Godwin 2018; Holden 2019; see also Whitley and Zhou 2020, 26). This, however, may be a step too far given how some men's organizations are ostensibly fronts for the less salubrious aspects of various MRA movements. For example, Barker (cited in Edwards 2017) makes that the point that "some [men's] groups may appear supportive of women's equality but actually promote an anti-feminist tone, emphasizing men as victims without talking about the power and privilege they have historically enjoyed." This book has shown not only the kinds of antifeminist and antiwomen sentiment promoted within the manosphere, but also how male supremacy and male victimism discursively manifest in these spaces. As Holden (2019) argues, "There is a real risk that men's groups can degenerate into hotbeds of male supremacy where alt-right talking points are parroted, especially when the members are overwhelmingly straight white men, which they often are." Addressing these issues will be one of the key challenges for masculinities scholars, activists, charities, and nongovernmental organizations in the years to come.

MEDIATED MASCULINITIES

While the book has examined how men use different forms of (mainly digital) media, it has also considered how men are represented across a range of other media outputs, including newspaper articles and television shows. For example, the analysis of 'tough' masculinity in Chapter 4 demonstrated how the image of the 'hard man' is deployed across two British newspapers, showing prevalent associations with crime and violence, but also across the spheres of politics, sports, and entertainment, reifying the identity of the 'hard man' as a potentially desirable one. Such representations are juxtaposed with what might be termed more 'sensitive' masculinities, as presented in the analysis of *Brooklyn Nine-Nine* in Chapter 7. Similarly, the analysis of fatherhood forums in Chapter 8 showed how men can demonstrate both emotional and personal vulnerability in public spheres, searching for help and guidance from others during difficult periods in their lives.

What the analysis of these mediated contexts has shown is that although the traditional image of masculinity based on domination, physicality, violence, and control endures, there is at least some shift away from the kinds of risky, toxic, and disruptive behaviors normatively associated with masculinity. These newer expressions of positive masculinities and more nuanced media representations of men suggest that content creators are engaging with the broader scope of masculinities, an especially important point given how mass media can shape public perceptions and attitudes toward men and masculinity via the characters crafted by writers and content creators. And again, such representations can play an important role in engaging men in equal opportunity efforts, challenging some of the problematic aspects of masculinity. As Edwards (2017) suggests, "Social movements with backing from influential figures, such as celebrities and religious leaders, and modelling new social norms through social media and 'edutainment' programs—such as television soap operas that criticize gender-based violence, for example—have a role in bringing about broader change."

FUTURE DIRECTIONS: THE PATH AHEAD

It is difficult, of course, to predict exactly how the field of language and masculinities studies might develop over the course of the next decade and beyond. But it is clear that there remains much more to investigate, over and above what has been covered in this book. So, what does the future hold?

First and foremost, masculinities are intimately bound up with an ever-changing global sociopolitical context. In the West, at least, we are seeing the continued growth of right-wing populism, increasing ethnic nationalism, rising social inequality, a changing material context of men's lives, and the reality of an ever more precarious economic future for many (partly compounded by the Coronavirus pandemic, the resultant economic shutdowns, and the present cost-of-living crisis). Add to this a 24/7 news cycle, with associated social media coverage, discussion, and debate, and an increasingly volatile culture war predicated along almost every axis imaginable, it is inevitable that ideologies of masculinity will come to the fore in different ways, shapes, and forms.

We are seeing some of these issues play out even now, particularly in the rise of the alt-right and a new wave of nationalist and supremacist organizations worldwide which exploit idealized notions of what constitutes manliness. This intersection of language, masculinity, and radicalization suggests a number of potentially productive avenues for future research. How are men convinced to join these movements? What linguistic strategies of persuasion and encouragement work and why? How might boys and men be educated to recognize and resist discourses of othering and marginalization? How can we chart the kinds of semantic prosodies prevalent across different extremist organizations? How might we be able to break the pattern of depersonalization which characterize extremist discourse? And how can we use what we know about language and masculinities to deradicalize members and offer them ways out of these movements? The fact that these extremist and radical movements exist almost entirely online introduces additional issues worthy of exploration, particularly in terms of how these spaces facilitate networked misogyny and online cyberhate (see also Ging and Murphy 2021 for their discussion of the future of manosphere and incel research).

Indeed, the growing importance of online spaces, and how they are becoming more deeply integrated into our everyday lives, has implications for how masculinity is constituted in those spaces and how gender relations are expressed in, for example, web forums, social media sites, photo-sharing apps, and more. Some of these issues are already being investigated; the collected papers in Ging and Siapera (2019) offer a detailed discussion of networked misogyny, while there is growing interest in the linguistic dimension of toxic masculinities (Mercer and McGlashan *in progress*), photographic harassment by men (Jones 2019), pick-up artists (Dayter and Rüdiger

2020, 2022), the alt-right (Norman 2020), and eco-misogyny (Lawson, Szenes, and Lamb *in progress*). There is also a need to investigate the intersections of masculinity with class, sexuality, and age within the manosphere to better understand how these issues affect participation and involvement. Finally, while attention has focused on the English-speaking manosphere (e.g. Farrell et al. 2019), we know very little about the manosphere in other international contexts, as well how Black, Asian and Minority Ethnic men engage with this online space. What are the differences? What are the convergences? How does ethnicity fit in to our understanding of online (and offline) masculinities (see, for example, Young 2022 for a discussion of the Black manosphere)?

As tempting as it might be to focus on the negative, sexist, and antagonistic practices within male-dominated digital spaces, we should also recognize the fact that men use digital spaces to engage in productive, positive, and socially inclusive action. For example, Chapter 7 examined some of the online discussion around positive masculinities in television comedies, suggesting that spaces are opening up where individuals can engage in (or at least discuss) alternative conceptualizations of masculinity, while Chapter 8 outlined how new fathers support one another through mutual encouragement and advice on a fatherhood forum. Masculinities at the nexus of digital spaces will continue to be of interest to scholars, especially as the range of technical and modal affordances available in digital and online spaces expands (see, for example, the collected chapters in Lawson *in progress*).

Finally, the role of print and televised media in promoting, reifying, and challenging different forms of masculinity will undoubtedly continue to be an important research area. As Chapter 4 and Chapter 7 demonstrated, we can productively draw on a range of linguistic methods to critically investigate representations and ideologies of masculinity in traditional media outputs. Research across a range of broadcast outputs, as well as newer media formats such as video games (Heritage 2021), can only help facilitate our understanding of how language in implicated in mediated constructions of masculinities.

Ultimately, it is unlikely that language and masculinities research (or masculinities studies more broadly) is in any danger of fading into obscurity, as evidenced by its strong research base, the range of ongoing projects, and the number of scholarly communities working on masculinities issues of all kinds. For example, the Masculinity, Sex and Popular Culture network (Birmingham City University and University of Sunderland) brings together an interdisciplinary group of scholars working at the nexus of masculinities, sexualities, and contemporary/popular culture, while the Masculinities Research Network (University of Exeter) supports research on the histories, theories, experiences, embodiments, performances, and representations of masculinity. These networks join a number of other research centers, including the Center for the Study of Men and Masculinities (Stony Brook University, New York), the Men and Masculinities Center (University of Massachusetts Amherst, Massachusetts), and the Center for Masculinities Studies (Aalborg University, Denmark). All of this suggests that the social, political, cultural, historical, economic, and linguistic dimensions of masculinities will remain on the research agenda for the foreseeable future.

FINAL THOUGHTS

In writing a book like this, it is very tempting to finish with a manifesto, a clarion call, a proclamation that **things must change**. While it would be nice to think that the discussion presented in this book might make even a small difference to the world, my main aim has been to show how we can develop a systematic and robust analysis of language and masculinities in different media contexts and analyze these contexts in relation to contemporary expressions of gender, identity, sociocultural politics, and more. We might be existing, as Kelan (2009) argues, in a permanent state of "gender fatigue," but it is now, perhaps more than any other time, that we should be fully onboard with interrogating and examining the intersection of language, masculinities, and society, since it is through language that lives are lived, that relationships are cultivated or torn down, that barriers are raised or bridges are built, and that connections are forged or severed. The gender culture wars which have dominated the media landscape show little sign of abating, while how men act, behave, and communicate has come under ever increasing public scrutiny. This book has been, I hope, one small step in setting out how we can investigate these issues through the prism of language.

REFERENCES

Addati, Laura, Naomi Cassirer, and Katherine Gilchrist. 2014. *Maternity and Paternity at Work: Law and Practice across the World*. Geneva: International Labour Office.

Agha, Asif. 2003. "The Social Life of Cultural Value." *Language & Communication* 23 (3): 231–273.

Agha, Asif. 2007. *Language and Social Relations*. Cambridge: Cambridge University Press.

Ahmed, Saifuddin, and Jörg Matthes. 2017. "Media Representation of Muslims and Islam from 2000 to 2015: A Meta-Analysis." *International Communication Gazette* 79 (3): 219–44.

Ainsworth, Claire. 2018. "Sex Redefined: The Idea of 2 Sexes Is Overly Simplistic." *Scientific American* 3 (5). https://www.scientificamerican.com/article/sex-redefined-the-idea-of-2-sexes-is-overly-simplistic1/.

Aisch, Gregor, Jon Huang, and Celicia Kang. 2016. "Dissecting the #PizzaGate Conspiracy Theories." *New York Times*, December 10, 2016. https://www.nytimes.com/interact ive/2016/12/10/business/media/pizzagate.html.

Aitken, Stuart C. 2000. "Fathering and Faltering: 'Sorry, but You Don't Have the Necessary Accoutrements.'" *Environment and Planning A: Economy and Space* 32 (4): 581–598.

Alexander, Susan M. 2003. "Stylish Hard Bodies: Branded Masculinity in *Men's Health* Magazine." *Sociological Perspectives* 46 (4): 535–554.

Alexandra, Rae. 2021. "Sarah Everard Is Forcing Men to Reckon with Violence Against Women." *KQED*, March 12, 2021. https://www.kqed.org/arts/13893889/sarah-ever ard-is-forcing-men-to-reckon-with-violence-against-women.

Alibhai-Brown, Yasmin. 2021. "MPs Calling for Legislation to End Trolling and Division Should Consider Their Own Behaviour." *Inews*, October 19, 2021. https://inews. co.uk/opinion/mps-calling-for-legislation-to-end-online-division-and-nastiness-should-first-consider-their-own-behaviour-1257804.

Alim, H. Samy, Jooyoung Lee, and Lauren Carris Mason. 2011. "Moving the Crowd, 'Crowding' the Emcee: The Coproduction and Contestation of Black Normativity in Freestyle Rap Battles." *Discourse & Society* 22 (4): 422–439.

Allegretti, Aubrey. 2021. "Beyond Equality Charity Works with Teenage Boys to 'Create Safer Streets.'" *The Guardian*, March 16, 2021. http://www.theguardian.com/uk-news/2021/mar/16/beyond-equality-charity-works-with-teenage-boys-to-create-safer-streets.

Allyn, Bobby. 2020. "Reddit Bans The_Donald, Forum of Nearly 800,000 Trump Fans, Over Abusive Posts." NPR.Org., June 29, 2020. https://www.npr.org/2020/06/29/884819923/reddit-bans-the_donald-forum-of-nearly-800-000-trump-fans-over-abusive-posts.

Ammari, Tawfiq, and Sarita Schoenebeck. 2015. "Understanding and Supporting Fathers and Fatherhood on Social Media Sites." In *Proceedings of the 33rd Annual ACM Conference on Human Factors in Computing Systems: CHI '15, 1905–1914*. Seoul, Republic of Korea: ACM Press.

Andersen, Gisle. 2012. "How to Use Corpus Linguistics in Sociolinguistics." In *The Routledge Handbook of Corpus Linguistics*, edited by Anne O'Keeffe and Michael McCarthy, 547–562. Oxon: Routledge.

Andersen, Pablo Dominguez, and Simon Wendt. 2015. "Introduction: Masculinities and the Nation." In *Masculinities and the Nation in the Modern World: Between Hegemony and Marginalization*, edited by Pablo Dominguez Andersen and Simon Wendt, 1–18. Global Masculinities. New York, NY: Palgrave Macmillan US.

Andersson, Kjerstin. 2008. "Constructing Young Masculinity: A Case Study of Heroic Discourse on Violence." *Discourse & Society* 19 (2): 139–161.

Andreasson, Jesper, and Thomas Johansson. 2016. "Global Narratives of Fatherhood. Fathering and Masculinity on the Internet." *International Review of Sociology* 26 (3): 482–496.

Anthony, Laurence. 2020. *AntConc* (version 3.5.8). OS X. Tokyo, Japan: Waseda University. http://www.antlab.sci.waseda.ac.jp/.

Archer, Nandini. 2018. "'Feminism Is Cancer': The Angry Backlash against Our Reporting on the Men's Rights Movement." *OpenDemocracy*, August 18, 2018. https://www.opendemocracy.net/en/5050/feminism-is-cancer-mens-rights-activists-online-backlash/.

Archibald, Maggie. 2019. "31 Jaw-Dropping Reddit Statistics in 2019." *Medium*. Strategic Content Marketing. July 17, 2019. https://medium.com/strategic-content-marketing/31-jaw-dropping-reddit-statistics-in-2019-1d50423addcd.

Ari. 2018. "Unconventional Masculinity and its Toxicity in Sitcoms." *THE GOBBLOG*, May 12, 2018. https://goblintrash.wordpress.com/2018/05/12/unconventional-masculinity-and-its-toxicity-in-sitcoms/.

Åsenhed, Liselotte, Jennie Kilstam, Siw Alehagen, and Christina Baggens. 2014. "Becoming a Father Is an Emotional Roller Coaster: An Analysis of First-Time Fathers' Blogs." *Journal of Clinical Nursing* 23 (9–10): 1309–1317.

Austad, Steven N. 2006. "Why Women Live Longer than Men: Sex Differences in Longevity." *Gender Medicine* 3 (2): 79–92.

Baele, Stephane J., Lewys Brace, and Travis G. Coan. 2019. "From 'Incel' to 'Saint': Analyzing the Violent Worldview behind the 2018 Toronto Attack." *Terrorism and Political Violence*, 33 (8): 1–25.

Baird, Adam. 2012. "The Violent Gang and the Construction of Masculinity amongst Socially Excluded Young Men." *Safer Communities* 11 (4): 179–190.

Bakar, Faima. 2019. "Why Do So Many Men Think Feminism Is a Cancer?" *Metro*, August 7, 2019. https://metro.co.uk/2019/08/07/why-do-some-men-deny-that-womens-lived-experiences-of-sexism-are-real-10137964/.

Baker, Paul. 2004. "Querying Keywords: Questions of Difference, Frequency, and Sense in Keywords Analysis." *Journal of English Linguistics* 32 (4): 346–359.

Baker, Paul. 2010. *Sociolinguistics and Corpus Linguistics*. Edinburgh: Edinburgh University Press.

Baker, Paul. 2015. "200 Years of the American Man." In *Language and Masculinities: Performances, Intersections, Dislocations*, edited by Tommaso M. Milani, 34–52. Oxon: Routledge.

Baker, Paul, and Helen Baker. 2019. "Conceptualising Masculinity and Femininity in the British Press." In *Journalism, Gender and Power*, edited by Cynthia Carter, Linda Steiner, and Stuart Allan, 363–382. Oxon: Routledge.

Baker, Paul, and Giuseppe Balirano, eds. 2018. *Queering Masculinities in Language and Culture*. London: Palgrave Macmillan.

Baker, Paul, and Erez Levon. 2015. "Picking the Right Cherries? A Comparison of Corpus-Based and Qualitative Analyses of News Articles about Masculinity." *Discourse & Communication* 9 (2): 221–236.

Baker, Paul, and Erez Levon. 2016. "'That's What I Call a Man': Representations of Racialised and Classed Masculinities in the UK Print Media." *Gender and Language* 10 (1): 106–139.

Bakharia, Aneesha, Peter Bruza, Jim Watters, Bhuva Narayan, and Laurianne Sitbon. 2016. "Interactive Topic Modeling for Aiding Qualitative Content Analysis." *Proceedings of the 2016 ACM on Conference on Human Information Interaction and Retrieval*, 213–222.

Baldoni, Justin. 2017. "Why I'm Done Trying to Be 'Man Enough.'" Presented at TEDxWomen2017. https://www.ted.com/talks/justin_baldoni_why_i_m_d one_trying_to_be_man_enough/transcript.

Baldwin, Kristen. 2018. "Huzzah for 'Brooklyn Nine-Nine', the Most Inclusive Show on TV." EW.Com., May 11, 2018. https://ew.com/tv/2018/05/11/brooklyn-nine-nine-b99-canceled-fox-inclusive/.

Bamberg, Michael. 2004. "Form and Functions of 'Slut Bashing' in Male Identity Constructions in 15-Year-Olds." *Human Development* 47 (6): 331–353.

Bandyopadhyay, Alakananda. 2019. "Brooklyn Nine-Nine's Terry Crews and Joe Lo Truglio Believe Masculinity Shouldn't Stop Men from Showing Affection." *Me Aww*, July 31, 2019. https://meaww.com/brooklyn-nine-nine-terry-crews-charles-boyle-terry-jeffords-unique-masculinity-joe-lo-truglio.

Banerjee, Sikata. 2005. *Make Me a Man!: Masculinity, Hinduism, and Nationalism in India*. Albany, NY: State University of New York Press.

Banerjee, Sikata. 2012. *Muscular Nationalism: Gender, Violence, and Empire in India and Ireland, 1914–2004*. New York, NY: NYU Press.

Banet-Weiser, Sarah. 2018. *Empowered: Popular Feminism and Popular Misogyny*. Durham, NC: Duke University Press Books.

Banet-Weiser, Sarah, and Kate M. Miltner. 2016. "#MasculinitySoFragile: Culture, Structure, and Networked Misogyny." *Feminist Media Studies* 16 (1): 171–174.

Barbarossaa. 2015. "A Rejection of The MGTOW 'Manifesto.'" *Shedding of the Ego*, September 26, 2015. http://sheddingoftheego.com/2015/09/26/a-rejection-of-the-mgtow-manifesto/.

Barber, Kristen. 2008. "The Well-Coiffed Man: Class, Race, and Heterosexual Masculinity in the Hair Salon." *Gender & Society* 22 (4): 455–476.

Barker, Richard W. 1994. *Lone Fathers and Masculinities*. Aldershot: Avebury.

Barnes, Luke. 2017. "Expose on Breitbart Proves the 'Alt-Right' Is Just a Euphemism for White Supremacists." *Think Progress*, October 5, 2017. https://thinkprogress.org/breitbart-expose-white-supremacists-e348021c491a/.

Baron, Alistair, Paul Rayson, and Dawn Archer. 2009. "Word Frequency and Key Word Statistics in Historical Corpus Linguistics." *Anglistik* 20 (1): 41–67.

Baron-Cohen, Simon. 2003. *The Essential Difference: Men, Women and the Extreme Male Brain*. London: Allen Lane.

Barr, Sabrina. 2019. "What Is Toxic Masculinity?" *The Independent*, January 17, 2019. https://www.independent.co.uk/life-style/toxic-masculinity-definition-what-boys-men-gillette-ad-behaviour-attitude-girls-women-a8729336.html.

Barrett, Rusty. 2017. *From Drag Queens to Leathermen: Language, Gender, and Gay Male Subcultures*. Oxford: Oxford University Press.

Barrow, Bill. 2016. "Trump Again Disavows Alt-Right, White Supremacists." *AP NEWS*, November 23, 2016. https://apnews.com/decb7c1cae4e4c19ba5cf117a2eaf04e.

Bartie, Angela, and Louise A. Jackson. 2011. "Youth Crime and Preventive Policing in Post-War Scotland (c. 1945–1971)." *Twentieth Century British History* 22 (1): 79–102.

Bartie, Angela, and Alistair Fraser. 2017a. "'It Wasnae Just Easterhouse': The Politics of Representation in the Glasgow Gang Phenomenon, c. 1965–1975." In *Youth Culture and Social Change: Making a Difference by Making a Noise*, edited by Keith Gildart, Anna Gough-Yates, Sian Lincoln, Bill Osgerby, Lucy Robinson, and John Street, 205–229. London: Palgrave Macmillan.

Bartie, Angela, and Alistair Fraser. 2017b. "Speaking to the 'Hard Men': Masculinities, Violence and Youth Gangs in Glasgow, c. 1965–1975." In *Nine Centuries of Man: Manhood and Masculinity in Scottish History*, edited by Lynn Abrams and Elizabeth L. Ewan, 258–277. Edinburgh: Edinburgh University Press.

Bauer, Laurie, and Peter Trudgill. 1998. *Language Myths*. London: Penguin.

Beauchamp, Zack. 2018. "Incel, the Misogynist Ideology That Inspired the Deadly Toronto Attack, Explained." *Vox*, April 25, 2018. https://www.vox.com/world/2018/4/25/17277496/incel-toronto-attack-alek-minassian.

Beckwith, Karen. 2001. "Gender Frames and Collective Action: Configurations of Masculinity in the Pittston Coal Strike." *Politics & Society* 29 (2): 297–330.

Bednarek, Monika. 2018. *Language and Television Series: A Linguistic Approach to TV Dialogue*. Cambridge: Cambridge University Press.

Bednarek, Monika. 2020. "The Sydney Corpus of Television Dialogue: Designing and Building a Corpus of Dialogue from US TV Series." *Corpora* 15 (1): 107–119.

Beeching, Kate. 2006. "Synchronic and Diachronic Variation: The How and Why of Sociolinguistic Corpora." In *Corpus Linguistics around the World*, edited by Andrew Wilson, Dawn Archer, and Paul Rayson, 49–61. Amsterdam: Rodopi.

Beekmans, Inge, Anne-Marie Sweep, Linmin Zheng, and Zhifang Yu. 2018. "Forgive Me Father, for I Hate Women: Anti-Feminism and Misogyny in the Manosphere." *Diggit Magazine*, June 1, 2018. https://www.diggitmagazine.com/papers/forgive-me-father-i-hate-women-anti-feminism-and-misogyny-manosphere.

Belfiore, Eleonora, and Anna Upchurch. 2013. "Introduction: Reframing the 'value' Debate of the Humanities." In *Humanities in the Twenty-First Century: Beyond Utility and Markets*, edited by Eleonora Belfiore and Anna Upchurch, 1–14. Basingstoke: Palgrave Macmillan.

Bem, Sandra L. 1974. "The Measurement of Psychological Androgyny." *Journal of Consulting and Clinical Psychology* 42 (2): 155–162.

Benwell, Bethan, ed. 2003. *Masculinity and Men's Lifestyle Magazines*. Oxford: Blackwell Publishing.

Berdahl, Jennifer L., Marianne Cooper, Peter Glick, Robert W. Livingston, and Joan C. Williams. 2018. "Work as a Masculinity Contest." *Journal of Social Issues* 74 (3): 422–448.

Bernard, Sam. 2021. "Political Fandom and the Myth of the Establishment: How a Politically Partisan Online Network Engaged with Dissonant Media Texts." Unpublished PhD thesis. Sussex: University of Sussex.

Bernstein, Joseph. 2017. "Here's How Breitbart and Milo Smuggled Nazi and White Nationalist Ideas into the Mainstream." *BuzzFeed News*, October 5, 2017. https://www.buzzfeednews.com/article/josephbernstein/heres-how-breitbart-and-milo-smuggled-white-nationalism.

Bhattarai, Abha. 2017. "Breitbart Lost 90 Percent of Its Advertisers in Two Months: Who's Still There?" *Washington Post*, June 8, 2017. https://www.washingtonpost.com/news/business/wp/2017/06/08/breitbart-lost-90-percent-of-its-advertisers-in-two-months-whos-still-there/.

Biber, Douglas, Susan Conrad, and Randi Reppen. 1998. *Corpus Linguistics: Investigating Language Structure and Use*. Cambridge: Cambridge University Press.

Billig, Michael. 1995. *Banal Nationalism*. London: SAGE Publications.

Bird, Sharon R. 1996. "Welcome to the Men's Club: Homosociality and the Maintenance of Hegemonic Masculinity." *Gender & Society* 10 (2): 120–132.

Blake, Mariah. 2014. "The Men's Rights Movement and the Women Who Love It." *Mother Jones*, August 11, 2014. https://www.motherjones.com/politics/2014/08/mens-rights-movement-women-who-love-it/.

Blei, David M, Andrew Y. Ng, and Michael I. Jordan. 2003. "Latent Dirichlet Allocation." *Journal of Machine Learning Research* 3: 993–1022.

Bliss, Shepard. 1987. "Revisioning Masculinity." *Gender: Fresh Visions & Ancient Roots* 16: 21–29.

Bloch, Katrina Rebecca, Tiffany Taylor, and Karen Martinez. 2020. "Playing the Race Card: White Injury, White Victimhood and the Paradox of Colour-Blind Ideology in Anti-Immigrant Discourse." *Ethnic and Racial Studies* 43 (7): 1130–1148.

Blommaert, Jan. 2018. "Online-Offline Modes of Identity and Community: Elliot Rodger's Twisted World of Masculine Victimhood." In *Cultural Practices of Victimhood*, edited by Martin Hoonderr, Paul Mutsaers, and William Arfman, 193–212. Oxon: Routledge.

Blondeel, Karel, Sofia de Vasconcelos, Claudia García-Moreno, Rob Stephenson, Marleen Temmerman, and Igor Toskin. 2018. "Violence Motivated by Perception of Sexual Orientation and Gender Identity: A Systematic Review." *Bulletin of the World Health Organization* 96 (1): 29–41.

Blumell, Lindsey E., and Jennifer Huemmer. 2017. "Silencing Survivors: How News Coverage Neglects the Women Accusing Donald Trump of Sexual Misconduct." *Feminist Media Studies* 17 (3): 506–509.

Boe, Bryce. 2019. "Python Reddit API Wrapper Documentation," 112.

Bogetić, Ksenija. 2013. "Normal Straight Gays: Lexical Collocations and Ideologies of Masculinity in Personal Ads of Serbian Gay Teenagers." *Gender and Language* 7 (3): 333–367.

Bohler, Damien. 2013. "A Weekend Initiation into Mature Masculinity." *The Good Men Project*, May 14, 2013. https://goodmenproject.com/featured-content/a-weekend-initiation-into-mature-masculinity/.

Boise, Sam de. 2019. "Editorial: Is Masculinity Toxic?" *NORMA: International Journal for Masculinity Studies* 14 (3): 147–151.

Bokhari, Allum, and Milo Yiannopoulos. 2016. "An Establishment Conservative's Guide to The Alt-Right." *Breitbart*, March 30, 2016. https://www.breitbart.com/tech/2016/03/29/an-establishment-conservatives-guide-to-the-alt-right/.

Bola, J. J. 2019. *Mask Off: Masculinity Redefined*. London: Pluto Press.

Bologna, Caroline. 2017. "Dad's Sweet Comics Promote Empathy, Tolerance and Love." *HuffPost*, November 27, 2017. https://www.huffpost.com/entry/lunarbaboon-comics_n_5a0f15d1e4b0e97dffed08aa.

Bonnar, Myles. 2019. "The Seduction Game." *BBC News*, October 7, 2019. https://bbc.co.uk/news/extra/tmZeuc7TX0/the-seduction-game.

Bonner-Thompson, Carl, and Linda McDowell. 2020. "Precarious Lives, Precarious Care: Young Men's Caring Practices in Three Coastal Towns in England." *Emotion, Space and Society* 35 (May): 100684.

Bonnett, Alastair. 1996. "The New Primitives: Identity, Landscape and Cultural Appropriation in the Mythopoetic Men's Movement." *Antipode* 28 (3): 273–291.

Bordieu, Pierre. 1979. "Symbolic Power." *Critique of Anthropology* 4 (13–14): 77–85.

Bosman, Julie, Kate Taylor, and Tim Arango. 2019. "A Common Trait Among Mass Killers: Hatred Toward Women." *The New York Times*, August 10, 2019. https://www.nytimes.com/2019/08/10/us/mass-shootings-misogyny-dayton.html.

Bothwell, Ellie. 2020. "The Emotional Challenges of Studying Online Hatred of Women." *Times Higher Education (THE)*, April 16, 2020. https://www.timeshighereducation.com/features/emotional-challenges-studying-online-hatred-women.

boyd, danah. 2019. "Facing the Great Reckoning Head-On." *Medium*, September 13, 2019. https://medium.com/@zephoria/facing-the-great-reckoning-head-on-8fe434e10630.

Boyle, Danny. 1996. *Trainspotting*. PolyGram.

Boyle, Jimmy. 1977. *A Sense of Freedom*. London: Ebury Press.

Boyle, Karen. 2019. *#MeToo, Weinstein and Feminism*. Basingstoke: Palgrave Macmillan.

Boyle, Maree V. 2002. "'Sailing Twixt Scylla and Charybdis': Negotiating Multiple Organisational Masculinities." *Women in Management Review* 17 (3/4): 131–141.

Bradshaw, Paul. 2017. "Why Journalists Ditch the Thesaurus When It Comes to 'Said' (for New Journalism Students Who Don't)." *Online Journalism Blog*, September 25, 2017. https://onlinejournalismblog.com/2017/09/25/using-said-in-journalism/.

Brandom, Russell. 2018. "Russian Troll Sites Infiltrated Donald Trump Subreddit as Recently as This Month." *The Verge*, September 24, 2018. https://www.theverge.

com/2018/9/24/17896586/reddit-the-donald-russia-troll-farm-ira-influence-operation.

Bratich, Jack, and Sarah Banet-Weiser. 2019. "From Pick-Up Artists to Incels: Con(Fidence) Games, Networked Misogyny, and the Failure of Neoliberalism." *International Journal of Communication* 13: 1–25.

Breland, Ali. 2019. "Why Reddit Is Losing Its Battle with Online Hate." *Mother Jones*, August 27, 2019. https://www.motherjones.com/politics/2019/08/reddit-hate-content-moderation/.

Brezina, Vaclav, Robbie Love, and Karin Aijmer. 2018. "Corpus Linguistics and Sociolinguistics: Introducing the Spoken BNC2014." In *Corpus Approaches to Contemporary British Speech: Sociolinguistic Studies of the Spoken BNC2014*, edited by Vaclav Brezina, Robbie Love, and Karin Aijmer, 3–9. Oxon: Routledge.

Brezina, Vaclav, Tony McEnery, and Stephen Wattam. 2015. "Collocations in Context: A New Perspective on Collocation Networks." *International Journal of Corpus Linguistics* 20 (2): 139–173.

Brezina, Vaclav, Matt Timperley, and Tony McEnery. 2018. *#LancsBox* (version 4.5). OS X. Lancaster: Lancaster University. http://corpora.lancs.ac.uk/lancsbox/.

Brigham, Bob. 2020. "Involuntary Celibates Are an 'Emerging Domestic Terrorism Threat'; Texas Warns of an 'Incel Rebellion.'" *Raw Story*, January 12, 2020. https://www.rawstory.com/2020/01/involuntary-celibates-are-an-emerging-domestic-terrorism-threat-texas-warns-of-an-incel-rebellion/.

Brindle, Andrew. 2016. *The Language of Hate: A Corpus Lingusitic Analysis of White Supremacist Language*. Oxon: Routledge.

Brizendine, Louann. 2008. *The Female Brain*. London: Bantam.

Brizendine, Louann. 2011. *The Male Brain*. London: Bantam.

Brock, André. 2018. "Critical Technocultural Discourse Analysis." *New Media & Society* 20 (3): 1012–1030.

Brooks, Virginia. 1982. "Sex Differences in Student Dominance Behavior in Female and Male Professors' Classrooms." *Sex Roles* 8 (7): 683–690.

Brookes, G., and McEnery, T. 2019. "The Utility of Topic Modelling for Discourse Studies: A Critical Evaluation." *Discourse Studies* 21 (1): 3–21.

Brown, Chip. 2017. "The Many Ways Society Makes a Man." *Magazine*, December 19, 2016. https://www.nationalgeographic.com/magazine/2017/01/how-rites-of-passage-shape-masculinity-gender/.

Brown, Katherine E. 2019. "Gender, Governance, and Countering Violent Extremism (CVE) in the UK." *International Journal of Law, Crime and Justice*, 100371.

Brown, Katherine E., and Tania Saeed. 2015. "Radicalization and Counter-Radicalization at British Universities: Muslim Encounters and Alternatives." *Ethnic and Racial Studies* 38 (11): 1952–1968.

Brown, Wendy. 1995. *States of Injury: Power and Freedom in Late Modernity*. Princeton, NJ: Princeton University Press.

Bruzzi, Stella. 2013. *Men's Cinema: Masculinity and Mise-En-Scene in Hollywood*. Edinburgh: Edinburgh University Press.

Buchbinder, David. 2012. *Studying Men and Masculinities*. New York, NY: Routledge.

Bucholtz, Mary. 1999. "You Da Man: Narrating the Racial Other in the Production of White Masculinity." *Journal of Sociolinguistics* 3 (4): 443–460.

Bucholtz, Mary. 2019. "The Public Life of White Affects." *Journal of Sociolinguistics* 23 (5): 485–504.

Bucholtz, Mary, and Kira Hall. 2005. "Identity and Interaction: A Sociocultural Linguistic Approach." *Discourse Studies* 7 (4–5): 585–614.

Bucholtz, Mary, and Kira Hall. 2016. "Embodied Sociolinguistics." In *Sociolinguistics*, edited by Nikolas Coupland, 173–198. Cambridge: Cambridge University Press.

Buckingham, David. 1993. *Reading Audiences: Young People and the Media*. Manchester: Manchester University Press.

Burdis, Ray. 2013. *The Wee Man*. London: Carnaby International.

Burgess, Adrienne, and Rebecca Goldman. 2018. *Who's the Bloke in the Room? Fathers during Pregnancy and at the Birth in the United Kingdom* (Full Report). Contemporary Fathers in the UK Series. Marlborough: Fatherhood Institute.

Burgess, Jean, and Ariadna Matamoros-Fernández. 2016. "Mapping Sociocultural Controversies across Digital Media Platforms: One Week of #gamergate on Twitter, YouTube, and Tumblr." *Communication Research and Practice* 2 (1): 79–96.

Burns, Jim. 2017. "Biopolitics, Toxic Masculinities, Disavowed Histories, and Youth Radicalization." *Peace Review* 29 (2): 176–183.

Burnett, Scott. 2022. "Circulation in the Manosphere: Mobile Matrices of Reactionary Masculinity." Working Papers in Urban Language and Literacies, 303.

Burrell, Stephen, Nicole Westmarland, and Sandy Buxton. 2021. "How Men Can Be Allies to Women Right Now." *The Conversation*, March 15, 2021. http://theconversation.com/how-men-can-be-allies-to-women-right-now-157126.

Buss, David M., and David P. Schmitt. 1993. "Sexual Strategies Theory: An Evolutionary Perspective on Human Mating." *Psychological Review* 100 (2): 204–232.

Butler, Judith. 1988. "Performative Acts and Gender Constitution: An Essay in Phenomenology and Feminist Theory." *Theatre Journal* 40 (4): 519–531.

Butler, Judith. 1990. *Gender Trouble: Feminism and the Subversion of Identity*. Oxon: Routledge.

Byrne, John. 1978. *The Slab Boys*. London: Penguin Books.

Byrne, John. 1979. *Cuttin' a Rug*. London: Penguin Books.

Byrne, John. 1982. *Still Life*. London: Penguin Books.

Byrnes, James P., David C. Miller, and William D. Schafer. 1999. "Gender Differences in Risk Taking: A Meta-Analysis." *Psychological Bulletin* 125 (3): 367–383.

C Sara. 2019. "The XX & XY Lie: Our Social Construction of a Sex and Gender Binary." *Medium*, December 22, 2019. https://medium.com/@QSE/the-xx-xy-lie-our-social-construction-of-a-sex-and-gender-binary-4eed1e60e615.

Caesar, Terry. 2008. "#1 Dad: Fatherhood, Reception, and Television in 'Seinfeld' and 'Curb Your Enthusiasm.'" *Studies in American Humor*, 18: 59–73.

Cahuasqui, Meagan. 2020. "Brooklyn Nine-Nine: 10 Reasons Jake and Charles Aren't Real Friends." *ScreenRant*, March 23, 2020. https://screenrant.com/brooklyn-nine-nine-reasons-jake-charles-arent-real-friends/.

CALM. n.d. "What Is CALM?" *Campaign Against Living Miserably*. Accessed January 17, 2020. https://www.thecalmzone.net/about-calm/what-is-calm/.

Cameron, Deborah. 1992. "'Not Gender Difference but the Difference Gender Makes': Explanation in Research on Sex and Language." *International Journal of the Sociology of Language* 94: 13–26.

Cameron, Deborah. 1994. "Problems of sexist and non-sexist language." In *Exploring Gender: Questions and Implications for English Language Education*, edited by Jane Sunderland, 26–33. Phoenix ELT: Hemel Hempstead.

Cameron, Deborah. 1997. "Performing Gender Identity: Young Men's Talk and the Construction of Heterosexual Masculinity." In *Language and Masculinity*, edited by Sally Johnson and Ulrike Hanna Meinhof, 47–65. Oxford: Wiley-Blackwell.

Cameron, Deborah. 2005. "Language, Gender, and Sexuality: Current Issues and New Directions." *Applied Linguistics* 26 (4): 482–502.

Cameron, Deborah. 2007. *The Myth of Mars and Venus*. Oxford: Oxford University Press.

Cameron, Deborah. 2018. "Language and the Brotherhood of Men." *Language: A Feminist Guide*, October 11, 2018. https://debuk.wordpress.com/tag/womens-language/.

Cameron, Deborah. 2020. "Banter, Male Bonding, and the Language of Donald Trump." In *Language in the Trump Era: Scandals and Emergencies*, edited by Janet McIntosh and Norma Mendoza-Denton, 158–167. Cambridge: Cambridge University Press.

Cameron, Deborah, Elizabeth Frazer, Penelope Harvey, Ben Rampton, and Kay Richardson. 1993. "Ethics, Advocacy and Empowerment: Issues of Method in Researching Language." *Language & Communication* 13 (2): 81–94.

Cameron, Deborah, and Don Kulick. 2003. *Language and Sexuality*. Cambridge: Cambridge University Press.

Cammaert, Bert. 2022. "The Abnormalisation of Social Justice: The 'Anti-Woke Culture War' Discourse in the UK." *Discourse & Society* 09579265221095407.

Carian, Emily. 2022. "'No Seat at the Party': Mobilizing White Masculinity in the Men's Rights Movement." *Sociological Focus* 55 (1): 27–47.

Carlson, Åsa. 2016. "Sex, Biological Functions and Social Norms: A Simple Constructivist Theory of Sex." *NORA: Nordic Journal of Feminist and Gender Research* 24 (1): 18–29.

Carney, Nikita. 2016. "All Lives Matter, but So Does Race: Black Lives Matter and the Evolving Role of Social Media." *Humanity & Society* 40 (2): 180–199.

Carroll, Rory. 2014. "Reddit Bans Groups behind Sharing of Leaked Celebrity Photos." *The Guardian*, September 7, 2014. https://www.theguardian.com/technology/2014/sep/07/reddit-bans-groups-behind-sharing-of-leaked-celebrity-photos.

Carter, Pelham, Matt Gee, Hollie McIlhone, Harkeeret Lally, and Robert Lawson. 2021. "Comparing Manual and Computational Approaches to Theme Identification in Online Forums: A Case Study of a Sex Work Special Interest Community." *Methods in Psychology* 5: 100065.

Carter, Pelham, Robert Lawson, Matt Gee, Hollie McIlhone, and Harkeeret Lally. 2019. "'I've Been Married for 30 Odd Years and the Sex Is Crap': Risk, Health and Identity in an Online Sex Work Forum." Presented at the Approaches to Digital Discourse Analysis, Turku, Finland.

CBS *This Morning*. 2019. "Is the Gillette Commercial on 'Toxic Masculinity' Misunderstood?" https://www.youtube.com/watch?v=0xmvDUhbktU.

Chafe, Wallace. 1994. *Discourse, Consciousness, and Time: The Flow and Displacement of Conscious*. Chicago: University of Chicago Press.

Chandrasekharan, Eshwar, Umashanthi Pavalanathan, Anirudh Srinivasan, Adam Glynn, Jacob Eisenstein, and Eric Gilbert. 2017. "You Can't Stay Here: The Efficacy of Reddit's 2015 Ban Examined Through Hate Speech." *Proceedings of the ACM on Human-Computer Interaction* 1 (CSCW): 1–22.

Chaney, Cassandra. 2016. "The Tears of Black Men: Black Masculinity, Sexuality, and Sensitivity in R&B and Hip Hop." In *Hyper Sexual, Hyper Masculine?: Gender, Race and Sexuality in the Identities of Contemporary Black Men*, edited by Brittany C. Slatton and Kamesha Spates, 103–132. Oxon: Routledge.

Chaney, Cassandra, and Ray V. Robertson. 2013. "Racism and Police Brutality in America." *Journal of African American Studies* 17 (4): 480–505.

Charness, Gary, and Uri Gneezy. 2012. "Strong Evidence for Gender Differences in Risk Taking." *Journal of Economic Behavior & Organization* 83 (1): 50–58.

Chasmar, Jessica. 2016. "Hilary Tone, D.C. Schools Spokeswoman, Says She Wants to 'Get Rid of' White Men." *Washington Times*, December 15, 2016. https://www.washingtontimes.com/news/2016/dec/15/hilary-tone-dc-schools-spokeswoman-says-she-wants-/.

Chawla, Ravish. 2018. "Topic Modeling with LDA and NMF on the ABC News Headlines Dataset." *Medium*, May 1, 2018. https://medium.com/ml2vec/topic-modeling-is-an-unsupervised-learning-approach-to-clustering-documents-to-discover-topics-fdfbf30e27df.

Chen, Yong, Hui Zhang, Rui Liu, Zhiwen Ye, and Jianying Lin. 2019. "Experimental Explorations on Short Text Topic Mining between LDA and NMF Based Schemes." *Knowledge-Based Systems* 163: 1–13.

Cheng, Cliff. 1999. "Marginalized Masculinities and Hegemonic Masculinity: An Introduction." *The Journal of Men's Studies* 7 (3): 295–315.

Chollet, Mona. 2016. "Trump's Macho Politics." *Le Monde Diplomatique*, August 2016. https://mondediplo.com/2016/08/15macho.

Christensen, Ann-Dorte. 2010. "Resistance and Violence: Constructions of Masculinities in Radical Left-wing Movements in Denmark." *NORMA: International Journal for Masculinity Studies* 5 (02): 152–168.

Christensen, Ann-Dorte, and Sune Qvotrup Jensen. 2010. "Men, Resistance and Political Radicalization." *NORMA: International Journal for Masculinity Studies* 5 (02): 77–84.

Christensen, Ann-Dorte, and Sune Qvotrup Jensen. 2014. "Combining Hegemonic Masculinity and Intersectionality." *NORMA: International Journal for Masculinity Studies* 9 (1): 60–75.

Clatterbaugh, Kenneth. 2004. "What Is Problematic about Masculinities?" In *Feminism and Masculinities*, edited by Peter Francis Murphy, 200–213. Oxford: Oxford University Press.

Coaston, Jane. 2019. "Audio Tape Reveals Richard Spencer Is, as Everyone Knew, a Racist." *Vox*, November 4, 2019. https://www.vox.com/identities/2019/11/4/20947833/richard-spencer-white-nationalism-audio-milo-alt-right.

Coates, Jennifer. 1997. "Competing Discourses of Femininity." In *Communicating Gender in Context*, edited by Helga Kotthoff and Ruth Wodak, 285–314. Amsterdam: John Benjamins Publishing.

Coates, Jennifer. 2003. *Men Talk: Stories in the Making of Masculinities*. Oxon: Blackwell Publishing.

Coates, Jennifer. 2013. "The Discursive Production of Everyday Heterosexualities." *Discourse & Society* 24 (5): 536–552.

Coffé, Hilda. 2019. "Gender, Gendered Personality Traits and Radical Right Populist Voting." *Politics* 39 (2): 170–185.

Coffey-Glover, Laura. 2015. "Ideologies of Masculinity in Women's Magazines: A Critical Stylistic Approach." *Gender and Language* 9 (3): 337–364.

Coffey-Glover, Laura. 2019. *Men in Women's Worlds: Constructions of Masculinity in Women's Magazines*. Basingstoke: Palgrave Macmillan.

Cohen, Stanley. 1972. *Folk Devils and Moral Panics: The Creation of the Mods and Rockers*. London: MacGibbon and Lee Ltd.

Cole, Mike. 2018. *Trump, the Alt-Right and Public Pedagogies of Hate and for Fascism: What Is to Be Done?* Oxon: Routledge.

Coleman, Daniel. 2015. "Traditional Masculinity as a Risk Factor for Suicidal Ideation: Cross-Sectional and Prospective Evidence from a Study of Young Adults." *Archives of Suicide Research* 19 (3): 366–384.

Collier, Richard, and Sally Sheldon. 2008. *Fragmenting Fatherhood: A Socio-Legal Study*. Bloomsbury Publishing.

Collins, Luke Curtis. 2019. *Corpus Linguistics for Online Communication: A Guide for Research*. Oxon: Routledge.

Confer, Jaime, Judith A. Easton, Diana S. Fleischman, Cari D. Goetz, David M.G. Lewis, Carin Perilloux, and David M. Buss. 2010. "Evolutionary Psychology: Controversies, Questions, Prospects, and Limitations." *American Psychologist* 65 (2): 110–126.

Coning, Alexis de. 2016. "Recouping Masculinity: Men's Rights Activists' Responses to Mad Max: Fury Road." *Feminist Media Studies* 16 (1): 174–176.

Connell, R. W. 1987. *Gender and Power: Society, the Person and Sexual Politics*. Cambridge: Polity Press.

Connell, R. W. 1992. "A Very Straight Gay: Masculinity, Homosexual Experience, and the Dynamics of Gender." *American Sociological Review* 57 (6): 735–751.

Connell, R. W. 1997. "Men, Masculinities and Feminism." *Social Alternatives* 16 (3): 7.

Connell, R. W. 2002. "On Hegemonic Masculinity and Violence." *Theoretical Criminology* 6 (1): 88–99.

Connell, R. W. 2003. "Scrambling in the Ruins of Patriarchy: Neo-Liberalism and Men's Divided Interests in Gender Change." In *Gender: from Costs to Benefits*, edited by Ursula Pasero, 58–69. Wiesbaden: VS Verlag für Sozialwissenschaften.

Connell, R. W. 2003. "The Role of Men and Boys in Achieving Gender Equality." United Nations, Division for the Advancement of Women, 21–24.

Connell, R. W. 2005. *Masculinities*. 2nd edition. Cambridge: Polity Press.

Connell, R. W., and James W. Messerschmidt. 2005. "Hegemonic Masculinity: Rethinking the Concept." *Gender & Society* 19 (6): 829–859.

Conover, Adam. 2017. *Adam Ruins Everything: Alpha Males Do Not Exist*. truTV. https://www.youtube.com/watch?v=0Ti86veZBjU.

Cook, Bethany. 2018. "'Wait until Your Father Gets Home': The Lasting Impact of How You Speak to Your Children about Their Other Parent." *Parentingadvice.Net*, August 31, 2018. https://www.parentingadvice.net/blog-1/wait-until-your-father-gets-home-the-lasting-impact-of-how-you-speak-to-your-children-about-their-other-parent.

Cooper, Frank Rudy. 2011. "Masculinities, Post-Racialism and the Gates Controversy: The False Equivalence Between Officer and Civilian." *Nevada Law Journal* 11 (1): 1–43.

Cooper, Frank Rudy. 2012. "The King Stay the Same: Multidimensional Masculinities and Capitalism in *The Wire*." In *Masculinities and the Law: A Multidimensional Approach*, edited by Ann C. McGinley and Frank Rudy Cooper, 96–118. New York, NY: NYU Press.

Cooper, Frank Rudy, and Ann C. McGinley. 2012. *Masculinities and the Law: A Multidimensional Approach*. NYU Press.

Cooper, Richard. 2020. "20 Red Flags to Avoid." *Entrepreneurs in Cars*. 2020. https://entrepreneursincars.com/wp-content/uploads/2020/01/20-Red-Flags-To-Avoid.pdf.

Cornelisse, Jimi. 2018. "Cucks, Keks, and Pepes: A Linguistic Approach to Studying User Migration from the Manosphere to the Alt-Right." Amsterdam: Universiteit van Amsterdam.

Cornwall, Andrea. 2016. "Introduction: Masculinities under Neoliberalism." In *Masculinities under Neoliberalism*, edited by Andrea Cornwall, Frank G. Karioris, and Nancy Lindisfarne, 1–28. London: Zed Books Ltd.

Cornwall, Andrea, Frank G. Karioris, and Nancy Lindisfarne, eds. 2017. *Masculinities under Neoliberalism*. London: Zed Books.

Cosslett, Rhiannon Lucy. 2022. "The Struggle of Fatherhood Is Real—so Why Are New Dads Often Invisible in NHS Advice?" *The Guardian*, August 22, 2022, sec. Opinion. https://www.theguardian.com/commentisfree/2022/aug/22/no-one-tells-you-how-hard-dad-new-parent-pregnancy-birth.

Cotto, Jessica H., Elisabeth Davis, Gayathri J. Dowling, Jennifer C. Elcano, Anna B. Staton, and Susan R. B. Weiss. 2010. "Gender Effects on Drug Use, Abuse, and Dependence: A Special Analysis of Results from the National Survey on Drug Use and Health." *Gender Medicine* 7 (5): 402–413.

Craig, Steve. 1992. *Men, Masculinity and the Media*. London: SAGE.

Crawford, Robert. 2009. *Scotland's Books: A History of Scottish Literature*. Oxford: Oxford University Press.

Crawford, William, and Eniko Csomay. 2015. *Doing Corpus Linguistics*. Oxon: Routledge.

Crawshaw, Paul. 2007. "Governing the Healthy Male Citizen: Men, Masculinity and Popular Health in Men's Health Magazine." *Social Science & Medicine (1982)* 65 (8): 1606–1618.

Crews, Terry. 2014. *Manhood: How to Be a Better Man or Just Live with One*. New York, NY: Penguin Random House USA.

Crombie, Neil, and Arthur Cary. 2016. "All Man." London: Swan Films. https://www.swanfilms.tv/productions/grayson-perry-all-man/.

Cross, Gary S. 2008. *Men to Boys: The Making of Modern Immaturity*. New York, NY: Columbia University Press.

Crump, Andy. 2017. "*Brooklyn Nine-Nine* Review: 'Moo Moo' Is One of the Best Episodes in the Series' Canon." *Pastemagazine*, May 2, 2017. https://www.pastemagazine.com/tv/brooklyn-nine-nine/brooklyn-nine-nine-review-the-sobering-moo-moo-is/.

Ćuklanz, Lisa, and Ali Erol. 2021. "The Shifting Image of Hegemonic Masculinity in Contemporary U.S. Television Series." *International Journal of Communication* 15: 545–562.

D'Onofrio, Annette. 2015. "Persona-Based Information Shapes Linguistic Perception: Valley Girls and California Vowels." *Journal of Sociolinguistics* 19 (2): 241–256.

dad.info. 2008. "About Us: DAD.Info." https://www.dad.info/about-us.

Dallesasse, Starla L., and Annette S. Kluck. 2013. "Reality Television and the Muscular Male Ideal." *Body Image* 10 (3): 309–315.

Davies, Andrew. 2013. *City of Gangs: Glasgow and the Rise of the British Gangster*. London: Hodder and Stoughton Ltd.

Davies, Helen. 2018. "All the Things Coffee Culture Tells Us about Gender." *Bitch Media*, August 29, 2018. https://www.bitchmedia.org/article/the-gendering-of-coffee-culture.

Davies, Jon A., David S. Shen-Miller, and Anthony Isacco. 2010. "The Men's Center Approach to Addressing the Health Crisis of College Men." *Professional Psychology: Research and Practice* 41 (4): 347–354.

Davies, William. 2020. "How the Humanities Became the New Enemy Within." *The Guardian*, February 28, 2020. https://www.theguardian.com/commentisfree/2020/feb/28/humanities-british-government-culture.

Day, Felicia. 2014. "Felicia's Melange: The Only Thing I Have to Say about Gamer Gate." October 22, 2014. https://thisfeliciaday.tumblr.com/post/100700417809/the-only-thing-i-have-to-say-about-gamer-gate.

Dayter, Daria, and Sofia Rüdiger. 2022. *The Language of Pick-Up Artists: Online Discourses of the Seduction Industry*. Oxon: Routledge.

Deckers, Erik. 2019. "The Flawed Psychology of the Middle-Aged Conservative White Man." *Medium*, November 23, 2019. https://medium.com/our-human-family/the-flawed-psychology-of-the-middle-aged-conservative-white-man-3a6ac2ca3d66.

Defoe, Daniel. 1753. *A Tour Thro' the Whole Island of Great Britain*: Vol. IV. London: Printed for S. Birt [and others]. http://archive.org/details/b3052796x_0004.

DeKeseredy, Walter S., and Martin D. Schwartz. 2005. "Masculinities and Interpersonal Violence." In *Handbook of Studies on Men and Masculinities*, edited by Michael S. Kimmel, Jeff Hearn, and R.W. Connell, 353–366. London: SAGE Publications Ltd.

Demetriou, Demetrakis Z. 2001. "Connell's Concept of Hegemonic Masculinity: A Critique." *Theory and Society* 30 (3): 337–361.

Densley, James, Ross Deuchar, and Simon Harding. 2020. "An Introduction to Gangs and Serious Youth Violence in the United Kingdom." *Youth Justice*, 1473225420902848.

Derksen, Christina, Anna Serlachius, Keith J. Petrie, and Nicola Dalbeth. 2017. "'What Say Ye Gout Experts?' A Content Analysis of Questions about Gout Posted on the Social News Website Reddit." *BMC Musculoskeletal Disorders* 18 (1): 1–5.

Dermott, Esther. 2008. *Intimate Fatherhood: A Sociological Analysis*. Oxon: Routledge.

Deschenes, Miguel A. 2016. "Man Up! Helping Adolescent Boys Breakthrough Gender Role Conflict Through Positive Masculinity." Unpublished MA dissertation. Seattle: City University of Seattle.

Desclos, Anne Cécile. 1954. *Histoire d'O (The Story of O)*. Paris: Jean-Jacques Pauvert.

Devega, Chauncey. 2015. "Dear White America: Your Toxic Masculinity Is Killing You." *Salon*, August 2, 2015. https://www.salon.com/2015/08/02/dear_white_america_your_toxic_masculinity_is_killing_you/.

Dickson-Swift, Virginia, Erica L. James, Sandra Kippen, and Pranee Liamputtong. 2007. "Doing Sensitive Research: What Challenges Do Qualitative Researchers Face?" *Qualitative Research* 7 (3): 327–353.

Dignam, Pierce Alexander, and Deana A. Rohlinger. 2019. "Misogynistic Men Online: How the Red Pill Helped Elect Trump." *Signs: Journal of Women in Culture and Society* 44 (3): 589–612.

Dill, Karen E., and Kathryn P. Thill. 2007. "Video Game Characters and the Socialization of Gender Roles: Young People's Perceptions Mirror Sexist Media Depictions." *Sex Roles* 57 (11–12): 851–864.

Dishy, Aaron. 2018. "Swallowing Misandry: A Survey of the Discursive Strategies of r/TheRedPill on Reddit." Unpublished MA dissertation. Toronto: University of Toronto.

Diviney, Leah. 2019. "James Bond Is Out; Jake Peralta Is In." *Medium*, November 13, 2019. https://medium.com/the-public-ear/james-bond-is-out-jake-peralta-is-in-d0d8374f3c4d.

Doucet, Andrea. 2016. "Foreword." In *Pops in Pop Culture: Fatherhood, Masculinity, and the New Man*, edited by Elizabeth Podnieks, ix–xii. Basingstoke: Palgrave Macmillan.

Doward, Jamie. 2016. "Men Much Less Likely to Seek Mental Health Help than Women." *The Observer*, November 5, 2016. https://www.theguardian.com/society/2016/nov/05/men-less-likely-to-get-help--mental-health.

Dragiewicz, Molly. 2008. "Patriarchy Reasserted: Fathers' Rights and Anti-VAWA Activism." *Feminist Criminology* 3 (2): 121–144.

Dragiewicz, Molly, and Yvonne Lindgren. 2009. "The Gendered Nature of Domestic Violence: Statistical Data for Lawyers Considering Equal Protection Analysis." *American University Journal of Gender, Social Policy and the Law* 17: 229–268.

Dragiewicz, Molly, and Ruth M. Mann. 2016. "Special Edition: Fighting Feminism—Organised Opposition to Women's Rights; Guest Editors' Introduction." *International Journal for Crime, Justice and Social Democracy* 5 (2): 1.

Duindam, Vincent. 1999. "Men in the Household: Caring Fathers." In *Gender, Power and the Household*, edited by Linda McKie, Sophia Bowley, Susan Gregory, and Jo Campling, 43–59. Basingstoke: Palgrave Macmillan.

Dumas, Tara M., Kathryn Graham, Matthew A. Maxwell-Smith, and Samantha Wells. 2015. "Being Cool Is Risky Business: Young Men's within-Peer-Group Status, Heavy Alcohol Consumption and Aggression in Bars." *Addiction Research & Theory* 23 (3): 213–222.

Dutton, Donald G. 2012. "The Case against the Role of Gender in Intimate Partner Violence." *Aggression and Violent Behavior* 17 (1): 99–104.

Eckert, Penelope. 1989. "The Whole Woman: Sex and Gender Differences in Variation." *Language Variation and Change* 1 (3): 245–267.

Eckert, Penelope. 2012. "Three Waves of Variation Study: The Emergence of Meaning in the Study of Sociolinguistic Variation." *Annual Review of Anthropology* 41: 87–100.

Eckert, Penelope. 2018. *Meaning and Linguistic Variation: The Third Wave in Sociolinguistics*. Cambridge: Cambridge University Press.

Eckert, Penelope, and Sally McConnell-Ginet. 1992. "Think Practically and Look Locally: Language and Gender as Community-Based Practice." *Annual Review of Anthropology* 21 (1): 461–488.

Eckert, Penelope, and Sally McConnell-Ginet. 2013. *Language and Gender*. 2nd edition. Cambridge: Cambridge University Press.

Eckert, Penelope, and Robert J. Podesva. 2011. "Sociophonetics and Sexuality: Toward a Symbiosis of Sociolinguistics and Laboratory Phonology." *American Speech* 86 (1): 6–13.

Economic and Social Research Council. 2015. "ESRC Framework for Research Ethics." Swindon: Economic and Social Research Council.

Edelsky, Carole. 1981. "Who's Got the Floor?" *Language in Society* 10 (3): 383–421.

Edley, Nigel, and Margaret Wetherell. 1997. "Jockeying for Position: The Construction of Masculine Identities." *Discourse & Society* 8 (2): 203–217.

Edley, Nigel, and Margaret Wetherell. 1999. "Imagined Futures: Young Men's Talk about Fatherhood and Domestic Life." *British Journal of Social Psychology* 38 (2): 181–194.

Edmond Jr., Alfred. 2019. "Why the Gillette 'Best Man A Man Can Be' Ad Misses So Badly." *Black Enterprise*, January 17, 2019. https://www.blackenterprise.com/gillette-best-men-ad-misses-so-badly/.

Edwards, Griffin Sims, and Stephen Rushin. 2018. "The Effect of President Trump's Election on Hate Crimes." SSRN Scholarly Paper ID 3102652. Rochester, NY: Social Science Research Network.

Edwards, Rosalind, Andrea Doucet, and Frank F. Furstenberg. 2009. "Fathering across Diversity and Adversity: International Perspectives and Policy Interventions." *The ANNALS of the American Academy of Political and Social Science* 624 (1): 6–11.

Edwards, Sophie. 2017. "Why Include Men and Boys in the Fight for Gender Equality?" *Devex*, May 15, 2017. https://www.devex.com/news/sponsored/why-include-men-and-boys-in-the-fight-for-gender-equality-90245.

Ehrenfreund, Max. 2016. "What the Alt-Right Really Wants, According to a Professor Writing a Book about Them." *Washington Post*, November 21, 2016. https://www.

washingtonpost.com/news/wonk/wp/2016/11/21/what-the-alt-right-really-wants-according-to-a-professor-writing-a-book-about-them/.

El Refaie, Elisabeth. 2014. "Looking on the Dark and Bright Side: Creative Metaphors of Depression in Two Graphic Memoirs." *A/b: Auto/Biography Studies* 29 (1): 149–174.

Elam, Paul. 2010. "Mission Statement: A Voice for Men." 2010. https://avoiceformen.com/policies/mission-statement/.

Elliott, Karla. 2016. "Caring Masculinities: Theorizing an Emerging Concept." *Men and Masculinities* 19 (3): 240–259.

Elliott, Kathleen. 2018. "Challenging Toxic Masculinity in Schools and Society." *On the Horizon* 26 (1): 17–22.

Ellis, Anthony. 2015. *Men, Masculinities and Violence: An Ethnographic Study*. Oxon: Routledge.

Elsherif, Mahmoud M., Sara L. Middleton, Jenny M. Phan, Flavio Azevedo, Bethan J. Iley, Magdalena Grose-Hodge, Samantha L. Tyler, et al. 2022. "Bridging Neurodiversity and Open Scholarship: How Shared Values Can Guide Best Practices for Research Integrity, Social Justice, and Principled Education." *MetaArXiv*. doi:10.31222/osf.io/k7a9p.

Ely, Kat. 2015. "The World is Designed for Men: How Bias Is Built into Our Daily Lives." *Medium*, September 8, 2015. https://medium.com/hh-design/the-world-is-designed-for-men-d06640654491.

Englar-Carlson, Matt, and Mark S. Kiselica. 2013. "Affirming the Strengths in Men: A Positive Masculinity Approach to Assisting Male Clients." *Journal of Counseling & Development* 91 (4): 399–409.

English, Otto. 2020. "Speaking Another Language: A Social Media Tale." *Byline Times*, February 6, 2020. https://bylinetimes.com/2020/02/06/speaking-another-language-a-social-media-tale/.

Enloe, Cynthia. 1998. "All the Men Are in the Militias, All the Women Are Victims: The Politics of Masculinity and Femininity in Nationalist Wars." In *The Women and War Reader*, edited by Lois Ann Lorentzen and Jennifer E. Turpin, 50–62. New York, NY: NYU Press.

Enloe, Cynthia. 2014. *Bananas, Beaches and Bases: Making Feminist Sense of International Politics*. Berkeley, CA: University of California Press.

Enloe, Cynthia. 2015. "The Recruiter and the Sceptic: A Critical Feminist Approach to Military Studies." *Critical Military Studies* 1 (1): 3–10.

Entenmen, Elizabeth. 2017. "John Legend Has Some Powerful Things to Say about What It Means to 'Be a Man' in 2017." *HelloGiggles*, August 25, 2017. https://uk.style.yahoo.com/john-legend-powerful-things-means-005921521.html.

Eriksson, Henrik, and Martin Salzmann-Erikson. 2013. "Supporting a Caring Fatherhood in Cyberspace: an Analysis of Communication about Caring within an Online Forum for Fathers." *Scandinavian Journal of Caring Sciences* 27 (1): 63–69.

Eriksson, Mia. 2017. "Breivik and I: Affective Encounters with 'Failed' Masculinity in Stories about Right-Wing Terrorism." *NORMA: International Journal for Masculinity Studies* 13 (3–4): 265–278.

European Commission. 2019. "Data Protection Rules as a Trust-Enabler in the EU and Beyond: Taking Stock." Koninklijke Brill NV.

Evaldsson, Ann-Carita. 2002. "Boys Gossip Telling: Staging Identities and Indexing (Unacceptable) Masculine Behavior." *Text & Talk* 22 (2): 199–225.

Evans, Joan, Frank Blye, John L. Oliffe, and David Gregoy. 2011. "Health, Illness, Men and Masculinities (HIMM): A Theoretical Framework for Understanding Men and Their Health." *Journal of Men's Health* 8 (1): 7–15.

Evans, Robert. 2018. "From Memes to Infowars: How 75 Fascist Activists Were 'Red-Pilled.'" *Bellingcat*, October 11, 2018. https://www.bellingcat.com/news/americas/2018/10/11/memes-infowars-75-fascist-activists-red-pilled/.

Evans, Roger, Alexander Gelbukh, Gregory Grefenstette, Patrick Hanks, Miloš Jakubíček, Diana McCarthy, Martha Palmer, et al. 2016. "Adam Kilgarriff's Legacy to Computational Linguistics and Beyond." In *International Conference on Intelligent Text Processing and Computational Linguistics*, edited by Alexander Gelbukh, 3–25. New York, NY: Springer.

Ezekilov, Jossif. 2017. "Gender 'Men-Streaming' CVE: Countering Violence Extremism By Addressing Masculinities Issues." *Reconsidering Development* 5 (1).

Fägersten, Kristy Beers, and Hanna Sveen. 2016. "SaMANtha: Language and Gender in *Sex in the City*." In *Watching TV with a Linguist*, edited by Kristy Beers Fägersten, 85–113. Syracuse, NY: Syracuse University Press.

Fahie, Declan. 2014. "Doing Sensitive Research Sensitively: Ethical and Methodological Issues in Researching Workplace Bullying." *International Journal of Qualitative Methods* 13 (1): 19–36.

Fairclough, Norman. 1989. *Language and Power*. Harlow: Pearson Education Limited.

Fairclough, Norman. 2001a. "Critical Discourse Analysis as a Method in Social Scientific Research." In *Methods of Critical Discourse Analysis*, edited by Ruth Wodak and Michael Meyer, 122–136. London: SAGE Publications.

Fairclough, Norman. 2001b. "The Discourse of New Labour: Critical Discourse Analysis." In *Discourse as Data: A Guide for Analysis*, edited by Margaret Wetherell, Stephanie Taylor, and Simeon J. Yates, 229–266. London: SAGE Publications.

Fairclough, Norman. 2012. "Critical Discourse Analysis." In *The Routledge Handbook of Discourse Analysis*, edited by James Paul Gee and Michael Handford, 9–20. Oxon: Routledge.

Faludi, Susan. 1992. *Backlash: The Undeclared War Against Women*. London: Chatto and Windus.

Farhi, Paul. 2019. "Whatever Happened to Breitbart? The Insurgent Star of the Right Is in a Long, Slow Fade." *The Washington Post*, July 4, 2019. https://www.washingtonp ost.com/lifestyle/style/whatever-happened-to-breitbart-the-insurgent-star-of-the- right-is-in-a-long-slow-fade/2019/07/02/c8f501a2-9cde-11e9-85d6-5211733f92c 7_story.html.

Farrell, Tracie, Miriam Fernandez, Jakub Novotny, and Harith Alani. 2019. "Exploring Misogyny across the Manosphere in Reddit." In *Proceedings of the 10ᵗʰ ACM Conference on Web Science*. Boston, Massachusetts, USA: ACM Press.

Farrell, Warren. 1993. *Myth of Male Power*. New York, NY: Berkley Trade.

Fausto-Sterling, Anne. 1987. "Society Writes Biology / Biology Constructs Gender." *Daedalus* 116 (4): 61–76.

Fausto-Sterling, Anne. 2000. *Sexing the Body: Gender Politics and the Construction of Sexuality*. New York, NY: Basic Books.

Fausto-Sterling, Anne. 2012. *Sex/Gender: Biology in a Social World*. New York, NY: Routledge.

Feasey, Rebecca. 2008. *Masculinity and Popular Television*. Edinburgh: Edinburgh University Press.

Feasey, Rebecca. 2009. "Spray More, Get More: Masculinity, Television Advertising and the Lynx Effect." *Journal of Gender Studies* 18 (4): 357–368.

Ferber, Abby L. 1998. *White Man Falling: Race, Gender, and White Supremacy*. Lanham: Rowman & Littlefield Publishers.

Ferber, Abby L. 2007. "The Construction of Black Masculinity: White Supremacy Now and Then." *Journal of Sport and Social Issues* 31 (1): 11–24.

Ferber, Abby L., and Michael S. Kimmel. 2000. "'White Men Are This Nation': Right-Wing Militias and the Restoration of Rural American Masculinity." *Rural Sociology* 65 (4): 582–604.

Ferguson, Harry. 2021. "By Breaking the Silence about Patriarchy, Men Can Help End Violence against Women." *The Guardian*, March 17, 2021. http://www.theguardian. com/commentisfree/2021/mar/17/breaking-silence-patriarchy-men-help-end-viole nce-against-women.

Ferris, Paul, and Reg McKay. 2001. *The Ferris Conspiracy*. Edinburgh: Mainstream Publishing.

Ferris, Paul, and Reg McKay. 2005. *Vendetta: Turning Your Back on Crime Can Be Deadly*. Edinburgh: Black and White Publishing.

Ferris, Paul, Stuart Wheatman, and Steve Wraith. 2018. *Unfinished Business: Putting the Conspiracy to Rest.* Newcastle: Mojo Risin' Publishing.

Fine, Cordelia. 2010. *Delusions of Gender: How Our Minds, Society, and Neurosexism Create Difference.* New York, NY: W. W. Norton & Company.

Firth, John Rupert. 1956. *Papers in Linguistics 1934-1951.* London: Oxford University Press.

Fishman, Pamela M. 1977. "Interactional Shitwork." *Heresies* 1: 99–111.

Fishman, Pamela M. 1978. "Interaction: The Work Women Do." *Social Problems* 25 (4): 397–406.

Fjordman. 2006. "How the Feminists' 'War against Boys' Paved the Way for Islam." *The Brussels Journal.* 2006. https://www.brusselsjournal.com/node/1300.

Fletcher, Richard, and Jennifer St George. 2011. "Heading into Fatherhood—Nervously: Support for Fathering from Online Dads." *Qualitative Health Research* 21 (8): 1101–1114.

Flood, Alison. 2020. "Author of Book about Victim Blaming Bombarded with Misogynist Abuse." *The Guardian*, April 24, 2020. http://www.theguardian.com/books/2020/apr/24/author-book-victim-blaming-misogynist-abuse-jessica-taylor.

Flood, Michael G. 2005. "Men's Collective Struggles for Gender Justice." In *Handbook of Studies on Men and Masculinities*, edited by Michael Kimmel, Jeff Hearn, and R.W. Connell, 458–466. London: SAGE Publications Ltd.

Flood, Michael G. 2008. "A Response to Bob Pease's 'Engaging Men in Men's Violence Prevention.'" *Australian Domestic & Family Violence Clearinghouse* 20: 1–11.

Flood, Michael G. 2008. "Men, Sex, and Homosociality: How Bonds between Men Shape Their Sexual Relations with Women." *Men and Masculinities* 10 (3): 339–359.

Flood, Michael G. 2010. "'Fathers' Rights' and the Defense of Paternal Authority in Australia." *Violence Against Women* 16 (3): 328–347.

Flood, Michael G. 2015. "Men and Gender Equality." In *Engaging Men in Building Gender Equality*, edited by Michael G. Flood and Richard Howson, 1–31. Newcastle: Cambridge Scholars Publishing.

Flood, Randy. 2019. "Talking About 'Toxic Masculinity.'" *Men's Resource Center* (blog). April 16, 2019. https://menscenter.org/toxic-masculinity/.

Ford, Clementine. 2018. "How Many Ways Can Men Say 'Not All Men'?" *Literary Hub*, October 25, 2018. https://lithub.com/how-many-ways-can-men-say-not-all-men/.

Formato, Federica, and Mandie Iveson. 2022. "'Soys Will Be Soys': Constructions of Masculinities in YouTube Responses to a Gillette Advert." *Discourse, Context & Media* 49: 100628.

Fox News. 2016. "Gavin McInnes: By Every Metric Men Have It Worse." https://www.youtube.com/watch?v=lsFFn9ttmMQ.

Fox, John. 2004. "How Men's Movement Participants View Each Other." *The Journal of Men's Studies* 12 (2): 103–118.

Franke-Ruta, Garance. 2013. "Niall Ferguson, Ted Cruz, and the Politics of Masculinity." *The Atlantic*, May 7, 2013. https://www.theatlantic.com/politics/archive/2013/05/niall-ferguson-ted-cruz-and-the-politics-of-masculinity/275580/.

Fraser, Alistair. 2013. "Street Habitus: Gangs, Territorialism and Social Change in Glasgow." *Journal of Youth Studies* 16 (8): 970–985.

Fraser, Alistair. 2015. *Urban Legends: Gang Identity in the Post-Industrial City.* Oxford: Oxford University Press.

Fraser, Alistair, M0ichele Burman, Susan Batchelor, and Susan McVie. 2010. "Youth Violence in Scotland: A Literature Review." *Research Reports or Papers*, November 2010. http://www.scotland.gov.uk/Publications/2010/10/07105517/0.

Freed, David, and James Millar. 2018. *Dads Don't Babysit: Towards Equal Parenting.* London: Ortus Press.

Friberg, Daniel. 2017. "5 Steps to Become a Real Man." *AltRight.Com*, 2017. https://web.archive.org/web/20180305005901/https://altright.com/2017/09/30/5-steps-to-become-a-real-man/.

Friedman, May. 2016. "Daddyblogs Know Best: Histories of Fatherhood in the Cyber Age." In *Pops in Pop Culture: Fatherhood, Masculinity, and the New Man*, edited by Elizabeth Podnieks, 87–103. New York, NY: Palgrave Macmillan US.

Friginal, Eric, ed. 2018. *Studies in Corpus-Based Sociolinguistics.* Oxon: Routledge.

Friginal, Eric, and Jack Hardy. 2014. *Corpus-Based Sociolinguistics: A Guide for Students.* Oxon: Routledge.

Furstenberg, Frank F. 1988. "Good Dads-Bad Dads: Two Faces of Fatherhood." In *The Changing American Family and Public Policy*, edited by Andrew J. Cherlin, 193–218. Washington, D.C.: The Urban Institute.

Futrelle, David. 2017. "Men's-Rights Activism Is the Gateway Drug for the Alt-Right." *The Cut*, August 17, 2017. https://www.thecut.com/2017/08/mens-rights-activism-is-the-gateway-drug-for-the-alt-right.html.

Gabrielatos, Costas. 2018. "Keyness Analysis: Nature, Metrics and Techniques." In *Corpus Approaches to Discourse: A Critical Review*, edited by Charlotte Taylor and Anna Marchi, Oxon, 225–258. Oxon: Routledge.

Gais, Hannah. 2019. "White Nationalist Richard Spencer Reportedly Spews Hate on Leaked Audio." Southern Poverty Law Center. 2019. https://www.splcenter.org/hatewatch/2019/11/07/white-nationalist-richard-spencer-reportedly-spews-hate-leaked-audio.

García-Favaro, Laura, and Rosalind Gill. 2016. "'Emasculation Nation Has Arrived': Sexism Rearticulated in Online Responses to Lose the Lads' Mags Campaign." *Feminist Media Studies* 16 (3): 379–397.

Garfinkel, Renee. 2007. "Personal Transformations: Moving from Violence to Peace." *United States Institute of Peace*, April 1, 2007. https://www.usip.org/publications/2007/04/personal-transformations-moving-violence-peace.

Garlick, Steve. 2003. "What Is a Man?: Heterosexuality and the Technology of Masculinity." *Men and Masculinities* 6 (2): 156–172.

Gärtner, Marc. 2007. "FOCUS: Fostering Caring Masculinities." Berlin: Hans Böckler Foundation. https://www.boeckler.de/pdf_fof/96720.pdf.

Gayle, Damien. 2018. "Arrest of Two Black Men at Starbucks for 'trespassing' Sparks Protests." *The Guardian*, April 16, 2018. https://www.theguardian.com/us-news/2018/apr/16/arrest-of-two-black-men-at-starbucks-for-trespassing-sparks-protests.

Geary, David C. 2010. *Male, Female: The Evolution of Human Sex Differences.* 2nd ed. Washington, DC: American Psychological Association.

Gee, James Paul. 2007. *Good Video Games + Good Learning: Collected Essays on Video Games, Learning, and Literacy.* Oxford: Peter Lang.

Gee, Matt. 2020. "Xtranscript." *Matt Gee's Blog.* http://mattgee.net/xtranscript/.

Gee, Matt. 2021. "ConcXML." *Matt Gee's Blog.* http://mattgee.net/concXML.

Genesoni, Lucia, and Maria Anna Tallandini. 2009. "Men's Psychological Transition to Fatherhood: An Analysis of the Literature, 1989–2008." *Birth* 36 (4): 305–318.

George, Kat. 2016. "'Brooklyn Nine-Nine' Deserves Applause for Refusing to Get Cheap Laughs from Gender Stereotypes." *Decider*, January 13, 2016. https://decider.com/2016/01/13/brooklyn-nine-nine-deserves-applause-for-refusing-to-get-cheap-laughs-from-gender-stereotypes/.

Gerald, J. P. B. 2021. "Slurring like a Real (n-Word)." *Medium*, October 8, 2021. https://jpbgerald.medium.com/slurring-like-a-real-n-word-e6549e929811.

Gerdes, Zachary T., and Ronald F. Levant. 2018. "Complex Relationships Among Masculine Norms and Health/Well-Being Outcomes: Correlation Patterns of the Conformity to Masculine Norms Inventory Subscales." *American Journal of Men's Health* 12 (2): 229–240.

Gill, Aisha K, and Karen Harrison. 2015. "Child Grooming and Sexual Exploitation: Are South Asian Men the UK Media's New Folk Devils?" *International Journal for Crime, Justice and Social Democracy* 4 (2): 34–49.

Gillette. 2019. "Our Commitment: The Best Men Can Be." 2019. https://gillette.com/en-us/our-committment.

Gilmore, David D. 1990. *Manhood in the Making: Cultural Concepts of Masculinity*. New Haven London: Yale University Press.

Gilpin, Caroline Crosson, and Natalie Proulx. 2018. "Boys to Men: Teaching and Learning About Masculinity in an Age of Change." *The New York Times*, April 12, 2018. https://www.nytimes.com/2018/04/12/learning/lesson-plans/boys-to-men-teaching-and-learning-about-masculinity-in-an-age-of-change.html.

Ging, Debbie. 2017. "Alphas, Betas, and Incels: Theorizing the Masculinities of the Manosphere." *Men and Masculinities* 22 (4): 638–657.

Ging, Debbie. 2019. "Bros v. Hos: Postfeminism, Anti-Feminism and the Toxic Turn in Digital Gender Politics." In *Gender Hate Online: Understanding the New Anti-Feminism*, edited by Debbie Ging and Eugenia Siapera, 45–68. Basingstoke: Palgrave Macmillan.

Ging, Debbie, and Eugenia Siapera. 2018. "Full Article: Special Issue on Online Misogyny." *Feminist Media Studies* 18 (4): 515–524.

Ging, Debbie, and Eugenia Siapera, eds. 2019. *Gender Hate Online: Understanding the New Anti-Feminism*. Basingstoke: Palgrave Macmillan.

Ging, Debbie, and Shane Murphy. 2021. "Tracking the Pilling Pipeline: Limitations, Challenges and a Call for New Methodological Frameworks in Incel and Manosphere Research." *AoIR Selected Papers of Internet Research*, September.

Giorgis, Hannah. 2018. "Terry Crews and the Discomfort of Masculine Anxiety." *The Atlantic*, June 29, 2018. https://www.theatlantic.com/entertainment/archive/2018/06/terry-crews-and-the-discomfort-of-masculine-anxiety/564047/.

Giroux, Henry A. 2001. "Private Satisfactions and Public Disorders: 'Fight Club', Patriarchy, and the Politics of Masculine Violence." *JAC* 21 (1): 1–31.

Godwin, Richard. 2018. "Men after #MeToo: 'There's a Narrative That Masculinity Is Fundamentally Toxic.'" *The Guardian*, March 9, 2018. https://www.theguardian.com/world/2018/mar/09/men-after-metoo-masculinity-fundamentally-toxic.

Goffman, Erving. 1963. *Stigma: Notes on the Management of Spoiled Identity*. Englewood Cliffs, NJ: Prentice Hall Inc.

Goffman, Erving. 1977. "The Arrangement between the Sexes." *Theory and Society* 4 (3): 301–331.

Goldberg, David Theo. 2009. *The Threat of Race: Reflections on Racial Neoliberalism*. Oxford: Blackwell Publishing.

Gor, Clarie. 2018. "The Men of Brooklyn Nine-Nine." *Clarie's Ramblings.*, July 2, 2018. https://clariesramblings.com/2018/07/02/the-men-of-brooklyn-99/.

Gordon, Matthew. 2005. "Research Aims and Methodology." In *Sociolinguistics*, edited by Ulrich Ammon, Norbert Dittmar, Klaus J. Mattheier, and Peter Trudgill, 955–964. Berlin: Walter de Gruyter.

Goss, Alex. 2016. *The First Season of Fatherhood: A Parenting Book for Dads*. Scott Valley, CA: CreateSpace Independent Publishing Platform.

Gotell, Lise, and Emily Dutton. 2016. "Sexual Violence in the 'Manosphere': Antifeminist Men's Rights Discourses on Rape." *International Journal for Crime, Justice and Social Democracy* 5 (2): 65–80.

Grant, Tim, and Nicci MacLeod. 2016. "Assuming Identities Online: Experimental Linguistics Applied to the Policing of Online Paedophile Activity." *Applied Linguistics* 37 (1): 50–70.

Grant, Tim, and Nicci MacLeod. 2020. *Language and Online Identities: The Undercover Policing of Internet Sexual Crime*. Cambridge: Cambridge University Press.

Gray, John. 1992. *Men Are from Mars, Women Are from Venus: The Classic Guide to Understanding the Opposite Sex*. New York, NY: Harper Collins.

Greengross, Gil. 2014. "Male Production of Humor Produced by Sexually Selected Psychological Adaptations." In *Evolutionary Perspectives on Human Sexual Psychology and Behavior*, edited by Viviana A. Weekes-Shackelford and Todd K. Shackelford, 173–196. New York, NY: Springer New York.

Gries, Stefan Th. 2013. "50-Something Years of Work on Collocations: What Is or Should Be Next . . . ." *International Journal of Corpus Linguistics* 18 (1): 137–166.

Griffin, Penny. 2013. "Gendering Global Finance: Crisis, Masculinity, and Responsibility." *Men and Masculinities* 16 (1): 9–34.

Grossmann, Igor, Anna Dorfman, Harrison Oakes, Henri Carlo Santos, Kathleen D. Vohs, and Abigail Scholer. 2021. "Training for Wisdom: The Illeist Diary Method." *Psychological Science* 32 (3): 381–394.

Grover, Ted, and Gloria Mark. 2019. "Detecting Potential Warning Behaviors of Ideological Radicalization in an Alt-Right Subreddit." *Proceedings of the International AAAI Conference on Web and Social Media* 13 (July): 193–204.

Habib, Hussam, Maaz Bin Musa, Fareed Zaffar, and Rishab Nithyanand. 2019. "To Act or React: Investigating Proactive Strategies for Online Community Moderation." *ArXiv:1906.11932*. http://arxiv.org/abs/1906.11932.

Haider, Syed. 2016. "The Shooting in Orlando, Terrorism or Toxic Masculinity (or Both?)." *Men and Masculinities* 19 (5): 555–565.

Hall-Lew, Lauren, Emma Moore, and Robert J. Podesva. 2021. "Social Meaning and Linguistic Variation: Theoretical Foundations." In *Social Meaning and Linguistic Variation: Theorizing the Third Wave*, edited by Lauren Hall-Lew, Emma Moore, and Robert J. Podesva, 1–24. Cambridge: Cambridge University Press.

Hall, Christopher M. 2019. "Merging Efforts: The Intersections of Domestic Violence Intervention, Men, and Masculinities." *Men and Masculinities* 22 (1): 104–112.

Hall, Steve. 2002. "Daubing the Drudges of Fury: Men, Violence and the Piety of the 'Hegemonic Masculinity' Thesis." *Theoretical Criminology* 6 (1): 35–61.

Halpin, Michael. 2022. "Weaponized Subordination: How Incels Discredit themselves to Degrade Women." *Gender & Society*, 08912432221128545.

Hamilton, Kirk. 2014. "Felicia Day and Gamergate: This Is What Happens Now." *Kotaku*, October 24, 2014. https://kotaku.com/felicia-day-and-gamergate-this-is-what-happens-now-1650544129.

Hampton, Rachelle. 2019. "The Black Feminists Who Saw the Alt-Right Threat Coming." *Slate*, April 23, 2019. https://slate.com/technology/2019/04/black-feminists-alt-right-twitter-gamergate.html.

Hanlon, Niall. 2008. "Masculinities and Affective Equality: Love Labour and Care Labour in Men's Lives." Unpublished PhD thesis. Dublin: University College Dublin.

Hanlon, Niall. 2009. "Caregiving Masculinities: An Exploratory Analysis." In *Affective Equality: Love, Care and Injustice*, edited by Kathleen Lynch, John Baker, and Maureen Lyons, 180–198. Basingstoke: Palgrave Macmillan.

Hanlon, Niall. 2012. *Masculinities, Care and Equality: Identity and Nurture in Men's Lives*. Basingstoke: Palgrave Macmillan.

Hansen, Andrew. 2011. "The Rationalization Hamster Is Now Immortal." *The Private Man*, December 13, 2011. https://theprivateman.wordpress.com/2011/12/12/the-rationalization-hamster-is-now-immortal/.

Hansen-Miller, Rosalind, and Rosalind Gill. 2011. "Lad Flicks: Discursive Reconstructions of Masculinity in Popular Film." In *Feminism at the Movies: Understanding Gender in Contemporary Popular Cinema*, edited by Hilary Radner and Rebecca Stringer, 36–50. Oxon: Routledge.

Hardaker, Claire. 2013. "'Uh . . . Not to Be Nitpicky . . . But . . . the Past Tense of Drag Is Dragged, Not Drug': An Overview of Trolling Strategies." *Journal of Language Aggression and Conflict* 1 (1): 58–86.

Hardaker, Claire, and Mark McGlashan. 2016. "'Real Men Don't Hate Women': Twitter Rape Threats and Group Identity." *Journal of Pragmatics* 91: 80–93.

Harper, Caroline, Rachel Marcus, Diana Jiménez Thomas Rodriguez, and Emilie Tant. 2022. "Is No Space Safe? Working to End Gender-Based Violence in the Public Sphere." ALIGN Briefing. London: ODI/ALIGN (www.alignplatform.org/resource/briefing-is-no-space-safe).

Harris, Sandra. 1995. "Pragmatics and Power." *Journal of Pragmatics* 23 (2): 117–135.

Harrison, Claire. 2008. "Real Men Do Wear Mascara: Advertising Discourse and Masculine Identity." *Critical Discourse Studies* 5 (1): 55–74.

Harry's. 2018. "'A Man Like You'. #WhatMakesAMan." Tweet. @harrys. March 9, 2018. https://twitter.com/harrys/status/972215743554125825.

Hartley, Ruth E. 1959. "Sex-Role Pressures and the Socialization of the Male Child." *Psychological Reports* 5 (2): 457–468.

Hartzell, Stephanie L. 2018. "Alt-White: Conceptualizing the 'Alt-Right' as a Rhetorical Bridge between White Nationalism and Mainstream Public Discourse." *Journal of Contemporary Rhetoric* 8 (1–2): 6–25.

Hasinoff, Amy Adele. 2009. "It's Sociobiology, Hon!: Genetic Gender Determinism in *Cosmopolitan* Magazine." *Feminist Media Studies* 9 (3): 267–283.

Hawkesworth, Mary. 1999. "Analyzing Backlash: Feminist Standpoint Theory as Analytical Tool." *Women's Studies International Forum* 22 (2): 135–155.

Hawley, George. 2017. *Making Sense of the Alt-Right*. New York, NY: Columbia University Press.

Haywood, Chris, and Thomas Johansson, eds. 2017. *Marginalized Masculinities: Contexts, Continuities and Change*. Oxon: Routledge.

Hearn, Jeff. 1999. "A Crisis in Masculinity, or New Agendas for Men?" In *New Agendas for Women*, edited by Sylvia Walby, 148–168. London: Palgrave Macmillan UK.

HEFCE (Higher Education Funding Council England). 2011. "Decisions on Assessing Research Impact." London: HEFCE. https://www.ref.ac.uk/2014/media/ref/content/pub/assessmentframeworkandguidanceonsubmissions/GOS%20includ ing%20addendum.pdf.

Held, Virginia. 2006. *The Ethics of Care: Personal, Political, and Global*. Oxford: Oxford University Press.

Heritage, Frazer. 2021. *Language, Gender and Videogames: Using Corpora to Analyse the Representation of Gender in Fantasy Videogames*. Cham: Palgrave Macmillan.

Heritage, Frazer, and Veronika Koller. 2020. "Incels, In-Groups, and Ideologies: The Representation of Gendered Social Actors in a Sexuality-Based Online Community." *Journal of Language and Sexuality* 9 (2): 152–178.

Hermansson, Patrik, David Lawrence, Joe Mulhall, and Simon Murdoch. 2020. *The International Alt-Right: Fascism for the 21st Century?* Oxon: Routledge.

Herrero, Sofia. 2019. "Exploring Textual Data with Topic Modelling and Topic Coherence." *Trifork Blog*, April 11, 2019. https://blog.trifork.com/2019/04/11/exploring-text ual-data-with-topic-modelling-and-topic-coherence/.

Hess, Aaron, and Carlos Flores. 2016. "Simply More than Swiping Left: A Critical Analysis of Toxic Masculine Performances on Tinder Nightmares." *New Media & Society* 20 (3): 1085–1102.

Hetherington, Norris S. 1983. "Just How Objective Is Science?" *Nature* 306 (5945): 727–730.

Hillman, Ben, and Lee-Anne Henfry. 2006. "Macho Minority: Masculinity and Ethnicity on the Edge of Tibet." *Modern China* 32 (2): 251–272.

Hillman, Nick, and Nicholas Robinson. 2016. "Boys to Men: The Underachievement of Young Men in Higher Education—and How to Start Tackling It." Oxford: Higher Education Policy Institute. https://www.hepi.ac.uk/wp-content/uploads/2016/05/Boys-to-Men.pdf.

Hilton, Phil. 2010. "The Cult of Fatherhood." *The Times*, March 27, 2010. https://www.thetimes.co.uk/article/the-cult-of-fatherhood-kkql3gpfd9n.

Hoang, Tu-Anh, Trang Thu Quach, and Tam Thanh Tran. 2013. "'Because I Am a Man, I Should Be Gentle to My Wife and My Children': Positive Masculinity to Stop Gender-Based Violence in a Coastal District in Vietnam." *Gender & Development* 21 (1): 81–96.

Hoffman, Bruce, Jacob Ware, and Ezra Shapiro. 2020. "Assessing the Threat of Incel Violence." *Studies in Conflict & Terrorism* 43 (7): 565–587.

Høiland, Thea. 2019. "Incels and the Stories They Tell. A Narrative Analysis of Incels' Shared Stories on Reddit." Unpublished MA dissertation. Oslo: University of Oslo. https://www.duo.uio.no/handle/10852/69841.

Holden, Madeleine. 2019. "Could a Real Men's Movement Be a Good Thing?" *MEL Magazine*, November 11, 2019. https://melmagazine.com/en-us/story/could-a-real-mens-movement-be-a-good-thing.

Holligan, Christopher, and Robert McLean. 2018. "Violence as an Environmentally Warranted Norm amongst Working-Class Teenage Boys in Glasgow." *Social Sciences* 7 (10): 207.

Holmes, Jack. 2016. "Are Young, White Males Being Radicalized Online?" *Esquire*, November 9, 2016. https://www.esquire.com/news-politics/news/a50513/young-trump-voters-undercover/.

Holtzman, Linda, and Leon Sharpe. 2014. *Media Messages*. Armonk, NY: Routledge.

hooks, bell. 2004. *The Will to Change: Men, Masculinity, and Love*. New York, NY: Washington Square Press.

HOPE Not Hate. 2020. "Conspiracy Theories: The Danger and the Appeal." HOPE Not Hate. 2020. https://www.hopenothate.org.uk/conspiracy-theories-the-danger-and-the-appeal/.

Hopf, G. Michael. 2016. *Those Who Remain: A Postapocalyptic Novel*. Scott Valley, CA: CreateSpace Independent Publishing Platform.

Horgan, John. 2008. "Deradicalization or Disengagement?" *Perspectives on Terrorism* 2 (4). http://www.terrorismanalysts.com/pt/index.php/pot/article/view/32.

Houbrick, Dan. 2019. "10 Best Terry Quotes from Brooklyn Nine-Nine." *ScreenRant*, March 17, 2019. https://screenrant.com/terry-jeffords-brooklyn-nine-nine-quotes/.

Howard, Kirsten. 2020. "Brooklyn Nine-Nine Season 8 Scripts Ditched After George Floyd Death." *Den of Geek*, June 24, 2020. https://www.denofgeek.com/tv/brooklyn-nine-nine-season-8-story-black-lives-matter/.

Howes, Lewis. 2017. *The Mask of Masculinity: How Men Can Embrace Vulnerability, Create Strong Relationships, and Live Their Fullest Lives*. Emmaus, PA: Macmillan USA.

Hughes, Tonda L., Sharon C. Wilsnack, and Lori Wolfgang Kantor. 2016. "The Influence of Gender and Sexual Orientation on Alcohol Use and Alcohol-Related Problems." *Alcohol Research: Current Reviews* 38 (1): 121–132.

Hunston, Susan. 2002. *Corpora in Applied Linguistics*. Cambridge: Cambridge University Press.

Hunston, Susan. 2007. "Semantic Prosody Revisited." *International Journal of Corpus Linguistics* 12 (2): 249–268.

Hunston, Susan. 2010. "How Can a Corpus Be Used to Explore Patterns?" In *The Routledge Handbook of Corpus Linguistics*, edited by Anne O'Keeffe and Michael McCarthy, 152–166. Oxon: Routledge.

Hunston, Susan. 2020. "Legitimate Interests." *ICO*, July 20, 2020. https://ico.org.uk/for-organisations/guide-to-data-protection/guide-to-the-general-data-protection-regulation-gdpr/lawful-basis-for-processing/legitimate-interests/.

Hunter, John D. 2007. "Matplotlib: A 2D Graphics Environment." *Computing in Science Engineering* 9 (3): 90–95.

Hunter, Sarah C., Damien W. Riggs, and Martha Augoustinos. 2017. "Hegemonic Masculinity versus a Caring Masculinity: Implications for Understanding Primary Caregiving Fathers." *Social and Personality Psychology Compass* 11 (3): e12307.

Hutchings, Kimberly. 2008. "Making Sense of Masculinity and War." *Men and Masculinities* 10 (4): 389–404.

Hutchinson, Darren Lenard. 1997. "Out yet Unseen: A Racial Critique of Gay and Lesbian Legal Theory and Political Discourse." *SSRN Electronic Journal*.

Hutchinson, Darren Lenard. 2000. "Identity Crisis: Intersectionality, Multidimensionality, and the Development of an Adequate Theory of Subordination." *Michigan Journal of Race and Law* 6: 285–320.

Hyde, Abbey, Jonathan Drennan, Etaoine Howlett, and Dympna Brady. 2009. "Young Men's Vulnerability in Constituting Hegemonic Masculinity in Sexual Relations." *American Journal of Men's Health* 3 (3): 238–251.

Iacuone, David. 2005. "'Real Men Are Tough Guys': Hegemonic Masculinity and Safety in the Construction Industry." *The Journal of Men's Studies* 13 (2): 247–266.

Ilbury, Christian. 2020. "'Sassy Queens': Stylistic Orthographic Variation in Twitter and the Enregisterment of AAVE." *Journal of Sociolinguistics* 24 (2): 245–264.

Incel. 2020. "Incel Wiki: Chad." Incel Wiki. 2020. https://incels.wiki/w/Chad.

Information Commissioner's Office. 2014. "Big Data, Artificial Intelligence, Machine Learning and Data Protection." Wilmslow: Information Commissioner's Office. https://marketinglaw.osborneclarke.com/data-and-privacy/big-data-and-data-pro tection-paper-from-ico/.

Inoue, Manami, Hiroyasu Iso, Seiichiro Yamamoto, Norie Kurahashi, Motoki Iwasaki, Shizuka Sasazuki, and Shoichiro Tsugane. 2008. "Daily Total Physical Activity Level and Premature Death in Men and Women: Results from a Large-Scale Population-Based Cohort Study in Japan (JPHC Study)." *Annals of Epidemiology* 18 (7): 522–530.

Irwin, Mary, and Gabrielle Smith. 2018. "'Ah Hink It's Time for Suttin Blue n a BAILEYS!' Subverting Scottish Male Identities in *Gary: Tank Commander*." *International Journal of Scottish Theatre and Screen* 11 (1): 51–66.

Isaac, Mike. 2021. "Reddit Is Valued at More than $10 Billion in Latest Funding Round." *The New York Times*, August 12, 2021. https://www.nytimes.com/2021/08/12/tec hnology/reddit-new-funding.html.

Jackson, Danny H. 2020. "The Subtle 'Copaganda' of *Brooklyn Nine-Nine*." *Medium*, June 8, 2020. https://medium.com/words-by-ellie/the-subtle-copaganda-of-brooklyn-nine-nine-95d37f1113e3.

Jackson, David. 2002. *The Fear of Being Seen as White Losers: White Working Class Masculinities*. Nottingham: Five Leaves Publications.

Jacobi, Carina, Wouter van Atttevelt, and Kasper Welbers. 2015. "Quantitative Analysis of Large Amounts of Journalistic Texts Using Topic Modelling." *Digital Journalism* 4 (1): 89–106.

Jacobsen, Kevin. 2018. "Emmy Spotlight: Renewed Love for 'Brooklyn Nine-Nine' after Cancellation Scare Could Help Awards Chances." *GoldDerby*, May 29, 2018. https://www.goldderby.com/article/2018/emmys-brooklyn-nine-nine-cancelled-andy-samb erg-andre-braugher-news/.

Jacobson, Erik. 2019. "Performing and Resisting Toxic Masculinities on Sports Comment Boards." In *Literacies, Sexualities, and Gender: Understanding Identities from Preschool to Adulthood*, edited by Barbara J. Guzzetti, Thomas W. Bean, and Judith Dunkerly-Bean, 169–181. Oxon: Routledge.

Jaki, Sylvia, Tom De Smedt, Maja Gwóźdź, Rudresh Panchal, Alexander Rossa, and Guy De Pauw. 2019. "Online Hatred of Women in the Incels.Me Forum: Linguistic Analysis and Automatic Detection." *Journal of Language Aggression and Conflict* 7 (2): 240–268.

Janik, Rachel. 2018. "'I Laugh at the Death of Normies': How Incels Are Celebrating the Toronto Mass Killing." Southern Poverty Law Center, April 24, 2018. https://www.splcenter.org/hatewatch/2018/04/24/i-laugh-death-normies-how-incels-are-cele brating-toronto-mass-killing.

Jaworska, Sylvia. 2018. "'Bad' Mums Tell the 'Untellable': Narrative Practices and Agency in Online Stories about Postnatal Depression on Mumsnet." *Discourse, Context & Media* 25: 25–33.

Jaworska, Sylvia, and Anupam Nanda. 2018. "Doing Well by Talking Good: A Topic Modelling-Assisted Discourse Study of Corporate Social Responsibility." *Applied Linguistics* 39 (3): 373–399.

Jefferson, Gail. 1990. "List-Construction as a Task and Resource." In *Interactional Competence*, edited by George Psathas, 63–92. New York, NY: Irvington Publishers.

Jeffrey, Robert. 2006. *Glasgow's Hard Men*. Edinburgh: Black & White Publishing.

Jeffrey, Robert. 2008. *Gangs of Glasgow: True Crime from the Streets*. Edinburgh: Black & White Publishing.

Jeffrey, Robert. 2011. *Glasgow's Godfather*. Edinburgh: Black & White Publishing.

Jennings, Rebecca. 2018. "Incels Categorize Women by Personal Style and Attractiveness." *Vox*, April 28, 2018. https://www.vox.com/2018/4/28/17290256/incel-chad-stacy-becky.

Jensen, Sune Qvotrup. 2010. "Masculinity at the Margins: Othering, Marginality and Resistance among Young Marginalized Ethnic Minority Men." *NORMA: International Journal for Masculinity Studies* 5 (01): 6–26.

Johansson, Thomas. 2011. "The Construction of the New Father: How Middle-Class Men Become Present Fathers." *International Review of Modern Sociology* 37 (1): 111–126.

Johansson, Thomas, and Jesper Andreasson. 2017. "Internet and the New Landscape of Fatherhood." In *Fatherhood in Transition: Masculinity, Identity and Everyday Life*, edited by Thomas Johansson and Jesper Andreasson, 103–117. Basingstoke: Palgrave Macmillan UK.

Johansson, Thomas, and Nils Hammarén. 2014. "'Imagine, Just 16 Years Old and Already a Dad!' The Construction of Young Fatherhood on the Internet." *International Journal of Adolescence and Youth* 19 (3): 366–381.

John, Arit, Laura M. Holson, Mihir Zaveri, and Emily S. Rueb. 2019. "Ed Buck Faces Federal Drug Charge in Death of Man in His Home (Published 2019)." *The New York Times*, September 19, 2019. https://www.nytimes.com/2019/09/19/us/ed-buck-charged-gemmel-moore.html.

Johns, Amelia. 2017. "Flagging White Nationalism 'After Cronulla': From the Beach to the Net." *Journal of Intercultural Studies* 38 (3): 349–364.

Johnson, Allyson. 2015. "The Quiet, Progressive Nature of Brooklyn Nine-Nine." *The Mary Sue*, September 13, 2015. https://www.themarysue.com/brooklyn-nine-nine-progressive/.

Johnson, Jessica. 2018. "Self-Radicalization of White Men: 'Fake News' and the Affective Networking of Paranoia." *Communication, Culture and Critique* 11 (1): 100–115.

Johnson, Sally. 1997. "Theorizing Language and Masculinity: A Feminist Perspective." In *Language and Masculinity*, 8–26. Oxford: Wiley-Blackwell.

Johnson, Sally, and Ulrike Hanna Meinhof, eds. 1997. *Language and Masculinity*. Oxford: Wiley-Blackwell.

Johnston, Lucy, Tracey McLellan, and Audrey McKinlay. 2014. "(Perceived) Size Really Does Matter: Male Dissatisfaction with Penis Size." *Psychology of Men & Masculinity* 15 (2): 225–228.

Johnston, Ronnie, and Arthur McIvor. 2004a. "Dangerous Work, Hard Men and Broken Bodies: Masculinity in the Clydeside Heavy Industries, c. 1930–1970s." *Labour History Review* 69 (2): 135–151.

Johnston, Ronnie, and Arthur McIvor. 2004b. "Oral History, Subjectivity, and Environmental Reality: Occupational Health Histories in Twentieth-Century Scotland." *Osiris* 19 (1): 234–249.

Johnston, Ronnie, and Arthur McIvor. 2007. "Narratives from the Urban Workplace: Oral Testimonies and the Reconstruction of Men's Work in the Heavy Industries in Glasgow." In *Testimonies of the City: Identity, Community and Change in a Contemporary Urban World*, edited by Richard Rodger and Joanna Herbert, 23–44. Oxon: Routledge.

Johnstone, Barbara. 2000. *Qualitative Methods in Sociolinguistics*. Oxford: Oxford University Press.

Johnstone, Barbara. 2013. *Speaking Pittsburghese: The Story of a Dialect*. Oxford: Oxford University Press.

Johnstone, Barbara. 2017. "Characterological Figures and Expressive Style in the Enregisterment of Linguistic Variety." In *Language and a Sense of Place*, 283–300. Cambridge: Cambridge University Press.

Jolivet, Kenneth. 2019. *Society Kills Men: Feminism Loses When Half Are Held Back*. Scott Valley, CA. CreateSpace. Independent Publishing Platform.

Jones, Callum, Verity Trott, and Scott Wright. 2019. "Sluts and Soyboys: MGTOW and the Production of Misogynistic Online Harassment." *New Media & Society* 22 (10): 1903–1921.

Jones, Lucy, Malgorzata Chałupnik, Jai Mackenzie, and Louise Mullany. 2022. "'STFU and Start Listening to How Scared We Are': Resisting Misogyny on Twitter via # NotAllMen." *Discourse, Context & Media*, 100596.

Jones, Rodney H. 2019. "Mediated Discourse Analysis in Language and Sexuality Research." In *The Oxford Handbook of Language and Sexuality*, by Rodney H. Jones, edited by Kira Hall and Rusty Barrett. Oxford: Oxford University Press.

Jordan, Ana. 2019. "Postfeminist Men's Movements: The Campaign Against Living Miserably and Male Suicide as 'Crisis.'" In *The New Politics of Fatherhood: Men's Movements and Masculinities*, edited by Ana Jordan, 165–191. Genders and Sexualities in the Social Sciences. London: Palgrave Macmillan UK.

Jordan, Ana. 2020. "Masculinizing Care? Gender, Ethics of Care, and Fathers' Rights Groups." *Men and Masculinities* 23 (1): 20–41.

Joshi, Meghana. 2021. "'I Do Not Want to Be a Weekend Papa': The Demographic 'Crisis', Active Fatherhood, and Emergent Caring Masculinities in Berlin." *Journal of Family Issues*, 0192513X21994154.

Kalish, Rachel, and Michael Kimmel. 2010. "Suicide by Mass Murder: Masculinity, Aggrieved Entitlement, and Rampage School Shootings." *Health Sociology Review* 19 (4): 451–464.

Kaminer, Debra, and John Dixon. 1995. "The Reproduction of Masculinity: A Discourse Analysis of Men's Drinking Talk." *South African Journal of Psychology* 25 (3): 168–174.

Karner, Tracy. 1996. "Fathers, Sons, and Vietnam: Masculinity and Betrayal in the Life Narratives of Vietnam Veterans with Post Traumatic Stress Disorder." *American Studies* 37 (1): 63–94.

Katz, Jackson. 2012. *Violence against Women: It's a Men's Issue*. San Francisco, CA: TED. https://www.ted.com/talks/jackson_katz_violence_against_women_it_s_a_men_s_issue.

Katz, Jason. 2019. "Why We Can No Longer See Sexual Violence as a Women's Issue." *TED Radio Hour*. NPR. https://www.npr.org/2019/02/01/689938588/jackson-katz-why-we-can-no-longer-see-sexual-violence-as-a-womens-issue.

Kaufman, Scott. 2014. "The Alpha Male Myth." *The Art of Manliness*, July 8, 2014. https://www.artofmanliness.com/articles/the-myth-of-the-alpha-male/.

Kaye, Linda. 2018. "Researcher Protection and Practices in Internet-Mediated Research." *The British Psychological Association*, August 24, 2018. https://www.bps.org.uk/blogs/linda-kaye/researcher-protection-and-practices-internet-mediated-research.

Kehoe, Andrew, and Matt Gee. 2007. "New Corpora from the Web: Making Web Text More 'Text-Like.'" *Studies in Variation, Contacts and Change in English* 2.

Keim, Amy. 2017. "15 Times Jake & Boyle from 'Brooklyn Nine-Nine' Were #Goals." *TheThings*, April 11, 2017. https://www.thethings.com/15-times-jake-boyle-were-goals/.

Kelan, Elisabeth K. 2009. "Gender Fatigue: The Ideological Dilemma of Gender Neutrality and Discrimination in Organizations." *Canadian Journal of Administrative Sciences / Revue Canadienne des Sciences de l'Administration* 26 (3): 197–210.

Kellner, Douglas. 2011. "Cultural Studies, Multiculturalism, and Media Culture." In *Gender, Race, and Class in Media: A Critical Reader*, edited by Gail Dines and Jean M. Humez, 7–18. London: SAGE Publications Ltd.

Kellner, Douglas. 2020. "Cultural Studies, Multiculturalism, and Media Culture." In *Gender, Race, and Class in Media: A Critical Reader*, edited by Bill Yousman, Lori Bindig Yousman, Gail Dines, and Jean McMahon Humez, 6th edition, 7–18. London: SAGE Publications Ltd.

Kelly, Annie. 2017. "The Alt-Right: Reactionary Rehabilitation for White Masculinity." *Soundings* 66 (66): 68–78.

Kelly, Megan, Alex DiBranco, and Julia DeCook. 2021. *Misogynist Incels and Male Supremacism: Overview and Recommendations for Addressing the Threat of Male Supremacist Violence.* Washington, D.C: New America. http://newamerica.org/politi cal-reform/reports/misogynist-incels-and-male-supremacism/.

Kemp, Rob. 2014. *The New Dad's Survival Guide: What to Expect in the First Year and Beyond.* London: Vermilion.

Kennedy, Francesca. 2017. "What Is Masculinity?" *The John Byrne Award*, July 16, 2017. https://www.johnbyrneaward.org.uk/entries/what-is-masculinity/.

Keskinen, Suvi. 2011. "Borders of the Finnish Nation: Media, Politics and Rape by 'foreign' Perpetrators." In *Media in Motion: Cultural Complexity and Migration in the Nordic Region*, edited by Elisabeth Eide and Kaarina Nikunen, 107–124. Oxon: Routledge.

Ketchum, Dr Alex. 2020. "Report on the State of Resources Provided to Support Scholars Against Harassment, Trolling, and Doxxing While Doing Public Media Work." *Medium*, July 4, 2020. https://medium.com/@alexandraketchum/report-on-the-state-of-resources-provided-to-support-scholars-against-harassment-trolling-and-401bed8cfbf1.

Kiesel, Laura. 2018. "Don't Blame Mental Illness for Mass Shootings; Blame Men." *POLITICO Magazine*. January 17, 2018. http://politi.co/2mFNPKf.

Kiesling, Scott F. 1997. "Power and the Language of Men." In *Language and Masculinity*, edited by Sally Johnson and Ulrike Hanna Meinhof, 65–85. Oxford: Wiley-Blackwell.

Kiesling, Scott F. 1998. "Men's Identities and Sociolinguistic Variation: The Case of Fraternity Men." *Journal of Sociolinguistics* 2 (1): 69–99.

Kiesling, Scott F. 2001. "Stances of Whiteness and Hegemony in Fraternity Men's Discourse." *Journal of Linguistic Anthropology* 11 (1): 101–115.

Kiesling, Scott F. 2004. "Dude." *American Speech* 79 (3): 281–305.

Kiesling, Scott F. 2005. "Homosocial Desire in Men's Talk: Balancing and Re-Creating Cultural Discourses of Masculinity." *Language in Society* 34 (5): 695–726.

Kiesling, Scott F. 2006. "Hegemonic Identity-Making in Narrative." In *Discourse and Identity*, 261–287. Cambridge University Press.

Kiesling, Scott F. 2007. "Men, Masculinities, and Language." *Language and Linguistics Compass* 1 (6): 653–673.

Kiesling, Scott F. 2018. "Masculine Stances and the Linguistics of Affect: On Masculine Ease." *NORMA: International Journal for Masculinity Studies* 13 (3–4): 191–212.

Kiesling, Scott F. 2019. *Language, Gender, and Sexuality: An Introduction.* Oxon: Routledge.

Kilgarriff, Adam. 1997. "Putting Frequencies in the Dictionary." *International Journal of Lexicography* 10 (2): 135–155.

Kilgarriff, Adam. 2009. "Simple Maths for Keywords." In *Proceedings of the Corpus Linguistics Conference*, 1–6.

Kilgarriff, Adam, Vít Baisa, Jan Bušta, Miloš Jakubíček, Vojtěch Kovář, Jan Michelfeit, Pavel Rychlý, and Vít Suchomel. 2014. "The Sketch Engine: Ten Years on." *Lexicography* 1 (1): 7–36.

Kilgo, Danielle K., Yee Man Margaret Ng, Martin J. Riedl, and Ivan Lacasa-Mas. 2018. "Reddit's Veil of Anonymity: Predictors of Engagement and Participation in Media Environments with Hostile Reputations." *Social Media + Society* 4 (4): 205630511881021.

Kim, Dorothy. 2019. "White Supremacists Have Weaponized an Imaginary Viking Past. It's Time to Reclaim the Real History." *Time*, April 15, 2019. https://time.com/5569399/viking-history-white-nationalists/.

Kimmel, Michael S. 1987. "Men's Response to Feminism at the Turn of the Century." *Gender & Society* 1 (3): 261–283.

Kimmel, Michael S. 1993. "Invisible Masculinity." *Society* 30 (6): 28–35.

Kimmel, Michael S. 1994. "Masculinity as Homophobia: Fear, Shame, and Silence in the Construction of Gender Identity." In *Theorizing Masculinities*, edited by Harry Brod and Michael Kaufman, 119–141. London: SAGE Publications.

Kimmel, Michael S. 2001. "Male Victims of Domestic Violence: A Substantive and Methodological Research Review." The Equality Committee of the Department of Education and Science. http://www.ncdsv.org/images/MaleVictimsOfDVaSubstanti veAndMethodologicalResearchReview_2001.pdf.

Kimmel, Michael S. 2017. *Angry White Men: American Masculinity at the End of an Era.* New York, NY: Nation Books.

Kimmel, Michael S. 2018. *Healing from Hate: How Young Men Get Into—and Out Of— Violent Extremism.* Oakland, CA: University of California Press.

Kimmel, Michael, and Michael Kaufman. 1993. "The New Men's Movement: Retreat and Regression with America's Weekend Warriors." *Feminist Issues* 13 (2): 3–21.

King, Sara. 2020. "Perceptions of an Osaka Father: How Regional Dialect Influences Ideas on Masculinity and Fatherhood." Unpublished MA dissertation. Eugene, OR: University of Oregon.

Kiselica, Mark S., and Matt Englar-Carlson. 2010. "Identifying, Affirming, and Building upon Male Strengths: The Positive Psychology/Positive Masculinity Model of Psychotherapy with Boys and Men." *Psychotherapy: Theory, Research, Practice, Training* 47 (3): 276–287.

Klee, Miles. 2019. "Desperate Incels Are Now 'Chadfishing' Women on Dating Apps." MEL Magazine, June 25, 2019. https://melmagazine.com/en-us/story/desperate-incels-are-now-chadfishing-making-themselves-even-more-miserable.

Klein, Viola. 1950. "The Stereotype of Femininity." *Journal of Social Issues* 6 (3): 3–12.

Koehler, Daniel. 2019. "Are There 'Best Practices' in Deradicalisation? Experiences from Frontline Intervention and Comparative Research." In *Terrorism, Radicalisation & Countering Violent Extremism: Practical Considerations & Concerns*, edited by Shashi Jayakumar, 59–68. Singapore: Springer.

Kohn, Isabelle. 2018. "The Growing Movement of Men Trying to Unlearn 'Toxic Masculinity.'" *Vice*, November 15, 2018. https://www.vice.com/en_us/article/vba d3y/toxic-masculinity-classes-rethinking-men.

Koller, Veronika, Frazer Heritage, Alexandra Krendel, and Mark McGlashan. 2019. "MANTRaP: A Corpus Approach to Researching Gender in Online Misogynist Communities." Presented at the 12th BAAL Language, Gender, and Sexuality Special Interest Group event, Birmingham, May 30, 2019.

Korobov, Neill. 2005. "Ironizing Masculinity: How Adolescent Boys Negotiate Hetero-Normative Dilemmas in Conversational Interaction." *The Journal of Men's Studies* 13 (2): 225–246.

Korobov, Neill. 2018. "Indirect Pursuits of Intimacy in Romantic Couples Everyday Conversations: A Discourse Analytic Approach." *Qualitative Social Research* 19 (2).

Kosse, Maureen. 2022. "'Ted Cruz Cucks Again': The Insult Term Cuck as an Alt-Right Masculinist Signifier." *Gender & Language* 16 (2): 99–124.

Krendel, Alexandra. 2020. "The Men and Women, Guys and Girls of the 'Manosphere': A Corpus-Assisted Discourse Approach." *Discourse & Society* 31 (6): 607–630.

Kupers, Terry A. 2005. "Toxic Masculinity as a Barrier to Mental Health Treatment in Prison." *Journal of Clinical Psychology* 61 (6): 713–724.

Labov, William. 1963. "The Social Motivation of a Sound Change." *Word* 19 (3): 273–309.

Labov, William. 1997. "Some Further Steps in Narrative Analysis." *Journal of Narrative and Life Experience* 7 (1–4): 395–415.

Labov, William, and Joshua Waletzky. 1967. "Narrative Analysis." In *Essays on the Verbal and Visual Arts*, edited by June Helm, 12–44. Seattle: University of Washington Press.

Lakoff, George. 2016. "Understanding Trump." *George Lakoff* (blog), July 24, 2016. https://georgelakoff.com/2016/07/23/understanding-trump-2/.

Lamoureux, Mack. 2015. "This Group of Straight Men Is Swearing Off Women." *Vice*, September 24, 2015. https://www.vice.com/en_us/article/7bdwyx/inside-the-glo bal-collective-of-straight-male-separatists.

Lankshear, Colin, and Michele Knobel. 2011. *New Literacies*. McGraw-Hill Education (UK).

LaRossa, Ralph. 1988. "Fatherhood and Social Change." *Family Relations* 37 (4): 451–457.

Lave, Jean, and Etienne Wenger. 1991. *Situated Learning: Legitimate Peripheral Participation*. Cambridge: Cambridge University Press.

Lavelle, Katherine L. 2010. "A Critical Discourse Analysis of Black Masculinity in NBA Game Commentary." *Howard Journal of Communications* 21 (3): 294–314.

LaViolette, Jack. 2017. "Cyber-Metapragmatics and Alterity on Reddit.com." *Tilburg Papers in Culture Studies*, 1–26.

LaViolette, Jack, and Bernie Hogan. 2019. "Using Platform Signals for Distinguishing Discourses: The Case of Men's Rights and Men's Liberation on Reddit." *Proceedings of the International AAAI Conference on Web and Social Media* 13: 323–334.

Lawler, Margaret, and Elizabeth Nixon. 2011. "Body Dissatisfaction Among Adolescent Boys and Girls: The Effects of Body Mass, Peer Appearance Culture and Internalization of Appearance Ideals." *Journal of Youth and Adolescence* 40 (1): 59–71.

Lawson, Robert. 2009. "Sociolinguistic Constructions of Identity among Adolescent Males in Glasgow." Unpublished PhD thesis. Glasgow, Scotland: University of Glasgow.

Lawson, Robert. 2011. "'It's Just a Waste of Money': The Role of Social and Traditional Media in Developing Public Engagement with Academic Research." Poster presented at the Interdisciplinary Linguistics Conference, Belfast, October 14, 2011.

Lawson, Robert. 2011. "Patterns of Linguistic Variation among Glaswegian Adolescent Males." *Journal of Sociolinguistics* 15 (2): 226–255.

Lawson, Robert. 2013. "The Construction of 'Tough' Masculinity: Negotiation, Alignment and Rejection." *Gender and Language* 7 (3): 369–395.

Lawson, Robert. 2015. "Fight Narratives, Covert Prestige, and Performances of 'Tough' Masculinity: Some Insights from an Urban Center." In *Language and Masculinities: Performances, Intersections, Dislocations*, edited by Tommaso Milani, 53–76. Oxon: Routledge.

Lawson, Robert. 2020. "Language and Masculinities: History, Development, and Future." *Annual Review of Linguistics* 6 (1): 409–434.

Lawson, Robert. 2022. "Tackling Online Radicalisation: Language, Masculinities, and the Role of the English Curriculum." *Teaching English* (28): 57–62.

Lawson, Robert. Forthcoming. "Risks in Working with Online Textual Data." In *Failures of Care*, edited by Julia DeCook, Ashley Mattheis, and Alexis de Coning. New Brunswick, NJ: Rutgers University Press.

Lawson, Robert, ed. in progress. *Discourses of Digital Masculinities*.

Lawson, Robert, and Ursula Lutzky. 2016. "Not Getting a Word in Edgeways? Language, Gender, and Identity in a British Comedy Panel Show." *Discourse, Context & Media* 13: 143–153.

Lawson, Robert, and Dave Sayers, eds. 2016a. "Where's We're Going, We Don't Need Roads: The Past, Present, and Future of Impact." In *Sociolinguistic Research: Application and Impact*, edited by Robert Lawson and Dave Sayers, 7–22. Oxon: Routledge.

Lawson, Robert, and Dave Sayers, eds. 2016b. *Sociolinguistic Research: Application and Impact*. Oxon: Routledge.

Lawson, Robert, Eszter Szenes, and Gavin Lamb. In progress. "A Multidisciplinary Linguistic Framework for Investigating Eco-Misogyny on Twitter: Greta Thunberg, Online Hate, and the (Anti)Climate Movement." *Discourse, Context & Media*.

Lazar, Michelle. 2000. "Gender, Discourse and Semiotics: The Politics of Parenthood Representations." *Discourse & Society* 11 (3): 373–400.

LeBlanc, Cameron. 2020. "Let's Talk About That 'Brooklyn Nine-Nine' Racial Profiling Scene." *Fatherly*, June 2, 2020. https://www.fatherly.com/news/brooklyn-99-moo-moo-racial-profiling-george-floyd-protest/.

Lee-Treweek, Geraldine, and Stephanie Linkogle. 2000. "Putting Danger in the Frame." In *Danger in the Field: Risk and Ethics in Social Research*, edited by Geraldine Lee-Treweek and Stephanie Linkogle, 8–25. London: Routledge.

Lee, Daniel D, and H Sebastian Seung. 2000. "Algorithms for Non-Negative Matrix Factorization." *Advances in Neural Information Processing Systems* 13: 556–562.

Lee, Yi-Tao. 2018. "Raised Online by Daddy: Fatherhoods and Childhoods in Taiwanese Father-Run Baby Blogs." Unpublished PhD thesis. Edinburgh: University of Edinburgh.

Leeuwen, Anne Ruth van. 2017. "Right on Time: Synchronization, Overlap, and Affiliation in Conversation." Unpublished PhD thesis. Utrecht: Universiteit Utrecht.

Leeuwen, Theo van. 2004. "Ten Reasons Why Linguists Should Pay Attention to Visual Communication." In *Discourse and Technology: Multimodal Discourse Analysis*, edited by Philip LeVine and Ron Scollon, 7–19. Washington, D.C.: Georgetown University Press.

Leeuwen, Theo van. 2014. "Critical Discourse Analysis and Multimodality." In *Contemporary Critical Discourse Studies*, edited by Christopher Hart and Piotr Cap, 281–296. London: Bloomsbury Publishing.

Leighton-Dore, Samuel. 2019. "6 Positive Male Role Models for International Men's Day." *SBS*, November 19, 2019. https://www.sbs.com.au/topics/voices/culture/article/2019/11/19/6-pretty-great-men-admire-even-when-its-not-internationalmensday.

Leslie, David. 2011. *Crimelord: The Licensee: The True Story of Tam McGraw*. Edinburgh: Mainstream Digital.

Levon, Erez, Tommaso M. Milani, and E. Dimitris Kitis. 2017. "The Topography of Masculine Normativities in South Africa." *Critical Discourse Studies* 14 (5): 514–531.

Lewis, Heather. 2021. "Weaponised Misogyny: Perspectives on Incel Extremism and Counter Terrorism." Unpublished MA dissertation. Birmingham, England: Birmingham City University.

Lien, Marianne Inéz, and Jørgen Lorentzen. 2019. "Violence Against Men in Intimate Relationships." In *Men's Experiences of Violence in Intimate Relationships*, edited by Marianne Inéz Lien and Jørgen Lorentzen, 1–12. Palgrave Studies in Victims and Victimology. Cham: Springer International Publishing.

Lin, Jie Liang. 2017. "Antifeminism Online: MGTOW (Men Going Their Own Way)." In *Digital Environments: Ethnographic Perspectives across Global Online and Offline Spaces*, edited by Urte Undine Frömming, Steffan Köhn, Samantha Fox, and Mike Terry, 77–96. Bielefeld, Germany: transcript Verlag.

Ling, Justin, Jill Mahoney, Patrick McGuire, and Colin Freeze. 2018. "The 'Incel' Community and the Dark Side of the Internet." *The Globe and Mail*, April 24, 2018. https://www.theglobeandmail.com/canada/article-the-incel-community-and-the-dark-side-of-the-internet/.

Litosseliti, Lia. 2006. *Gender and Language Theory and Practice*. London: Routledge.

Livingstone, Sonia, and Elisabetta Locatelli. 2012. "Ethical Dilemmas in Qualitative Research with Youth On/Offline." *International Journal of Learning and Media* 4 (2): 67–75.

Locke, John. 2011. *Duels and Duets: Why Men and Women Talk So Differently*. Cambridge: Cambridge University Press.

Lockwood, Penelope. 2006. "'Someone Like Me Can Be Successful': Do College Students Need Same-Gender Role Models?" *Psychology of Women Quarterly* 30 (1): 36–46.

Loesche, Dyfed. 2017. "The Prison Gender Gap." *Statista*, October 22, 2017. https://www.statista.com/chart/11573/gender-of-inmates-in-us-federal-prisons-and-general-population/.

Lohan, Maria, and Wendy Faulkner. 2004. "Masculinities and Technologies: Some Introductory Remarks." *Men and Masculinities* 6 (4): 319–329.

Lomas, Tim, Tina Cartwright, Trudi Edginton, and Damien Ridge. 2016. "New Ways of Being a Man: 'Positive' Hegemonic Masculinity in Meditation-Based Communities of Practice." *Men and Masculinities* 19 (3): 289–310.

Loofbourow, Lili. 2018. "Brett Kavanaugh and the Cruelty of Male Bonding." *Slate Magazine*, September 25, 2018. https://slate.com/news-and-politics/2018/09/brett-kavanaugh-allegations-yearbook-male-bonding.html.

Lorber, Judith. 1993. "Believing Is Seeing: Biology as Ideology." *Gender & Society* 7 (4): 568–581.

Lord, Annie. 2020. "Brooklyn Nine-Nine Cast Help Black Lives Matter by Donating $100k to National Bail Fund Network." *The Independent*, June 3, 2020. https://www.inde pendent.co.uk/arts-entertainment/tv/news/brooklyn-nine-nine-black-lives-mat ter-national-bail-fund-network-a9545901.html.

Lotz, Amanda D. 2014. *Cable Guys: Television and Masculinities in the 21st Century*. New York, NY: NYU Press.

Louw, Bill. 1993. "Irony in the Text or Insincerity in the Writer? The Diagnostic Potential of Semantic Prosodies." In *Text and Technology: In Honour of John Sinclair*, edited by Mona Baker, Gill Francis, and Elena Tognini-Bonelli, 157–176. Amsterdam: John Benjamins Publishing.

Lupton, Deborah, and Lesley Barclay. 1997. *Constructing Fatherhood: Discourses and Experiences*. London: SAGE Publications.

Lynskey, Dorian. 2018. "How Dangerous Is Jordan B. Peterson, the Rightwing Professor Who 'Hit a Hornets' Nest'?" *The Guardian*, February 7, 2018. https://www.theguard ian.com/science/2018/feb/07/how-dangerous-is-jordan-b-peterson-the-rightwing-professor-who-hit-a-hornets-nest.

Lyons, Matthew N. 2017. "Ctrl-Alt-Delete: The Origins and Ideology of the Alternative Right." *Political Research Associates*, January 20, 2017. https://www.politicalresea rch.org/2017/01/20/ctrl-alt-delete-report-on-the-alternative-right#sthash.pyfXk ALX.uO2xtz0b.dpbs.

Lyons, Matthew N. 2018. *Insurgent Supremacists: The U.S. Far Right's Challenge to State and Empire*. Oakland, CA: PM Press.

Maas, Jennife. 2019. "'Brooklyn Nine-Nine' Renewed for Season 8 by NBC." *TheWrap*, November 14, 2019. https://www.thewrap.com/brooklyn-nine-nine-season-8-rene wed-season-7-premiere-february/.

Mac an Ghaill, Máirtín. 1996. "'What about the Boys?': Schooling, Class and Crisis Masculinity." *The Sociological Review* 44 (3): 381–397.

Macarro, Antonia Sánchez. 2002. "Series Editor's Preface." In *Windows on the World: Media Discourse in English*, edited by Antonia Sánchez Macarro, 13–14. València: Universitat de València.

Macaulay, R. S. 1977. *Language, Social Class and Education*. Edinburgh: Edinburgh University Press.

Machin, Anna. 2018. *The Life of Dad: The Making of a Modern Father*. London: Simon & Schuster.

Machin, David, and Andrea Mayr. 2012. *How to Do Critical Discourse Analysis: A Multimodal Introduction*. London: SAGE Publications.

MacInnes, John. 1998. *End of Masculinity: The Confusion of Sexual Genesis and Sexual Difference in Modern Society*. Buckingham: Open University Press.

Mackenzie, Jai. 2017. "Identifying Informational Norms in Mumsnet Talk: A Reflexive-Linguistic Approach to Internet Research Ethics." *Applied Linguistics Review* 8 (2–3): 293–314.

Mackenzie, Jai. 2018. "'Good Mums Don't, Apparently, Wear Make-up': Negotiating Discourses of Gendered Parenthood in Mumsnet Talk." *Gender and Language* 12 (1): 114–135.

Mackenzie, Jai. 2019. *Language, Gender and Parenthood Online: Negotiating Motherhood in Mumsnet Talk*. Oxon: Routledge.

MacKinnon, Gillies. 1995. Small Faces. Pathé. https://www.imdb.com/title/tt0114474/.

Maclean, Kate. 2016. "Gender, Risk and the Wall Street Alpha Male." *Journal of Gender Studies* 25 (4): 427–444.

Mactavish, Scott. 2005. *The New Dad's Survival Guide: Man-to-Man Advice for First-Time Fathers*. New York, NY: Little, Brown and Company.

Magdy, Walid, Kareem Darwish, Norah Abokhodair, Afshin Rahimi, and Timothy Baldwin. 2016. "#ISISisNotIslam or #DeportAllMuslims? Predicting Unspoken Views."

In *Proceedings of the 8th ACM Conference on Web Science*, 95–106. New York, NY, USA: Association for Computing Machinery.

Magrath, Rory, and Ryan Scoats. 2019. "Young Men's Friendships: Inclusive Masculinities in a Post-University Setting." *Journal of Gender Studies* 28 (1): 45–56.

Mahlberg, Michaela, Peter Stockwell, Johan de Joode, Catherine Smith, and Matthew Brook O'Donnell. 2016. "CLiC Dickens: Novel Uses of Concordances for the Integration of Corpus Stylistics and Cognitive Poetics." *Corpora* 11 (3): 433–463.

Mair, Christian. 2009. "Corpus Linguistics Meets Sociolinguistics: The Role of Corpus Evidence in the Study of Sociolinguistic Variation and Change." In *Corpus Linguistics: Refinements and Reassessments*, edited by Antoinette Renouf and Andrew Kehoe, 7–32. Amsterdam: Rodopi.

Makhija, Sonal. 2019. "APN This Week: Finland Wants More Dads to Take Paternity Leave, but Foreign Stay-at-Home Fathers Struggle to Find Support." *Yle Uutiset*, October 16, 2019. https://yle.fi/uutiset/osasto/news/apnthis_week_finland_wants_more_dads_to_take_paternity_leave_but_foreign_stay-at-home_fathers_struggle_to_find_support/11021690.

Maldoff, Gabe. 2016. "How GDPR Changes the Rules for Research." *Iapp*. https://iapp.org/news/a/how-gdpr-changes-the-rules-for-research/.

Maney, Donna L. 2016. "Perils and Pitfalls of Reporting Sex Differences." *Philosophical Transactions of the Royal Society B: Biological Sciences* 371 (1688): 20150119.

Mantilla, Karla. 2013. "Gendertrolling: Misogyny Adapts to New Media." *Feminist Studies* 39 (2): 563–570.

Marantz, Andrew. 2017. "The Alt-Right Branding War Has Torn the Movement in Two." *The New Yorker*, July 6, 2017. https://www.newyorker.com/news/news-desk/the-alt-right-branding-war-has-torn-the-movement-in-two.

Marantz, Andrew. 2019. *Antisocial: Online Extremists, Techno-Utopians, and the Hijacking of the American Conversation*. New York: Viking.

Marche, Stephen. 2016. "Swallowing the Red Pill: A Journey to the Heart of Modern Misogyny." *The Guardian*, April 14, 2016. https://www.theguardian.com/technology/2016/apr/14/the-red-pill-reddit-modern-misogyny-manosphere-men.

Marcotte, Amanda. 2016. "Overcompensation Nation: It's Time to Admit That Toxic Masculinity Drives Gun Violence." *Salon*, June 13, 2016. https://www.salon.com/2016/06/13/overcompensation_nation_its_time_to_admit_that_toxic_masculinity_drives_gun_violence/.

Marcus, Simon. 2020. "Failing White Working-Class Boys." *Spiked*, January 22, 2020. https://www.spiked-online.com/2020/01/22/failing-white-working-class-boys/.

Markham, Annette. 2012. "Fabrication as Ethical Practice." *Information, Communication & Society* 15 (3): 334–353.

Markham, Annette, and Elizabeth Buchanan. 2012. "Ethical Decision-Making and Internet Research: Recommendations from the AoIR Ethics Working Committee (Version 2.0)." https://aoir.org/reports/ethics2.pdf.

Marshall, Harriette. 1991. "The Social Construction of Motherhood: An Analysis of Childcare and Parenting Manuals." In *Motherhood: Meanings, Practices and Ideologies*, edited by Ann Phoenix, Anne Woollett, and Eva Lloyd, 66–85. London: SAGE Publications.

Martin, Audrey. 2020. "What Is Copaganda and Can I Keep Watching *Brooklyn Nine-Nine*?" *Study Breaks*, June 14, 2020. https://studybreaks.com/tvfilm/copaganda-brooklyn-nine-nine/.

Martin, Trevor. 2017. "Dissecting Trump's Most Rabid Online Following." *Five Thirty Eight*, March 23, 2017. https://fivethirtyeight.com/features/dissecting-trumps-most-rabid-online-following/.

Martino, Wayne. 1999. "'Cool Boys', 'Party Animals', 'Squids' and 'Poofters': Interrogating the Dynamics and Politics of Adolescent Masculinities in School." *British Journal of Sociology of Education* 20 (2): 239–263.

Marwick, Alice. 2022. "What People Misunderstand about Red-Pilling." *Slate*, May 19, 2022. https://slate.com/technology/2022/05/red-pill-buffalo-shooter-online-hate-groups-research.html.

Marwick, Alice E., and Rebecca Lewis. 2017. "Media Manipulation and Disinformation Online." New York, NJ: Data & Society Research Institute.

Marwick, Alice E., Lindsay Blackwell, and Katherine Lo. 2016. "Best Practices for Conducting Risky Research and Protecting Yourself from Online Harassment." New York, NY: Data & Society Research Institute.

Marwick, Alice E., and Robyn Caplan. 2018. "Drinking Male Tears: Language, the Manosphere, and Networked Harassment." *Feminist Media Studies* 18 (4): 543–559.

Mashabane, Bridgetti, and Neil Henderson. 2020. "Ulwaluko: 'Rights' of Passage of Gay Men in South Africa." *Journal of GLBT Family Studies* 16 (2): 163–175.

Massanari, Adrienne L. 2015. *Participatory Culture, Community, and Play*. New York, NY: Peter Lang Publishing.

Massanari, Adrienne L. 2017. "#Gamergate and The Fappening: How Reddit's Algorithm, Governance, and Culture Support Toxic Technocultures." *New Media & Society* 19 (3): 329–346.

Massanari, Adrienne L. 2018. "Rethinking Research Ethics, Power, and the Risk of Visibility in the Era of the 'Alt-Right' Gaze." *Social Media + Society* 4 (2): 1–9.

Mautner, Gerlinde. 2009. "Checks and Balances: How Corpus Linguistics Can Contribute to CDA." In *Methods for Critical Discourse Analysis*, edited by Ruth Wodak and Michael Meyer, 122–143. London: SAGE Publications.

Maxwell, Karen J. 2018. "Fatherhood in the Context of Social Disadvantage: Constructions of Fatherhood and Attitudes towards Parenting Interventions of Disadvantaged Men in Scotland." Unpublished PhD thesis. Glasgow, Scotland: University of Glasgow.

May, Rob, and Matthew Feldman. 2019. "Understanding the Alt-Right: Ideologues, 'Lulz' and Hiding in Plain Sight." In *Post-Digital Cultures of the Far Right: Online Actions and Offline Consequences in Europe and the US*, edited by Maik Fielitz and Nick Thurston, 25–36. Bielefeld, Germany: transcript Verlag.

McArthur, Alexander, and Herbert Kingsley-Long. 1935. *No Mean City: A Story of the Glasgow Slums*. London: Longmans.

McCammon, Ross. 2019. "I Became a Better Dad When I Stopped Worrying About Being 'Manly.'" *Men's Health*, May 30, 2019. https://www.menshealth.com/health/a27651457/how-to-be-a-nicer-dad/.

McCarthy, Tyler. 2019. "The Best 25 Episodes of 'Brooklyn Nine-Nine,' Ranked." *Thrillist*, August 20, 2019. https://www.thrillist.com/entertainment/nation/best-brooklyn-nine-nine-episodes.

McCrea, Aisling. 2019. "The Magical Thinking of Guys Who Love Logic." *The Outline*, February 15, 2019. https://theoutline.com/post/7083/the-magical-thinking-of-guys-who-love-logic.

McDowell, Linda. 2000. "The Trouble with Men? Young People, Gender Transformations and the Crisis of Masculinity." *International Journal of Urban and Regional Research* 24 (1): 201–209.

McEnery, Tony, and Andrew Hardie. 2012. *Corpus Linguistics: Method, Theory and Practice*. Cambridge: Cambridge University Press.

McEnery, Tony, and Andrew Wilson. 2001. *Corpus Linguistics: An Introduction*. Edinburgh: Edinburgh University Press.

McEnery, Tony, Richard Xiao, and Yukio Tono. 2006. *Corpus-Based Language Studies: An Advanced Resource Book*. Milton Park: Taylor & Francis.

McGarth, Tom, and Jimmy Boyle. 1977. *The Hard Man*. Edinburgh: Canongate Books.

McGinley, Ann C. 2016. *Masculinity at Work: Employment Discrimination Through a Different Lens*. New York, NY: NYU Press.

McGlashan, Mark. 2015. "The Representation of Same-Sex Parents in Children's Picturebooks: A Corpus-Assisted Multimodal Critical Discourse Analysis." Unpublished PhD thesis. Lancaster, England: Lancaster University.

McGuire, Colin. 2017. "Footage & Recordings." Colin McGuire Poet. http://www.colin mcguirepoet.co.uk/recordings.html.

McIntosh, Janet. 2020. "Introduction: The Trump Era as a Linguistic Emergency." In *Language in the Trump Era: Scandals and Emergencies*, edited by Janet McIntosh and Norma Mendoza-Denton, 1–43. Cambridge: Cambridge University Press.

McIntyre, Dan, and Hazel Price. 2018. *Applying Linguistics: Language and the Impact Agenda*. Oxon: Routledge.

McKay, Brett, and Kate McKay. 2010. "Male Rites of Passages from Around the World." *The Art of Manliness*. https://www.artofmanliness.com/articles/male-rites-of-pass age-from-around-the-world/.

McKay, Reg. 2006. *Murder Capital: Life and Death on the Streets of Glasgow's*. Edinburgh: Black and White Publishing.

McKay, Reg. 2007. *The Last Godfather: The Life and Crimes of Arthur Thompson*. Edinburgh: Black and White Publishing.

McKeown, Kieran, Harry Ferguson, and Rooney Dermot. 1997. *Fathers: Irish Experience in an International Context*. Dublin: Commission on the Family.

McLean, Robert, and Chris Holligan. 2018. "The Semiotics of the Evolving Gang Masculinity and Glasgow." *Social Sciences* 7 (8): 125.

McMillen, Kyle. 2018. "Between a Cuck and a Hard Place: Masculinity and Online Uses of the Word 'Cuck.'" *The Activist History Review*, November 19, 2018. https://activist history.com/2018/11/19/between-a-cuck-and-a-hard-place-masculinity-and-onl ine-uses-of-the-word-cuck/.

McNeill, Lisa S., and Katie Douglas. 2011. "Retailing Masculinity: Gender Expectations and Social Image of Male Grooming Products in New Zealand." *Journal of Retailing and Consumer Services* 18 (5): 448–454.

Mearns, Adam, and Karen P. Corrigan, eds. 2016. *Creating and Digitizing Language Corpora*. Basingstoke: Palgrave Macmillan.

Mech, L. David. 1970. *Wolf: The Ecology and Behavior of an Endangered Species*. New York, NY: American Museum of Natural History.

Megarry, Jessica. 2014. "Online Incivility or Sexual Harassment? Conceptualising Women's Experiences in the Digital Age." *Women's Studies International Forum* 47: 46–55.

Mellström, Ulf. 2004. "Machines and Masculine Subjectivity: Technology as an Integral Part of Men's Life Experiences." *Men and Masculinities* 6 (4): 368–382.

Mendoza-Denton, Norma. 2008. *Homegirls: Language and Cultural Practice Among Latina Youth Gangs*. Malden, MA: Wiley-Blackwell.

Mendoza-Denton, Norma. 2017. "Bad Hombres: Images of Masculinity and the Historical Consciousness of US-Mexico Relations in the Age of Trump." *HAU: Journal of Ethnographic Theory* 7 (1): 423–432.

Mendoza-Denton, Norma, Scarlett Eisenhauer, Wesley Wilson, and Cory Flores. 2017. "Gender, Electrodermal Activity, and Videogames: Adding a Psychophysiological Dimension to Sociolinguistic Methods." *Journal of Sociolinguistics* 21 (4): 547–575.

Mercer, John, and Mark McGlashan, eds. in progress. *Toxic Masculinity: Men, Meaning and the Media*. Oxon: Routledge.

Merkouris, Stephanie S., Anna C. Thomas, Kerrie A. Shandley, Simone N. Rodda, Erin Oldenhof, and Nicki A. Dowling. 2016. "An Update on Gender Differences in the Characteristics Associated with Problem Gambling: A Systematic Review." *Current Addiction Reports* 3 (3): 254–267.

Merullo, Jack, Luke Yeh, Abram Handler, Alvin Grissom II, Brendan O'Connor, and Mohit Iyyer. 2019. "Investigating Sports Commentator Bias within a Large Corpus of American Football Broadcasts." *ArXiv:1909.03343*. http://arxiv.org/abs/1909.03343.

Messer-Davidow, Ellen. 1993. "Manufacturing the Attack on Liberalized Higher Education." *Social Text*, no. 36: 40–80.

Messner, Michael. 1990. "When Bodies Are Weapons: Masculinity and Violence in Sport." *International Review for the Sociology of Sport* 25 (3): 203–220.

Messner, Michael. 2016. "Forks in the Road of Men's Gender Politics: Men's Rights vs Feminist Allies." *International Journal for Crime, Justice and Social Democracy; Brisbane* 5 (2): 6–20.

MGTOW. 2020. "The History of Men Going Their Own Way." MGTOW. 2020. https://www.mgtow.com/history/.

MGTOW. n.d. "The Manosphere." *MGTOW*, Accessed December 18, 2020. https://www.mgtow.com/manosphere/.

Milani, Tommaso. 2011. "Introduction: Re-Casting Language and Masculinities." *Gender and Language* 5 (2): 175–186.

Milani, Tommaso. 2015. "Theorizing Language and Masculinities." In *Language and Masculinities: Performances, Intersections, Dislocations*, 8–33. Oxon: Routledge.

Milani, Tommaso, ed. 2015. *Language and Masculinities: Performances, Intersections, Dislocations*. Oxon: Routledge.

Miller, Tina. 2011. *Making Sense of Fatherhood: Gender, Caring and Work.* Cambridge: Cambridge University Press.

Mills, Sara. 2008. *Language and Sexism.* Cambridge: Cambridge University Press.

Milton, Colin. 1997. "Ma Language Is Disgraceful: Tom Leonard's Glasgow Dialect Poems." In *Englishes Around the World: General Studies, British Isles, North America*, edited by Edgar Schneider, 1:185–210. Amsterdam: John Benjamins Publishing.

Mitchell, Wendy, and Annie Irvine. 2008. "I'm Okay, You're Okay?: Reflections on the Well-Being and Ethical Requirements of Researchers and Research Participants in Conducting Qualitative Fieldwork Interviews." *International Journal of Qualitative Methods* 7 (4): 31–44.

Möller-Leimkühler, Anne Maria. 2018. "Why Is Terrorism a Man's Business?" *CNS Spectrums* 23 (2): 118–119.

Mooney, Gerry. 2004. "Cultural Policy as Urban Transformation? Critical Reflections on Glasgow, European City of Culture 1990." *Local Economy: The Journal of the Local Economy Policy Unit* 19 (4): 327–340.

Moore, Jeremy. 2019. "The Missing Piece: Fathers' Role in Stemming Youth Radicalization." *United States Institute of Peace*, October 16, 2019. https://www.usip.org/blog/2019/10/missing-piece-fathers-role-stemming-youth-radicalization.

Morgan, David. 2006. "The Crisis in Masculinity." In *Handbook of Gender and Women's Studies*, edited by Kathy Davis, Mary Evans, and Judith Lorber, 109–124. London: SAGE Publications.

Morgan, George. 2016. *Global Islamophobia: Muslims and Moral Panic in the West.* Oxon: Routledge.

Morgan, Max. 2021. "Not All Men: Dismantling the Pyramid." *Spiller of Tea*, March 11, 2021. https://spilleroftea.com/2021/03/11/not-all-men-dismantling-the-pyramid/.

Mort, F. C. 1988. "Boy's Own? Masculinity, Style and Popular Culture." In *Male Order: Unwrapping Masculinity*, edited by Rowena Chapman and John Rutherford, 193–224. London: Lawrence and Wishart.

Moss, Mark. 2012. *The Media and the Models of Masculinity.* Lexington Books.

Mosse, George L. 1996. *The Image of Man: The Creation of Modern Masculinity.* Oxford: Oxford University Press.

Mudde, Cas. 2018. "Why Is the Far Right Dominated by Men?" *The Guardian*, August 17, 2018. https://www.theguardian.com/commentisfree/2018/aug/17/why-is-the-far-right-dominated-by-men.

Mulcahy, Clare, Hannah McGregor, and Marcelle Kosman. 2017. "Digital Feminist Counter-Publics." *Atlantis: Critical Studies in Gender, Culture & Social Justice* 38 (2): 134–136.

Mulholland, Jon, Nicola Montagna, and Erin Sanders-McDonagh, eds. 2018. *Gendering Nationalism: Intersections of Nation, Gender and Sexuality.* Basingstoke: Palgrave Macmillan.

Mullan, Peter. 2010. *Neds.* E1 Entertainment.

Mullen, Amanda. 2019. "Terry Crews and Joe Lo Truglio Talk Masculinity on Brooklyn Nine-Nine." *Fansided*, July 29, 2019. https://culturess.com/2019/07/29/terry-crews-and-joe-lo-truglio-talk-masculinity-on-brooklyn-nine-nine/.

Mundy, Robert, and Harry Denny. 2020. *Gender, Sexuality, and the Cultural Politics of Men's Identity: Literacies of Masculinity*. Oxon: Routledge.

Munn, Luke. 2019. "Alt-Right Pipeline: Individual Journeys to Extremism Online." *First Monday* 24 (6).

Murakami, Akira, Paul Thompson, Susan Hunston, and Dominik Vajn. 2017. "'What Is This Corpus about?': Using Topic Modelling to Explore a Specialised Corpus." *Corpora* 12 (2): 243–277.

Murphy, Bróna. 2010. *Corpus and Sociolinguistics: Investigating Age and Gender in Female Talk*. Amsterdam: John Benjamins Publishing.

Murray, Christopher J. L., Alan D. Lopez, Mohsen Naghavi, and Haidong Wang. 2016. "Global, Regional, and National Life Expectancy, All-Cause Mortality, and Cause-Specific Mortality for 249 Causes of Death, 1980–2015: A Systematic Analysis for the Global Burden of Disease Study 2015." *The Lancet* 388 (10053): 1459–1544.

Musser, Amber Jamilla. 2015. "BDSM and the Boundaries of Criticism: Feminism and Neoliberalism in *Fifty Shades of Grey* and *The Story of O*." *Feminist Theory* 16 (2): 121–136.

Mutua, Athena. 2013. "Multidimensionality Is to Masculinities What Intersectionality Is to Feminism." *Nevada Law Journal* 13: 341–367.

Myketiak, Chrystie. 2016. "Fragile Masculinity: Social Inequalities in the Narrative Frame and Discursive Construction of a Mass Shooter's Autobiography/Manifesto." *Contemporary Social Science* 11 (4): 289–303.

Nagel, Emily van der. 2017. "From Usernames to Profiles: The Development of Pseudonymity in Internet Communication." *Internet Histories* 1 (4): 312–331.

Nagel, Emily van der. 2020. "Embodied Verification: Linking Identities and Bodies on NSFW Reddit." In *Mediated Interfaces: The Body on Social Media*, edited by Katie Warfield, Crystal Abidin, and Carolina Cambre, 51–64. London: Bloomsbury.

Nagel, Joane. 1998. "Masculinity and Nationalism: Gender and Sexuality in the Making of Nations." *Ethnic and Racial Studies* 21 (2): 242–269.

Nagle, Angela. 2017. *Kill All Normies: Online Culture Wars From 4Chan And Tumblr To Trump And The Alt-Right*. Winchester: Zero Books.

Nartey, Mark, and Isaac N. Mwinlaaru. 2019. "Towards a Decade of Synergising Corpus Linguistics and Critical Discourse Analysis: A Meta-Analysis." *Corpora* 14 (2): 203–235.

Neiwert, David. 2017. *Alt-America: The Rise of the Radical Right in the Age of Trump*. London: Verso.

Nicholas, Lucy, and Christine Agius. 2018. "#Notallmen, #Menenism, Manospheres and Unsafe Spaces: Overt and Subtle Masculinism in Anti-'PC' Discourse." In *The Persistence of Global Masculinism: Discourse, Gender and Neo-Colonial Re-Articulations of Violence*, edited by Lucy Nicholas and Christine Agius, 31–59. Cham: Springer International Publishing.

Niedzielski, Nancy A., and Dennis R. Preston. 2010. *Folk Linguistics*. Berlin: Walter de Gruyter.

Nishida, Toshisada, Toshikazu Hasegawa, Hitoshige Hiyaki, Yukio Takahata, and Shigeo Uehara. 1992. "Meat Sharing as a Coalition Strategy by an Alpha Male Chimpanzee." In *Topics in Primatology*, edited by Toshisada Nishida, William C. McGrew, and Peter Marler, 1: 159–174. Tokyo: University of Tokyo Press.

Nissenbaum, Helen. 2004. "Privacy as Contextual Integrity." *Washington Law Review* 79 (1): 119–158.

Noble, Greg. 2012. "Where's the Moral in 'Moral Panic'? Islam, Evil and Moral Turbulence." In *Global Islamophobia: Muslims and Moral Panic in the West*, edited by George Morgan and Scott Poynting, 215–232. Oxon: Routledge.

Noonan, Laura, Alan Smith, David Blood, and Martin Stabe. 2017. "How Are Financial Services Firms Doing on Gender Equality?" *Financial Times*, April 4, 2017. https://ig.ft.com/managements-missing-women-data.

Norman, Chelsey. 2020. "The Alt-Right Arc: Identity Construction and Audience Uptake on YouTube." Presentation presented at the 114th American Anthropological Association Annual Meeting, Denver, March 29, 2020. https://aaal.confex.com/aaal/2020/meetingapp.cgi/Session/4151.

Norocel, Ov Christian, Tuija Saresma, Tuuli Lähdesmäki, and Maria Ruotsalainen. 2018. "Discursive Constructions of White Nordic Masculinities in Right-Wing Populist Media." *Men and Masculinities* 23 (3–4): 425–446.

O'Keeffe, Anne, and Michael McCarthy. 2010. "Historical Perspective: What Are Corpora and How Have They Evolved." In *The Routledge Handbook of Corpus Linguistics*, edited by Anne O'Keeffe and Michael McCarthy, 3–13. Oxon: Routledge.

O'Malley, Harris. 2016. "The Difference Between Toxic Masculinity and Being A Man." *The Good Men Project*, June 27, 2016. https://goodmenproject.com/featured-content/the-difference-between-toxic-masculinity-and-being-a-man-dg/.

O'Malley, Harris. 2017. "What Does It Take to Be a Good Man?" *Paging Dr. NerdLove*, October 9, 2017. https://www.doctornerdlove.com/be-a-better-man/.

O'Neil, James M. 2008. "Summarizing 25 Years of Research on Men's Gender Role Conflict Using the Gender Role Conflict Scale: New Research Paradigms and Clinical Implications." *The Counseling Psychologist* 36 (3): 358–445.

O'Neil, James M. 2010. "Is Criticism of Generic Masculinity, Essentialism, and Positive-Healthy-Masculinity a Problem for the Psychology of Men?" *Psychology of Men & Masculinity* 11 (2): 98–106.

O'Neil, James M. 2012. "The Psychology of Men." In *The Oxford Handbook of Counseling Psychology*, edited by Elizabeth M. Altmaier and Jo-Ida C. Hansen, 375–408. Oxford: Oxford University Press.

Ochs, Elinor, Ruth Smith, and Carolyn Taylor. 1989. "Detective Stories at Dinnertime: Problem-Solving through Co-Narration." *Cultural Dynamics* 2 (2): 239–259.

Office for National Statistics. 2021a. "The Nature of Violent Crime in England and Wales." February 25, 2021. https://www.ons.gov.uk/peoplepopulationandcommunity/crimeandjustice/articles/thenatureofviolentcrimeinenglandandwales/yearendingmarch2020#long-term-trends-in-violent-crime.

Office for National Statistics. 2021b. "The Lasting Impact of Violence against Women and Girls." November 24, 2021. https://www.ons.gov.uk/peoplepopulationandcommunity/crimeandjustice/articles/thelastingimpactofviolenceagainstwomenandgirls/2021-11-24.

Ohlheiser, Abby. 2015. "Why 'Social Justice Warrior,' a Gamergate Insult, Is Now a Dictionary Entry." *The Washington Post*, October 7, 2015. https://www.washingtonpost.com/news/the-intersect/wp/2015/10/07/why-social-justice-warrior-a-gamergate-insult-is-now-a-dictionary-entry/.

Oksanen, Atte, Magdalena Celuch, Rita Latikka, Reetta Oksa, and Nina Savela. 2022. "Hate and Harassment in Academia: The Rising Concern of the Online Environment." *Higher Education* 84 (3): 541–567.

Okun, Rob. 2018. "Men Listening to Women and to Each Other." *Feminist*, 2018. https://www.feminist.com/resources/artspeech/mensvoices8.html.

O'Malley, Roberta Liggett, and Brenna Helm. 2022. "The Role of Perceived Injustice and Need for Esteem on Incel Membership Online." *Deviant Behavior* DOI: 10.1080/01639625.2022.2133650

Oransky, Matthew, and Jeanne Marecek. 2009. "'I'm Not Going to Be a Girl': Masculinity and Emotions in Boys' Friendships and Peer Groups." *Journal of Adolescent Research* 24 (2): 218–241.

Orchard, Treena. 2019. "Bumble Article Comments Indicate the Rise of a Far-Right Feminist-Backlash." *The Conversation*, September 30, 2019. http://theconversation.

com/bumble-article-comments-indicate-the-rise-of-a-far-right-feminist-backlash-121652.

Orenstein, Peggy. 2020. *Boys & Sex: Young Men on Hook-Ups, Love, Porn, Consent and Navigating the New Masculinity*. London: Souvenir Press.

Osborn, Jacob. 2019. "21 Best Dad Blogs." *Man of Many*, September 30, 2019. https://manofmany.com/lifestyle/advice/21-best-dad-blogs.

Page, Ruth. 2017. "Ethics Revisited: Rights, Responsibilities and Relationships in Online Research." *Applied Linguistics Review* 8 (2–3): 315–320.

Paglia, Camille. 1993. "Challenging the Male Mystique." *Washington Post*, July 25, 1993. https://www.washingtonpost.com/archive/entertainment/books/1993/07/25/challenging-the-male-mystique/31b3a4da-3b8b-4f11-9252-01058c385a99/.

Papacharissi, Zizi. 2015. *Affective Publics: Sentiment, Technology, and Politics*. Oxford: Oxford University Press.

Parent, Mike C., Teresa D. Gobble, and Aaron Rochlen. 2019. "Social Media Behavior, Toxic Masculinity, and Depression." *Psychology of Men & Masculinities* 20 (3): 277–287.

Park, Albert, and Mike Conway. 2018. "Harnessing Reddit to Understand the Written-Communication Challenges Experienced by Individuals with Mental Health Disorders: Analysis of Texts From Mental Health Communities." *Journal of Medical Internet Research* 20 (4): e121.

Park, Jennifer. 2018. "'Brooklyn Nine-Nine' Is How All Shows Should Do Inclusivity." *SBS*, March 28, 2018. https://www.sbs.com.au/guide/article/2018/03/26/brooklyn-nine-nine-how-all-shows-should-do-inclusivity.

Parker, yan. 2018. "Terry Crews Condemns 'Toxic Masculinity' in Senate Testimony on Sexual Assault." *The Hollywood Reporter*, June 26, 2018. https://www.hollywoodreporter.com/news/terry-crews-senate-testimony-sexual-assault-1123360.

Parsons, Talcott. 1940. "An Analytical Approach to the Theory of Social Stratification." *American Journal of Sociology* 45 (6): 841–862.

Partington, Alan, Alison Duguid, and Charlotte Taylor. 2013. *Patterns and Meanings in Discourse: Theory and Practice in Corpus-Assisted Discourse Studies (CADS)*. Amsterdam: John Benjamins Publishing.

Patton, Desmond Upton, Robert D. Eschmann, and Dirk A. Butler. 2013. "Internet Banging: New Trends in Social Media, Gang Violence, Masculinity and Hip Hop." *Computers in Human Behavior* 29 (5): A54–A59.

Pearson, Elizabeth. 2019. "Extremism and Toxic Masculinity: The Man Question Re-Posed." *International Affairs* 95 (6): 1251–1270.

Pease, Allan, and Barbara Pease. 2001. *Why Men Don't Listen and Women Can't Read Maps*. London: Orion.

Pease, Bob. 2000. "Researching Profeminist Men's Narratives: Participatory Methods in a Postmodern Frame." In *Practice and Research in Social Work: Postmodern Feminist Perspectives*, edited by Barbara Fawcett, Brid Featherstone, Jan Fook, and Amy Rossiter, 138–161. Oxon: Routledge.

Pease, Bob. 2008. "Engaging Men in Men's Violence Prevention: Exploring the Tensions, Dilemmas and Possibilities." *Australian Domestic and Family Violence Clearinghouse* 17: 1–20.

Pedregosa, Fabian, Gael Varoquaux, Alexandre Gramfort, Vincent Michel, Bertrand Thirion, Olivier Grisel, Mathieu Blondel, et al. 2011. "Scikit-Learn: Machine Learning in Python." *Machine Learning in Python* 12: 2825–2830.

Pennycook, Alastair. 1990. "Towards a Critical Applied Linguistics for the 1990s." *Issues in Applied Linguistics* 1 (1): 8–28.

Perry, Grayson. 2016. *The Descent of Man*. London: Penguin Books.

Peters, Michael A., and Tina Besley. 2019. "Weinstein, Sexual Predation, and 'Rape Culture': Public Pedagogies and Hashtag Internet Activism." *Educational Philosophy and Theory* 51 (5): 458–464.

Pichler, Pia. 2021. "'I've Got a Daughter Now Man It's Clean Man': Heteroglossic and Intersectional Constructions of Fatherhood in the Spontaneous Talk of a Group of Young Southeast London Men." *Language in Society* 1–28.

Pinkett, Matt, and Mark Roberts. 2019. *Boys Don't Try? Rethinking Masculinity in Schools*. Oxon: Routledge.

Pleasants, Robert K. 2011. "Men Learning Feminism: Protecting Privileges Through Discourses of Resistance." *Men and Masculinities* 14 (2): 230–250.

Pleck, Joseph H. 1998. "Families in the U.S.: Kinship and Domestic Politics." In *Families in the U.S.: Kinship and Domestic Politics*, edited by Karen V. Hansen and Anita Ilta Garey, 351–362. Philadelphia: Temple University Press.

Pleck, Joseph H. 2010. "Fatherhood and Masculinity." In *The Role of the Father in Child Development*, edited by Michael E. Lamb, 27–57. John Wiley & Sons.

Pleck, Elizabeth H., and Joseph H. Pleck. 1997. "Fatherhood Ideals in the United States: Historical Dimensions." In *The Role of the Father in Child Development*, edited by Michael E. Lamb, 33–48. New York, NY: John Wiley & Sons.

Plowright, Marcus. 2020. "Football, Prince William and Our Mental Health." *BBC*. https://www.bbc.co.uk/programmes/m000jkbr.

Podnieks, Elizabeth. 2016a. "Introduction." In *Pops in Pop Culture: Fatherhood, Masculinity, and the New Man*, edited by Elizabeth Podnieks, 1–27. New York, NY: Palgrave Macmillan US.

Podnieks, Elizabeth. 2016b. *Pops in Pop Culture: Fatherhood, Masculinity, and the New Man*. Springer.

Poland, Bailey. 2016. *Haters: Harassment, Abuse, and Violence Online*. Lincoln, NE: University of Nebraska Press.

Poling, J. Ryan. 2013. "New Masculinity: Exploring the Effects of a Men's Initiation Weekend." Unpublished MA dissertation. Pasadena, CA: Fuller Theological Seminary.

Pomerantz, Anita. 1984. "Agreeing and Disagreeing with Assessments: Some Features of Preferred/Dispreferred Turn Shapes." In *Structures of Social Action*, edited by J. Maxwell Atkinson and John Heritage, 57–101. Cambridge: Cambridge University Press.

Prasad, Ritu. 2019. "How Trump Talks about Women—and Does It Matter?" *BBC News*, November 29, 2019. https://www.bbc.com/news/world-us-canada-50563106.

Preece, Siân, ed. 2016. *The Routledge Handbook of Language and Identity*. Oxon: Routledge.

Price, Lee. 2018. *The GoodFather: Expectant Dad Survival Guide*. Oakamoor: Dark River.

Prinsloo, Jeanne. 2006. "Where Have All the Fathers Gone? Media(Ted) Representations of Fatherhood." In *Baba: Men and Fatherhood in South Africa*, edited by Linda M. Richter and Robert Morrell, 132–146. Cape Town: HSRC Press.

Proctor, Keith, and Dyan Mazurana. 2019. "The Role of Gender in Mobilizing and Countering Fundamentalist Violent Extremist Organizations." In *Routledge Handbook of Gender and Security*, edited by Caron E. Gentry, Laura J. Shepherd, and Laura Sjoberg, 227–238. Oxon: Routledge.

Proudfoot, Jenny. 2021. "'If You're Using the #NotAllMen Hashtag, You're Part of the Problem.'" *Marie Claire*, March 12, 2021. https://www.marieclaire.co.uk/opinion/not-all-men-hashtag-731556.

Queen, Robin. 2012. "The Days of Our Lives: Language, Gender and Affluence on a Daytime Television Drama." *Gender and Language* 6 (1): 153–180.

Quinn, Zoë. 2017. *Crash Override: How Gamergate (Nearly) Destroyed My Life, and How We Can Win the Fight Against Online Hate*. New York, NY: PublicAffairs.

/r/MensRights FAQs. n.d. "FAQ: MensRights." Reddit. Accessed December 21, 2020. https://www.reddit.com/r/MensRights/wiki/faq.

Rafanell, Irene, Robert McLean, and Lynne Poole. 2017. "Emotions and Hyper-Masculine Subjectivities: The Role of Affective Sanctioning in Glasgow Gangs." *NORMA: International Journal for Masculinity Studies* 12 (3–4): 187–204.

Randles, Jennifer. 2018a. "'Manning Up' to Be a Good Father: Hybrid Fatherhood, Masculinity, and U.S. Responsible Fatherhood Policy." *Gender & Society* 32 (4): 516–539.

Randles, Jennifer. 2018b. "Making Men into 'Responsible' Fathers." *Contexts* 17 (2): 34–39.

Randles, Jennifer. 2018c. "Taking Time to Be a Manly Dad: Gender Inequality and the Politics of Fatherhood." *Gender & Society* (blog). August 21, 2018. https://gender society.wordpress.com/2018/08/21/taking-time-to-be-a-manly-dad-gender-inequal ity-and-the-politics-of-fatherhood/.

Ranson, Gillian. 2015. *Fathering, Masculinity and the Embodiment of Care.* Basingstoke: Palgrave Macmillan.

Rational Wiki. 2019. "Manosphere Glossary." *Rational Wiki*, November 6, 2019. https:// rationalwiki.org/wiki/Manosphere_glossary#All_women_are_like_that.

Read, Max. 2019. "How The Matrix's Red Pill Became the Internet's Delusional Drug of Choice." *Vulture*, February 8, 2019. https://www.vulture.com/2019/02/the-matrix-red-pill-internet-delusional-drug.html.

Real, Terrence, and Adam Verner. 2011. *I Don't Want to Talk about It: Overcoming the Secret Legacy of Male Depression.* Unabridged edition. Old Saybrook, CT: Tantor Media Inc.

Reddit Inc. 2019. "Reddit Wiki Content Policy." 2019. https://www.reddit.com/wiki/ contentpolicy.

Reddit Inc. 2020. "Content Policy: Reddit." Reddit. 2020. https://www.redditinc.com/polic ies/content-policy.

Reddit Inc. 2020. "Privacy Policy." 2020. https://www.redditinc.com/policies/privacy-policy.

Reeser, Todd W. 2010. *Masculinities in Theory: An Introduction.* Chichester: Wiley-Blackwell.

Reigeluth, Christopher S., and Michael E. Addis. 2016. "Adolescent Boys' Experiences with Policing of Masculinity: Forms, Functions, and Consequences." *Psychology of Men & Masculinity* 17 (1): 74–83.

Reisigl, Martin, and Ruth Wodak. 2016. "Critical Discourse Studies: A Sociocognitive Approach." In *Methods of Critical Discourse Studies*, edited by Ruth Wodak and Michael Meyer, 3rd edition, 23–61. London: SAGE Publications.

Ren, Yi. 2019. "Masculinity, Fatherhood, and Beyond: Potential Social Indices Behind Osaka Dialect." Unpublished MA dissertation. Eugene, OR: University of Oregon.

Renouf, Antoinette. 1996. "The ACRONYM Project: Discovering the Textual Thesaurus." In *Papers from English Language Research on Computerized Corpora (ICAME 16)*, edited by Ian Meyer, Charles Percy, and Carol Percy, 171–187. Amsterdam: Rodopi.

Rensin, Emmett. 2015. "The Internet Is Full of Men Who Hate Feminism. Here's What They're like in Person." *Vox*, February 5, 2015. https://www.vox.com/2015/2/5/ 7942623/mens-rights-movement.

Rhodes, Nancy, and Kelly Pivik. 2011. "Age and Gender Differences in Risky Driving: The Roles of Positive Affect and Risk Perception." *Accident Analysis & Prevention* 43 (3): 923–931.

Rhymes, Edward. 2014. "Woman as Aggressor: The Unspoken Truth Of Domestic Violence." *MintPress News*, September 19, 2014. https://www.mintpressnews.com/ woman-aggressor-unspoken-truth-domestic-violence/196746/.

Riabov, Oleg, and Tatiana Riabov. 2014. "The Remasculinization of Russia?: Gender, Nationalism, and the Legitimation of Power Under Vladimir Putin." *Problems of Post-Communism* 61 (2): 23–35.

Ribeiro, Manoel Horta, Raphael Ottoni, Robert West, Virgílio A. F. Almeida, and Wagner Meira. 2019. "Auditing Radicalization Pathways on YouTube." *ArXiv:1908.08313.* http://arxiv.org/abs/1908.08313.

Ricciardelli, Rosemary, Kimberley A. Clow, and Philip White. 2010. "Investigating Hegemonic Masculinity: Portrayals of Masculinity in Men's Lifestyle Magazines." *Sex Roles* 63 (1–2): 64–78.

Rice-Oxley, Mark. 2017. "The 'masculine Mystique': Why Men Can't Ditch the Baggage of Being a Bloke." *The Guardian*, November 21, 2017. https://www.theguardian.com/money/2017/nov/21/the-masculine-mystique-why-men-cant-ditch-the-baggage-of-being-a-bloke.

Richardson, John. 2007. *Analysing Newspapers: An Approach from Critical Discourse Analysis*. London: Red Globe Press.

Rickford, John. 1993. "Comments on Ethics, Advocacy and Empowerment." *Language & Communication* 13 (2): 129–31.

Rickford, Russell. 2016. "Black Lives Matter: Toward a Modern Practice of Mass Struggle." *New Labor Forum* 25 (1): 34–42.

Riley, Tonya. 2018. "Why the Government Should Fund Research on Incel Culture." *Mother Jones*, November 2018. https://www.motherjones.com/politics/2018/11/why-the-government-should-fund-research-on-incel-culture/.

Robertson, Adi. 2019. "Reddit Has Broadened Its Anti-Harassment Rules and Banned a Major Incel Forum." *The Verge*, September 30, 2019. https://www.theverge.com/2019/9/30/20891920/reddit-harassment-bullying-threats-new-policy-change-rules-subreddits.

Robertson, Adi. 2019. "Should We Treat Incels as Terrorists?" *The Verge*, October 5, 2019. https://www.theverge.com/2019/10/5/20899388/incel-movement-blueprint-toronto-attack-confession-gender-terrorism.

Robertson, Emma. 2010. *Chocolate, Women and Empire: A Social and Cultural History*. Manchester: Manchester University Press.

Robinson, Sally. 2000. *Marked Men: White Masculinity in Crisis*. New York, NY: Columbia University Press.

Robinson, Stefan, Adam White, and Eric Anderson. 2017. "Privileging the Bromance: A Critical Appraisal of Romantic and Bromantic Relationships." *Men and Masculinities* 22 (5): 850–871.

Rodrick, Stephen. 2014. "Andre Braugher, the Undercover Comedian of 'Brooklyn Nine-Nine.'" *The New York Times*, October 3, 2014. https://www.nytimes.com/2014/10/05/magazine/andre-braugher-the-undercover-comedian-of-brooklyn-nine-nine.html.

Romaine, Suzanne. 2001. "A Corpus-Based View of Gender in British and American English." In *Gender across Languages: The Linguistic Representation of Women and Men*, edited by Marlis Hellinger and Hadumod Bußmann, 153–176. *Studies in Language and Society*. Amsterdam: John Benjamins Publishing.

Romano, Aja. 2016. "Milo Yiannopoulos's Twitter Ban, Explained." *Vox*, July 20, 2016. https://www.vox.com/2016/7/20/12226070/milo-yiannopoulus-twitter-ban-explained.

Romano, Aja. 2018. "How the Alt-Right's Sexism Lures Men into White Supremacy." *Vox*, April 25, 2018. https://www.vox.com/culture/2016/12/14/13576192/alt-right-sexism-recruitment.

Roose, Joshua M., Michael Flood, and Mark Alfano. 2020. "Challenging the Use of Masculinity as a Recruitment Mechanism in Extremist Narratives: A Report to the Victorian Department of Justice and Community Safety." Melbourne: Deakin University.

Roose, Josha M., Michael Flood, Alan Greig, Mark Alfano, and Simon Copland. 2022. *Masculinity and Violent Extremism*. Basingstoke: Palgrave Macmillan.

Rossetti, Polly, Tamar Dinisman, and Ania Moroz. 2016. "An Easy Target?: Risk Factors Affecting Victimisation Rates for Violent Crime and Theft." *Victim Support*. https://www.victimsupport.org.uk/sites/default/files/VS%20Insight%20Report%20-%20An%20easy%20target.pdf.

Rossum, Guido van. 2020. *Python Reference Manual* (version 3.8.6). OS X. Virginia: Python Software Foundation. https://dl.acm.org/doi/book/10.5555/869369.

Roth-Gordon, Jennifer. 2012. "Linguistic Techniques of the Self: The Intertextual Language of Racial Empowerment in Politically Conscious Brazilian Hip Hop." *Language & Communication* 32 (1): 36–47.

Roth-Gordon, Jennifer. 2017. *Race and the Brazilian Body: Blackness, Whiteness, and Everyday Language in Rio de Janeiro*. Oakland, CA: University of California Press.

Rüdiger, Sofia, and Daria Dayter. 2017. "The Ethics of Researching Unlikeable Subjects." *Applied Linguistics Review* 8 (2–3): 251–269.

Rüdiger, Sofia, and Daria Dayter. 2020. "Talking about Women: Elicitation, Manual Tagging, and Semantic Tagging in a Study of Pick-up Artists' Referential Strategies." In *Corpus Approaches to Social Media*, 63–88. Amsterdam: John Benjamins Publishing.

Rüehlemann, Christoph, and Matt Gee. 2017. "Conversation Analysis and the XML Method." *Online-Zeitschrift Zur Verbalen Interaktion* 18: 274–296.

Ruiz, Rebecca. 2018. "You Haven't Heard of This Masculinity Movement, but It's Exactly What Men Need Right Now." *Mashable*, June 16, 2018. https://mashable.com/2018/06/16/how-to-be-a-better-man-healthy-masculinity/.

Russell, Eric. 2021. *Alpha Masculinity: Hegemony in Language and Discourse*. Basingstoke: Palgrave Macmillan.

Russell, Graeme. 1978. "The Father Role and Its Relation to Masculinity, Femininity, and Androgyny." *Child Development* 49 (4): 1174–1181.

Russell, Nicole. 2017. "The 'Toxic Masculinity' Trend Blames Boys for Being Born Male." *The Federalist*, April 12, 2017. https://thefederalist.com/2017/04/12/toxic-masculinity-trend-blames-boys-born-male/.

Rymes, Betsy. 2020. *How We Talk about Language: Exploring Citizen Sociolinguistics*. Cambridge: Cambridge University Press.

Saad, Gad. 2018. "Is Toxic Masculinity a Valid Concept?" *Psychology Today*, March 8, 2018. https://www.psychologytoday.com/blog/homo-consumericus/201803/is-toxic-masculinity-valid-concept.

Säily, Tanja, and Jukka Suomela. 2017. "Types2: Exploring Word-Frequency Differences in Corpora." *Studies in Variation, Contacts and Change in English* 19.

Salzmann-Erikson, Martin, and Henrik Eriksson. 2013. "Fathers Sharing about Early Parental Support in Health-care-virtual Discussions on an Internet Forum." *Health & Social Care in the Community* 21 (4): 381–390.

Sattel, Jack. 1983. "Men, Inexpressiveness and Power." In *Language, Gender, and Society*, edited by Barry Thorne, Cheris Kramarae, and Nancy Henley, 119–124. Rowley, MA: Newbury House Publishers.

Scalzi, John. 2012. "Straight White Male: The Lowest Difficulty Setting There Is." *Whatever*, 2012. https://whatever.scalzi.com/2012/05/15/straight-White-male-the-lowest-difficulty-setting-there-is/.

Scharrer, Erica. 2001. "From Wise to Foolish: The Portrayal of the Sitcom Father, 1950s-1990s." *Journal of Broadcasting & Electronic Media* 45 (1): 23–40.

Scharrer, Erica. 2012. "More Than 'Just the Facts'?: Portrayals of Masculinity in Police and Detective Programs Over Time." *Howard Journal of Communications* 23 (1): 88–109.

Scharrer, Erica, and Greg Blackburn. 2018. "Cultivating Conceptions of Masculinity: Television and Perceptions of Masculine Gender Role Norms." *Mass Communication and Society* 21 (2): 149–177.

Scheibling, Casey. 2019a. "Digital Dads: The Culture of Fatherhood 2.0." Unpublished PhD thesis. Hamilton, Ontario: McMaster University.

Scheibling, Casey. 2019b. "The Culture of Fatherhood 2.0: Exploring the 'Tiny Public' of Dad Bloggers in North America." *Feminist Media Studies*, 1–18.

Scheibling, Casey. 2020. "'Real Heroes Care': How Dad Bloggers Are Reconstructing Fatherhood and Masculinities." *Men and Masculinities* 23 (1): 3–19.

Schmitz, Rachel M., and Emily Kazyak. 2016. "Masculinities in Cyberspace: An Analysis of Portrayals of Manhood in Men's Rights Activist Websites." *Social Sciences* 5 (2): 18.

Schneider, Klaus P. 2012. *Diminutives in English*. Walter de Gruyter.

Schrock, Douglas, and Michael Schwalbe. 2009. "Men, Masculinity, and Manhood Acts." *Annual Review of Sociology* 35 (1): 277–295.

Schroeder, Stan. 2020. "Reddit's Former CEO Slams Reddit for 'Amplifying Hate, Racism and Violence.'" *Mashable*, June 2, 2020. https://mashable.com/article/ellen-pao-reddit-amplifying-hate/.

Scott, Marni. 2019. "Brooklyn Nine-Nine: Breaking Down Stereotypes." *The Digital Impact on Feminism*, January 9, 2019. http://www.blogs2018.buprojects.uk/marniscott/brooklyn-99-stereotypes/.

Scott, Mike. 1997. "PC Analysis of Key Words: And Key Key Words." *System* 25 (2): 233–245.

Scott, Mike. 2020. *WordSmith Tools* (version 8.0). Stroud: Lexical Analysis Software. https://lexically.net/wordsmith/index.html.

Schwalbe, Michael. 2005. "Identity Stakes, Manhood Acts, and the Dynamics of Accountability." In *Studies in Symbolic Interaction*, edited by N. Denzin, 65–81. New York: Elsevier.

Sculos, Bryant W. 2017a. "Who's Afraid of 'Toxic Masculinity'?" *Class, Race and Corporate Power* 5 (3).

Sculos, Bryant W. 2017b. "We Are the Beast: On Toxic Masculinity and Social Responsibility in Disney's Beauty and the Beast." *Class, Race and Corporate Power* 5 (2).

Seager, Martin, and John A. Barry. 2019. "Positive Masculinity: Including Masculinity as a Valued Aspect of Humanity." In *The Palgrave Handbook of Male Psychology and Mental Health*, edited by John A. Barry, Roger Kingerlee, Martin Sager, and Luke Sullivan, 105–122. Cham: Springer International Publishing.

Sedgwick, Eve Kosofsky. 1985. *Between Men: English Literature and Male Homosocial Desire*. New York, NY: Columbia University Press.

Seidler, Victor J. 1989. *Rediscovering Masculinity: Reason, Language, and Sexuality*. London: Routledge.

Shapiro, Ben. 2017. "The 'Toxic Masculinity' Smear." *National Review*, June 7, 2017. https://www.nationalreview.com/2017/06/masculinity-not-toxic-stop-blaming-men-everything/.

Shary, Timothy. 2012. *Millennial Masculinity: Men in Contemporary American Cinema*. Wayne State University Press.

Shontell, Alyson. 2013. "What It's Like When Reddit Wrongly Accuses Your Loved One Of Murder." *Business Insider*, July 26, 2013. https://www.businessinsider.com/reddit-falsely-accuses-sunil-tripathi-of-boston-bombing-2013-7.

Siapera, Eugenia. 2019. "Online Misogyny as Witch Hunt: Primitive Accumulation in the Age of Techno-Capitalism." In *Gender Hate Online: Understanding the New Anti-Feminism*, edited by Debbie Ging and Eugenia Siapera, 21–43. Basingstoke: Palgrave Macmillan.

Sidnell, Jack. 2011. "'D'you Understand That Honey?': Gender and Participation in Conversation." In *Conversation and Gender*, edited by Susan A. Speer and Elizabeth Stokoe, 183–209. Cambridge: Cambridge University Press.

Sigle-Rushton, Wendy. 2005. "Young Fatherhood and Subsequent Disadvantage in the United Kingdom." *Journal of Marriage and Family* 67 (3): 735–753.

Simpson, Z. B. 2015. "Brooklyn Nine-Nine: A Character Development Masterclass, Part 2—Raymond Holt." *Z.B Simpson*, December 15, 2015. https://zbsimpsonwriter.wordpress.com/2015/12/15/brooklyn-nine-nine-a-character-development-masterclass-part-2-raymond-holt/.

Sinclair, John. 1998. "The Lexical Item." In *Contrastive Lexical Semantics*, edited by Edda Weigand, 1–24. Amsterdam: John Benjamins Publishing.

Sinclair, Neil. 2012. *Commando Dad: How to Be an Elite Dad or Carer. From Birth to Three Years*. Chichester: Summersdale.

Singal, Jesse. 2016. "How America Became Infatuated with a Cartoonish Idea of 'Alpha Males.'" *New York Magazine*, May 18, 2016. https://nymag.com/article/2016/05/the-rise-of-the-alpha-beta-male.html.

Sisley, Marta Parszeniew, Dominique. 2019. "The Story of the Incel Is the Story of the 2010s." *Vice*, December 13, 2019. https://www.vice.com/en_uk/article/m7qqen/what-is-an-incel-how-incel-culture-grew-2010s.

Skott, Sara, and Susan McVie. 2019. "Reduction in Homicide and Violence in Scotland Is Largely Explained by Fewer Gangs and Less Knife Crime." *Applied Quantitative Methods Network Research Briefing* 13: 5.

Sledge, Charles. n.d. "Who Else Wants to Become The Man They've Always Dreamed Of Becoming?" Charles Sledge. Accessed December 16, 2019. http://charlessledge.com/membership-benefits/.

Slootmaeckers, Koen. 2019. "Nationalism as Competing Masculinities: Homophobia as a Technology of Othering for Hetero- and Homonationalism." *Theory and Society* 48 (2): 239–265.

Smith-Lovin, Lynn, and Charles Brody. 1989. "Interruptions in Group Discussions: The Effects of Gender and Group Composition." *American Sociological Review* 54 (3): 424–435.

Smith, C. Brian. 2018. "This Man Leads the Most 'Hateful' Men's Rights Group in the Country." *MEL Magazine*, March 9, 2018. https://melmagazine.com/en-us/story/this-man-leads-the-most-hateful-mens-rights-group-in-the-country.

Smith, Evan. 2021. "The Conservatives Have Been Waging Their 'War on Woke' for Decades." *The Guardian*, 21 April 2021. http://www.theguardian.com/commentisfree/2021/apr/21/conservatives-war-on-woke-loony-left-political-correctness.

Smith, Helen, Alpaslan Bulbul, and Christina J. Jones. 2017. "Can Online Discussion Sites Generate Quality Data for Research Purposes?" *Frontiers in Public Health* 5: 1–4.

Smith, Jeremy Adam, Heather M. Bryant, Heather Gibbs Flett, Shawn Taylor, and Jason Sperber. 2018. "Seven TV Shows That Highlight the Best in Fatherhood." *Greater Good*, June 13, 2018. https://greatergood.berkeley.edu/article/item/seven_tv_shows_that_highlight_the_best_in_fatherhood.

Snyder, Emily. 2017. "Defining 'Toxic Masculinity,' or, Terms of Enragement." *Defining "Toxic Masculinity," or, Terms of Enragement*, December 19, 2017. http://emilycasnyder.blogspot.com/2017/12/whats-so-toxic-about-masculinity-anyway.html.

Solnit, Rebecca. 2017. "Silence and Powerlessness Go Hand in Hand: Women's Voices Must Be Heard." *The Guardian*, March 8, 2017. https://www.theguardian.com/commentisfree/2017/mar/08/silence-powerlessness-womens-voices-rebecca-solnit.

Sonnad, Nikhil, and Tim Squirrell. 2017. "The Alt-Right Is Creating Its Own Dialect. Here's the Dictionary." *Quartz*, October 30, 2017. https://qz.com/1092037/the-alt-right-is-creating-its-own-dialect-heres-a-complete-guide/.

Southern Poverty Law Center. 2012. "Misogyny: The Sites." Southern Poverty Law Center, March 1, 2012. https://www.splcenter.org/fighting-hate/intelligence-report/2012/misogyny-sites.

Southern Poverty Law Center. 2017. "Alt-Right." Southern Poverty Law Center. https://www.splcenter.org/fighting-hate/extremist-files/ideology/alt-right.

Southern Poverty Law Center. 2018. "Daryush 'Roosh' Valizadeh." Southern Poverty Law Center. 2019. https://www.splcenter.org/fighting-hate/extremist-files/individual/daryush-roosh-valizadeh.

Southern Poverty Law Center. 2021. "Male Supremacy." Southern Poverty Law Center. https://www.splcenter.org/fighting-hate/extremist-files/ideology/male-supremacy.

Spaaij, Ramón. 2008. "Men Like Us, Boys Like Them: Violence, Masculinity, and Collective Identity in Football Hooliganism." *Journal of Sport and Social Issues* 32 (4): 369–392.

Speer, Susan A. 2005. "The Interactional Organization of the Gender Attribution Process." *Sociology* 39 (1): 67–87.

Spender, Dale. 1980. *Man Made Language*. London: Rivers Oram Press.

Spilioti, Tereza, and Caroline Tagg. 2017. "The Ethics of Online Research Methods in Applied Linguistics: Challenges, Opportunities, and Directions in Ethical Decision-Making." *Applied Linguistics Review* 8 (2–3): 163–167.

Spock, Benjamin. 2013. *The Common Sense Book of Baby and Child Care*. Edited by Dorothea Fox and Sam Sloan. Bronx, NY: Ishi Press.

Spratt, Vicky. 2021. "Is It Acceptable to Use the Phrase 'Men Are Trash'?" *Refinery29*, April 24, 2021. https://www.refinery29.com/en-gb/2021/04/10255113/men-are-trash-meaning.

Spring, Marianna. 2021. "I Get Abuse and Threats Online: Why Can't It Be Stopped?" *BBC News*, October 18, 2021. https://www.bbc.co.uk/news/uk-58924168.

Squirrell, Tim. 2017. "Linguistic Data Analysis of 3 Billion Reddit Comments Shows the Alt-Right Is Getting Stronger." *Quartz*, August 18, 2017. https://qz.com/1056 319/what-is-the-alt-right-a-linguistic-data-analysis-of-3-billion-reddit-comments-shows-a-disparate-group-that-is-quickly-uniting/.

Squirrell, Tim. 2017. "Slurred Lines: How 'Cuck' Took over Reddit." *Tim Squirrell, PhD*, July 6, 2017. https://www.timsquirrell.com/blog/2017/7/6/slurred-lines-cuckography-or-how-to-analyse-the-genealogy-and-spread-of-a-word-across-reddit.

Squirrell, Tim. 2018. "A Definitive Guide to Incels Part Two: The A-Z Incel Dictionary." *Tim Squirrell, PhD*, 2018. https://www.timsquirrell.com/blog/2018/5/30/a-definitive-guide-to-incels-part-two-the-blackpill-and-vocabulary.

Stamarski, Cailin Susan, and Leanne S. Son Hing. 2015. "Gender Inequalities in the Workplace: The Effects of Organizational Structures, Processes, Practices, and Decision Makers' Sexism." *Frontiers in Psychology* 6: 1–20.

Stamou, Anastasia G., Katerina S. Maroniti, and Konstantinos D. Dinas. 2012. "Representing 'Traditional' and 'Progressive' Women in Greek Television: The Role of 'Feminine'/'Masculine' Speech Styles in the Mediation of Gender Identity Construction." *Women's Studies International Forum* 35 (1): 38–52.

Staples, Louis. 2020. "Men Are Complaining That Snack Branding Isn't Sexist Anymore and Masculinity Is Very Fragile." *Indy100*, June 14, 2020. https://www.indy100.com/article/snack-branding-sexist-lad-culture-mccoys-yorkie-pot-noodle-9565251.

Starbird, Kate. 2022. Twitter post, 6 October 2022, 5:50pm, https://twitter.com/katestarbird/status/1578065130654351364.

Starling, Boris. 2016. *Babies: Haynes Explains*. Sparkford: J H Haynes & Co Ltd.

Stemple, Lara, Andrew Flores, and Ilan H Meyer. 2017. "Sexual Victimization Perpetrated by Women: Federal Data Reveal Surprising Prevalence." *Aggression and Violent Behavior* 34: 302–311.

Steward, Melissa. 2015. "How Mass Media Portray Dads & What You Can Do About It." *Fatherhood*, July 5, 2015. https://www.fatherhood.org/fatherhood/americas-fatherhood-problem-mass-media-and-how-we-can-fix-it.

Stewart, Emily. 2019. "Reddit Restricts Its Biggest Pro-Trump Board over Violent Threats." *Vox*, June 26, 2019. https://www.vox.com/recode/2019/6/26/18760288/reddit-the-donald-trump-message-board-quarantine-ban.

Stibbe, Arran. 2004. "Health and the Social Construction of Masculinity in Men's Health Magazine." *Men and Masculinities* 7 (1): 31–51.

Stokoe, Elizabeth. 2008. "Dispreferred Actions and Other Interactional Breaches as Devices for Occasioning Audience Laughter in Television 'Sitcoms.'" *Social Semiotics* 18 (3): 289–307.

Stout, Dustin. 2019. "Social Media Statistics: Top Social Networks by Popularity." *Dustin Stout* (blog), July 8, 2019. https://dustinstout.com/social-media-statistics/.

Stolworthy, Jacob. 2017. "Brooklyn Nine-Nine Finally Tackled Police Racism in the Sitcom's Latest Episode." *The Independent*, May 4, 2017. http://www.independent.co.uk/arts-entertainment/tv/news/brooklyn-nine-nine-polcie-racism-racial-profiling-terry-holt-dan-goor-terry-crews-andrew-braugher-a7717566.html.

Stommel, Wyke, and Lynn de Rijk. 2021. "Ethical Approval: None Sought. How Discourse Analysts Report Ethical Issues around Publicly Available Online Data." *Research Ethics* 17 (3): 275–297.

Strauss, Neil. 2005. *The Game: Undercover in the Secret Society of Pickup Artists*. Edinburgh: Canongate Books.

Sturge, Georgina. 2018. "UK Prison Population Statistics." Library Briefing Paper Number CBP-04334. London: House of Commons. https://researchbriefings.files.parliament.uk/documents/SN04334/SN04334.pdf.

SturtzSreetharan, Cindi. 2017a. "Resignifying the Japanese Father: Mediatization, Commodification, and Dialect." *Language & Communication* 53: 45–58.

SturtzSreetharan, Cindi. 2017b. "Language and Masculinity: The Role of Osaka Dialect in Contemporary Ideals of Fatherhood." *Gender and Language* 11 (4): 552–574.

Sugiura, Lisa. 2021. *The Incel Rebellion: The Rise of the Manosphere and the Virtual War Against Women*. Bingley: Emerald Publishing Limited.

Sunderland, Jane. 2000. "Baby Entertainer, Bumbling Assistant and Line Manager: Discourses of Fatherhood in Parentcraft Texts." *Discourse & Society* 11 (2): 249–274.

Sunderland, Jane. 2004. *Gendered Discourses*. Basingstoke: Palgrave Macmillan.

Sunderland, Jane, and Mark McGlashan. 2012. "The Linguistic, Visual and Multimodal Representation of Two-Mum and Two-Dad Families in Children's Picturebooks." *Language and Literature* 21 (2): 189–210.

Sunderland, Jane, and Mark McGlashan. 2015. "Heteronormativity in EFL Textbooks and in Two Genres of Children's Literature (*Harry Potter* and Same-Sex Parent Family Picturebooks)." *The ESOL Journal* 26 (2): 17–26.

Sunderland, Jane. 2022. "Fighting for Masculine Hegemony: Contestation Between Alt-Right and White Nationalist Masculinities on Stormfront.org." *Men and Masculinities* 0(0), 1097184X221120664.

Tait, Amelia. 2017. "Spitting out the Red Pill: Former Misogynists Reveal How They Were Radicalised Online." *New Statesman*, February 27, 2017. https://www.newstatesman.com/science-tech/internet/2017/02/reddit-the-red-pill-interview-how-misogyny-spreads-online.

Tajfel, Henri, John C. Turner, William G. Austin, and Stephen Worchel. 1979. "An integrative theory of intergroup conflict." *Organizational Identity* 56 (65).

Talbot, Kirsten, and Michael Quayle. 2010. "The Perils of Being a Nice Guy: Contextual Variation in Five Young Women's Constructions of Acceptable Hegemonic and Alternative Masculinities." *Men and Masculinities* 13 (2): 255–278.

Talbot, Mary. 2019. *Language and Gender*. 3rd edition. Cambridge: Polity Press.

Taylor, Alex. 2021. "The Matrix's Real-World Legacy: From Red Pill Incels to Conspiracies and Deepfakes." *BBC News*, December 21, 2021. https://www.bbc.com/news/entertainment-arts-57572152.

Taylor, Charles. 2019. "Why Gillette's New Ad Campaign Is Toxic." *Forbes*, January 15, 2019. https://www.forbes.com/sites/charlesrtaylor/2019/01/15/why-gillettes-new-ad-campaign-is-toxic/.

Taylor, Magdalene. 2019. "Welcome to Simp Nation, TikTok's New Softboi Club." *MEL Magazine*, October 16, 2019. https://melmagazine.com/en-us/story/why-is-the-simp-sucka-who-idolizes-mediocre-pussy-so-hated.

Taylor, Paul, June Keeling, and Richard Mottershead. 2019. "Intimate Partner Violence and Abuse Against Men: Voices of Victimization Among Ex-Servicemen of the British Armed Forces." *Illness, Crisis & Loss* 27 (2): 119–142.

Texas Department of Public Safety. 2020. "Texas Domestic Terrorism Threat Assessment." Austin, TX: Texas Fusion Center Intelligence & Counter Terrorism Division. http://www.dps.texas.gov/director_staff/media_and_communications/2020/txTerrorThreatAssessment.pdf.

Thébaud, Sarah. 2010. "Masculinity, Bargaining, and Breadwinning: Understanding Men's Housework in the Cultural Context of Paid Work." *Gender & Society* 24 (3): 330–354.

ThePlagueDoctor0. 2015. "The Protocols of the Elders of MGTOW: The Original MGTOW Manifesto Revealed!" Reddit. 2015. https://www.reddit.com/r/MGTOW/comments/3ust22/the_protocols_of_the_elders_of_mgtow_the_original/.

Todd, Richard Watson. 2016. *Discourse Topics*. Amsterdam: John Benjamins Publishing.

Tolentino, Jia. 2018. "The Rage of the Incels." *The New Yorker,* May 15, 2018. https://www.newyorker.com/culture/cultural-comment/the-rage-of-the-incels.

Tomassi, Rollo. 2019. "Remove the Man 2019." *The Rational Male*, January 9, 2019. https://therationalmale.com/2019/01/08/remove-the-man-2019/.

Tranchese, Alessia. 2019. "Using Corpus Analysis to Investigate 'Extreme' Incel Misogyny Online." Presented at the 12th BAAL Language, Gender, and Sexuality Special Interest Group event, Birmingham, May 30, 2019.

Trott, Verity Anne. 2020. "'Gillette: The Best a Beta Can Get': Networking Hegemonic Masculinity in the Digital Sphere." *New Media & Society*, 1–18.

Trudgill, Peter. 1972. "Sex, Covert Prestige and Linguistic Change in the Urban British English of Norwich." *Language in Society* 1 (2): 179–195.

Tufail, Waqas. 2015. "Rotherham, Rochdale, and the Racialised Threat of the 'Muslim Grooming Gang.'" *International Journal for Crime, Justice and Social Democracy* 4 (3): 30–43.

Tufail, Waqas. 2018. "Media, State and 'Political Correctness': The Racialisation of the Rotherham Child Sexual Abuse Scandal." In *Media, Crime and Racism*, edited by Monish Bhaia, Scott Poynting, and Waqas Tufail, 49–72. Basingstoke: Palgrave Macmillan.

TV Tropes. n.d. "Violent Glaswegian." *TV Tropes*. Accessed December 14, 2020. https://tvtropes.org/pmwiki/pmwiki.php/Main/ViolentGlaswegian.

UK Copyright Service. 2020. "P-27: Using the Work of Others: The UK Copyright Service." *Copyright Service*. https://copyrightservice.co.uk/copyright/p27_work_of_others.

UK Research and Innovation. 2020. "GDPR and Research: An Overview for Researchers." *UKRI*, October 25, 2020. https://www.ukri.org/wp-content/uploads/2020/10/UKRI-020920-GDPR-FAQs.pdf.

University of Chicago Press Editorial Staff. 2020. "Black and White: A Matter of Capitalization." *CMOS Shop Talk* (blog). June 22, 2020. https://cmosshoptalk.com/2020/06/22/black-and-white-a-matter-of-capitalization/.

Vagianos, Alanna. 2018. "Terry Crews: Black Men Aren't Allowed to Be Victims Until They're Dead." *HuffPost*, September 5, 2018. https://www.huffpost.com/entry/terry-crews-black-men-arent-allowed-to-be-victims-until-theyre-dead_n_5af1e510e4b041fd2d2bbea2.

Valizadeh, Daryush. 2015. "Women Must Have Their Behavior and Decisions Controlled by Men." *Return of Kings*, November 4, 2015. https://www.returnofkings.com/73131/women-must-have-their-behavior-and-decisions-controlled-by-men.

Van Valkenburgh, Shawn P. 2018. "Digesting the Red Pill: Masculinity and Neoliberalism in the Manosphere." *Men and Masculinities*, 1097184X1881611.

Van Valkenburgh, Shawn P. 2019. "'She Thinks of Him as a Machine': On the Entanglements of Neoliberal Ideology and Misogynist Cybercrime." *Social Media + Society* 5 (3): 205630511987295.

VanArendonk, Kathryn. 2018. "An Ode to Brooklyn Nine-Nine." *Vulture*, May 10, 2018. https://www.vulture.com/2018/05/brooklyn-nine-nine-ode.html.

Vandello, Joseph A., and Jennifer K. Bosson. 2013. "Hard Won and Easily Lost: A Review and Synthesis of Theory and Research on Precarious Manhood." *Psychology of Men & Masculinity* 14 (2): 101–113.

van Dijk, Teun A. 1993. "Principles of Critical Discourse Analysis." *Discourse & Society* 4 (2): 249–283.

van Dijk, Teun A. 2016. "Critical Discourse Studies: A Sociocognitive Approach." In *Methods of Critical Discourse Studies*, edited by Ruth Wodak and Michael Meyer, 62–85. London: SAGE Publications.

Veissière, Samuel Paul Louis. 2018. "'Toxic Masculinity' in the Age of #MeToo: Ritual, Morality and Gender Archetypes across Cultures." *Society and Business Review* 13 (3): 274–286.

Veiszadeh, Mariam. 2018. "Equality for Women Does Not Mean Oppression For Men." *10 Daily*, September 7, 2018. https://10daily.com.au/views/a180907qlh/equality-for-women-does-not-mean-oppression-for-men-20180907.

Veletsianos, George, Shandell Houlden, Jaigris Hodson, and Chandell Gosse. 2018. "Women Scholars' Experiences with Online Harassment and Abuse: Self-Protection, Resistance, Acceptance, and Self-Blame." *New Media & Society* 20 (12): 4689–4708.

Vigdor, Neil, and Niraj Chokshi. 2019. "Reddit Restricts Pro-Trump Forum Because of Threats." *The New York Times*, June 26, 2019. https://www.nytimes.com/2019/06/26/us/politics/reddit-donald-trump-quarantined.html.

Vinopal, Lauren. 2018. "There's No Such Thing as Toxic Masculinity." *Fatherly*, November 24, 2018. https://www.fatherly.com/health-science/toxic-masculinity-fake-male-insecurity/.

Vinopal, Lauren. 2019. "Masculinity Is Not All Bad, According to New Research on Positive Masculine Traits." *Fatherly*, January 18, 2019. https://www.fatherly.com/health-science/what-are-positive-masculinity-norms-study/.

Viruet, Pilot. 2017. "'Brooklyn Nine-Nine' Finally Tackled Racist Cops." *Vice*, May 4, 2017. https://www.vice.com/en_uk/article/jpyx4b/brooklyn-nine-nine-finally-tackled-racist-cops.

Visser, Richard O. de, and Jonathan A. Smith. 2007. "Alcohol Consumption and Masculine Identity among Young Men." *Psychology & Health* 22 (5): 595–614.

Vito, Christopher, Amanda Admire, and Elizabeth Hughes. 2018. "Masculinity, Aggrieved Entitlement, and Violence: Considering the Isla Vista Mass Shooting." *NORMA* 13 (2): 86–102.

Vivenzi, Laura, Gabriela de la Vega, and Lennart Driessen. 2017. "Infiltrating the Manosphere: An Exploration of Male-Oriented Virtual Communities from the Inside." *Diggit Magazine*, November 3, 2017. https://www.diggitmagazine.com/articles/infiltrating-manosphere-exploration-male-oriented-virtual-communities-inside.

Voigt, Rob, Nicholas P. Camp, Vinodkumar Prabhakaran, William L. Hamilton, Rebecca C. Hetey, Camilla M. Griffiths, David Jurgens, Dan Jurafsky, and Jennifer L. Eberhardt. 2017. "Language from Police Body Camera Footage Shows Racial Disparities in Officer Respect." *Proceedings of the National Academy of Sciences* 114 (25): 6521–6526.

VOX-Pol Network of Excellence. 2020. "Researcher Resources: VOX-Pol." *VOX-Pol*. https://www.voxpol.eu/researcher-resources/.

Waal, Frans B. M. de. 1986. "The Brutal Elimination of a Rival among Captive Male Chimpanzees." *Ethology and Sociobiology* 7 (3): 237–251.

Wade, Lauren. 2018. "Meet the Inspiring Projects Making Life Better for Men." *EachOther*, March 17, 2018. https://eachother.org.uk/gender-justice-empowerment-men/.

Wade, Lisa. 2018. "The Big Picture: Confronting Manhood after Trump." *Public Books*, January 11, 2018. https://www.publicbooks.org/pb-staff-favorites-2017-big-picture-confronting-manhood-trump/.

Walsh, Fintan. 2010. *Male Trouble: Masculinity and the Performance of Crisis*. Basingstoke: Palgrave Macmillan.

Walsh, Kate. 2011. "Migrant Masculinities and Domestic Space: British Home-Making Practices in Dubai." *Transactions of the Institute of British Geographers* 36 (4): 516–29.

Ward, Antonia. 2019. "To Ensure Deradicalisation Programmes Are Effective, Better Evaluation Practices Must First Be Implemented." *Rand Corporation*, March 4, 2019. https://www.rand.org/blog/2019/03/to-ensure-deradicalisation-programmes-are-effective.html.

Warraich, Haider Javed, and Robert Califf. 2017. "Men Still Die before Women. Is Toxic Masculinity to Blame?" *The Guardian*, June 26, 2017. http://www.theguardian.com/commentisfree/2017/jun/26/men-die-before-women-toxic-masculinity-blame.

Warzell, Charlie. 2019. "How an Online Mob Created a Playbook for a Culture War." *Medium*, August 19, 2019. https://web.archive.org/web/20190819235030/https://medium.com/new-york-times-opinion/how-an-online-mob-created-a-playbook-for-a-culture-war-d4c3310f07bc.

Waterson, Jim. 2020. "Virtue Signalling: The Culture War Phrase Now in BBC Guidelines." *The Guardian*, October 30, 2020. https://www.theguardian.com/media/2020/oct/30/virtue-signalling-the-culture-war-phrase-now-in-bbc-guidelines.

Webb, Robert. 2017. *How Not to Be a Boy*. Edinburgh: Canongate Books.

Welch, Kelly. 2007. "Black Criminal Stereotypes and Racial Profiling." *Journal of Contemporary Criminal Justice* 23 (3): 276–288.

Wells, Adam. 2017. "Floyd Mayweather: Donald Trump Is a 'Real Man' for P---y Grabbing Comments." Bleacher Report. September 14, 2017. https://bleacherreport.com/articles/2733250-floyd-mayweather-donald-trump-is-a-real-man-for-p-y-grabbing-comments.

Wells, David. 2003. *Guidelines for Medico-Legal Care for Victims of Sexual Violence*. Geneva: World Health Organization. http://whqlibdoc.who.int/publications/2004/924154628X.pdf.

West, Candace. 1984. "When the Doctor Is a 'Lady': Power, Status and Gender in Physician-Patient Encounters." *Symbolic Interaction* 7 (1): 87–106.

Wetherell, Margaret, and Nigel Edley. 1999. "Negotiating Hegemonic Masculinity: Imaginary Positions and Psycho-Discursive Practices." *Feminism & Psychology* 9 (3): 335–356. https://doi.org/10.1177/0959353599009003012.

White, Michele. 2019. *Producing Masculinity: The Internet, Gender, and Sexuality*. Oxon: Routledge.

Whitley, Rob, and JunWei Zhou. 2020. "Clueless: An Ethnographic Study of Young Men Who Participate in the Seduction Community with a Focus on Their Psychosocial Well-Being and Mental Health." *PLOS ONE* 15 (2): e0229719.

Whyte, Lara. 2018. "'Young Men Should Be Furious': Inside the World's Largest Gathering of Men's Rights Activists." *OpenDemocracy*, July 25, 2018. https://www.opendemocracy.net/en/5050/young-men-should-be-furious-inside-worlds-largest-mens-rights-activism/.

Wijngaard, Marianne van den. 1997. *Reinventing the Sexes: Feminism and Biomedical Construction of Femininity and Masculinity, 1959-1985*. Bloomington, IN: Indiana University Press.

Wilkinson, Abi. 2016. "We Need to Talk about the Online Radicalisation of Young, White Men." *The Guardian*, November 15, 2016. http://www.theguardian.com/commentisfree/2016/nov/15/alt-right-manosphere-mainstream-politics-breitbart.

Wilkinson, Sue. 1997. "Feminist Psychology." In *Critical Psychology: An Introduction*, edited by Dennis Fox and Isaac Prilleltensky, 247–264. London: SAGE Publications.

Williams, Byron Edward. 2018. "The Nature of the Alt-Right." Unpublished PhD thesis. Wellington, New Zealand: Victoria University of Wellington.

Williams, Quentin E., and Christopher Stroud. 2014. "Battling the Race: Stylizing Language and Coproducing Whiteness and Colouredness in a Freestyle Rap Performance." *Journal of Linguistic Anthropology* 24 (3): 277–293.

Willott, Sara, and Antonia C. Lyons. 2012. "Consuming Male Identities: Masculinities, Gender Relations and Alcohol Consumption in Aotearoa New Zealand." *Journal of Community & Applied Social Psychology* 22 (4): 330–345.

Wilson, John K. 1995. *The Myth of Political Correctness: The Conservative Attack on Higher Education*. Durham, NC: Duke University Press.

Wilton, Robert, Geoffrey DeVerteuil, and Joshua Evans. 2014. "'No More of This Macho Bullshit': Drug Treatment, Place and the Reworking of Masculinity." *Transactions of the Institute of British Geographers* 39 (2): 291–303.

Winder, Robert. 1994. "Book Review / Hapless Underdogs in a Bitchy World: 'The Myth of Male.'" *The Independent*, March 11, 1994. http://www.independent.co.uk/voices/book-review-hapless-underdogs-in-a-bitchy-world-the-myth-of-male-power-warren-farrell-4th-estate-699-1428367.html.

Wingfield, Adia M. Harvey. 2019. "Special Session on Social Justice and Social Media." Presented at the Annual Meeting of the American Sociological Association, New York. https://www.asanet.org/annual-meeting-2019/special-sessions.

Winton, Tim. 2018. "About the Boys: Tim Winton on How Toxic Masculinity Is Shackling Men to Misogyny." *The Guardian*, April 9, 2018. https://www.theguardian.com/books/2018/apr/09/about-the-boys-tim-winton-on-how-toxic-masculinity-is-shackling-men-to-misogyny.

Wodak, Ruth. 2004. "Critical Discourse Analysis." In *Qualitative Research Practice*, 185–202. London: SAGE Publications.

Wodak, Ruth. 2015. *The Politics of Fear: What Right-Wing Populist Discourses Mean.* London: SAGE Publications.

Wolfram, Walt. 2016. "Public Sociolinguistic Education in the United States: A Proactive, Comprehensive Program." In *Sociolinguistic Research: Application and Impact,* edited by Robert Lawson and Dave Sayers, 87–108. Oxon: Routledge.

Wong, Alex. 2019. "What Are the Biggest Problems Women Face Today?" POLITICO Magazine. https://www.politico.com/magazine/story/2019/03/08/women-biggest-problems-international-womens-day-225698.

Woods, Mark. 2018. *Pregnancy for Men: The Whole Nine Months.* Richmond: White Ladder.

Wordsworth, Dot. 2019. "Illeism." *The Spectator,* January 12, 2019. https://www.spectator.co.uk/article/illeism.

World Health Organization. 2015. *WHO Recommendations on Health Promotion Interventions for Maternal and Newborn Health.*

Worth, Nancy. 2020. "Public Geographies and the Gendered Experience of Saying 'Yes' to the Media." *The Professional Geographer* 72 (4): 547–555.

Wright, Charlotte. 2018. "What Is Toxic Masculinity, Anyway?" *The Cultch,* October 5, 2018. https://thecultch.com/what-is-toxic-masculinity-anyway/.

Wright, Scott, Verity Trott, and Callum Jones. 2020. "'The Pussy Ain't Worth It, Bro': Assessing the Discourse and Structure of MGTOW." *Information, Communication & Society* 23 (6): 908–925.

Wu, Brianna. 2019. "I Wish I Could Tell You It's Gotten Better. It Hasn't." *The New York Times,* August 15, 2019. https://www.nytimes.com/interactive/2019/08/15/opinion/brianna-wu-gamergate.html, https://www.nytimes.com/interactive/2019/08/15/opinion/brianna-wu-gamergate.html.

Wyles, Liza. 2018. "Why Are We Still Pretending Dads Have No Clue?" *Romper,* June 15, 2018. https://www.romper.com/p/fathers-deserve-better-than-the-bumbling-dad-stereotype-onscreen-9351057.

Wyllie, Clare, Stephen Platt, Julie Brownlie, Amy Chandler, Sheelah Connolly, Rhiannon Evans, Brendan Kennelly, et al. 2012. "Men, Suicide and Society: Why Disadvantaged Men in Mid-Life Die by Suicide." Surrey: Samaritans. https://xyonline.net/sites/xyonline.net/files/Whyllie%2C%20Men%2C%20Suicide%20and%20Society%20-%20Samaritans%20Report.pdf.

X-man. 2019. "A Brief Organization of The Men's Movement." *Medium,* July 6, 2019. https://medium.com/@moint/a-brief-organization-of-the-mens-movement-891916b2e13.

Xiao, Richard, and Hongyin Tao. 2007. "A Corpus-Based Sociolinguistic Study of Amplifiers in British English." *Sociolinguistic Studies* 1 (2): 241–273.

Xu, Guandong, Yu Zong, and Zhenglu Yang. 2013. *Applied Data Mining.* Boca Raton, FL: CRC Press.

Yader, A.V. 2014. "The Deadly Consequences of Feminist Propaganda in the US Navy." *Return of Kings,* July 14, 2014. https://www.returnofkings.com/39218/the-deadly-consequences-of-feminist-propaganda-in-the-us-navy.

Yglesias, Matthew. 2019. "The Case for Taking Trump's Black Outreach Seriously." *Vox,* November 13, 2019. https://www.vox.com/policy-and-politics/2019/11/13/20960203/black-voices-for-trump-african-american-polling.

Yiannopoulos, Milo. 2014. "Feminist Bullies Tearing the Video Game Industry Apart." *Breitbart,* September 1, 2014. https://www.breitbart.com/europe/2014/09/01/lying-greedy-promiscuous-feminist-bullies-are-tearing-the-video-game-industry-apart/.

Yiannopoulos, Milo. 2016. "Teenage Boys with Tits: Here's My Problem With Ghostbusters." *Breitbart,* 2016. https://www.breitbart.com/tech/2016/07/18/milo-reviews-ghostbusters/.

Yogachandra, Natascha. 2014. "Teaching Positive Masculinity." *The Atlantic,* May 14, 2014. https://www.theatlantic.com/health/archive/2014/05/becoming-men-teaching-positive-masculinity/361739/.

Young, Danielle M., Laurie A. Rudman, Helen M. Buettner, and Meghan C. McLean. 2013. "The Influence of Female Role Models on Women's Implicit Science Cognitions." *Psychology of Women Quarterly* 37 (3): 283–292.

Young, Hilary. 2007. "Hard Man, New Man: Re/Composing Masculinities in Glasgow, c.1950-2000." *Oral History* 35 (1): 71–81.

Young, Nicole. 2022. "How a Bad Zoom Date Led Me to the 'Black Manosphere.'" *ELLE*, January 25, 2022. https://www.elle.com/life-love/a38819237/black-manosphere-online-dating/.

Zafimehy, Marie. 2019. "Black Masculinity and White-Cast Sitcoms: Unraveling Stereotypes in *New Girl*." Unpublished MA dissertation. Linköping, Sweden: Linköping University.

Zanettin, Federico. 2012. *Translation-Driven Corpora: Corpus Resources for Descriptive and Applied Translation Studies*. Oxon: Routledge.

Zatychies, Maki. 2020. "What Fans Don't Know About Terry Jeffords from Brooklyn Nine-Nine." *TheThings*, May 10, 2020. https://www.thethings.com/brooklyn-nine-nine-terry-jeffords-facts/.

Zhang, Qing. 2008. "Rhotacization and the 'Beijing Smooth Operator': The Social Meaning of a Linguistic Variable." *Journal of Sociolinguistics* 12 (2): 201–222.

Ziegler, Ashley. 2019. "'Brooklyn Nine-Nine's Terry Is a Great Example of What Modern Masculinity Could Be." *Femestella*, October 14, 2019. https://www.femestella.com/brooklyn-99-terry-modern-masculinity/.

Zimman, Lal. 2014. "The Discursive Construction of Sex: Remaking and Reclaiming the Gendered Body in Talk about Genitals among Trans Men." In *Queer Excursions: Retheorizing Binaries in Language, Gender, and Sexuality*, edited by Lal Zimman, Jenny Davis, and Joshua Raclaw, 13–34. Oxford: Oxford University Press.

Zimman, Lal. 2017a. "Transgender Language Reform: Some Challenges and Strategies for Promoting Trans-Affirming, Gender-Inclusive Language." *Journal of Language and Discrimination* 1 (1): 84–105.

Zimman, Lal. 2017b. "Gender as Stylistic Bricolage: Transmasculine Voices and the Relationship between Fundamental Frequency and /s/." *Language in Society* 46 (3): 339–370.

Zimmer, Franziska, Katrin Scheibe, Mechtild Stock, and Wolfgang G. Stock. 2019. "Fake News in Social Media: Bad Algorithms or Biased Users?" *Journal of Information Science Theory and Practice* 7 (2): 40–53.

Zimmerman, Don H, and Candace West. 1975. "Sex Roles, Interruptions and Silences in Conversation." In *Language and Sex: Difference and Dominance*, edited by Barrie Thorne and Nancy Henley, 105–129. Rowley, MA: Newbury House Publishers.

Zuckerberg, Donna. 2018. *Not All Dead White Men: Classics and Misogyny in the Digital Age*. Cambridge, MA: Harvard University Press.

INDEX

For the benefit of digital users, indexed terms that span two pages (e.g., 52–53) may, on occasion, appear on only one of those pages.

4chan, 87–88, 94–95

absolutism, 24
academic performance, 3–4, 23–24
Adam Ruins Everything, 143
addiction, 3–4, 227
    see also alcohol; drugs; gambling
        problems
Admire, Amanda, 134
advertising
    family campaigns, 205
    Gillette, 12–14, 121–22
affinity spaces, 224
affirmation, 21
African American Vernacular English
    (AAVE), 34
aggressive masculinity, 3, 6, 18
Agha, Asif, 70–71
alcohol, 3–4, 66t, 68, 69t, 80–82, 122–
    23, 227
    violence, interpersonal, 231
    see also addiction,
Alexander, Susan M., 26–27
alimony, 127, 130–31, 135–36, 160
alpha male/masculinity, 142–44, 144t, 175
    see also betas,
alt-right movement, 5, 18, 37, 85–119,
    224, 233–34
    definition, 86–89
    nationalism and, 90–92
    Reddit and, 92–95
alternative right *see* alt-right movement
Alternative Right, The (webzine), 86–87
Amazon Prime, 172–73
American Sociological Association, 55–56
Ammari, Tawfiq, 206
Anderson, Malcolm, xviii
Andreasson, Jesper, 37–38
AntConc, 42–43, 63, 71, 73, 147, 179, 181

anthropology, linguistic, 9–10, 14–15, 26
antisemitism, 87, 93
anxiety, 3–4, 167–68
    see also mental health
Application Programming Interface (API),
    96
appraisal theory, 138
Ari, 176
Åsenhed, Liselotte, 206
At It, 60
attitudinal preference, 44
attractiveness, sexual, 8, 142, 148
austerity measures, 228–29
AWALT (all women are like that), 24, 160,
    161

'backlash' politics, 56
Bad Boys, 175
Baker, Helen, 43–44, 62, 71–72
Baker, Paul, 24, 41–42, 43–44, 61–62, 71–
    72, 83, 99, 104–5, 117
Banerjee, Sikita, 37, 90
Balston, Antony, 71
BAME (Black, Asian and Minority Ethnic),
    181, 233–34
Band of Brothers, A, 167–68, 169–70
Banet-Weiser, Sarah, 95, 130–31
Bannon, Steven, 89
banter, 2
    see also locker room banter
Barclay, Lesley, 201–2
Barr, Sabrina, 123
Barrett, Rusty, 21
BBC (British Broadcasting Corporation)
    iPlayer, 172–73
    Scotland, 76n.5
beauty products, 26–27
Bednarek, Monika, 50, 172, 173
Beierle, Scott P., 133–34

Bem, Sandra L., 168
Benjamin, Owen, 87n.3
Berdahl, Jennifer L., 22–23
betas, 143–44
  see also alpha males/masculinity
Beyond Equality, 167–68, 169–70
bias, male, 31–32
biological determinism, 134–35
biological sex, 20, 21, 23, 25–26
Black Eyed Peas, 190
Black Lives Matter (BLM), 114, 115, 116,
    196–97n.9
Black masculinity, 114–18, 118t, 193–94
Blake, Mariah, 230
Bliss, Shepherd, 4, 122, 168
Bly, Robert, 4–5
Bogetić, Ksenija, 43–44, 46
Boise, Sam de, 4–5, 168, 229
Boko Haram, 128
Bola, J. J., 124
Boston Marathon bombing, 93
boxing, 69t, 79t
boyd, danah, 56
Boyle, Danny, 60
Boyle, Jimmy, 60
Boyle, Karen, 11
Boyle, Maree V., 203
branded masculinity, 26–27
Brazilian men, 30
breadwinner status, 4
Breaking Bad, 174
Breitbart News, 87–88, 89
British Association of Applied Linguistics
    (BAAL), 57
British National Corpus (BNC), 73
broadsheet newspapers, 17
bromance, 176, 185–92
Brookes, G., 49
Brooklyn Nine-Nine, 18, 40, 49–50, 167–
    98, 232
  Black masculinity, construction of, 194f
  bromance and heterosexual friendship,
    185–92
  close up shot visual analysis, 189f
  concordance lines, 186t, 187t, 195t
  keywords, 181–85
  masculinities in, 174–77
  overview of corpus by season, 178t
  positive masculinity and, 167–72
  radar chart of keyword categories, 183f
  speech, amount of, 179–81
  television and masculinity, 172–74
  top keywords, 182t
  turns by speaker, number of, 180f
  vulnerability and masculinity, 193–97

  wide shot visual analysis, 189f, 191f
  word frequency by speaker, 180f
Brown, Chip, 28n.3
Brown, Gordon, 64t
Brown, Katherine E., 225, 226
Brown, Wendy, 228
Buchanan, Elizabeth, 53
Buck, Ed, 116
Buckingham, David, 173
bullying, 12, 15, 121–22
  see also cyberbullying
Bunch, Ted, 13
Burgess, Jean, 88, 200–1, 203–4
Burnistoun, 60, 82–83
Bush, Billy, 1, 2–3, 36
Buss, David M., 23–24
Butler, Judith, 8, 33

Call to Men, A, 13, 169–70
Cameron, Deborah, 2, 9, 25, 52, 138, 220
Campaign Against Living Miserably
    (CALM), 167–68, 169–70
cancer, prostate/testicular, 167–68
capitalism, 26–27, 120, 229
Caplan, Robyn, 129–30, 227–28
caregiving, 14
caring masculinities, 1, 19, 36–37, 203–4
  definition, 37–38
  see also fatherhood
Carlyle, Robert, 76
Carter, Pelham, 206–7
catcalling, 12
CDA see Critical Discourse Analysis
Center for Masculinities Studies, 234
Center for the Study of Men and
    Masculinities, 234
Chads, 151, 151t
Chafe, Wallace, 221
Chaney, Cassandra, 116, 193
'changing' masculinities, 4–6
charity organisations, 13, 14, 167–
    68, 169–70
Chateau Heartiste, 126–27
chauvinism, 37, 123
Cheng, Cliff, 29–30
Chewin' the Fat, 60, 82
Child Maintenance Service (CMS), 210t
Child Support Agency (CSA), 210t
children, 22, 157
  childbirth, narrative accounts of, 213–17
  childcare, 202–3
  custody, 120, 127, 131, 148–49
  maintenance/support, 127, 130–31,
    148–49, 209t, 209, 210t, 218
  rearing, 23–24

sex trafficking/grooming, 93, 111–12
sexual abuse, 110
see also fatherhood,
Children and Family Court Advisory and
    Support Service (CAFCASS), 210*t*
chronic illness, 3–4
cisgender, 11, 129–30
Clatterbaugh, Kenneth, 19–20, 29
CLiC Dickens Corpus, 42–43
climate change, 3
Clinton, Hillary, 2, 93, 116–18, 125
cloud-based storage systems, 50–51
Coaston, Jane, 87n.2
Coates, Jennifer, 7, 142–43, 204
Coffey-Glover, Laura, 7, 43–44
cognitive turn, 41
Cole, Mike, 93
Coleridge, Samuel Taylor, 194
Collett, Mark, 87n.3
collocation, 46–48, 77–80
    Black men, 118*t*
    connectivity, 46, 47
    criteria for identifying, 46–47
    DadInfo corpus, 212*t*
    directionality, 46, 47
    dispersion, 46, 47
    distance, 46
    exclusivity, 46
    frequency, 46
    graphical *see* GraphColl
    Guardian, The, 79*t*
    manosphere corpus, 147*t*, 157*t*
    men, 101*t*
    Muslim men, 112*t*
    Scotsman, 81*t*
    type-token distribution, 46, 47
    White men, 106*t*
common-law partnerships, 5
communal belonging, 165
communication studies, 10
Community of Practice, 224
composite accounts, 213
concordance lines, 48*t*, 79*t*
    Brooklyn Nine-Nine, 186*t*, 187*t*, 195*t*
    DadInfo corpus, 211*t*
    Incels subcorpus, 150*t*, 151*t*, 164*t*
    manosphere corpus, 141*t*, 145*t*, 152*t*,
        153*t*, 154*t*, 155*t*, 156*t*, 161*t*, 162*t*
    men subcorpus, 102*t*
    Mens Rights subcorpus, 163*t*
    MGTOW subcorpus, 149*t*
    Muslim men, 113*t*
    Red Pill subcorpus, 144*t*, 149*t*, 163*t*
    White men subcorpus, 107*t*, 108*t*, 109*t*
ConcXML, 179

confidentiality, 52–53, 92–93
Conley, Chris, 2
Connell, R. W., 14, 27, 28–30, 35–36, 153,
    173, 227, 228, 230–31
Connelly, Billy, 66*t*, 69*t*
Conover, Adam, 143
consent, 2–3, 55
conspiracy theory, 128
constructivism, 34
consumerism, 120
contemporary masculinities, 1–3
contextual integrity, 53
contrarian communities, 87n.3
conversation analysis (CA), 185, 198
    conversational dominance, 31–32
    conversational floor, control of, 31–32
    conversational maxim of quality, 191–92
Conway, Mike, 52–53
cool solidarity, 140
Cooper, Frank Rudy, 34–35, 128–29
copyright, 49–52
Coronavirus pandemic, 233
corpus linguistics (CL), 9–10, 39, 40, 41–
    44, 61–62, 198, 217
    CDA and, 42
    data and corpus construction, 62–63,
        96–97, 137–38, 177–79, 207–8
    definition, 42
    fatherhood studies, 206–7
    features of, 42–43
    frequency analysis, 69–73, 72*f*
    sociolinguistics and, 43
    see also collocation; keywords; word lists
Corpus of Historical American English,
    43–44
cost-of-living crisis, 233
COVID-19 *see* Coronavirus pandemic
crafts, 4–5
Craig, Steve, 173
Crawford, Robert, 60
Cray, Ronnie, 66*t*
Crews, Terry, 176n.5, 194
crime,
    environmental, 3
    inner-city, 3
    writers, 60
    see also murder; violence,
criminology, 10, 55–56, 61
crisis of masculinity discourse, 4–5, 28
Critical Discourse Analysis (CDA), 8, 9, 39,
    40–42, 61–62
    corpus-assisted, 42
critical media literacy, 231–32
critical technocultural discourse analysis,
    42

Critics' Choice Awards, 174–75
Cross, Gary S., 168
Crowder, Steven, 87
crowdsourced abuse, 88
Crump, Andy, 196
cucks, 8–9, 101–2, 111, 132
    definition, 152
cyberbullying, 56
    see also bullying; harassment: online,
cyber-ethnographic approach, 206
cyberhate, 233

DadInfo, 40, 54, 207–8, 213, 218
    analysis, 208–12
    collocates, 212*t*
    concordance lines, 211*t*, 212*t*
    corpus overview of, 209*t*
    top keywords, 210*t*
dads *see* fatherhood
Daily Stormer, 87–88
Daniel, Jamie, 60
data, 39–40
    corpus construction and, 62–63, 96–97,
        137–38, 177–79, 207–8
    protection and regulation of *see* General
        Data Protection Regulation (GDPR)
    scraping programs, 207
dating, 120, 127, 132, 134–35
Davies, Andrew, 60
Davies, Helen, 22
Davies, William, 223
Davison, Jake, 133–34
Day, Felicia, 88
Dayter, Daria, 55–56, 160
Debt Collector, The, 68
deficit approach, 31
definition of masculinity, 6–7, 19–20
Defoe, Daniel, 60
dehumanization, 94–95, 112–13
Demetriou, Demetrakis, 30–31
democracy, 90
Democratic Party (US), 93, 107–8, 116–18
depression, 3–4, 121–22, 127, 167–68
    see also mental health
Depression Quest, 88
deprivation, 3–4
Derksen, Christina, 52–53
Dermot, Rooney, 199n.1
Dermott, Esther, 202–3
Desclos, Anne Cécile, 126n.3
deterministic approach, 23
Dewar, Donald, 75
Dexter, 174
dictatorship, 90
Die Hard, 175

digital literacies, 224–25
digital research, ethics of, 52–54
diminutive form, 185–86
direct speech, 71–72
disability, 3–4
discourse-historical approach, 41
discourse prosody, 44
discrimination, 1, 38, 106, 196
    accent, 220
    ethnic, 88–89
    legal and educational, 130–31
    racial, 117
    see also misogyny; racism; sexism
dislocated masculinity, 28, 29
Diviney, Leah, 198
divorce, 24, 120, 127, 130–31, 132, 135–
        36, 139–40, 208–9, 223, 228
    see also marriage
'dogpiling', 132
domestic violence, 3, 35–36, 123–24, 228
    against males, 131
dominance framework, 31–32
Donald, The, 17, 40, 55, 85–119, 120,
        224, 225
    corpus breakdown, 97*t*
    men and masculinities, 95–96
#DontBottleItUp, 169–70
doxing, 14–15, 16–17, 55–56
drag queens, 21
Dragiewicz, Molly, 202–3
drinks consumption,
    gendered distribution of, 22
    see also alcohol
driving, 3–4
Dropbox, 50–51
drugs, 92–93, 116, 227
    abuse, 231
    addiction, 3–4, 229
    see also addiction
Duca, Lauren, 106
Dunham, Lena, 107–8
Dutton, Emily, 3, 130–31, 147

EastEnders, 64*t*, 66, 66*t*, 69*t*, 77, 78, 79–80
Eckert, Penelope, 8, 21, 25–27, 32, 33
Economic and Social Research Council
        (ESRC), 57
Edley, Nigel, 34, 205
education, 10, 228–29
    public programs, 231–32
    see also literacy
edutainment, 232–33
El Refaie, Elisabeth, 85–86
emasculation, 125, 227–28
Emmy Awards, 174–75

Englar-Carlson, Matt, 14, 37, 168–69, 172
English Defence League (EDL), 226
Enloe, Cynthia, 37, 90
entitlement, 'aggrieved', 91
Entourage, 174
environmental crime, 3
equality discourse, 132
    see also inequality
essentialist definition of masculinity,
    28–29
ethics, 17
    digital research, 52–54
    ethical principles, 54–55
    online, 14–15
ethnicity, 13–14, 85
    ethnic diversity, 174–75, 181
    ethnic identity, 85–119
    ethnic minorities, 8, 30, 86
ethnography, 55–56
ethno-nationalism, 55
ethnopluralism, 85–86
European City of Culture, 82
European Commission (EC), 50–51
European Union (EU) regulations
    see General Data Protection
    Regulation (GDPR)
Everard, Sarah, 11–12
extremism, 55, 83–84, 225–26, 229, 233
    see also radicalization

Facebook, 11, 86, 93, 101, 110, 133–34
'faggot', 152
Fahie, Declan, 57
failure of masculinity, 11, 28, 40–41, 133
fair use, 49–52
Fairclough, Norman, 41
fake news, 93
Families Need Fathers, 207–8
family
    nuclear, 159
    courts, 131, 209
    unity, 157
    see also children; fatherhood
Farrell, Warren, 128, 227
fascism, 100*f*
fatherhood, 14, 224–25, 232, 234
    affective, 205
    biological fathers, 211–12
    Black men, 205
    caring masculinities and, 203–4
    childcare, 202–3
    dad blogs, 206, 207
    dad books, 200
    definition, 199
    digital lives, 213

discourses of, 205
domestic responsibilities, 203–4
egalitarianism, 205
emotion, 217
false paternity claims, 148–49
Fatherhood 2.0, 201, 205–7
Incels subcorpus, concordance lines of,
    150*t*, 151*t*
in Ireland, 201–2
language of, 199–218
masculinity and, 201–3
media representations, 200, 202
narratives of personal experience,
    213–17
new dads, challenges for, 213–17
online construction of, 201
online spaces, 205–6
parentcraft and, 200–1
parenting and, 204–5
research studies, 201
rights activism, 127, 202–3
in Scandinavia, 206
single, 130–31, 148–49
workshops, 200
    see also children; *DadInfo*;
    motherhood
Fausto-Sterling, Anne, 14–15, 20, 25–26
Feasey, Rebecca, 174
female masculinities, 11
female terms
    negative, 159–64, 160*f*, 163*f*
    neutral/generic, 155–58, 156*f*
    neutral/relational, 158–59, 159*f*
    positive, 154–55
feminazis (portmanteau), 99–100, 161–62
femininity
    cultural gendered practices, 22–23
    feminine type, 23
feminism, 16–17, 25, 31, 32, 35, 85, 88–
    89, 91, 93, 99–100, 110, 120, 158,
    164, 165–66, 193–94, 220, 222, 224–
    25, 227–29
    antifeminism, 4–5, 126–27, 128, 131,
    132, 135–36, 137
    backlash against, 230–31
    'cult' of, 128
    men's rights activism and, 129–30
    'problem' of, 129
    propaganda, 128
    sex and power, 132
femoid (portmanteau), 162
Ferber, Abby L., 86, 90
Ferguson, Alex, 75
Ferguson, Harry, 199n.1, 201–2
Ferris, Paul, 60

financial crisis *see* global financial
   crisis (GFC)
Fine, Cordelia, 24, 25
Firth, John Rupert, 46
Fish, Phil, 88
fitness, physical, 120
Fletcher, Richard, 205–6
Flood, Alison, 16–17
Flood, Michael G., 202–3
Flood, Randy, 124
Floyd, George, 196–97n.9
folk linguistics, 220
food consumption
   gendered distribution of, 22
football, 64*t*, 66*t*, 68, 69*t*, 72–73, 74*t*, 75
   hooligans, 37
Ford, Clementine, 11
Forsyth, Michael, 75
Fournier, Ryan, 99
Fox News, 178–79, 227
Fox, John, 4–5
fragile masculinity, 6
Fraser, Alistair, 60, 61
fraternity men, 34
fraud, 3
free speech, 223
Friberg, Daniel, 85–86, 222
friendship, 4–5, 18, 198
   heterosexual, 14, 185–92
   homosocial, 176
Futrelle, David, 120–21
Future Men, 200

Gabrielatos, Costas, 45n.1, 73
gambling problems, 3–4
   see also addiction
Game, The, 142
Gamergate Controversy, 56, 88
games *see* video games
gang culture, 61, 66, 76
gangster literature, 60
García-Favaro, Laura, 91, 227–28
Garfinkel, Renee, 226
Garlick, Steve, 26–27
Gary: Tank Commander, 82–83
gay masculinities, 8, 11, 30
GDPR *see* General Data Protection
   Regulation (GDPR)
Geary, David C., 20
Gee, James Paul, 46, 224
gender
   concepts, 20–26
   definition, 17, 19–26
   digital literacies and, 224–25
   equality activism and, 12–13

fatigue, 235
identity and, 6–7, 16
manosphere and, 120–66
parenting and, 204–5
pay gap, 101
politics, 8–9, 10, 18, 19, 35–36
studies, 223
twenty-first century relations,
   18, 230–32
see also cisgender; LGBTQ+ community;
   sexuality; transgender issues; women
General Data Protection Regulation
   (GDPR), 39, 49–52, 54
genetics, 134–35
genital mutilation
   male circumcision, 130–31, 146–47
Ghostbusters, 88–89
Gill, Rosalind, 91, 114, 227–28
Gillette, 12–14, 13*f*, 106, 121–22, 124
Gilmore, David D., 27–28, 123–24
Ging, Debbie, 128, 129, 165, 219, 226,
   228–29, 233–34
Giroux, Henry A., 173
Glasgae Boys, The, 82
Glasgow gang complex, 61
Global Environmental Change, 48
global financial crisis (GFC), 3
globalism, 93
globalization, 95
Goffman, Erving, 21, 29–30, 33
Goldberg, David Theo, 113
Golden Globe Awards, 174–75
Golden One, The, 87n.3
Goldy, Faith, 87n.3
Good Lad Initiative, 167–68, 169–70
Good Men Project, 6, 169–70
GoodFellas, 83
goodness, concept of, 124
Google, 50–51, 55, 57, 92, 106, 207
Gor, Clarie, 175, 176
gossip, male, 32
Gottel, Lise, 147
grammar of particularity, 12
GraphColl, 47–48, 77, 78
   collocation networks, 47*f*
   Guardian corpus, 78*f*
   Scotsman corpus, 61–62
Greengross, Gil, 23–24
Gries, Stefan Th., 46, 47
groping, 2
Guardian, The, 40, 49–50, 63
   collocates, 79*t*
   concordance lines, 79*t*, 80*t*
   corpus breakdown, 63*t*
   frequency analysis, 72*f*

GraphColl results, 78*f*
'hard man' variants, 70*t*, 79*t*, 80*t*
top keywords, 74*t*
topic comparison, 69*t*
topic model analysis, 64*t*
gun violence, 69*t*, 117–18
gym membership, 26–27
gynocentrism, 135–36, 169–70n.2

hacking, 16–17, 56, 88
  photo, 93
Hall, Christopher M., 172
Hall, Steve, 82
Hamish Macbeth, 76n.5
Hammaren, Nils, 206
Hanlon, Niall, 37–38, 203
harassment, 11, 18, 35–36, 39–40, 88
  digital, 231
  institutional, 196
  online, 16–17, 55–56, 227–28
  photographic, 233–34
  sexual, 2–3, 121–22
Hard Man, The, 60
hard man masculinity, 17, 37, 40, 59–
  84, 232
  Glasgow hard man, 60–61
  Scottish media representations, 80–83
Hardie, Andrew, 73
Hartzell, Stephanie L., 109–10
hate
  crimes, 115
  mail, 16–17, 55–56
  speech, 55, 92–94, 106
HBOS fraud case, 3
health, 66*t*, 120
  care, 61
  industry, 26–27
  issues, 167–68
  men's, 3–4, 167–68, 169–70
HEFCE (Higher Education Funding Council
  England), 222
hegemonic masculinity, 1, 19, 29–31,
  40, 43–44, 59, 133, 134–35, 142,
  203, 217
hegemony, 18
  internal, 8
  see also hegemonic masculinity
Heritage, Frazer, 134–35, 140
Hermansson, Patrik, 126
heroism, 99–100
heteronormativity, 34–35, 91, 123,
  159, 175
heterosexism, 34–35
heterosexuality, 121
  friendship, 185–92

Hilton, Phil, 200–1
history studies, 10, 61
Hogan, Bernie, 131, 157, 164
Holden, Madeleine, 231–32
Hollywood masculinity, 127, 165–66
Holocaust, 87–88
Holtzman, Linda, 173
homelessness, 131, 227
homophobia, 34–35, 37, 91, 134–35, 168–
  69, 175
homosexuality, 87–88
homosociability, 18, 142
  male bonding, 165
homosociality, 14, 198
  toxic, 36
HOPE Not Hate, 128
Hopf, Michael, 101
Hopkins, Katie, 2
Horgan, John, 226
Houbrick, Dan, 193
Howe, Lewis, 6–7
HSBC, 3
Huddle Up program, 231–32
Huffman, Steve, 94
Hughes, Elizabeth, 134
Hultgreen, Kara, 128
Hulu, 172–73
human trafficking,
  pizzagate conspiracy, 93
humanities research,
  impact agenda, 222
humor, 23–24, 87–88, 93, 174–75
Hunston, Susan, 44
Hutchinson, Darren Lenard, 34–35
hypermasculinity, 193

iCloud, 50–51
identity, 9–10, 16
  masculine, 6, 7, 33–35
  gendered, 8
  language and, 7–8
  national, 17
  politics of, 18
  see also nationalism
illeism, 194
immigration, 85, 90, 95, 120
incarceration, 227
  rates of, 3–4, 127, 130–31
Incel Wiki, 151
Incels, 5, 40, 129
  concordance lines, 164*t*
  masculine status, 140
  research, 233
indexical social meaning,
  concept of, 33–34

inequality, 1
  discourses of, 227–29
  structural, 31, 32
  see also equality discourse
Information Commissioner's Office, 51
injury, physical, 227
  rates, 3–4
insider trading, 3
Instagram, 161
Intellectual Dark Web, 87n.3
International Men's Day, 101
intersectionality theory, 10, 34–35
IRA (Irish Republican Army), 68
Ireland, 201–2
ISIS (Islamic State), 128
Isla Vista shooting (2014), 133–34
Islamophobia, 93, 94, 96, 98–99, 110,
  113, 114

Jacobson, Erik, 225
Jaki, Sylvia, 134–35
Jaworska, Sylvia, 204–5
Jeffrey, Robert, 62
Jewish gay community, 87–88
Johansson, Thomas, 37–38, 206
Johnson, Boris, 74t
Johnson, Kevin, 117
Johnson, Sally, 175
Johnstone, Barbara, 12
jokes *see* humour
Jolivet, Kenneth, 227, 230
Jones, Leslie, 88–89
Jones, Vinnie, 66, 66t, 68, 69t, 77, 79–80
JPMorgan Chase, 3
Just a Boy's Game, 76
Just Another Saturday, 76

Kazyak, Emily, 131
Kehoe, Andrew, 46, 207
Kelan, Elisabeth K., 235
Kellner, Douglas, 173
Kelly, Gerry, 70
Kelly, Megan, 231n.3
Kemp, Ross, 64t, 69t
Kennedy, Francesca, 82
Kennedy, Mick, 70
Keskinen, Suvi, 111
Ketchum, Alex, 56, 57
Key Words in Context (KWIC), 48
  see also concordance lines
keywords, 45, 73–77, 181–85
  radar charts, 183f
Kiesling, Scott, 21, 23, 27, 28, 29, 32, 33–
  34, 140, 184–85
Kilgarriff, Adam, 45

Kim, Dorothy, 35, 86n.1
Kimmel, Michael S., 91–92, 225
Kiselica, Mark S., 14, 37, 123, 168–69, 172
Klein, V., 23
knife crime, 66t, 68, 69t
Knobel, Michele, 224
Koller, Veronika, 134–35, 140
Korobov, Neill, 22, 34
Kosse, Maureen, 152
Krendel, Alexandra, 138
Kuchibhotla, Srinivas, 98, 99
Kupers, Terry A., 123

laboring jobs, 4
Labour Party (UK), 60
lad culture, 91
Lahren, Tomi, 100–1
Lakoff, George, 31–32, 95–96
Lancaster-Oslo-Bergen (L-O-B) corpus,
  47–48
LancsBox, 42–43, 44, 63, 69, 71, 77, 97–
  98, 138, 179
language and masculinity studies (LMS),
  19, 32, 218
  future prospects, 219–35
language attitudes, 220
language change, 220
language myths, 220
Lankshear, Colin, 224
LaRossa, Ralph, 203
Lave, Jean, 224
LaViolette, Jack, 131, 157, 164
Lazar, Michelle, 205
Leeuwen, Theo van, 188, 205
'leftist' ideology, 228–29
Lehman Brothers, 3
Lethal Weapon, 175
Levon, Erez, 41–42, 43–44, 61–62, 83, 99,
  104–5, 117
LexisNexis, 62–63
LGBTQ + community, 174–75, 228–29
liberal philosophy, 16–17
liberalism, 85, 93, 228–29
LIBOR case, 3
Lieu, Ted, 116–17
life expectancy, 3–4, 231
Lin, Jie Liang, 136
linguistic anthropology *see* anthropology,
  linguistic
linguistic variation, 9–10
linguistics training, 221
literacy
  digital, 224–25
  education, 225
  new literacies, 224

Litosseliti, Lia, 20
Lo Truglio, Joe, 176
Loaded, 91
Lock, Stock and Two Smoking Barrels, 66
locker room banter, 2, 36
Lomas, Tim, 169
Loofbourow, Lili, 36
Lorber, Judith, 25–26
Lotz, Amanda D., 174
Lunarbaboon, 171*f*
Lupton, Deborah, 201–2
Lyons, Matthew N., 86–87

Macarro, Antonio S., 62
Machin, David, 42
macho masculinity, 34
MacIntyre, Donal, 64*t*, 66, 69*t*
MacIntyre's Underworld: Gangster, 66
magazines, 26–27, 43–44, 91
Maher, Bill, 100–1
Make America Great Again (MAGA), 95
male supremacism, 5
   websites, 6
male terms, 26–28, 139–53
   biological category, 26–27
   negative, 150–53, 150*f*
   neutral/generic, 146*f*, 146–48
   neutral/relational, 148*f*, 148–49
   positive, 139–46, 140*f*
male violence *see* violence
man hating, 11
man shaming, 124–25
ManCave Project, 169–70
Maney, Donna L., 23, 26
manhood, precarious, 123–24
ManKind project, 169–70, 231–32
Manogrid, 130*f*
manosphere, 8, 18, 91, 119, 120–21, 224,
      225, 233
   collocates, 147*t*, 157*t*
   communities, 24
   concordance lines, 141*t*, 145*t*, 152*t*,
      153*t*, 154*t*, 155*t*, 156*t*, 161*t*, 162*t*
   corpus breakdown, 138*t*
   definition, 5, 126–29
   Incels, 133–35
   international contexts, 233–34
   male and female referents compared,
      165*f*
   MensRights, 129–31
   MGTOW, 135–37
   negative female terms, 160*f*, 163*f*
   negative male terms, 150*f*
   neutral/generic female terms, 156*f*
   neutral/generic male terms, 146*f*

neutral/relational female terms, 159*f*
neutral/relational male terms, 148*f*
online communities, 36
positive male terms, 140*f*
Reddit, spaces on, 129–37
RedPill, 131–32
Marantz, Andrew, 93
Marcus, Simon, 228–29
marginalization, 39–40
marketing strategies, 12–14
Markham, Annette, 53, 213
marriage, 5, 120, 127, 135–36, 139–40
   see also divorce
Marshall, Harriette, 204
Marshall, Kendall, 2
Martin, Trevor, 94
Marwick, Alice E., 129–30, 227–28
Marxism, cultural, 89
masculine ease, 140, 184–85
Masculinities Research Network, 234
masculinity
   analytic approaches, 39–58
   caring/parental *see* fatherhood
   definitions, 17, 19–20, 26–29
   hard man *see* hard man masculinity
   hegemonic, 29–31
   language, history of, 31–32
   mediated, 232–33
   positive *see* positive masculinity
   public eye, in the, 3–4
   research publications, 61–62
   theories of, 36–38
   toxic *see* toxic masculinity
Masculinity, Sex and Popular Culture
      network, 234
maskcraft/mask metaphor, 6–7
mass media, 62
   control of, 128
mass shootings, 3, 133–34
Massanari, Adrienne L., 56, 132
maternal health, 199–200
Matrix, The, 24–25, 131–32
Mautner, Gerlinde, 220–21
Maxwell, Karen J., 203
Mayr, Andrea, 42
Mayweather, Floyd, 2–3
McCammon, Ross, 203–4
McCarthy, Michael, 42
McCrea, Aisling, 161
McDougall, Peter, 76
McEnery, Tony, 42–43, 46, 47–48, 49
McGlashan, Mark, 204, 233–34
McGraw, Thomas, 60
McGuire, Colin, 82
McInnes, Gavin, 87

McKeown, Kieran, 199n.1, 201–2
McMillen, Kyle, 95
McNab, Andy, 64t, 69t
Mead, Michael, 4–5
Mech, David, 142
media, 10
    bias, 127
    language, 9–10
    mass *see* mass media
    social *see* social media
mediated masculinities, 232–33
Meinhof, Ulrike Hanna, 32
memes, 87–88, 93
Men and Masculinities Center, 234
Men Going Their Own Way, 6
men
    definition, 17, 19–20, 26–28
    masculinities *vs.*, 12–14
men subcorpus,
    collocates, 101t, 106t
    concordance lines, 102t, 104t, 105t
    top 3-grams, 103t
Men's Health magazine, 41–42
Men's Health Network, 6
Men's Movement, 4–5
    Men's Movement 2.0, 169–70
Men's Rights Activists (MRA), 129–31, 231–32
Men's Rights Movement, 120, 146–47, 230
MenCare, 167–68, 169–70
Mens Rights subcorpus, 40, 129, 137
    concordance lines, 163t
mental health, 3–4, 54, 56–57, 121–22, 130–31, 133, 167–68, 169–70, 226, 231
    see also anxiety; depression; stress; suicide
mental illness, 228–29
Messner, Michael, 229
#metoo movement, 2–3, 11–12, 231
MGTOW movement (men going their own way), 5, 24, 40, 127, 128–29
    concordance lines, 149t
    sex, approaches to, 135–36n.6
migration, 85–86
    see also immigration
Milani, Tommaso, 11, 29, 34, 43–44
militarism, 90
military service, 130–31
    conscription, 131, 230–31
    fraternal relationships, 140–42
military violence, 230–31
Miller, Johnny Lee, 76
Minassian, Alek, 133–34

misogyny, 3, 9, 11, 30–31, 37, 38, 55, 56, 87, 88, 90, 93, 94, 109–10, 114, 123, 130–31, 134–35, 158, 160, 164–65, 168–69, 223, 227–28, 231
    eco-misogyny, 233–34
    networked, 92, 128, 233–34
Molyneux, Stefan, 87
money laundering, 3
monogamy, 159
Mooney, Gerry, 82
morality, 95–96
Morgan, Piers, 12–13, 13f, 99
Mort, F. C., 29
Moss, Mark, 198
Mosse, George L., 90
motherhood, 201, 204
    single, 159
    see also fatherhood
Movember project, 167–68
movies, 26–27
    see also Hollywood masculinity
MRA *see* Men's Rights Activists
Mudde, Cas, 91
multiculturalism, 85–87, 89, 90, 93, 98
multidimensionality theory, 34–35
multimodal analysis, 42, 198
Mumsnet, 204–5, 207
Munn, Luke, 94–95
Murakami, Akira, 48, 49, 64
murder, 3, 35–36, 68, 133–34, 227
    see also serial killers
Murphy, Brona, 43
Murphy, Shane, 233
music,
    Black masculinity, 193–94
    festivals, 66t
Muslim men, 110–14
    collocates, 112t
    concordance lines, 113t
    see also Islamophobia
Mutual Information (MI), 77
Mwinlaaru, Issac N., 42
mythopoetic men's movement, 122, 129–30, 168–69, 170

Nagel, Emily van der, 37, 90
Nartey, Mark, 42
National Bail Fund Network, 196–97n.9
National Childbirth Trust (NCT), 207
National Consortium for Academics and Sports, 231–32
National Policy Institute, 87n.2
National Review, 124–25
nationalism, 17, 85, 228
    alternative right and, 90–92

banal, 86
  ethnic, 18
  right-wing, 37
  White nationalist discourse, 86
NAWALT (not all women are like that),
  154–55, 156
Nazism, 99–100
  neo-, 87, 89, 91
NBC, 178–79
NCIS, 175
Neds, 60
neoliberalism, 18
Nesbitt, Rab C., 60
Nessa, Sabina, 11–12
Netflix, 172–73
neuroscientific discourse, 24
neurosexism, 25
Newsom, Gavin, 116
newspaper discourse, 63
Niedzielski, Nancy A., 220
Nip/Tuck, 174
Nissenbaum, Helen, 53
No Ma'am website, 135
No Mean City, 60
Nonnegative Matrix Factorization (NMF),
  48–49
non-tender masculinity, 125
normative masculinities, 28–29, 74
Northern Vanguard, 90–91
Norval, Walter, 60
#notallmen movement, 11–12
Nuts magazine, 91

O'Grady, Christopher: 'Real', 171*f*
O'Keeffe, Anne, 42
O'Malley, Harris, 124
O'Neil, James M., 168–70, 171–72, 229
Obama, Barack, 116, 117–18
Ocasio-Cortez, Alexandria, 107–8
Occidental Observer, 87–88
Ochs, Elinor, 124
Office for National Statistics (ONS), 3
Okun, Rob, 231
Oliver, John, 2
online communities, 52–54
oppression, discourse of, 227–28
optical character recognition (OCR), 62–63
Otherness concept, 91, 114–15
outdoor pursuits, 3–4

Paglia, Camille, 230
Papacharissi, Zizi, 110
paramilitary discourses, 99–100
parenthood, 174–75, 204–5
  see also fatherhood

Park, Albert, 52–53
Parsons, Talcott, 23
paternity leave, 200
patriarchy, 31
  patriarchal dividend, 14, 228
  patriarchal masculinity, 95
patriotism, 99–100
Pearson, Elizabeth, 226
Pennycook, Alastair, 41
performativity theory, 21, 33
Perry, Grayson, 6–7
personal data protection *see* General Data
    Protection Regulation (GDPR)
Peterson, Jordan, 87
photographic harassment, 233–34
physical assault, 35–36, 123–24
Pichler, Pia, 205
pick-up artists (PUA), 126–27, 142,
  160, 233–34
  see also seduction artists
Pinkett, Matt, 125, 226
pitch *see* vocal pitch
Planned Parenthood, 125
Podnieks, Elizabeth, 200, 202
poetry, 4–5
police, 36, 55–56
  brutality, 115, 116, 196–97n.9
political correctness (PC), 86–87, 93, 223
politics, 74, 74*t*, 75*t*, 79*t*
  British, 64*t*, 66*t*, 69*t*
  French, 69*t*
  Irish, 64*t*, 69*t*
  Russian, 64*t*, 69*t*
poll tax, 72
Pomerantz, Anita, 191–92
populism, 90, 95, 233
pornography, 92–93
positionality, 14–15
positive masculinity, 14, 18, 19, 36–37, 40,
  166, 167–98, 234
  definition, 37, 168–72
  see also Brooklyn Nine-Nine
Positive Psychology/Positive Masculinity
  Model (PPPM), 168–69
positivism, 24
  definition of masculinity, 28–29
'possible' masculinities, 169
power, 19, 35–36, 227–28
  dominance approach, 32, 41
  gender politics and, 35
  identity and, 33
  male, 32
  patterns of, 55
  sexual privilege, 2–3
  types of, 34

Prasad, Ritu, 95
preferred response, 191–92
prehistoric behavior, 25
Preston, Dennis R., 220
primatology research, 142
probabilistic modelling, 48–49
professional conduct, 2
#Project84, 169–70
promiscuity, sexual, 8
protectionism, 17, 225
Proud Boys, 87
Proudfoot, Jenny, 11
psychology, 23–24, 28–29, 168–69
    evolutionary, 23–24, 125–26, 131–32
    of men, 14
puberty, 20
public policy, 10
Pussygate, 1–3
Putin, Vladimir, 66, 74, 74t, 75
Python, 64
Python Reddit API Wrapper (PRAW), 96–
    97, 137–38

queer
    masculinities, 11, 21
    representation, 175
    theory, 11
Quinn, Zoë, 56, 88

Rab C. Nesbitt, 82
race
    hegemonic masculinity and, 30
    racial bias, 115
    social class and, 43–44
    see also Black men; Muslim men;
        White men
racism, 9, 55, 56, 88–89, 92–93, 94, 105,
    106, 109–10, 134–35, 223
    discrimination and, 117
    institutional, 174–75
    police, 196
radical dualism, 134–35
radicalization, 91–92, 225–26
    deradicalization programs, 225–26
    online, 18, 38, 93, 94–95, 112–13
    see also extremism
Radix Journal, 87–88
Rafanell, Irene, 61
Randles, Jennifer, 203–4
rape, 3, 35–36, 95, 110, 111, 114, 115,
    125, 157
    false allegations of, 127, 130–31
    threats, 94–95
    see also sexual assault
Rational Wiki, 24

real masculinity, 85–86
Red Pill, The, 6, 24–25, 40, 116, 129, 131–
    32, 139–40, 165–66, 229
    concordance lines, 144t, 149t, 163t
    manosphere, 131–32
Reddit, 17, 18, 40, 51, 52–54, 55, 85, 86,
    92–93, 94, 121, 128, 133–34, 138,
    139–40, 224–25
    alternative right and, 92–95
    manosphere, 129–37
    subreddits, 92, 93
Ren, Yi, 205
reproductive rights, 130–31
Research Excellence Framework (REF), 222
researcher risk, 55–58
    see also safety, researcher
Return of Kings, The, 6
Ribeiro, Manoel Horta, 87n.3, 94–95
Rickford, Russell, 52
right-wing ideology
    masculinity, 17, 86
    nationalism, 37
risk
    management, 39
    researcher, 55–58
    risk-taking behavior, 3–4, 28–
        29, 125–26
rituals, 4–5
roastie, definition, 162
robbery, 3
Roberts, Mark, 125, 226
Robertson, Adi, 93, 134
Robertson, Ray V., 116
Rodger, Elliot, 133–34
role models, 171, 226
Romano, Aja, 88
Roth-Gordon, Jennifer, 30
Royal Bank of Scotland (RBS), 3
Rüdiger, Sofia, 55–56, 160
rugby, 66t, 69t
Rush Hour, 175
Russell, Eric, 14–15, 24, 142
Russell, Graeme, 201–2
Russell, Lin, 68n.3
Russell, Megan, 68n.3
Russell, Nicole, 124
Russian politics, 64t
Ryan, Paul, 2
Rymes, Betsy, 220

Saad, Gad, 125–26
Saeed, Tania, 225
safety, researcher, 17, 39, 57
    see also researcher risk
Salzmann-Erikson, Martin, 206

same-sex relationships, 18
  parenthood, 204
Sarkeesian, Anita, 56, 88
Sarkozy, Nicolas, 74, 74t
Scalzi, John, 5
Scharrer, Erica, 174–75, 177, 200
Scheibling, Casey, 199, 206, 207
Schiff, Adam, 116–17
Schlichter, Kurt, 100–1
Schmitz, Rachel M., 131
Schneider, Klaus P., 185–86
Schoenebeck, Sarita, 206
scientific discourse strategies, 24
Scikit-learn, 64
Scotsman, The, 40, 63
  corpus breakdown, 63t
  frequency analysis, 72f
  GraphColl results, 81f
  'hard man', collocates of, 81t
  'hard man' variants, 70t
  top keywords, 75t
  topic comparison, 69t
  topic model analysis, 66t
Scrubs, 174
Sculos, Bryant W., 37, 56, 123
sectarianism, 76
seduction communities, 5, 24, 126–
  27, 142
  see also pick-up artists (PUA)
self-harm, 3–4
  see also suicide
self-image, 121–22, 123–24
semantic preference, 44
semantic prosody, 44
semiotic definition of masculinity, 28–
  29, 30
Separated Dads, 207–8
serial killers, 64t, 69t, 116
  see also murder
sex, 3–4
  biological *see* biological sex
  concepts, 20–26
  definition, 17, 19–20
  reproductive function, 5
Sex-Role Inventory, 168
sex role theory, 23–24
sexism, 9, 14, 39–40, 55, 56, 88, 90, 93,
  109–10, 114, 123, 138, 160, 164–65,
  171–72, 223
  casual, 12, 13
  discrimination, 35
  institutional, 3
  workplace, 3, 174–75
sexual abuse, 2–3, 11, 18, 56, 114, 123–
  24, 176n.5

sexual assault, 2, 3, 11, 35–36, 111, 114
  see also rape
Sexual Assault Survivors' Bill of Rights,
  176n.5
sexual attractiveness, 8
sexual deviancy, 55
sexual harassment *see* harassment
sexual relations, 4
sexuality, 9–10, 13–14, 17, 18, 19, 86,
  106–7, 175, 201, 230–31, 233–34
  see also gender
Sexy Beast, 66
Shapiro, Ben, 87, 124–25
Sharpe, Leon, 173
Shield, The, 175
'shitposting', 93, 95
Sidnell, Jack, 34
simp, definition, 152
Simpsons, The, 60
Sinclair, John, 46
Sinclair, Neil, 200
Sinn Féin (SF), 70
Sketch Engine, 42–43
Slab Boys, The, 60
Sledge, Charles, 127
Slootmaeckers, Koen, 90
Small Faces, 60
Smith, Ruth, 124
'snowflake' culture, 89
social actor theory, 205
social advantage, 16
social class, 13–14
social constructionism, 24, 34
  see also constructionism
social disadvantage, 3–4
social justice, 86–87, 220
  warriors, 87, 93, 132, 223
social media, 17, 233
  advertising and marketing campaigns,
    12–14
  alt-right movement and, 86
  #metoo movement and, 11–12
  monitoring and security, 57
social sciences, 28–29
social status, 123–24
sociobiology, 23–24
sociolinguistics, 9–10, 14–15, 26, 31, 43,
  52, 57, 61–62
  'citizen', 220
  theory, 8
  third wave, 21
sociology, 10, 15, 23–24, 55–56, 61
Sopranos, The, 83, 174
Southern Poverty Law Center, 5, 6, 86–87,
  129, 131, 169–70n.2

spam, 92–93
Spencer, Richard, 86–87
Spilioti, Tereza, 14–15
spiritualism, 4–5
Spock, Benjamin, 203
sport, 2, 3–5, 37, 64*t*, 69*t*, 74*t*, 75*t*, 79*t*, 81*t*
   Black masculinity and, 193–94
   see also see also football; locker room
     talk; rugby
'standards' of masculinity, 6–7
Staples, Louis, 22
Starbird, Kate, 56
Starbucks, 117
Stark, Johnnie, 60
Stein, Jock, 75
STEM subjects (Science, Technology,
   Engineering, Maths), 221–22
stereotypes
   advertising campaigns, 12–13
   female, 25
   tough masculinity and, 171
   working-class characteristics, 33
Still Game, 82–83
Stone Age Myth, 25
Stone, Michael, 66*t*, 68
storytelling, 4–5
street gangs, 37
street violence, 11, 16, 61, 80–82
stress, 3–4, 227
Students for Trump, 99
SturtzSreetharan, Cindi, 205
stylistics, 9–10
successful masculinity, 11
suicide, 3–4, 127, 130–31, 167–68, 169–
   70, 227, 231
   see also self-harm
Sunderland, Jane, 22–23, 204, 205
supremacism, male, 55, 169–70n.2
   see also White supremacism
Swan, Andy, 99, 100*f*

Tagg, Caroline, 14–15
Taggart, 60
Talbot, Mary, 20
tax evasion, 3
Taylor, Carolyn, 124
Taylor, Charles, 12
Taylor, Jessica, 56
tech industry, 56
television shows, 26–27
   language and masculinities, 172–74
   on-demand services, 172–73
   see also Brooklyn Nine-Nine
Telfer, Jim, 75

terrorism, 3, 68, 70, 225–26
testosterone, 25, 26–27, 222
Texas Department of Public Safety, 134
TheDadsNet, 207–8
theft, 3
threats, online, 55–56
Tone, Hillary, 101
topic analysis, 48–49
topic management, 31–32
topic model analysis, 64–69
   Guardian corpus, 64*t*
   Scotsman corpus, 66*t*
tough masculinity, 17, 37, 40, 59–84,
   192, 232
   see also hard man masculinity; violence
toxic behavior, 124
toxic femininity, 124
toxic masculinity, 1, 3, 6, 12, 18, 19,
   30–31, 36–37, 56, 106, 120–66,
   175, 233–34
   beverage orders, 22*f*
   definition, 37, 121–26
   smear, 124–25
toxic technocultures, 56, 132
traditional masculinity, 135, 169, 203, 231
Trainspotting, 60, 66*t*, 68, 69*t*, 76, 79–80
Tranchese, Alessia, 151
transgender issues
   sports, 101
trolling, 16–17, 56, 92, 93, 95
Trudgill, Peter, 220
Trump, Donald, 1–3, 35, 36, 40, 74*t*, 74,
   75, 89, 93, 95–96, 98, 100–1, 114–15,
   116, 117–18
   Trumpism, 228
   see also Donald, The; Students for Trump
Trump, Eric, 75, 100–1
Trump, Melania, 100–1
Trumpism, 228
Twitter, 11, 86, 88–89, 93, 99, 106, 128,
   134–35, 137
   tweets, analysis of, 13*f*, 22*f*, 100*f*

unemployability, discourses of, 220–21
United Kingdom (UK),
   Copyright Service, 50
   Government *Prevent* strategy, 226
   Research and Innovation, 46, 51
United States (US)
   culture, 110, 119, 122–23
   Declaration of Independence, 97
   exceptionalism, 89, 95, 112–13
   protectionism, 89
'unlikeable' subjects, 55–58

Valizadeh, Daryush (Roosh V), 5–6, 128
van Dijk, Teun A., 41, 221
Van Valkenburgh, Shawn P., 229
VanArendonk, Kathryn, 175
Vandello, Joseph, 123–24, 230
Veissière, Samuel Paul Louis, 124, 170
Very British Gangster, A, 66
victimhood
    discourses, 130–31, 143, 219–
        20, 227–29
    victim-blaming, 11
    victimism, 228, 229
    White men, 5
video games, 26–27, 56, 88, 224, 234
Vietnam war, 122–23
violence, 19, 35–36, 37, 39–40
    casual, 68
    crime and, 3–4
    culture of, 83
    discourses of, 35–36, 60–61
    domestic *see* domestic violence
    glorification of, 123
    gun *see* gun violence
    homophobic, 6
    incels, 134
    intergenerational, 76
    interpersonal, 30–31
    male against female, 11–12
    masculinity, violent, 59
    men against men, 6
    military *see* military violence; war
    political, 90
    street *see* street violence
    symbolic, 36
    terrorist *see* terrorism
    toxic masculinity and, 37, 38
    transphobic, 6
    types of, 59
    urban spaces, 60–61
virginity, 133–34
Vito, Christopher, 134
vocal pitch, 33–34
Voice for Men, A, 6, 169–70n.2
Voigt, Rob, 116
VOX-Pol Research Network, 57
vulnerability, 193–97
    emotional, 6–7, 12, 37–38, 54, 175
    positive masculinity and, 193–97

Wade, Lauren, 169–70
Wade, Lisa, 95
Walker, Donald, 62–63
Walton, Jessica, 22f
war, 3, 37

Warren, Elizabeth, 100–1
Warzell, Charlie, 56
Washington Summit
    Publishers, 87n.2
Watson, Paul Joseph, 87n.3
Wayne, John, 217
Webb, Robert, 6–7
Wee Man, The, 60
Weidmann, James C., 126–27
wellbeing industry, 26–27
Welsh, Irvine, 60, 76
Wenger, Etienne, 224
Wetherell, Margaret, 34, 205
whelk tool, 44, 69
white knights, 132
    definition, 152
White masculinity, 2–3, 11, 37, 85–86, 90,
    108, 114, 119, 225
White men, 3, 5, 104–10
    collocates, 106t
    concordance lines, 107t, 108t, 109t
White supremacism, 86–87, 90–91, 94,
    95, 109–10
Whyte, Lara, 230
Wikipedia, 96–97
Williams, Byron Edward, 89, 99–100
Willis, Paul, 15
Winstone, Ray, 66, 69t
Wire, The, 175
Wodak, Ruth, 41, 90
'woke'-ness, 105, 223
wolf packs, 142
Wolfram, Walt, 220
women
    caregiving role, 8–9
    infantilization of, 123
    maternity and *see* children;
        motherhood
    objectification of, 123
    sexual behavior, 8
    see also gender
word lists, 44–45
WordPress, 126–27
WordSmith Tools, 42–43
working-class identity, 34, 43–44, 59, 60–
    62, 82–83, 203
workplace
    deaths, 130–31
    sexism, 3
World Health Organization (WHO),
    199–200
Wu, Brianna, 56, 88

X-man, 127

XML (eXtensible Markup Language), 177–78
XPath, 179
XTranscript tool, 177–78
Xu, Guandong, 49

Yang, Zhenglu, 49
Yglesias, Matthew, 117–18
Yiannopoulos, Milo, 88–89, 100–1
Young, Nicole, 233–34
youth crime, 61

YouTube, 12–13, 88, 92, 96–97, 121–22, 133–34, 172–73, 184n.7

Zacarias, Moussaoui, 74t
Zafimehy, Marie, 193–94
Zatychies, Maki, 195
Zimman, Lal, 21
Zimmer, Franziska, 93
Zong, Yu, 49
Zoo, 91
zoology, 142, 143